POPE PIUS XII LIBRARY, ST. JOSEPH COLLEG

3 2528 05175 2675

Springer Series on Social Work
Albert R. Roberts, D.S.W., Series Editor
Graduate School of Social Work, Rutgers, The State University of New Jersey

Advisory Board: Joseph D. Anderson, D.S.W., Barbara Berkman, D.S.W., Paul H. Ephross, Ph.D., Sheldon R. Gelman, Ph.D., Paul H. Glasser, Ph.D., and Julia Watkins, Ph.D.

Vol. 1 **Battered Women and Their Families:** Intervention Strategies and Treatment Programs, *Albert R. Roberts, D.S.W.*

Vol. 2 **Disability, Work, and Social Policy:** Models for Social Welfare, *Aliki Coudroglou, D.S.W., and Dennis L. Poole, Ph.D.*

Vol. 3 **Social Policy and the Rural Setting** *Julia M. Watkins, Ph.D., and Dennis A. Watkins, Ph.D.*

Vol. 4 **Clinical Social Work in Health Settings:** A Guide to Professional Practice with Exemplars, *Thomas Owen Carlton, D.S.W.*

Vol. 5 **Social Work in the Emergency Room** *Carole W. Soskis, M.S.W., J.D.*

Vol. 6 **Task-Centered Practice with Families and Groups** *Anne E. Fortune, Ph.D.*

Vol. 7 **Widow-to-Widow** *Phyllis R. Silverman, Ph.D.*

Vol. 8 **Elder Abuse and Neglect:** Causes, Diagnosis, and Intervention Strategies, *Mary Joy Quinn, R.N., M.A., and Susan K. Tomita, M.S.W.*

Vol. 9 **Law and Social Work Practice** *Raymond Albert, M.S.W., J.D.*

Vol. 10 **Information and Referral Networks:** Doorways to Human Services, *Risha W. Levinson, D.S.W.*

Vol. 11 **Social Work in the Workplace:** Practice and Principles, *Gary M. Gould, Ph.D., and Michael Lane Smith, Ph.D.*

Vol. 12 **Foundations of Social Work Practice** *Joseph Anderson, D.S.W.*

Vol. 13 **The Human Bond:** Support Groups and Mutual Aid, *Harry Wasserman, D.S.W., and Holly E. Danforth, M.S.W.*

Vol. 14 **Social Work: The Membership Perspective** *Hans S. Falck, Ph.D.*

Vol. 15 **Social Work Practice in Maternal and Child Health** *Terri Combs-Orme, Ph.D.*

Vol. 16 **Program Evaluation in the Human Services** *Michael J. Smith, D.S.W.*

Vol. 17 **Journeys to Recovery** *Milton Trachtenberg, A.C.S.W., C.A.C.*

Vol. 18 **Evaluating Your Practice:** A Guide to Self-Assessment, *Catherine Alter, Ph.D., and Wayne Evens, M.S.W.*

Vol. 19 **Violence Hits Home:** Comprehensive Treatment Approaches to Domestic Violence, *Sandra M. Stith, Ph.D., Mary Beth Williams, L.C.S.W., and Karen Rosen, M.S.*

Sandra M. Stith, Ph.D., earned her doctorate in marriage and family therapy from Kansas State University. She is currently an Assistant Professor in the Marriage and Family Therapy Program at Virginia Tech's Northern Virginia Campus, Falls Church, Virginia. She is a Licensed Professional Counselor for the State of Virginia and maintains a private practice in Vienna, Virginia. She is a Clinical Member and Approved Supervisor of the American Association for Marriage and Family Therapy. Dr. Stith has worked in the field of domestic violence for seven years and has co-led a group for battered women for three years. She has several publications on spouse abuse and presents nationally on issues related to domestic violence.

Mary Beth Williams, L.C.S.W., is earning her doctorate in human and organizational development from the Fielding Institute. Her research focuses on post-traumatic stress disorder symptoms in adults as long-term effects of childhood sexual abuse. She is currently a school social worker for Falls Church, Virginia, public schools. Ms. Williams is a licensed clinical social worker for the state of Virginia and has been in private practice for eight years. She is a member of NASW Society for Traumatic Stress Studies and the American Psychological Association. A Phi Beta Kappa member, Ms. Williams has authored several publications on issues related to divorce and divorce mediation. She is also an oral examiner for the State Board of Licensure and co-chaired the Northern Virginia Conference on treatment of family violence, Violence Hits Home.

Karen Rosen, M.S., is a Licensed Professional Counselor in Virginia and a Clinical Member of the American Association for Marriage and Family Therapy. She is on the faculty at the Department of Family and Child Development, Virginia Tech's Northern Virginia Graduate Center. Ms. Rosen is a supervisor and the Assistant Director of the Center for Family Services at Virginia Tech. She has worked as a volunteer counselor in child abuse prevention programs sponsored by the Community Department of Social Services. Ms. Rosen is also currently in private practice at PIERRS (Pilot Information, Education, Resources, and Referral Services) in Fairfax, Virginia.

Violence Hits Home

Comprehensive Treatment Approaches to Domestic Violence

Sandra M. Stith, Ph.D.
Mary Beth Williams, L.C.S.W.
Karen Rosen, M.S.

Editors

Springer Publishing Company
New York

Copyright © 1990 by Springer Publishing Company, Inc.

All rights reserved

No part of this publication may be reproduced, stored in a retrieval system, or transmitted in any form or by any means, electronic, mechanical, photocopying, recording, or otherwise, without the prior permission of Springer Publishing Company, Inc.

Springer Publishing Company, Inc.
536 Broadway
New York, NY 10012

90 91 92 93 94 / 5 4 3 2 1

Printed in the United States of America

Library of Congress Cataloging-in-Publication Data

Violence hits home: comprehensive treatment approaches to
    domestic violence / Sandra M. Stith, Mary Beth Williams, Karen
    H. Rosen, editors.
        p.   cm.
    Includes bibliographical references.
    ISBN 0-8261-7270-9
    1. Family violence—United States. 2. Problem families—
Counseling of—United States. 3. Family social work—
United States. I. Stith, Sandra M. II. Williams, Mary Beth.
III. Rosen, Karen H.
    [DNLM: 1. Child Abuse. 2. Child Abuse, Sexual. 3. Elder
Abuse. 4. Family Therapy. 5. Spouse Abuse. HQ 809 V7947]
HQ809.3.U5V566   1990
362.82'92—dc20
DNLM/DLC
for Library of Congress   90-9459
                                                               CIP

Dedicated to
those who live or have lived in violent homes
and
those who work to end domestic violence

Contents

II Treatment of Child Abuse

III Treatment of Child Sexual Abuse

IV Treatment of Adults Molested as Children

V   Treatment of Elder Abuse and Neglect

VI   Conceptual Models and Conclusion

Foreword

The editors and their prominent team of authors offer no magical solution to eliminating the pervasive problem of family violence in today's society. Those involved in treating victims of family violence and their abusers know that although innovative intervention strategies can lessen the extent and recurrence of family violence, it can never totally eliminate this major social problem.

For many years, human service practitioners, family therapists, and mental health professionals have been searching for a book that provides an examination of the latest techniques and strategies for intervening with victims of all forms of family violence. This unique sourcebook provides a complete step-by-step review of the essential treatment approaches necessary for timely and effective intervention with abused and neglected children, battered women and their children, elder abuse victims, batterers, and victims of child sexual abuse.

Sandra Stith, Mary Beth Williams, and Karen Rosen have done a masterful job of compiling and editing *Violence Hits Home*. It is rare indeed for practitioners to plan and conduct a major conference on family violence and then to diligently keep after the presenters to prepare full-length chapters appropriate for a book. But this is precisely the accomplishment that the editors have achieved with this outstanding volume.

Stith, Williams, and Rosen have collaborated on a valuable reference for anyone interested in working in the family violence field, including graduate students, practitioners, and policymakers. This highly readable and practical book contains a wealth of case examples, descriptive information, and practice techniques. The editors should be applauded for this important addition to the social work and family violence literature.

I invite the reader to explore the wide range of treatment programs for survivors of family violence included here. This book provides an insider's view of clinical issues, intervention methods, and techniques that have been developed to facilitate the recovery of survivors of violence in the home.

ALBERT R. ROBERTS, D.S.W.

Contributors

Daniel R. Clow, Ed.D., is a Licensed Professional Counselor affiliated with North Roanoke Family Counselors in Roanoke, Virginia. He is a therapist with the Roanoke Area Sex Offender Program. Dan is an authority on issues related to domestic violence and spouse abuse and has been qualified as an expert witness in sex abuse cases. Dan earned his bachelor's degree at Houghton College, New York, his master's degree at Gordon-Conwell, Massachusetts, and his Doctor of Education at Virginia Tech.

Mary Froning, Psy.D., is a Licensed Psychologist and has been in private practice in Silver Spring, Maryland, and Washington, D.C. specializing in sexual abuse since 1984. She has presented both nationally and regionally on child sexual abuse and is currently writing a chapter on male victims of sexual abuse for a forthcoming book. Mary received her Psy.D. from the Illinois School of Professional Psychology.

Janet C. Fulmer, L.C.S.W., is a partner and senior therapist at The Therapy Center in Alexandria and Falls Church, Virginia. She received her master's degree in social work from Catholic University and has been in private practice for the past 15 years. Ms. Fulmer is a Licensed Clinical Social Worker in Virginia and Maryland. Her main focus in the past 5 years has been in working with adults molested as children. She helped found the partial hospitalization program at Woodburn Center for Community Mental Health and was the first worker at Woodburn Center Emergency Services. Ms. Fulmer has done numerous workshops and presentations in the community.

Eliana Gil, Ph.D., is the director of Gil and Associates, Child Abuse Treatment and Training Programs, in Pleasant Hill, California. She has been active in child abuse counseling and education for over 12 years. She is a graduate of the California Graduate School of Marital and Family Therapy in San Rafael, California, and is a Licensed Marriage, Family, and Child Counselor. Dr. Gil has written several pamphlets and journal articles. Her most recent publication is *Outgrowing the Pain: A Book For and About Adults Abused as Children*. She has made lecturing appearances throughout the United States.

David E. Hutchins, Ph.D., is an Associate Professor in the Counselor Education Program at Virginia Tech. He is a Licensed Professional Counselor, past Chairman and current member of the Virginia Board of Professional Counselors. Dr. Hutchins has distinguished himself as the developer of *TFA Systems™*, an innovative approach to counseling and human development. He is the author of numerous professional articles and book chapters. His internationally used counseling techniques textbook, *Helping Relationships and Strategies*, is now in its second edition. Dr. Hutchins earned his B.A. and M.A. degrees in psychology and counseling, respectively, at the University of Iowa. His Ph.D. is from Ohio University, where his major was counselor education with a minor in behavior systems analysis from the College of Engineering.

Martha L. Jones, A.C.S.W., is President of Common Sense Associates, Inc., in Mechanicsburg, Pennsylvania, a private organization providing counseling, therapy, training, and consultation. She has an undergraduate degree in sociology and is a graduate of the University of Maryland School of Social Work. Ms. Jones is a Board Certified Social Work Diplomate and Registered Social Worker with 20 years experience in the field. She has published numerous articles and has conducted presentations and training sessions throughout the United States and Canada.

Anthony P. Jurich, Ph.D., received his B.S. in psychology from Fordham University in 1969 and his M.S. and Ph.D. in human development and family studies from Penn State in 1971 and 1972, respectively. He is presently a professor of human development and family studies at Kansas State University, where he is also the Clinical Director for Marriage and Family Therapy. Dr. Jurich has taught Family Crisis for 12 years and was named the Kansas State University Outstanding Teacher in 1976 and the Osborne Award winner of the National Council on Family Relations in 1987. He is a Fellow in the American Association for Marriage and Family Therapy. Dr. Jurich has 93 publications in various journals and books covering the topics of family crisis, adolescence, and marriage and family therapy, and is co-editor of *New Perspectives in Marriage and Family Therapy*.

Shelley Kramer-Dover, Ph.D., is a Licensed Clinical Psychologist in private practice at the Virginia Psychiatric Institute in Fairfax, Virginia. Her clinical practice includes evaluation and treatment of children and adults and related consultative work. Dr. Kramer-Dover has worked extensively in the areas of sexual abuse, child custody, and special-needs children. She has given presentations and conducted workshops in these areas, and, having been court qualified as a expert witness, has provided testimony in numerous litigations. Dr. Kramer-Dover received her bachelor's degree Summa Cum Laude from Harvard University and her doctorate in clinical psychology from George Washington University. Prior to establishing her practice in the Washington, D.C. area, Dr. Kramer-Dover conducted research on schizophrenia in Copenhagen, Denmark, and served as Assistant Dean of Freshmen at Harvard University.

Lana R. Lawrence, L.F.D., is a survivor of child sexual abuse. She has been active in forming self-help groups for incest survivors, has appeared on several national television shows, and has made numerous presentations on issues related to incest survival. Her first article about her experience was published in the *Washington Post Health Section.* Lana is also a licensed funeral director.

Linda F. Little, Ph.D., is a Licensed Psychologist in Virginia and an Approved Supervisor of the American Association for Marriage and Family Therapy. She is an Associate Professor and Program Director for the Master's and Post Master's Certificate Program in Marriage and Family Therapy, Department of Family and Child Development, Virginia Tech's Northern Virginia Graduate Center. Dr. Little has served as a volunteer psychologist for a battered women's shelter and has presented at numerous national conferences on intervention strategies.

Lisa McCann, Ph.D., received an M.S.W. from Columbia University and a Ph.D. in clinical psychology from the University of Kansas. She is the founder and Clinical Director of The Traumatic Stress Institute. She is also Assistant Clinical Professor of Psychiatry at the University of Connecticut Health Center. Her research and clinical interests include understanding psychological adaptation to a wide variety of traumatic stresses, including incest, family violence, and war. She is co-author, with Dr. Laurie Pearlman, of the book *Through a Glass Darkly: Understanding the Adult Trauma Survivor through Constructivist Self Development Theory* as well as other articles on interventions with trauma survivors.

Barry W. McCarthy, Ph.D., is a Diplomate in Clinical Psychology, a Certified Sex Educator and Sex Therapist, and a Clinical Member of the American Association for Marriage and Family Therapy. He is a Professor of Psychology at American University and has presented human sexuality workshops in the United States and abroad. Dr. McCarthy practices in clinical psychology, marital therapy, and sex therapy at the Washington Psychological Center. He is the author of over 20 articles and 4 books, the most recent being *Sexual Awareness: Sharing Sexual Pleasure.*

Robert Nevin, Ph.D., is an Associate Professor at the Indiana University School of Social Work. His doctorate and master's degree in public health are from the University of Minnesota and his master's degree in social work is from the University of Denver. His primary specializations are child welfare, health policy, maternal and child health, planning and management, addictions, and substance abuse. Dr. Nevin is a successful grant writer and has published many articles and book chapters on family stress and coping, elderly services, and child welfare.

Laurie Anne Pearlman, Ph.D., is a clinical psychologist and Research Director of The Traumatic Stress Institute. Her research and clinical work focus on adult trauma survivors. She is co-author, with Dr. Lisa McCann, of the book *Through a Glass Darkly: Understanding the Adult Trauma Survivor through Constructivist Self Development Theory*. Dr. Pearlman received her bachelor's degree from the University of Michigan and her doctorate in clinical psychology from the University of Connecticut.

Mary Joy Quinn, M.A., is a registered nurse and court investigator in San Francisco for the Superior Court of California. She is a Licensed Marriage, Family and Child Counselor and is an instructor for the Gerontology Certificate Program at San Francisco State University. She is associated with the American Society on Aging in San Francisco as a faculty member for the Community Education in Aging Project. Ms. Quinn has made numerous lectures and presentations and has contributed to several publications. She is the author of *Elder Abuse and Neglect* and co-author of *Elder Abuse and Neglect: Causes, Diagnosis, and Intervention Strategies*.

Albert R. Roberts, D.S.W., is an Associate Professor of Social Work and Criminal Justice at the School of Social Work, Rutgers, New Brunswick, New Jersey. His doctorate is from the School of Social Work, University of Maryland at Baltimore, and his master's degree in sociology is from Long Island University in Brookville, New York. Dr. Roberts is a fellow of the American Orthopsychiatric Association and founding and current editor of the Springer Publishing Company's prestigious social work series. Dr. Roberts is a prolific writer and scholar, with over 60 publications, including 12 books and numerous articles in international social work, criminal justice, and public health journals. He is the editor of *Battered Women and Their Families: Intervention Strategies and Treatment Programs*, which is Volume 1 in the Springer Series on Social Work. Dr. Roberts recently completed a national survey of the organizational structure and functions of 184 victim service and witness assistance programs. Prior to returning to his home state of New Jersey, Dr. Roberts lived in the Midwest for five years, where he taught at the Indiana University School of Social Work and conducted clinical research with batterers and battered women in cooperation with local social service and criminal justice agencies in Indianapolis.

Beverly Schenkman Roberts, M.Ed. is the Project Director of Mainstreaming Medical Care for the New Jersey Association for Retarded Citizens in North Brunswick, New Jersey. While working as a Planning Consultant for the Community Service Council of Central Indiana, Ms. Roberts authored several reports, including *Housing Options for Seniors in Marion County* and *Legal Guardianship in Indiana: A Report on the Existing Resources and the Need for Services*. She also wrote the chapter on "Funding Sources" for *Sheltering Battered Women: A National Study and Service Guide*, published by Springer Publishing Company.

Meriam S. Rogan, M.S.Ed., received her undergraduate degree in psychology and graduated from the master's program in counseling at St. Bonaventure. She has 15 years experience in the social work field, with 10 years experience working with the multidisciplinary team concept. Ms. Rogan has been with the Fairfax County Department of Social Services for the past 4 years, where she has supervised the sexual abuse intake unit. She is also the Coordinator and Facilitator of Parents United in Fairfax, Virgina.

Jana Staton, Ph.D., earned her doctorate at UCLA in 1984 in counseling and educational psychology. She had two years of postdoctoral training in marriage and family therapy at the Center for Family Services, Virginia Tech's Northern Virginia Graduate Center. Dr. Staton is now studying the use of art and sandtray therapy with children from the perspective of Jungian psychology. Her primary interest is in developing new approaches for working with young children who have experienced trauma, severe loss, or abuse, within a family system framework. She is currently in private practice as a family therapist in Northern Virginia at the Center for Therapy and Education and is an instructor at Virginia Tech.

Daniel E. Vogler, Ed.D., is a consultant with the Delta Management Group. Dr. Vogler has been involved in various leadership positions in education for 25 years. He is currently a graduate faculty member at Virginia Tech. His professional contributions include authoring or co-authoring 9 books and more than 150 articles, monographs, and technical papers. He also has considerable experience as a policy and instructional consultant. Dr. Vogler earned his Bachelor of Science, Master of Education, and Doctor of Education degrees from the University of Illinois at Champaign.

Acknowledgments

The idea for this book was conceived as a result of the conference on domestic violence, "Violence Hits Home," held in Fairfax, Virginia in April 1988. It was from this conference that the enthusiasm for and the structure of this book emerged. There is much yet to be done to end domestic violence, and we are pleased to take one more step with this book.

We have many people to thank for their assistance in the development of this book. First, we extend special thanks to the Junior League of Northern Virginia, which sponsored the conference in 1988. Many of the chapters in this volume spring directly from that conference. We would also like to thank Virginia Tech and particularly the Northern Virginia Graduate Center for their contribution in hosting the conference and for their continued institutional support for this project. We thank Dr. Linda Little, Director of the Marriage and Family Therapy Program in Northern Virginia, for her inspiration and encouragement.

We extend our deepest appreciation to Pat Meneely, who was crucial to the coordination between editors and contributors and to the word processing of numerous drafts of chapters. We are also grateful to Al Roberts, who encouraged us to undertake this project and who has skillfully guided our efforts throughout. Finally, we thank the contributors who devoted countless hours to refining their work and responded to deadlines in a timely fashion.

Introduction

Domestic violence is recognized as one of the most serious problems facing contemporary families. Child abuse reporting has increased dramatically in recent years; the law enforcement system is beginning to recognize that spouse abuse is a crime; and abuse of the elderly is emerging from the closet. As a consequence, demands on mental health services for treatment of the various forms of domestic violence have also increased dramatically. However, many mental health providers remain ill-prepared to treat these important problems.

Working from the assumption that domestic violence is a multicausal problem with multiple points of intervention, this book provides readers with an overview of treatment approaches dealing with specific forms of domestic violence, that is, spouse abuse, child physical and sexual abuse, elder abuse, and treatment of adults molested as children. It is not intended to present the final word on assessment and treatment of domestic violence. Instead, it compiles the expertise of human service professionals who provide domestic violence treatment.

This text emphasizes the practical rather than the theoretical aspects of intervention. Contributors to this volume are family therapists, social workers, psychologists, or human service workers who have been recognized for their expertise with various forms of domestic violence. Each contributor was asked to write a chapter that included both a review of the literature and his or her therapeutic perspective on treatment, drawing heavily on his or her own clinical work.

These authors do not present a unified perspective on treatment of domestic violence. Four contributors are professional psychologists, four are family therapists, eight are social workers, three are counselors, one is a nurse, and one is a survivor of incest. Their treatment approaches illustrate their own perspectives as well as their own educational, experiential, and theoretical backgrounds. This diversity of perspectives enriches our understanding of treatment issues and demonstrates the value of multidisciplinary approaches.

The book begins with an overview of the problem of domestic violence by Sandra Stith and Karen Rosen. This chapter concentrates on the theoretical aspects of intervention, laying the groundwork for the subsequent chapters, which have a more practical emphasis.

The rest of the book is divided into six parts, each focusing on a specific treatment area: (1) treatment of spouse abuse, (2) treatment of child abuse, (3) treatment of child sexual abuse, (4) treatment of adults molested as children, (5) treatment of elder abuse and neglect, and (6) a general treatment model and summary chapter.

According to Straus and Gelles (1986), 1,620,000 women were beaten by their husbands in 1985. As a result of increasing attention to the problem of spouse abuse, many communities are changing their legal response to this problem. Police officers are being encouraged, and in some cases required, to arrest spouse abusers. More judges are mandating treatment for abusers. Yet many mental health providers are not prepared to treat this population. Thus, Part I addresses treatment issues regarding spouse abuse.

The first chapter in Part I, written by Dr. Albert Roberts and Beverly Schenkman Roberts, presents a comprehensive crisis intervention model for battered women and their children. Roberts discusses early intervention by police-based crisis teams and victim assistance units, assessment and detection in the hospital emergency room, specific intervention techniques used by crisis hotlines and battered women's shelters, and short-term treatment for the children of women receiving shelter.

The second chapter, by Dr. Linda Little, presents a Gestalt therapy approach for working with female victims of spouse abuse. Gestalt therapy goals and action-oriented therapeutic techniques are introduced to aid clinicians in their work with battered women.

Drs. Daniel Clow, David Hutchins, and Daniel Vogler wrote the third chapter in this section. They present a group treatment approach for male batterers based on changing men's thoughts, feelings, and actions.

The final chapter in Part I, by Dr. Sandra Stith and Karen Rosen, describes a comprehensive treatment approach for marital violence. The authors describe a multistage intervention approach to marital violence when the couple chooses to remain together.

Part II presents treatment approaches for working with child abuse. The enactment of more stringent child abuse reporting laws nationwide has led to a dramatic increase in the need for mental health treatment of children and families impacted by child abuse.

The first chapter, written by Meriam Rogan, discusses the multidisciplinary team approach to child abuse and neglect. Rogan emphasizes the importance of coordination among agencies involved with the same abusing family and describes the use of a multidisciplinary team to coordinate expertise and services among agencies that share the goal of protecting children.

The next chapter, written by Martha Jones, helps professionals assess and deal with the unmotivated child-abusing client. The author presents suggestions for working with the involuntary client who does not ask for or want help.

Dr. Anthony Jurich wrote the third chapter in this section, "Families Who Physically Abuse Adolescents." In this chapter, Dr. Jurich presents a typology of families who abuse adolescents and suggests specific intervention strategies based on the typology of the specific family.

The final chapter in Part II was written by Dr. Al Roberts and Dr. Robert Nevins. In this chapter they present models of community coordination in developing relevant treatment for children. Specifically, they discuss the child protection model, the medical model, the legal model, and interdisciplinary models.

Part III deals with treatment of child sexual abuse. As sexual abuse prevention programs are becoming more common, children are breaking the cultural ban against talking about their victimizations. School personnel, medical personnel, neighbors, and others are reporting child abuse more frequently. Yet many mental health providers lack experience and specific information on treating child physical and sexual abuse.

The first chapter of Part III, by Dr. Barry McCarthy, describes a cognitive-behavioral approach to the treatment of incest families. Interventions used with victimized children, nonvictimized siblings, mothers, and abusive fathers are introduced. General guidelines for working with incest families that do not increase trauma to the family are offered.

The second chapter in this section, by Dr. Shelley Kramer-Dover, describes the multidimensional nature of the treatment responsibilities facing the therapist who works with children who have been sexually abused. Specific issues covered include coordination and consultation with those involved in the case as well as the therapist's role in litigation and work with child victims who have special needs.

Dr. Jana Staton, in the final chapter of this section, presents guidelines for treatment of young children involved in cases of incest and sexual abuse using symbolic and nonverbal communication. Suggestions for using these same strategies to involve family members in the treatment process are also included.

Part IV discusses treatment issues with adults who were molested as children. As therapists begin to ask their adult clients about past victimizations, a growing part of the clientele is revealing histories of sexual abuse. Therapists need to become familiar with the unique therapeutic issues that these clients present to serve this population.

The first chapter in Part IV, by Lana Lawrence and Dr. Mary Froning, includes a firsthand account of the trauma of incest and the recovery process experienced by a survivor of incest and a response to this treatment process by the first author's therapist. The first author describes her childhood incest experience and the response of professionals to the disclosure. Additionally, she describes her recovery process, the impact the abuse has had on her adult life, and how treatment has changed her life. The second author addresses specific treatment issues pertaining to this work.

The disguised presentation of adult survivors of incest and other child molestations are discussed by Janet Fulmer in the second chapter of Part IV. Incest survivors frequently consciously or unconsciously avoid revealing victimizations. This chapter provides clues to early sexual victimization and emphasizes the importance of exploring the possibility of sexual abuse with all clients. Treatment issues after the abuse is revealed are also examined.

The final chapter in Part IV, by Dr. Eliana Gil, presents a specific treatment approach for working with adults molested as children. The literature review found in the chapter summarizes the known psychological problems correlated with childhood sexual abuse. Specific attention is given to dissociation, posttraumatic stress disorder, and multiple personality as consequences of childhood sexual abuse.

Part V of this book includes two chapters by Mary Joy Quinn examining abuse of the elderly. Elder abuse and neglect are the most recent forms of domestic violence to be recognized as social problems. Research elucidating the problem and treatment suggestions are in their infancy, but as increasing numbers of elderly abuse cases come to light, professionals working with families need to develop clear guidelines and specific interventions for working with this population.

Ms. Quinn reviews the literature on elder abuse and neglect and discusses the response of society to this problem. Next, she describes assessment approaches and presents profiles of elderly victims and their offenders. Finally, in the second chapter in this section, she offers general principles of intervention as well as specific interventions for treating elder abuse and neglect.

Next, Drs. Lisa McCann and Laurie Anne Pearlman present an innovative, contextual theoretical model for assessing and treating victims of a variety of traumatic stressors. It enables clinicians to conceptualize the unique experience of victims, formulate valuable hypotheses, and plan appropriate and beneficial treatment strategies.

Finally, the book concludes with a general treatment model for working with victims of trauma and with a summary chapter that demonstrates the organizing principles illustrated throughout the book and points the way for future work.

SANDRA M. STITH, PH.D.
KAREN ROSEN, M.S.

REFERENCE

Straus, M., and Gelles, R. (1986). Societal change and change in family violence from 1975 to 1985 as revealed by two national surveys. *Journal of Marriage and the Family* 48(August), 465–479.

1 Overview of Domestic Violence

Sandra M. Stith
Karen H. Rosen

Effective clinical intervention in abusive families requires a basic understanding of the issues involved. This chapter lays the groundwork for understanding domestic violence from an interactive theoretical framework that is useful for assessment and treatment. What is domestic violence? Why are families susceptible to domestic violence? What factors increase or decrease the risk of domestic violence? How can individual and family vulnerabilities, resources, and situational stressors operating within the larger sociocultural context be viewed as sources for assessing and treating domestic violence? These are some of the issues addressed in this chapter.

DEFINITION OF DOMESTIC VIOLENCE

Domestic violence is defined broadly as violent acts carried out by persons in a marital, sexual, parental, or caregiving role toward others in reciprocal roles. Thus, the term "spouse abuse" may apply to couples engaged in a sexual relationship outside of marriage. Additionally, child abuse may be perpetrated by parents, siblings, stepparents, or live-in boyfriends or girlfriends of the abused child's parent. Elder abuse includes abuse perpetrated by spouses, children, siblings, or caregivers in institutional settings. Assaults by strangers or nonfamily members not in a caregiving role are not encompassed within this definition.

Violence involves any act of violation, including emotional violence, that attacks the individual's self-concept. Sexual abuse of children includes covert or overt abuse in which adult relatives, caregivers, stepparents, lovers of a child's parent, or older, more powerful siblings attempt to receive sexual gratification from the child or attempt to gratify the child sexually. Physical abuse includes any act of aggression within a family from hitting, shoving, or pushing, to using a weapon or murdering another family member. Elder abuse encompasses physical abuse, psychological abuse, neglect, financial abuse, and violation of the rights of the elderly person.

Although this book will cite many statistics regarding the extent of the violence occurring in the United States today, these statistics remain ambiguous for several reasons. First, although reporting of all types of domestic violence is increasing, violence frequently remains a family secret. And violence flourishes in privacy. Second, the reported data have been gathered using a variety of methodologies, making comparisons between studies very difficult. Finally, researchers have used different definitions of violence. Thus, no one statistic reveals exactly how much violence is really occurring. However, it is clear that violence is a common, yet extremely destructive, aspect of life for many families in the United States today.

FAMILY CHARACTERISTICS THAT
ENHANCE SUSCEPTIBILITY

Except for the police and the military, the family is perhaps the most violent social group and the home the most violent social setting in our society. A person is more likely to be hit or killed in his or her own home by another family member than anywhere else or by anyone else (Gelles & Straus, 1979). Persons who treat family violence, study family violence, or live within violent families frequently question why family members are consistently more violent to each other than they are to their friends or to strangers. Gelles and Straus (1979, pp. 552–553) suggested that 12 characteristics of families make them particularly susceptible to violence.

1. Time at risk: Family members spend more time together than members of most other groups.
2. Range of activities and interests: Because a wide range of activities and interests exists within a family, a wide range of possible conflictual situations exists.
3. Intensity of involvement: Family members have a great deal of emotional investment in each other and thus respond

more intensely when internal conflict occurs than when a similar conflict occurs outside the family.

4. Impinging activities: Conflict is structured into most choices made by family members, because each person's choice may impinge on choices made by other family members. Thus, activities chosen by one family member may impinge on the right of another family member to engage in his or her chosen activity.

5. Right to influence: Family membership carries with it an implicit right to influence the behavior of others.

6. Age and sex discrepancies: The family is composed of people of differing ages and sexes, which makes the family an arena for cultural conflict.

7. Ascribed roles: Family role and status are frequently assigned on the basis of biological characteristics rather than on the basis of competencies and interests. This method of ascribing roles frequently leads to conflict and mismatches between talent and role.

8. Family privacy: The high level of privacy of the urban family insulates the unit from both social control and external assistance to cope with intrafamily conflict.

9. Involuntary membership: Social, emotional, material, and legal constraints make it difficult to leave the family when conflict is high.

10. High level of stress: The nuclear family is continuously undergoing major changes in structure as a result of processes inherent in the family life cycle. The family is likely to be the locus of more serious stresses than are other groups.

11. Normative approval: Deeply rooted cultural norms legitimize the rights of parents to use physical force with their children and also make the marriage license a hitting license.

12. Socialization into violence and its generalization: Through physical punishment, children learn to associate love with violence. This association carries forward into marital relationships.

Because these characteristics are present, at least to some extent, in all families, families are at higher risk for violence than are other groups. However, many of these characteristics point practitioners to potential areas of investigation when a family is being treated for violence between its members.

THEORETICAL PERSPECTIVE
ON DOMESTIC VIOLENCE

In addition to the characteristics that make families in general more at risk for violence, certain families at certain times are at greater risk for violence than are other families. An interactive model illustrating this point has been developed. The model, presented in Figure 1.1, explores the multicausal factors involved in domestic violence from an interactive framework that takes into account family and individual vulnerabilities (e.g., socialization experiences of adults), situational stressors (e.g., life cycle nodal events), individual and family resources to overcome vulnerabilities and/or situational stressors (e.g., strong social networks), and the larger sociocultural context that envelopes all.

This model suggests that sociocultural values relating to violence and sex roles affect vulnerabilities, situational stressors, and coping resources as well as the definition of and perception of the violence itself. It also suggests that there is a tendency for violence, once it has been used as a way of getting needs met, to exacerbate already existing vulnerabilities and stressors, thus contributing to its maintenance.

This framework is a tool to assess the potential for the expression of violence as well as a guide for the development of intervention strategies. While each of the following chapters examines specific forms of domestic violence, this model presents a general theory of domestic violence illustrating that it is multicausal, with a variety of points for intervention.

Sociocultural Context

Families who share the same community and culture are influenced by certain shared values and norms. Values relating to the acceptability of violence, the role of men and women in society, and the respect given to the elderly all influence the level of violence in individual families.

Acceptability of Violence

Media, government, and society in general affect the values and beliefs of each individual. The high incidence of violence on television, in movies, in legal and governmental systems, and in communities influences the level of violence within families. Straus

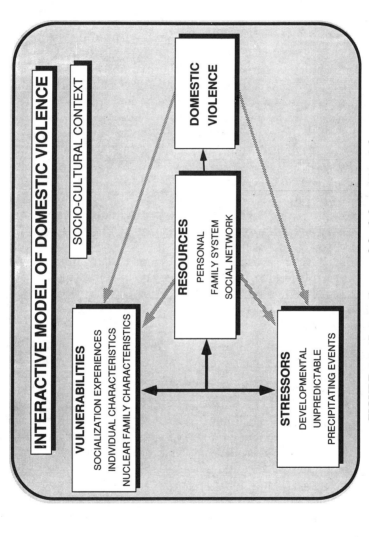

FIGURE 1.1 Interactive model of domestic violence.

(1977) suggests that violence portrayed in the media both reflects the high level of aggression in American society and perpetuates the pattern. Societies that tolerate and even glorify violence outside the family can expect to have high levels of violence within the family (Straus 1977).

Parents receive messages from society that encourage the use of corporal punishment of children. There is a prevalent belief in western Judeo-Christian culture that infants are easily spoiled and may have innate tendencies to be stubborn and willful (Steele, 1976). Accompanying this is the belief that physical punishment is the only way to prevent this "willful behavior." Abusive parents may quote passages from the Bible such as "Withhold not correction from the child: for if thou beatest him with the rod, he shall not die. Thou shalt beat him with the rod, and shalt deliver his soul from hell" (Proverbs 23:13–14).

Parents also receive messages from the school implying that physical punishment is an integral part of child rearing. For example, in 1986, all but eight states allowed school personnel to physically discipline children who misbehaved (Van Dyke, 1986, in Radin, 1988). This not only reinforces beliefs of adults that physical punishment is an acceptable way to deal with children who misbehave but also reinforces childrens' beliefs that adults who hurt them have a right to do so when they are bad, thus blurring the lines between what is appropriate discipline and what is abuse (Steele, 1976).

Subordinate Status of Women

Cultural values regarding male and female roles also influence the level of violence in families. The subordinate status of women in most of the world's communities, including the United States, is well recorded (Blumberg, 1978; Chafetz, 1984). Straus (1976) has suggested that physical force is the ultimate resort used to keep subordinate groups in their place.

The United States today remains a patriarchal society. In general, a higher value is placed on work done by men than on work done by women. Men continue to hold the majority of leadership positions in business, government, and the legal system. Children receive clear messages that women are not as important or valued as men. These messages may lead women in abusive relationships to believe that their needs, even their lives, are not as important as the needs of their children or husbands. Thus, women may remain in abusive homes to assure that their children have financial support or to protect their husbands. Many men continue to believe that they own their wives and their children and that they have the right to "use" their wives or children in any way that gratifies them.

Ageism

Cultural values in the United States that emphasize youth, work, independence, education, and progress result in the elderly being perceived as being relatively unimportant (Kosberg, 1985). Rather than viewing the elderly as respected members of our society with much to offer the young, ageism is rampant. "The history of violence in American society, the general treatment of dependent individuals, and the perception of the aged can result in cultural legitimacy for the victimization of the elderly" (Kosberg, 1985, 380).

Cultural values relating to violence, male–female and parent–child relationships, and the elderly provide the context that supports domestic violence. This sociocultural support affects individuals' and families' vulnerabilities and how they deal with situational stressors. The degree to which each individual and family accepts the cultural messages varies and is reflected in their behavior.

Vulnerabilities

For the model presented, individual and family vulnerabilities include socialization experiences, individual characteristics, and nuclear family characteristics.

Socialization Experiences

Exposure to and experience with violence in one generation increases the likelihood of violence occurring in the next generation. Adults who have witnessed violence in their families as children or who were themselves victims of violence are affected throughout the life span in different ways, depending on their own developmental stage at the time the acts of violence occurred (Wilson, 1985). Wilson, noting the effects on Vietnam veterans of participation in violence and atrocities, states that individuals exposed to violence or who have participated in violence at younger ages may be affected in a regressive manner (i.e., causing them to utilize violent behaviors in an immature manner against others) for the rest of their lives.

Children who observe their father hitting their mother are much more likely to continue this pattern in their own marriages than are children growing up in nonviolent homes (Parke & Collmer, 1975; Straus et al., 1980; Bernard & Bernard, 1983; Kalmuss, 1984). Likewise, Hotaling and Sugarman (1986), in their review of factors predictive of marital violence, found that the only factor that consistently differentiated battered women from nonbattered women was that battered women were more likely to have witnessed violence between parents/caregivers while growing up (Hotaling & Sugarman, 1986; Coleman et al., 1980; Kalmuss, 1984; Parker & Schumacher, 1977; Rosenbaum & O'Leary, 1981).

A transgenerational violence theory has also been purported in the case of elder abuse (Fulmer, 1988). Reversing roles, the abused child becomes an elder abuser, completing a cyclical family pattern. Steinmetz (1980) found that 1 in 400 children who were raised nonviolently physically abused their parents later in life, compared to 1 in 2 children who were treated violently by their parents. Compared to the learned behavior transmitted in cases of witnessing spousal violence or being on the receiving end of child abuse, there may be different psychological processes involved in elder abuse— elements of retaliation as well as imitation are thought to contribute (Pillemer, 1985).

In summary, adults physically or sexually abused in their homes as children are much more likely to abuse their children or marry spouses who abuse their children than are those who did not experience abuse. Adults who felt devalued as a result of constant emotional abuse or neglect as children are more likely to have problems imparting strong positive self-concepts to their children than are those who grew up in nurturing homes. Indeed, investigators believe that the type of care that parents received in their childhood is the most consistent predictor of how they will treat their children and whether the abuse will be generational in nature (Belsky, 1980).

Individual Characteristics

Early research on factors predicting domestic violence focused on the psychopathology of perpetrators. Later studies, however, have indicated that individual psychopathology accounts for only a small number of abuse cases (Parke & Collmer, 1975). However, Pillemer (1985) argues that there is a greater likelihood that psychopathology is related to elder abuse than to other forms of domestic violence. Since it is generally held that it is a more socially deviant act to strike an impaired elderly person, the perpetrator may be more disturbed. Even when psychopathology has not been found to be more prevalent among abusers than nonabusers, certain personality characteristics, such as higher overall violent behavior, negativity, lower self-concepts, inability to relate to peers, etc., do seem to be more prevalent.

Hotaling and Sugarman (1986) report that physically violent husbands are "generally violent and aggressive within the family" (Hotaling & Sugarman, 1986, p. 111). Rouse (1984) has also found a greater likelihood of nonfamily violence among batterers than nonbatterers.

Abusive parents seem to have poorer parenting skills than nonabusive parents. Burgess and Conger (1977) found that abusive mothers displayed more negative behavior toward their children than did nonabusive mothers. In addition, abusive parents seemed to use punishment more frequently than did nonabusive parents (Disbrow et al., 1977; Trickett & Kuczynski, 1986).

Abusive family members have lower self-concepts, often feel powerless, and use violence to gain feelings of power (Steele, 1975; Conger et al., 1979). Hotaling and Sugarman (1986) also report that male batterers are less assertive and possess fewer educational and economic resources than do nonviolent men. Additionally, men who sexually abuse their children may have trouble relating to adult women and may turn toward their children to assure themselves of their masculinity. Incest perpetrators often find sexual relationships with a child safer, less threatening, less demanding, and less problematic than adult sexual relationships (Sgroi, 1982, p. 27).

Spouse abusers have been described as more possessive and jealous of partners than nonabusers (Coleman, 1980; Roy, 1982; Walker, 1979). Extreme suspiciousness may be related to the male batterer's dependency and jealousy (Sonkin et al., 1985).

Individuals also vary in their abilities to deal with stress. Abusers deal with stress by using various coping mechanisms such as denial, repression of the effects of their abusive behaviors, and splitting. These defensive coping operations give meaning to the abusive acts and are used by abusers to justify their behaviors (Hartman & Burgess, 1988). Moos (1986) also describes the various coping processes that persons use to deal with life crises, noting that the appraisal given to behaviors (i.e., the abusive acts) varies due to exposure to abuse, beliefs about the effectiveness and role of the abuse in the relationship, and roles in the family.

The conceptualizations individuals have about themselves (including their self-worth, their roles in life, and what the world "owes" them) and about others are known as belief systems. Violence (exposure to, perpetration of, and participation in) modifies belief systems. Victims quite frequently have negative beliefs about themselves and their power over events in their lives (i.e., their locus of control), as well as their chances to obtain future happiness. Perpetrators, while frequently having negative belief systems about themselves as well, also believe that their own feelings of inadequacy entitle them to hurt others or to force others to conform to their will (McCann et al., in press).

Other, more general characteristics of all people, including age and gender, have also been shown to be related to domestic violence. Studies have been unclear as to the relationship between age and domestic violence. Some studies have indicated that teenage mothers may be at greater risk of becoming child abusers than are older mothers (Oppel & Royston, 1971; Bolton, 1981). This increased risk may result from youth or inexperience or from increased situational stress in the lives of those mothers. Spouse abuse is also more likely when the abuser is younger (Hotaling & Sugarman, 1986). Two studies reported finding that "old old" individuals, 75 years of age and older, run a greater risk of being abused (Fulmer, 1988; King, 1984). However, Pillemer and Finkelhor (1988), in an extensive study of elderly in the Boston metropolitan area, did not find any particular age group within the population over 65 to be at higher risk of elder abuse. In any case, all forms of family violence (physical abuse, sexual abuse, emotional abuse, and neglect) occur between people of all ages.

Studies looking at the impact of gender on family violence have reported that husbands and wives hit each other with similar frequency (Straus & Gelles, 1986). However, the consequences of the violence perpetrated by husbands is very different from that perpetrated by wives. Male violence has much more serious health and emotional consequences for families than does violence perpetrated by women. Men do not suffer from what Walker (1979) has called the "battered woman's syndrome." Battered women suffering from this syndrome become increasingly paralyzed in their abilities to make changes in their lives. They live in fear of the next attack. However, they may remain unable to seek help.

While men may be hit by their wives, typically they have outside contacts, do not become isolated, and are, generally, larger and stronger than their wives. Furthermore, much of the violence perpetrated by women against men is done in retaliation or self-defense (Straus, 1980; Saunders, 1986). Although the consequences and causes of violence by women may be very different from those for violence perpetrated by men, both male and female violence have serious consequences for the family.

Elder abuse also generally tends to be directed at females (Fulmer, 1988; King, 1984). At greatest risk are women who are physically and/or mentally "impaired" and who are dependent in some way on their abuser. Longer life expectancy of females may contribute to this occurrence.

Overall, the data indicate that mothers are slightly more likely to physically abuse their children than are fathers (Gil, 1970). However, Gil reported that in two-parent families, about two-thirds of the abusing parents were fathers. The higher overall incidence of child abuse perpetrated by women may result from women being the primary caregivers of young children (who tend to be abused more frequently) and being the single caregivers of children after a divorce. Thus, women are more likely to have to deal with the added economic and social stressors of single parenting than are men.

Similarly, women are usually charged with the primary responsibility of caring for their elderly parents; hence some studies have suggested that the majority of elder abuse is committed by middle-aged females who are typically offspring of the abused (Pedrick-Cornell & Gelles, 1982).

Although reports of child sexual abuse perpetrated by women are increasing, the primary offenders seem to be men. This appears to be true even when the victims are boys. For example, Finkelhor (1979) reported that 80% of the sexually abused boys in his study were abused by men, and Risin and Koss (1987) reported that 53% of the boys in their study were abused by men.

Finally, research has consistently found links between chemical dependency and all types of family violence (Coleman et al., 1980; Coleman & Straus, 1983; Rosenbaum & O'Leary, 1981; Fulmer, 1988), although the exact relationship is unclear. It does not appear that alcoholism causes domestic violence, and there is no evidence that merely treating the substance abuse substantially reduces the level of violence in an individual. However, chemically dependent individuals are more likely to be abusive than are people who are not chemically dependent.

Thus, it is clear that individual characteristics impact on the level of violence within the family. Individuals who are generally violent, feel powerless, appear possessive and jealous, have low self-esteem, lack coping moderators, or are chemically dependent are at greater risk for domestic violence. Individual characteristics interact with situational stressors including precipitating events to increase the likelihood that domestic violence will occur.

Nuclear Family Characteristics

The quality of the marital relationship influences the likelihood of child abuse (Martin, 1976). When husbands and wives have warm, loving relationships, child abuse is rare. Child physical and sexual abuse are much more likely to flourish when marital relationships are deteriorating or destructive. One study (Paveza, 1988) found that families in which the marital relationship is unsatisfactory are at 7.19 times greater risk for incest than are families in which the marital relationship is satisfactory. Furthermore, marital violence seems to occur more frequently when marital stress is higher (Stith, 1990). In addition, father–daughter incest seems to occur more frequently when the mother–daughter relationship is more distant (Paveza, 1988).

A variety of structural factors within the family also seem to influence the incidence of violence. Studies have found that families with greater numbers of children are more likely to experience child abuse (Gil, 1970; Parke & Collmer, 1975; Elmer, 1967; Straus et al., 1980). The risk of family violence is increased when children are unwanted (Martin, 1976), "difficult" (Martin, 1976; George & Main, 1979), or premature (Martin, 1976; Elmer, 1967; Lynch, 1975). Although no children "ask for" or deserve abuse, some may be at greater risk than are others because of their individual characteristics and behaviors.

Stressors

A variety of events that affect the family as it proceeds through time, including developmental and unexpected stressors and immediate precipitating events, may increase the likelihood of family violence (Conger et al., 1979).

Developmental Stressors

Carter and McGoldrick (1988) outline the normative life cycle changes that families face as they move through time. Family anxiety is greater around life cycle transition points and thus the likelihood of the development of symptomatic behavior and dysfunction is also greater. Gelles and Straus (1979) include these stressors among those that make families more susceptible to violence. For example, studies have been reported that suggest that an increase in violence perpetrated by men to their partner occurs during pregnancy (Gelles, 1975). This abuse can also be considered prenatal child abuse and may grow out of the stress of the family situation being compounded when the family has other preexisting stresses (Gelles, 1975).

The birth of the infant can also be a time of increased stress and increased likelihood of abuse. Often the stress is the result of an unwanted pregnancy that is extremely inconvenient and/or draining to the family resources (Watkins & Bradbard, 1982).

The stage of the life cycle of the nuclear family can also contribute to the incidence of elder abuse. Care of elderly parents has customarily been the socially assigned responsibility of adult daughters and daughters-in-law (King, 1984). By the time their parents require assistance and care, these women may be experiencing stressful age-related changes. The timing of added responsibility for their parents may coincide with the launching stage of their own children, a period of college and wedding expenses, as well as a time when many women are looking forward to fulfilling their own educational and career plans (Katz, 1980). Sometimes an older parent moves in with an adult child who is nearing retirement age and looking forward to a more carefree and relaxed lifestyle. In both cases, caring for an elderly parent exacts a heavy financial and psychological toll, which may lead to elder abuse.

Unpredictable Stressors

Throughout the life cycle the family is also affected by unpredictable stressors such as unemployment, chronic illness, untimely death, and divorce. Any of these unpredictable events may push families already under strain over the line to abuse. Life crises such as loss of job, divorce, change in residence, and decrease in income can have a detrimental effect on family members' ability to care for their elders and may trigger abuse (Douglas et al., 1980). Since old age is accompanied by many negative life events, including the death of loved ones, reduced income, and ill health, stress has been postulated as a possible causal factor in elder abuse and neglect (Wolf 1987).

Unemployment increases the risk of all forms of abuse (Gil, 1970; Parke & Collmer, 1975; Peterson, 1980; Straus et al., 1980). Losing a job or not being able to find an appropriate job seems to have deleterious effects on the individual's self-esteem.

In addition to specific unexpected stressors, the pile-up of stressors has been shown to be related to increased incidence of both child abuse and spouse abuse (Garbarino, 1976; Neidig & Friedman, 1984). Neidig and Friedman (1984) report that in their study of military subjects, those who received a higher score on an overall measure of stress reported higher frequency of violent episodes. Straus (1980), in his investigation of the relationship between violence and stress, concludes that stress does not cause violence but acts as a mediating variable that increases the likelihood of violence occurring. Thus, individuals who show certain vulnerabilities to violence and who are under higher stress, both normative and unexpected, seem to be at higher risk for violence.

Immediate Precipitating Events

All of the various factors in this model influence the individual's response to stressful situations. When abuse occurs in a family, the perpetrator generally blames the abuse on a specific precipitating factor. For example, the mother may say that she hit her child because the child was disobedient. The husband may attribute his violence to his wife's insult. The father may say that he molested his daughter because his wife worked nights and was unavailable to him.

Although at times all children misbehave, all spouses let their partners down, all adults get their feelings hurt, and all families leave children at home with only one parent, the outcome of these experiences is generally not abuse. It is clear that the immediate precipitating event—for example, the child's misbehavior—is not the *cause* of the abuse. The abuse is caused by a multitude of factors, unique to each individual family, which have been delineated in this model.

Resources

Resources refer to the capabilities of individuals and families to meet the demands of everyday life and overcome vulnerabilities without resorting to violence or other dysfunctional behavior (McCubbin & Figley, 1983). These are divided into categories: personal resources, family system resources, and social support.

Personal Resources

Personal resources refer to the broad range of characteristics of family members that are potentially available to them in times of crisis

(McCubbin & Figley, 1983). When family members have sufficient appropriate resources, they are more able to deal with stressors and vulnerabilities. "There are four basic components of personal resources: financial (economic well-being), education (contributing to cognitive ability that facilitates realistic stress perception and problem-solving skills), health (physical and emotional well-being), and psychological resources (personality characteristics)" (McCubbin & Figley, 1983, p. 16). Each of the factors that have been noted as vulnerabilities or stressors can also be recognized as being resources. For example, poverty can be considered a stressor that increases the likelihood of violence occurring. Violence occurs at all socioeconomic strata and is not simply a problem caused by poverty. However, it is clear that poverty increases the risk of violence in families (Gelles, 1974; Gayford, 1975; Elmer, 1967; Parke and Collmer, 1975; Straus et al., 1980). Poverty-level families may not have the resources needed to deal with normal stressors of family life. Additionally, poverty attacks self-esteem and leads to despair. This despair may become a breeding ground for violence in the family. Therefore, an important personal resource is financial stability. A woman with financial resources may leave an abusive husband or may hire a babysitter in order to get time away from a fussy baby. A family with resources that is having marital or parenting problems may seek out and pay for therapy before violence escalates. A middle-aged couple needing a break from an elderly parent can hire someone to help.

Education can serve as a resource in many ways. For example, programs to prevent sexual victimization of children are widely available throughout the United States. It is clear that "no single set of activities will create a society in which the vulnerable need not protect themselves because they are in fact not vulnerable. However, efforts by prevention professionals directed toward making the vulnerable strong and changing the social conditions associated with vulnerability will go a long way in preventing sexual abuse of children" (Conte et al., 1986). Thus, education and primary prevention efforts are seen as vital resources in combating all forms of domestic violence.

Emotional and physical health and psychological resources are also important factors in reducing the likelihood that abuse will occur. For example, individuals who have high self-esteem, good coping skills, and who are generally nonviolent will be able to deal with stress more competently without resorting to domestic violence.

Family System

Family cohesion and adaptability seem to be two important family resources in managing stress and overcoming vulnerabilities (Olson et al., 1979). Cohesion refers to the emotional bonding family members have with each other. Adaptability refers to the amount of flexibility to change a family typically demonstrates. It appears that families functioning moderately along the dimensions of cohesion and adaptability are likely to make a more successful adaptation to crisis. Too much cohesion can lead to enmeshment and too much adaptability is chaotic for the family. Likewise, too little cohesion leads to disengagement and too little adaptability leads to rigidity (McCubbin & Patterson, 1983).

One study examining the relationship between family adaptability and cohesion with incestuous families was conducted by Saunders et al. (1987). These authors found that both mothers and incestuous fathers viewed their families as being disengaged in their level of cohesion and rigid in their level of adaptability.

Another important family resource is clear, open communication. "Conflict avoidance, secretiveness, hostility, and double-binding communication patterns are commonly present in sexually abusing families" (Trepper & Barrett, 1986, p. 20). Dysfunctional communication patterns between husband and wife and between mother and daughter are often seen in sexually abusive families. Thus, openness and clarity in communication can be a great resource in preventing family violence.

The balance of power between family members seems to be important in leading to healthy family functioning. Hierarchy refers to the graduated system of membership in the family. "In healthy families, clear boundaries exist separating parents from children. In many incest families, these boundaries are blurred" (Barrett et al., 1986). Not only is the boundary between parents and children important for preventing child sexual abuse, the balance of power between the parental couple seems to be important in preventing spouse abuse. Coleman and Straus (1983) reported that egalitarian marriages (in which the power is shared) have the lowest rates of intrafamily conflict and violence.

Social Network

Another potential resource is a strong social network. Families who have relationships with neighbors or others are much less likely to have problems with domestic violence than are families with no outside relationships. Social isolation is related to child abuse, spouse abuse, and elder abuse (Steele, 1975; Straus et al., 1980; Kosberg, 1985). Isolation plays a particularly significant role in elder abuse, since infirm elders have little or no contact with people outside the home who might be alert to symptoms of signs of abuse (Kosberg, 1985; King, 1984). Young (1964) found that 85% of the severely abusing and 83% of the moderately abusing families in her study had no continuing relationship with people outside the nuclear family. Numerous investigators have also noted that these families receive little or no support from relatives (Parke & Collmer 1975). Garbarino (1976) reported that the degree to which mothers were subjected to socioeconomic stress without adequate support systems accounted for a substantial proportion of the variance in rates of child abuse in his study of 58 counties in New York.

Incest families also protect their sexual secret by constructing barriers between the family system and its social environment (Larson & Maddock, 1986). This isolation fosters inappropriate overdependence among family members. Therefore, providing social supports is a vital part of any treatment program designed to eliminate violence.

SUMMARY

Whether the violence involves a single physical assault, repeated assaults, psychological violence, or sexual abuse, many factors interact leading to its emergence and maintenance. The interactive framework described above elucidates a number of potential avenues for intervention. For example, large-scale education programs can be developed to change cultural values that permit and even encourage violence to continue. Programs designed to prevent violence in this generation can free the next generation from the vulnerability caused by being socialized into violence. Programs can be developed to reduce stressors experienced by families. Individual, family system, and social network resources can be enhanced. However, regardless of which avenue is chosen for intervention, it is useful if the helper is cognizant of the myriad of issues involved and how they relate to each other. For example, when a therapist works to end child abuse by focusing only on the immediate precipitating event, that is, teaching the abused child to behave more appropriately, without examining each of the factors in the proposed model and without examining the role of other family members, his or her myopic vision may actually increase the level of violence in the family. The goal of this book is to present a multidimensional perspective to the treatment of domestic violence.

REFERENCES

Barrett, M. J., Sykes, C., & Byrnes, W. (1986). A systemic model for the treatment of intrafamily child sexual abuse. *Journal of Psychotherapy and the Family, 2,* 67–82.

Belsky, J. (1980). Child maltreatment, an ecological integration. *American Psychologist, 35,* 320–335.

Bernard, M., & Bernard, J. (1983). Violent intimacy: The family as a model of love relationships. *Family Relations, 32,* 283–286.

Blumberg, R. (1978). *Stratification: Socioeconomic and sexual inequality.* Dubuque, IA: William C. Brown.

Bolton, F. (1981). *The pregnant adolescent,* Newbury Park, CA: Sage Publications.

Burgess, R., & Conger, R. (1977). Family interaction patterns related to child abuse and neglect: Some preliminary findings. *Child Abuse and Neglect: The International Journal, 1,* 269–277.

Carter, B., & McGoldrick, M. (1988). *The changing family life cycle: A framework for family therapy.* New York: Gardner.

Chafetz, J. (1984). *Sex and advantage: A comparative macrostructural theory of sex stratification.* Totowa, NJ: Rowman and Allanheld.

Coleman, D., & Straus, M. (1983). Alcohol abuse and family violence. In E. Gottheil, A. Durley, I. Skolada & H. Waxman (Eds.). *Alcohol, drug abuse and aggression* (pp. 104–123). Springfield, IL: Charles C. Thomas.

Coleman, K. (1980). Conjugal violence: What 33 men report. *Journal of Marriage and Family Therapy, 6,* 207–213.

Coleman, K., Weinman, M., & Hsi, B. (1980). Factors affecting conjugal violence. *Journal of Psychology, 105,* 197–202.

Conger, R., Burgess, R., & Barrett, C. (1979). Child abuse related to life change and perceptions of illness: Some preliminary findings. *The Family Coordinator, 28,* 73–78.

Conte, J., Rosen, C., & Saperstein, L. (1986). An analysis of programs to prevent the sexual victimization of children. *Journal of Primary Prevention, 6*(3), 141–155.

Disbrow, M., Doerr, H., & Caulfield, C. (1977). Measuring the components of parents' potential for child abuse and neglect. *International Journal of Child Abuse and Neglect, 1,* 279–296.

Douglas, R. L., Hickey, T., & Noel, L. (1980). *A study of maltreatment of the elderly and other vulnerable adults.* Ann Arbor, MI: Institute of Gerontology, University of Michigan.

Elmer, E. (1967). *Children in jeopardy: A study of abused minors and their families.* Pittsburgh: University of Pittsburgh Press.

Finkelhor, D. (1979). *Sexually victimized children.* New York: Free Press.

Fulmer, T. (1988). Elder abuse. In M. Straus (Ed.), *Abuse and victimization across the life span.* Baltimore, MD: Johns Hopkins University Press.

Garbarino, J. (1976). A preliminary study of some ecological correlates of child abuse: The impact of socioeconomic stress on mothers. *Child Development, 47,* 178–185.

Gayford, J. (1975). Wife beating: A preliminary survey of 100 cases. *British Medical Journal, 1*, 194–197.

Gelles, R. (1974). *The violent home.* Beverly Hills, CA: Sage.

Gelles, R. (1975). Violence and pregnancy: A note on the extent of the problem and needed services. *The Family Coordinator, 24*, 81–86.

Gelles, R. (1979). Child abuse as psychopathology: A sociological critique and reformulation. In R. Gil (Ed.), *Child abuse and violence.* New York: AMS Press.

Gelles, R. J., & Straus, M. A. (1979). Determinants of violence in the family: Toward a theoretical integration. In W. R. Burr, R. Hill, F. I. Nye, & I. L. Reiss (Eds.) *Contemporary theories about the family* (pp. 549–581). New York: The Free Press.

George, C., & Main, M. (1979). Social interactions of young abused children: Approach, avoidance, and aggression. *Child Development, 50*, 308–318.

Gil, D. (1970). *Violence against children: Physical child abuse in the United States.* Cambridge, MA: Harvard University Press.

Hartman, C., & Burgess, A. (1988). Information processing of trauma: Case application of a model. *Journal of Interpersonal Violence, 3*(4), 443–457.

Hotaling, G., & Sugarman, D. (1986). An analysis of risk markers in husband to wife violence: The current state of knowledge. *Violence and Victims, 1*(2), 101–123.

Kalmuss, D. (1984). The intergenerational transmission of marital aggression. *Journal of Marriage and the Family, 46*(1), 11–19.

Katz, K. (1980). Elder abuse. *Journal of Family Law, 18*, 695–722.

King, N. (1984). Exploitation and abuse of older family members: An overview of the problem. In Costa J. (Ed.), *Abuse of the elderly: A guide to resources and services.* Lexington, MA: Lexington Books.

Kosberg, J. (1985). Victimization of the elderly: Causation and prevention. *Victimology: An International Journal, 10*, 376–396.

Larson, N., & Maddock, J. (1986). Structural and functional variables in incest family systems: Implications for assessment and treatment. *Journal of Psychotherapy and the Family, 2*(2), 27–44.

Lynch, M. (1975). Ill-health and child abuse. *Lancet, 2*, 317–319.

Martin, H. (1976). *The abused child: A multidisciplinary approach to developmental issues and treatment.* Cambridge, MA: Ballinger Publishing Co.

McCann, L., Pearlman, L. A., & Abrahamson, D. J. (in press). *Through a glass darkly: Transforming the inner experience of trauma.* New York: Brunner/Mazel.

McCubbin, H., & Figley, C. (1983). *Stress and the family:* Vol. 1. *Coping with normative transitions.* New York: Brunner/Mazel.

McCubbin, H., & Patterson, J. (1983). Family transitions: Adaptations to stress. In McCubbin, H., & Figley, C. (Eds.), *Stress and the family:* Vol. 1. *Coping with normative transitions.* New York: Bruner/Mazel.

Moos, R. H. (Ed.) (1986). *Coping with life crises: An integrated approach.* New York: Plenum Press.

Neidig, P., Freidman, D., & Collins, B. (1984). *Attitudinal characteristics of males who have engaged in spouse abuse.* Paper presented at the Second National Conference for Family Violence Researchers, University of New Hampshire, Durham, NH.

Olson, D., Russell, C., & Sprenkle, D. (1979). Circumplex model of marital and family systems: II. Empirical studies and clinical intervention. In J. Vincent (Ed.), *Advances in family intervention, assessment and theory.* Greenwich, CT: JAI Press.

Oppel, W., & Royston, A. (1971). Teenage births: Some social, psychological, and physical sequelae. *American Journal of Public Health,* 61, 751–756.

Parke, R., & Collmer, C. (1975). Child abuse: An interdisciplinary analysis. In M. Hetherington (Ed.), *Review of child development research* (Vol. 5, pp. 1–102). Chicago: University of Chicago Press.

Parker, B., & Schumacher, D. (1977). The battered wife syndrome and violence in the nuclear family of origin: A controlled pilot study. *American Journal of Public Health,* 67, 760–761.

Paveza, G. (1988). Risk factors in father daughter child sexual abuse: A case-control study. *Journal of Interpersonal Violence,* 3(3), 290–306.

Pedrick-Cornell, C., & Gelles, R. (1982). Elder abuse: The status of current knowledge. *Family Relations,* 31, 457–465.

Peterson, R. (1980). Social class social learning and wife abuse. *Social Service Review,* 54, 390–406.

Pillemer, K. (1985). *Domestic violence against the elderly: A case-control study.* Unpublished doctoral dissertation, Department of Sociology, Brandeis University, Waltham, MA.

Pillemer, K., & Finkelhor, D. (1988). The prevalence of elder abuse: A random sample survey. *The Gerontologist,* 28(1), 51–57.

Radin, N. (1988). Alternatives to suspension and corporal punishment. *Urban Education,* 22(4), 476–495.

Risin, L., & Koss, M. (1987). The sexual abuse of boys: Prevalence and descriptive characteristics of childhood victimizations. *Journal of Interpersonal Violence,* 2(3), 309–323.

Rosenbaum, A., & O'Leary, K. (1981). Marital violence: Characteristics of abusive couples. *Journal of Consulting and Clinical Psychology,* 49(1), 63–71.

Rouse, L. (1984). *Conflict tactics used by men in marital disputes.* Paper presented at the Second National Conference for Family Violence Researchers, University of New Hampshire, Durham, NH.

Roy, M. (1982). Four thousand partners in violence: A trend analysis. In M. Roy (Ed.), *The abusing partner: An analysis of domestic battering.* New York: Van Nostrand Reinhold.

Saunders, B., McClure, S., & Murphy, S. (1987). Structure, function, and symptoms in father-child sexual abuse families: A multilevel-multirespondent empirical assessment. Paper presented at the Family Violence Research Conference, University of New Hampshire, Durham, NH.

Saunders, D. (1986). When battered women use violence: Husband-abuse or self-defense? *Violence and Victims,* 1, 47–60.

Sgroi, S. (1982). A conceptual framework for child sexual abuse, In S. M. Sgroi (Ed.), *A handbook of clinical intervention in child sexual abuse*. Lexington, MA: Lexington Books.

Sonkin, D., Martin, D., & Walker, L. (1985). *The male batterer: A treatment approach*. New York: Springer Publishing Co.

Steele, B. (1975). Working with abusive parents: From a psychiatric point of view. Washington, DC: U.S. Department of Health, Education, and Welfare, Office of Child Development, #0H075–70.

Steele, B. (1976). Violence within the family. In R. E. Helfer & C. H. Kempe (Eds.), *Child abuse and neglect: The family and the community*. Cambridge, MA: Ballinger Publishing Co.

Steinmetz, S. (1980). Elder abuse: Society's double dilemma. Testimony before the Joint Senate Hearing Special Committee on Aging and House Select Committee on Aging, June 11, 1–18.

Stith, S. (1990). The relationship between the male police officer's response to victims of domestic violence and his personal and family experiences. In E. Viano (Ed.), *The victimology research handbook*. New York: Garland Publishing Co.

Straus, M. (1976). Sexual inequality, cultural norms, and wife-beating. *Victimology*, 1(1); 54–76.

Straus, M. (1977). A sociological perspective on the prevention and treatment of wifebeating. In M. Roy (Ed.), *Battered women*. New York: Van Nostrand Reinhold.

Straus, M. (1980). Victims and aggressors in marital violence. *American Behavioral Scientist*, 23, 681–704.

Straus, M., & Gelles, R. (1986). Societal change and change in family violence from 1975 to 1985 as revealed by two national surveys. *Journal of Marriage and the Family*, 48(August), 465–479.

Straus, M., Gelles, R., & Steinmetz, S. (1980). *Behind closed doors*. Garden City, NY: Doubleday.

Trepper, T., & Barrett, M. J. (1986). Vulnerability to incest: A framework for assessment. *Journal of Psychotherapy and the Family*, 2(2), 13–24.

Trickett, P., & Kuczynski, L. (1986). Children's misbehaviors and parental discipline strategies in abusive and nonabusive families. *Developmental Psychology*, 22(1), 115–123.

Walker, L. (1979). *The battered woman*. New York: Harper and Row.

Watkins, H., & Bradbard, M. (1982). Child maltreatment: An overview with suggestions for intervention and research. *Family Relations, 31*, 323–333.

Wilson, J. P. (1985). Predicting post-traumatic stress disorders among Vietnam veterans. In W. E. Kelly (Ed.), *Post-traumatic stress disorder and the war veteran patient* (pp. 102–147). New York: Brunner/Mazel.

Wolf, R. (1987, July), *Spouse abuse and neglect in the aging*. Paper presented at the Third National Family Violence Conference, University of New Hampshire, Durham, NH.

Young, L. (1964). *Wednesday's children: A study of child neglect and abuse*. New York: McGraw-Hill.

I   Treatment of Spousal Abuse

A Comprehensive Model for Crisis Intervention with Battered Women and Their Children*

2

Albert R. Roberts
Beverly Schenkman Roberts

> Do you know what some women get for their birthdays? A black eye; a punch in the ribs; or a few teeth knocked out. It's so frightening because it doesn't just happen on their birthday. It may be every month, every week, or even every day. It's so frightening because some times he abuses the kids, too. Or maybe she's pregnant and he kicks her in the stomach in the same spot where, just a few minutes ago, she felt the baby moving. It's so frightening because the woman doesn't know what to do. She feels so helpless. He's in control. She prays he'll come to his senses and stop. He never does. She prays he won't hurt their kids. He threatens to. She prays he won't kill her. He promises he will. . . . (Haag, undated).

The above description of the fear and anguish to which battered women are repeatedly subjected comes from a training manual for crisis counselors prepared by the Domestic Violence Intervention Program of Brown County, Wisconsin. It is included in the manual to acquaint staff and volunteers with the painful history of the women they will be counseling. Increasingly, battered women are turning to emergency shelters and telephone crisis intervention services for help.

Recognition of the need for and actual establishment of crisis intervention for victims of the battering syndrome has increased dramatically since the mid-1970s. While there were only seven emergency shelters for battered women in 1974 (Roberts, 1981), by 1986

*Adapted with permission from Roberts, A. D., & Roberts, B. S. (1990). A comprehensive model for crisis intervention with battered women and their children. In A. R. Roberts (Ed.), *Crisis Intervention Handbook: Assessment, Treatment, and Research* (pp. 105–123). Belmont, CA: Wadsworth.

there were more than 800 shelters coast-to-coast for battered women and their children (National Coalition Against Domestic Violence, 1986). Through crisis intervention, many women are able to regain control of their lives by identifying current options and goals and by working to attain those goals. The children of battered women may also be in crisis, but their plight has often been overlooked as the domestic violence programs focused their efforts on emergency intervention for the women. The progressive programs now incorporate crisis intervention for children (as well as for the mothers) in the treatment plan.

Battered women are usually subjected to a prolonged pattern of abuse coupled with a recent severe attack so that by the time the victim makes contact with a shelter, she is generally in need of crisis intervention. Abused women are subjected to an extended period of stress and trauma that results in a continual loss of energy. The woman is in a vulnerable position, and when a particularly severe beating takes place or when other factors occur (e.g., the abuser starts to hurt the children), the woman may be thrust into a state of crisis (NOVA, 1983).

Effective treatment for battered women and their children in crisis requires an understanding of crisis theory and the techniques of crisis intervention. According to Caplan (1964), Aguilera and Messick (1978), and Janosik (1984), a crisis state can occur rapidly when the following four things happen:

1. The victim experiences a precipitating or hazardous incident.
2. The incident is perceived by the woman as threatening to her or her children's safety and, as a result, tension and distress intensifies.
3. The battered woman attempts to resolve the situation by using customary coping methods and fails to resolve the situation.
4. The emotional discomfort and turmoil worsens and the victim feels that the pain or anguish is unbearable.

At this point of maximum discomfort, when the woman perceives the pain and torment as unbearable, she is in an active crisis state. During this time there is an opportunity for change and growth, and some women are mobilized to seek help from a 24-hour telephone crisis intervention service, the police, the hospital emergency room, or a shelter for battered women.

The emphasis in crisis assessment is on identifying the nature of the precipitating event and the woman's cognitive and affective reaction to it. The three most common precipitating events that lead battered women in crisis to seek the help of a domestic violence program are (1) an acute battering incident resulting in serious physical injury, (2) a serious abusive injury inflicted on the woman's child, (3) temporary impairment of hearing, sight, or thought process as a direct result of severe batterment. Often the precipitating event is perceived by the woman in crisis as being the final incident or "last straw" in a long history of violence (L. Edington, executive director, SOJOURNER, Indianapolis, personal communication, Feb. 19, 1987; Houston, 1987; R. Podhorin, director, Womanspace, Inc., Lawrenceville, NJ, personal communication, Feb. 12, 1987; M. Schiller-Ramirez, executive director, St. Martha's Hall, St. Louis, personal communication, Mar. 4, 1987).

Crisis intervention with battered women needs to be done in an orderly, structured, and humanistic manner. The process is the same for victims of other violent crimes, but it is particularly important to respond quickly to abused women because they may continue to be in danger the longer they remain in a place where the batterer can locate them. Crisis intervention activities can result in the person returning to her precrisis state or growing from the crisis intervention so that she learns new coping skills to utilize in the future.

This chapter will describe the following types of crisis intervention: early intervention by police-based crisis teams and victim assistance units, assessment and detection in the hospital emergency room, specific intervention techniques used by crisis hotlines and battered women's shelters, and short-term treatment for the children. The chapter will also discuss the importance of referrals.

CRISIS INTERVENTION BY POLICE-BASED CRISIS TEAMS AND VICTIM ASSISTANCE UNITS

Surveys of police departments around the United States indicate that approximately 80 to 90% of the police officers' time is spent on service calls, also known as order maintenance activities, such as assaults among family members, neighbor disputes, bar fights, traffic accidents, and individuals who are drunken and disorderly. The police may have the skills to intervene and resolve a dispute among neighbors, a bar fight, or a traffic accident, but they are rarely skilled to provide crisis intervention and follow-up counseling with victims of domestic violence.

In recognition of the large amount of time police spend respond-

ing to repeat family assault calls and their lack of clinical skills,
several police departments have developed crisis intervention teams
staffed by professional social workers and trained volunteers.

Victims often turn to their local city or county police department when confronted with the life-threatening danger posed by
domestic violence. As a result of the Thurman case (in which a
battered women was awarded $2.3 million in her lawsuit against the
Torrington, Connecticut, police department for its failure to protect
her from her violent husband), more police departments are re-
sponding to calls from domestic violence victims. Police can respond quickly to domestic violence calls and can transport the
victim to the local hospital emergency room or the battered women's
shelter. In some cities, police receive backup from the crisis team,
which arrives at the home shortly after the police. The first such
crisis team began in 1975 at the Pima County District Attorney's
Office in Tucson, Arizona. The acceptance of and growing reliance
on this program by the Tucson Police Department is revealed by the
significantly increased number of police referrals to the crisis team
— there were a total of 840 police referrals in 1977 compared to
4,734 referrals in 1984. It should be noted that these figures reflect
referrals for all types of crime victims, but most referrals are for
domestic violence cases. Since violence in the home constitutes a
considerable percentage of police calls, abused women are frequent
beneficiaries of this innovative system.

The following descriptions of programs in Tucson, Arizona, and
Houston, Texas, will illustrate the intervention procedures utilized
by victim assistance programs.

The Pima County Victim Witness Program has received national
recognition for providing immediate crisis intervention to battered
women and other crime victims. It has served as a model for similar
programs in other cities.

The program was initiated in 1975 with a grant from the Law
Enforcement Assistance Administration (LEAA). The grant-funded
program was so successful that when the grant expired, the city and
county officials agreed to pay for its continuation.

The crisis intervention staff use two police vehicles (unmarked
and radio-equipped) to travel to the crime scene. The mobile crisis
teams are on patrol every night between 6:00 p.m. and 3:00 a.m. At
all other times they are contacted via a beeper system (Roberts,
1987).

Domestic violence cases are potentially the most dangerous for
the crisis counselors. The staff work in pairs, generally in a team of
a male and a female. They are given an intensive training program

in which they are taught self-defense, escape driving, and the way to use a police radio, as well as crisis intervention techniques.

Houston Program

In 1983, the Houston Police Department developed a program (modeled after the Tucson program) to provide immediate crisis counseling to victims of domestic violence as well as to victims of other violent crimes such as rape. The Crisis Intervention Team (CIT) provides the following services: crisis counseling, advocacy, transportation to and from medical centers and shelters, and referrals to social service agencies. An estimated 40% of their clients are battered women (Roberts, 1990).

The CIT staff are civilian employees of the Houston Police Department, and all of the referrals come from the police. A crisis team (always working in groups of two) is notified of a crisis situation via the police radio, and the counselors meet the police at the crime scene. The police, after determining that the counselors will not be in danger, leave the home. The counselors utilize a basic crisis intervention model of assessing the situation, discussing the options, forming a plan of action, and aiding the victim in implementing the plan. The Houston program has 12 full-time staff members and 2 to 4 graduate student interns each semester, and has recently recruited volunteer workers. The program director, Margaret Hardman-Muye, has a master's degree in social work and is an advanced clinical practitioner with specialization in treating battered women and victims of sexual assault.

The program is funded by a state criminal justice grant and by the city of Houston. Initially, 100% of the budget came from the state grant, but the city is expected to fund an additional 20% of the cost each year until it is totally city-funded. In its first year, the program was budgeted at $159,000. This amount had increased to $351,000 in its third year of operation.

As of 1986, similar types of crisis intervention programs had been developed under the auspices of the police departments in many cities, including South Phoenix, Arizona; Santa Ana, California; Stockton, California; Indianapolis, Indiana; Detroit, Michigan; Omaha, Nebraska; Las Vegas, Nevada; Rochester, New York; Houston, Texas; and Salt Lake City, Utah. However, there are still many communities that have not initiated this type of crisis intervention program. It is hoped that the success of the newly developed programs will encourage other localities to establish a similar type of service.

ASSESSMENT AND INTERVENTION
IN THE EMERGENCY ROOM

A visit to the emergency room may provide the initial opportunity for some victims to recognize the life-threatening nature of the violent relationship and to begin making important plans to change their situation. At a growing number of large hospitals in urban areas, crisis intervention is being provided to battered women by emergency room staff.

A recommended way for emergency rooms to handle detection and assessment of battery is through the use of an adult abuse protocol. Two of the pioneers in the development of these protocols are K. S. Klingbeil and V. D. Boyd of Seattle, who initiated plans in 1976 for emergency room intervention with abused women. The Social Work Department of the Harborview Medical Center in Seattle developed an adult abuse protocol that provides specific information on the assessment to be made by the involved staff: the triage nurse, the physician, and the social worker. Using a protocol serves two purposes: first, it alerts the involved hospital staff to provide the appropriate clinical care, and second, it documents the violent incident so that if the woman decides to file a legal complaint, "reliable, court-admissible evidence" (including photographs) is available (Klingbeil & Boyd, 1984).

Although this protocol was developed for use by emergency room social workers, it can easily be adapted for use by other health care personnel. The following case example describes the way in which the adult abuse protocol has been successfully used:

> Mrs. J was admitted to the emergency room accompanied by her sister. This was the second visit within the month for Mrs. J and the emergency room triage nurse and social worker realized that her physical injuries were much more severe on this second visit. Mrs. J was crying, appeared frightened, and in spite of the pain, she constantly glanced over her shoulder. She indicated that her husband would follow her to the emergency room and that she feared for her life. The social worker immediately notified Security. . . .
>
> Mrs. J indicated that she just wanted to rest briefly and then leave through another entrance. She was four months pregnant and concerned about her unborn child. She reported that this had been the first time Mr. J had struck her in the abdomen. The social worker spent considerable time calming Mrs. J in order to obtain a history of the assaultive event. Consent for photography was obtained and Mrs. J indicated that she *would* press charges. "The attack on my child" seemed to be a turning

point in her perception of the gravity of her situation, even though Mr. J had beaten her at least a dozen times over the previous two years.

While the social worker assisted in the history taking, a physician provided emergency medical care: several sutures over the right eye.

With Mrs. J's permission, an interview was conducted with her sister who agreed to let Mrs. J stay with her and also agreed to participate in the police reporting. When Mrs. J felt able, the social worker and sister helped her complete necessary forms for the police who had been called to the emergency room.

Although the physician had carefully explained the procedures and rationale to Mrs. J, the social worker repeated this information and also informed her of the lethality of the battering, tracing from her chart her last three emergency room visits. Mrs. J was quick to minimize the assaults but when the social worker showed her photographs from those visits, documenting bruises around her face and neck, she shook her head and said, "No more, not any more." Her sister provided excellent support and additional family members were on their way to the emergency room to be with Mrs. J. When the police arrived Mrs. J was able to give an accurate report of the day's events. . . . She realized there would be difficult decisions to make and readily accepted a follow-up counseling appointment for a Battered Women's group. (Klingbeil & Boyd, 1984, pp. 16–24)

It should be noted that all cases are not handled as easily as the one cited above. The two aspects of Mrs. J's situation that led to a positive resolution were (1) the immediate involvement of emergency room staff and their discussion with the patient of her history and injuries, and (2) the availability of supportive relatives.

Before the woman leaves the emergency room, the social worker should talk with her about whether to return home or to seek refuge with friends, with family, or at a shelter for abused women. The emergency room staff should be able to provide names and phone numbers of referral sources. It is helpful if the pertinent information is printed on a small business-size card (which would be easy to tuck away in a pocket or purse) and given to all abuse victims as well as to suspected victims (Klingbeil & Boyd, 1984). Even if a woman refuses to acknowledge that her current bruises are the result of batterment, she may keep the card for use in the future.

Merely having an adult-abuse protocol does not ensure that it will be used. A study conducted by Flaherty et al. (1985) at four Philadelphia hospitals found that the protocol was used selectively, mainly for victims who volunteered that they had been battered. The medical staff thus ignored the opportunity to help batterment victims who were not able to volunteer the information. The researchers cited the following reasons for underutilization of the protocol:

1. Some physicians and nurses did not regard battering as a medical problem.
2. They believed that it would be an invasion of privacy to ask a woman questions about how she was injured.
3. Many of the emergency room staff viewed completing the protocol as an additional burden when they were already overworked.

Of those medical personnel who did recognize battery as a legitimate problem, the intervention technique used most often was the tear-off list of referral sources that was printed at the bottom of the protocol.

There is a major difference between the Philadelphia study conducted by Flaherty et al. (1985) and the procedures described previously by Klingbeil and Boyd (1984) in Seattle. The Philadelphia study requested the cooperation of nurses and physicians but did not involve medical social workers. In contrast, the Harborview Medical Center protocol was created and implemented by the hospital social work department. It emphasized a multidisciplinary team approach, with the social workers taking the lead role in conducting screening and assessment, often talking to the victim while the physician provided medical treatment.

The information just presented would indicate that the involvement of medical social workers is advisable (and perhaps necessary) for the successful implementation of a system for crisis assessment and intervention with battered women in the hospital emergency room.

INTERVENTION TECHNIQUES USED BY TELEPHONE HOTLINES AND BATTERED WOMEN'S SHELTERS

Battered women in crisis may reach out for help in any of a number of ways. The initial contact is generally by telephone, making the phone line into a lifeline for many women. Violence often occurs late in the evening, on weekends, or during holidays, and shelter staff are usually available 24 hours a day to respond to a crisis call. But a woman in crisis who has just been brutally beaten probably does not know the name or phone number of the local shelter. A frequent scenario is that a woman and her children hastily escape from home late in the evening and flee to a neighbor's home to make an emergency call for help. Not having the number of the local shelter, these women generally contact the police or the area-wide crisis hotline (which aids people in all types of crises). If the woman contacts the area-wide hotline, there is generally a brief delay while the worker gathers some basic information and then gives the caller the phone number of the closest shelter. An alternative is for the crisis counselor to take the caller's phone number and have the shelter worker call her back.

When a battered woman in crisis calls a hotline, it is essential that she be able to talk immediately to a trained crisis counselor— not put on "hold" or confronted with an answering machine. If she is not able to talk to a caring and knowledgeable crisis counselor, she may just give up, and a valuable opportunity for intervening in the cycle of violence will have been lost. In these situations time is of the essence because if the violent male is still on the rampage, he is likely to go searching for her, thereby endangering not only his mate but the neighbor as well.

Hotline workers distinguish between a "crisis call"—one in which the woman is in imminent danger or has just been beaten— and other types of calls in which the individual is not in immediate danger but is anxious or distressed and is seeking information or someone to talk to. The overriding goal of crisis intervention is ensuring the safety of the woman and her children. To determine whether the call is a crisis call, the worker asks such questions as:

Are you or your children in danger now?
Is the abuser there now?
Do you want me to call the police?
Do you want to leave and can you do so safely?
Do you need medical attention?

Programs have different policies regarding transporting women who need refuge but have no way to get there. While some shelters will send staff to pick up the woman at her home, it is more common for shelter policy to prohibit staff from doing so because of the possibility of the staff member being attacked by the abuser. In cities that have a Crisis Intervention Team affiliated with the police department (such as those described earlier in this chapter) the shelter staff can contact the police, who will investigate the situation and radio for the crisis workers to transport the victim and her children to the shelter. Sometimes the police themselves are prevailed upon to provide the transportation.

The Marital Abuse Project of Delaware County in Pennsylvania encourages battered women to call the police themselves but there are circumstances in which they are not able to do so. In those cases, shelter workers call the police (with the woman's permission) and then contact the woman again. If the facility has two phone lines, there may be times when it is advisable for the worker to keep the woman on the line while the worker calls the police on the other line. Staff are advised to follow-up on the woman's call to law enforcement by waiting a few minutes and then also calling the police to find out where they will be taking her (i.e., to the police station, hospital, etc.). If it is too soon for the police to have this information, the worker asks the officer to call her back when they do know. If 30 minutes have elapsed without a call from the police, the worker contacts the police department again (Roberts, 1981).

Once the urgent issues pertaining to the woman's physical safety have been resolved, the crisis counselor can begin to help the victim talk about her situation and discuss possible courses of action. Throughout this process it is important for the counselor to remember that she can present different alternatives but that the client must make her own decisions.

The following is a step-by-step guide to intervention with battered women (originally developed by Jones, 1968) that is included in the training manual prepared by the Abuse Counseling and Treatment, Inc. (ACT) program in Ft. Myers, Florida. It is referred to as the ABC Process of Crisis Management—the "A" referring to "Achieving Contact," the "B" to "Boiling Down the Problem," and the "C" to "Coping."

A. *Achieving Contact*
   1. Introduce yourself: name, role and purpose.
   2. If a phone call, ask the client if she is safe and protected now.
   3. Ask client how she would like to be addressed: first name, surname, or nickname; this helps client regain control.
   4. Collect client data—breaks the ice and allows the client and counselor to get to know each other and develop trust.
   5. Ask client if she has a counselor or if she is taking any medication.
   6. Identify client's feelings and ask for perception check.
B. *Boiling Down the Problem*
   1. Ask client to describe briefly what has just happened.
   2. Encourage client to talk about the here and now.
   3. Ask client what is the most pressing problem.
   4. Ask client if it were not for said problem, would she feel better right now.

      5. Ask client if she has been confronted with a similar type of problem before, and if so, how did she handle it then? What worked and what didn't?

      6. Review with the client what you heard as the primary problem.

   C. Coping with the Problem

      1. What does the client want to happen?

      2. What is the most important need—the bottom line?

      3. Explore what the client feels is the best solution.

      4. Find out what the client is willing to do to meet her needs.

      5. Help client formulate plan of action: resources, activities, time.

      6. Arrange follow-up contact with client. (Jones, 1968)

Careful recruitment and thorough training of crisis intervention staff is essential to a program's success. It is also necessary for an experienced clinician to be on call at all times for consultation in difficult cases. In addition to knowing what to say, the workers need to learn about the tone of voice and attitude to be used while handling crisis calls. Crisis workers are advised to speak in a steady, calm voice, to ask open-ended questions, and to refrain from being judgmental.

A shelter's policies and procedures manual should include guidelines for crisis staff. For example, the ACT program in Ft. Myers, Florida, has developed a 45-page training manual that includes sections on shelter policies and procedures, referral procedures, and background information on domestic violence that discusses both the victims and the abusers. The ACT manual explains the wide variation in the emotional reaction of the women who call for help. The client's speaking style may be "fast, slow, hesitant, loud, barely audible, rambling, loss of words [or] normal." Her emotional reaction may be "angry, highly upset, hysterical, withdrawn, fearful, laughing, calm, icy, guilty, or a combination of these" (Houston, 1987). No matter what characteristics the caller exhibits, the crisis worker's task is to try to help the victim cope with the immediate situation. However, the guidelines also advise crisis counselors to avoid the pitfall of believing they need to provide the caller with immediate, expert solutions to her problems. Crisis workers should not subject themselves to guilt feelings if they cannot help an abused woman resolve her situation. If the worker suspects child abuse or neglect, she is required to notify the supervisor and then report the suspected abuse to the appropriate agency (Houston, 1987).

Shelter staff are confronted with a dilemma when the caller is an abused woman who is under the influence of drugs or alcohol or who has psychiatric symptoms. Although the women are victims of battery, they also have a significant problem that the staff is not trained to treat. Shelter policy generally requires crisis counselors to screen out battered women who are under the influence of alcohol or drugs, but there are exceptions. At Womanspace (in central New Jersey) women with drug/alcohol problems are accepted provided that they are simultaneously enrolled in a drug or alcohol treatment program (R. Podhorin, personal communication, Feb. 12, 1987). Likewise, it is the crisis counselor's responsibility to determine whether a woman's behavior is excessively irrational or bizarre or whether she is likely to be a danger to herself or others. If a woman is suspected of having psychiatric problems, she is generally referred to the psychiatric screening unit of a local hospital or to a mental health center for an evaluation.

Another policy issue relates to battered women in crisis who have no psychiatric or drug problems but are denied admission to a shelter because they have a son aged 12 or older who needs shelter also. Many programs subscribe to the belief that by the time a boy from a violent family reaches the age of 12 he will have adopted his father's violent behavior patterns, and they want to avoid the possibility of violent outbursts at the shelter. However, not all shelters have such a policy. There is a minority view that an abused woman in crisis should be helped regardless of whether or not she has a young adolescent son (Arbour, 1987).

Telephone Log

Battered women's shelters usually maintain a written record of all phone calls, whether or not they are crisis calls. In addition to seeking such routine information as name, address, phone number, marital status, and ages of children, the form may also include the following: Are you in immediate danger? Do you want me to call the police? How did you get our number? Action taken by crisis worker, and follow-up action (R. Podhorin, personal communication, Feb. 12, 1987). Shelters that are often overcrowded may also have a section on the form where the counselor can indicate whether the family is able to be housed immediately, is to be referred to another shelter or safe home, or needs to be put on a waiting list.

Womanspace developed a one-page telephone log form that asks many of the questions listed above on the front and, on the reverse side, contains further screening questions and an explanation of their policies. An example is the printed statement cited below, which explains the program's policy on weapons:

We do not allow weapons in the shelter.
    We ask that you not bring a weapon or anything that may be used
as a weapon with you.
    Do you own a weapon? _____
    If yes, do you agree to let us keep it in a safe place for you? (R.
Podhorin, personal communication, Feb. 12, 1987).

The advantage of printing this and other procedural statements on
every telephone form is to ensure that all crisis workers impart the
same basic information.

At the bottom of each form is a list of nine of the most frequently used telephone numbers, including those of three area police departments. The advantage of having those phone numbers on
every form is that during a crisis, those numbers are always readily
available, and valuable time will not be lost searching for them.

Group Therapy

Once the woman and her children have arrived at a shelter or other
safe place and the immediate danger of further violence has passed,
group counseling can be initiated. Rhodes and Zelman (1986) have
developed group therapy sessions based on a crisis intervention
model that are *intended for mothers as well as their children.* The
sessions are provided for current and former residents of a spouse
abuse shelter in White Plains, New York, and are led by staff from a
local mental health clinic. The clinic staff believes that the families
who come to the shelter are in crisis; therefore, group treatment
focuses on crisis intervention principles. The group sessions emphasize the following: (1) relieving feelings of isolation and alienation of
persons in crisis and (2) strengthening the relationship between the
mother and children, which is viewed as the "natural support
group."

When the women come to the shelter, the group leader talks to
them individually and develops a treatment plan for the woman and
her children. The group sessions are one component of the treatment
plan. The group leader is careful not to overlook the needs of the
children during group sessions. As a result of the children's presence, special types of intervention are included such as playing,
educating parents, modeling of appropriate parent–child interactions, and encouraging the children to facilitate an exchange of ideas
and feelings.

The 1-hour sessions are held at the shelter two afternoons a
week. During the first 45 minutes of each meeting there is discussion, while the last 15 minutes are reserved for play activities that
the children have chosen.

TREATMENT FOR THE CHILDREN

Battered women who seek temporary shelter to escape from the violence at home generally have children who come to the shelter with them. The children often feel confused, afraid, and angry. They miss their father and do not know if or when they will see him again. It is not uncommon for children to be misinformed or uninformed about the reason that they were suddenly uprooted from their home, leaving their personal possessions, friends, and school to stay at a crowded shelter. Similarly, the children may not realize that all of the other children have come to the shelter for the same reason.

Moreover, large numbers of these children have, at one time or another, also been victims of physical abuse. The 1986 Annual Report from the Family Violence Center, Inc. in Green Bay, Wisconsin, provided data on child abuse committed by the batterer. They found that close to half (73) of the 148 woman abusers had on one or more occasions also beaten their children (S. Prelipp, director, Family Violence Center, Green Bay, WI, personal communication, Feb. 13, 1987).

The following is a true story written by a 10-year-old girl who came to a shelter after her father's violent attack on her mother:

MY LIFE
by Lisa, a ten-year-old shelter resident

One day around two months ago my mom and dad got into a fight. First, my mom and I came home from the mall. We had a really nice time there. But, when we came home our nice time got to be terrible. I knew they were going to get into a fight so I went into my bedroom and did my homework. I knew he was going to talk to her about something, but I didn't know what. Then I heard my mom start screaming and I went to the door and asked what was wrong. My dad said, "Oh, nothing is wrong. Go do your homework." But I knew something was wrong so I went and prayed to God. My dad was really mean that night. I hated him so bad. My mom did not deserve to get hurt. I love her more than anything else in the entire world. Then I heard my mom scream something but I didn't understand what she said because my dad covered her mouth with his hand. Afterward she told me she said call the cops. Anyway, I went back to the door by the bedroom and told my mom I needed help on my homework, but I didn't. I just wanted my mom to come out of the bedroom because I was afraid. Then they both came out. And I hugged my mom and went to bed. Then my dad started to strangle my mom. So I went out and told my dad to stop. he told me to go back to the bedroom and go to sleep. So, I did. But I was so stupid. Then I heard my mom screaming. So I went back into the living room and he was kicking my mom. He wouldn't stop, he kept kicking her in her arm and legs. I told him to stop. He told me to go back to bed but I said, No! Then he took his guitar and was gonna hit her over the head. But I went on top of my mother. He told me to get off. But I said, No! So he put down the guitar, then he got her ice for her arm. Then I went to sleep crying. They next morning I didn't go to school and she didn't go to work. Then he called up the house and talked to her for a while. He threatened to kill her. So we left to go to the shelter. And here I am now. (*Disabuse, Newsletter* 1986, p. 4)

This girl was fortunate in that her mother brought her to the Jersey Battered Women's Service, Inc. (in northern New Jersey), which has a carefully developed counseling program for battered mothers and their children. Sadly, however, the majority of shelters offer only basic child care services; they do not provide the crisis counseling needed to help the children deal with the turmoil of recent events (Alessi & Hearn, 1984).

Nevertheless, innovative techniques for helping the children have been incorporated into the program of the more progressive shelters. At St. Martha's Hall (a shelter in St. Louis, Missouri), in addition to providing counseling for the children, the shelter requires mothers to participate in parenting classes and to meet with the coordinator of the Children's Program about establishing family goals and meeting the child's individual needs. The program also provides opportunities for mother and child to participate jointly in relaxing recreational activities (Schiller-Ramirez, 1987). Group therapy for mothers and children was discussed in the previous section. Two other types of intervention—coloring books and groups for children—will be described below.

Coloring Books as Part of an Individualized Treatment Approach

Some shelters utilize specially designed coloring books that discuss domestic violence in terms children can understand. Laura Prato of the Jersey Battered Women's Service, Inc. (JBWS) in Morristown, New Jersey, has created two coloring books—one for children aged 3 to 5 entitled "What Is a Shelter?" (26 pages), and another for 6- to 11-year-olds called "Let's Talk It Over" (22 pages). In addition to the children's books, Prato has also written two manuals for shelter workers that serve as a discussion guide for the counselors. The books contain realistic, sensitive illustrations that depict the confused, sad, and angry emotions that the children are feeling. They are illustrated in black and white so that the children can color the pictures if they wish. Funding for the preparation and printing of the books and manuals came from the New Jersey Division of Youth and Family Services and NORWES CAP.

The purpose of the coloring books and the way in which they are to be used is explained in the introduction to the counselors' manuals. The manuals state that the books are used as part of the "Intake and Orientation process" for all children who stay at the JBWS shelter. The stated objectives of the books are as follows:

To provide assurances of the child's continued care and safety.
To encourage children to identify and express their feelings.
To provide information needed for children to understand what is happening in their family.
To provide information that will improve each child's ability to adapt to the shelter setting.
To begin to assess the individual child's needs and concerns.

The counselors' manuals stress the importance of the way in which the book is presented to the child, as shown in the following passage:

The process surrounding the use of the orientation books is extremely important. It is likely to be the initial contact between the counselor and the newly arrived family and one that will set the tone for future interactions. Consistent with the JBWS Children's Program philosophy, this initial meeting communicates respect for mother and child and acceptance of their feelings. (Prato, undated)

Before meeting with the child, the counselor meets privately with the mother to show her the book, explain its purpose, and ask for her permission to read the book to her child. The counselors are advised to read any available intake information prior to meeting with the child so that the counselor is better able to "anticipate the individual child's special concerns and place the child's responses in a meaningful context" (Prato, undated).

The books have been prepared in a way that encourages the child's active participation. Throughout both books there are several places where the child is given the opportunity to write his or her thoughts on the page. For example, one of the pages in the "Let's Talk It Over" book focuses on a child staying at a shelter who misses her father. The caption under the picture states

Many children at the shelter think a lot about their fathers, and that's okay. You may not see your father for a while until everyone in your family has a chance to think about things carefully. The little girl in the picture is wondering about her father. . . . What questions do you think she is asking? (Prato, undated).

There is a place on that page for the child's response to the question asked in the above quote. The response could be written by the child or dictated to the counselor, who would write it in the book. On the next page of the book is a large blank space and a caption that reads, "You may use this page to draw a picture of your father." (Prato, undated).

Books such as those developed by the Jersey Battered Women's Service are very appropriate in helping children cope with the crisis that has led to their staying at the shelter.

Group Treatment for Children

Another way to help children cope is through therapeutic groups such as the approach developed at Haven House, a shelter for battered women and their children in Buffalo, New York. Alessi and Hearn (1984) initiated the group approach when they observed the maladaptive ways in which the children reacted to the crisis they were experiencing. The children tended to be aggressive and attempted to resolve problems through hitting. They had considerable anxiety, "biting their fingernails, pulling their hair, and somaticizing feelings as manifested by complaints of headaches and 'tight' stomachs" (Alessi & Hearn, 1984). They had ambivalent feelings toward their father—loving him as well as hating him.

The two group leaders established a six-session treatment program for children ages 8 to 16, focusing on the following topics: "1) the identification and expression of feelings; 2) violence; 3) unhealthy ways to solve problems; 4) healthy ways to solve problems; 5) sex, love and sexuality; and 6) termination and saying goodbye" (Alessi & Hearn, 1984).

To provide an indication of the scope of the group sessions, the content of the session on "violence" is summarized below:

> Violence. The purpose of the session on violence is to give children an opportunity to explore and express feelings about the violence in their families and how it has affected them. This helps children break down their denial and minimization of the problem. It also gives children a chance to learn that other families have similar problems and that many families do not. The following questions are presented to each of the children for reflection and discussion:
> 1. Why did you come to Haven House?
> 2. Do you think it's right for a man to hit a woman or a woman to hit a man, and why?
> 3. Do you think it's right for a parent to hit a child, and why?

4. How do you think you've been affected by the violence in your family?
5. Do you think you'll grow up to be violent or accept violence in intimate relationships? (Alessi & Hearn, 1984)

The children are always given "homework" to "keep the session alive" between meetings. For example, after the discussion on "violence" they are asked to develop a "minidrama" on family violence to be presented the next week. Following the session on healthy problem-solving, they are asked to prepare a list of healthy ways of coping with their problems.

REFERRAL

Knowledge of referral sources is essential. It is just as important for the police, hospitals, and human service agencies to know about and refer to programs helping beaten women and their children as it is for staff at domestic violence treatment programs to refer clients to appropriate community resources.

It is frequently determined that the battered woman needs a variety of services such as job training and placement, low-cost housing, daycare, and ongoing counseling; therefore, referral should be made to the appropriate service providers. In its 1986 *Year End Report*, St. Martha's Hall in St. Louis itemized the agencies to which their clients had been referred (Schiller-Ramirez, 1987). Most women were referred to three or more agencies, while several clients were given nine or more referrals, depending on their individual needs. The most frequently used referral sources were

Legal aid
Medical care
Careers for Homemakers
Job Bank
Daycare programs
Women in Need (WIN), long-term housing for single women
Alcoholics Anonymous
Women's Self-Help Center, providing counseling and support groups
St. Pat's, a Catholic social service agency that finds low-cost housing and provides classes in budgeting money and other life skills

Examples of other, less frequently used, referral sources were

A shelter in another state
Alateen
Al Anon
Literacy Council
Big Brothers
Dental care
GED program
Crisis Nursery
Victim Services
Red Cross

There are two ways in which programs providing crisis intervention services can facilitate the referral process: (1) publicizing their services to the population at large and to other service providers; and (2) becoming knowledgeable about community services needed by their clients and, in some instances, accompanying them to the agency.

Publicize the program through the following methods:

1. Printing brochures that describe the program's services and having business cards that provide the program's name and phone number. They should be made available in large quantity to police officers, emergency room staff, and other potential sources of referral to the program.
2. Participating in interdisciplinary workshops and seminars on family violence so that the program can become widely known. (In addition, this enables the staff to learn about appropriate programs to which their clients can be referred.)
3. Attending in-service training programs for police officers, county-wide hotline staff, emergency room staff, and others to discuss referral of abused women and to resolve any problems in the referral process that may have occurred.
4. Alerting the public through newspaper articles and public service announcements on radio and television, with the program's phone number prominently mentioned.

Become familiar with community resources. Information for crisis counselors on appropriate referral sources should be available in several ways:

1. The phone number of the most urgently needed agencies—such as the police, victim assistance program, drug/alcohol treatment programs, and psychiatric screening unit—should

be readily available, preferably printed on each intake sheet or telephone log form.

2. The program's training manual should contain a section on the most frequently used referral sources. For example, the manual of the ACT program in Ft. Myers, Florida, contains eight pages of often-used referral sources that list the address, phone number, office hours, and services provided for each source.

3. Most of the major metropolitan areas have a comprehensive resource guide (published by the local United Way or an affiliate such as Call for Action) that provides a comprehensive listing of all of the community services in that area. All programs serving abused women and their children should have a copy of and be familiar with their community's resources handbook.

The way in which referrals are made is extremely important since it may affect the outcome. All too often, victims in crisis do not follow through in making the initial contact with the referral agency. Counselors at St. Martha's Hall and other shelters provide support by accompanying the client to the agency in order to demonstrate how to obtain services. This is viewed as a positive alternative to the often intimidating and frustrating experience encountered by women who are given a referral but are expected to fend for themselves.

CONCLUSION

A number of important issues and techniques relating to crisis intervention with battered women and their children have been examined. Specific methods for crisis intervention in different settings have also been discussed. As increased numbers of women in acute crisis seek help, crisis counselors and victim advocates must be prepared to respond without delay. Crisis counseling for battered women and their children may do much to alleviate the emotional distress and anguish experienced by those exposed to the trauma of domestic violence. Because of their experience and specialized training, crisis counselors and medical social workers can play a vital role in assisting women and children in crisis.

Law enforcement officers, victim advocates, hospital emergency room staff, and counselors at area-wide crisis lines and battered women's shelters often come in contact with beaten women who are experiencing a crisis. Effective crisis intervention requires an understanding by these service providers of the value and methods of crisis intervention as well as the community resources to which referrals should be made.

Battered women are often motivated to change their lifestyle only during the crisis or post-crisis period. Therefore, it is important for service providers at community agencies to offer immediate assistance to battered women in crisis. With an estimated 2 million couples involved in battering episodes annually, policymakers and program developers should give priority to expanding urgently needed crisis-oriented and follow-up services for battered women and their children.

REFERENCES

Alessi, J. J., & Hearn, K. (1984). Group treatment of children in shelters for battered women. In A. R. Roberts (Ed.), *Battered women and their families* (pp. 49–61). New York: Springer Publishing Co.

Aquilera, D. C., & Messick, J. M. (1984). *Crisis intervention: Theory and methodology.* St. Louis: C. V. Mosby.

Caplan, G. (1964). *Principles of preventive psychiatry.* New York: Basic Books.

Disabuse Newsletter (1986, December): Morristown, NJ. Jersey Battered Women's Service.

Flaherty, E. W., et al. (1985). *Identification and intervention with battered women in hospital emergency departments: Final report.* Philadelphia: Philadelphia Health Management Corp.

Haag, R. (Undated). The birthday letter. In S. A. Prelipp (Ed.), *Training manual.* Green Bay, WI: Family Violence Center, Inc.

Houston, S. (1987). Abuse Counseling and Treatment, Inc. (ACT) manual. Ft. Myers, FL: ACT.

Janosik, E. H. (1984). *Crisis counseling.* Belmont, CA: Wadsworth.

Jones, W. A. (1968). The A-B-C method of crisis management. *Mental Hygiene, 52,* 87–89.

Klingbeil, K. S., & Boyd, V. D. (1984). Emergency room intervention: Detection, assessment and treatment. In A. R. Roberts (Ed.), *Battered women and their families: Intervention strategies and treatment programs* (pp. 7–32). New York: Springer Publishing Co.

National Coalition Against Domestic Violence. (1986). *Director of shelters and services for battered women.* Washington, DC: Author.

National Organization for Victim Assistance (NOVA). (1983). *Victim services: A guide to action.* Washington, DC: Author.

Prato, L. (Undated). What is a shelter?; Let's talk it over; What is a shelter? A shelter worker's manual; Let's talk it over: A shelter worker's manual. Morristown, NJ: Jersey Battered Women's Service, Inc.

Rhodes, R. M., & Zelman, A. B. (1986). An ongoing multi-family group in a women's shelter, *American Journal of Orthopsychiatry*, 56: 120–130.

Roberts, A. R. (1981). *Sheltering battered women: A national study and service guide.* New York: Springer Publishing Co.

Roberts, A. R. (Ed.), (1984). *Battered women and their families. Intervention strategies and treatment programs.* New York: Springer Publishing Co.

Roberts, A. R. (1987). *National survey of victim service and witness assistance programs: Final report.* Indianapolis, IN: Indiana University School of Social Work.

Roberts, A. R. (1990). *Helping crime victims: Research, policy and practice:* Newbury Park, CA: Sage.

Schiller-Ramirez, M. (1987). Year-end Report 1986. St. Louis: St. Martha's Hall.

3 Gestalt Therapy with Females Involved in Intimate Violence

Linda F. Little

Writings suggesting intervention strategies in cases of intimate violence typically focus on the crisis aspect of the abuse. Individual safety of the victim is considered more important than relationship reconstruction; therefore, separate sessions for abuser and abused are recommended until the crisis has passed and there is decreased danger that violence will occur again. Consistent recommendations for crisis interventions include working with females in sheltered environments (Weitzman & Dreen, 1982) and males in group settings (Gondolf, 1985). Individual and/or same-sex group therapy is recommended until after the crisis is past and there is some assurance that violent behavior is being effectively controlled. Female therapists are recommended for working with females, and male therapists or a male/female therapy team for working with males.

Therapy for females most often focuses on self-sufficiency, skill enhancement, strength building, career planning, independent functioning from batterer, assertion training, and feminist counseling. Walker (1989) emphasizes the strengthening focus on ". . .reempowerment rather than adjustment or merely continuous personal growth without first working through and integrating the victimizing experience" (p. 699).

Feminist therapists have succeeded in redefining ". . .the problem of violence against women as one of misuse of power by men who have been socialized into believing that they have the right to control the women in their lives, even through violent means" (Walker, 1989, p. 695). Therapy for males stresses anger control, personal responsibility, problem solving, contracting for change

(Neidig & Freidman 1984), stress reduction, communication training, and alteration of sex-role stereotypes (Gondolf, 1985).

A smaller body of literature is emerging that focuses on the systemic process of abuse and the relationship issues that revolve around the violent acts. Systemic-oriented couples therapy and family-of-origin work are recommended after partners are sufficiently differentiated so that relationship issues can be worked on in tandem without escalating possibilities of violence (Cook & Frantz-Cook, 1984). Family therapy is not seen as an initial appropriate setting that can allow the victim of abuse to express her fears and recover from the trauma of the abuse. Systems therapists who have not adopted the feminist perspective of unequal distribution of power in abusive relationships can in fact work to maintain a setting for continued abuse (Walker, 1989).

According to National Crime Survey data (U.S. Department of Justice, 1983), men commit 95% of the assaults on spouses. Women receive more frequent and serious injuries from males than vice versa, and women who are violent toward males are more generally reactive rather than active/aggressive (Walker, 1989). Incidences of wife abuse are estimated as occurring in up to 16% of all marriages annually (Straus, Gelles, & Steinmetz 1980) and in 50 to 60% of all marriages at some point (Straus, 1978). There is also growing evidence that conjugal violence flourishes at all socioeconomic levels (Gullatte, 1979). Considering these findings, community-based clinicians have a great likelihood of confronting women who experience abuse either on a regular or irregular basis prior to the point when crisis intervention is mandatory.

It is not uncommon for helping professionals working with families in the context of parent–child relationship or personal problems to discover after several sessions that battering is an integral part of the family dynamics. Clinicians in community settings often find that abuse is admitted reluctantly, that the importance of it is downplayed, and that its contribution to the presenting problem is omitted or slighted. Based on the clinical experience of this author, even with specific questions routinely targeted to reveal abuse at intake, the revelation is usually (a) made in the absence of the male spouse, (b) made in a phone call when the female partner wishes to convey a "secret" to the therapist that she thinks relevant but doesn't want talked about, or (c) boldly asserted in the session by the male as a necessary part of keeping the upper hand in the spousal relationship. After admission of abuse, family members are hesitant to continue discussion of the subject (McG Mullen & Carroll, 1983).

While the suggestions for intervention with battered women in sheltered environments mentioned above can apply and are usually continued outside those environments, community-based clinicians need a theoretical framework, therapeutic goals, and intervention techniques with which to work with victims of abuse. Similar needs are evidenced by helpers in sheltered environments. Estimates suggest that 50 to 75% of the women who separate from their abusers return to live with them. Many return to their relationships after numerous episodes of seeking shelter due to escalation of abuse (Hendricks-Matthews, 1982). Shelter workers find it common to expend large amounts of energy to secure safety, legal rights, employment possibilities, and residential provisions for their residents only to find that the women leave the shelters just as the workers are encouraged about their abilities to function on their own. Professional burnout, bitterness, resentment, and discouragement run high with workers in women's shelters.

The purpose of this chapter is to present to clinicians, whether they work in community settings or shelter environments, a Gestalt therapy approach to intervening in cases of intimate violence that goes beyond crisis intervention. Gestalt therapy is systemically oriented. It recognizes the individual as a unique system (of thoughts, behaviors, beliefs; physical and psychological components) that accounts for the "internal" processes usually dealt with in therapy and stresses that the individual cannot be separated from the larger environmental systems with which he/she consistently interacts (Yontef, 1983).

This chapter focuses on the female's roles (both internal and interactional) in intimate violence as supported in the related literature. Similar papers applying Gestalt therapy theory and techniques to perpetrators of violence or intervention with the couple system would be equally appropriate. The goal of therapy is to clarify the female's role in conjugal violence, increase her responsibility in the relationship, and provide her options for future interactions—both with her partner and other authority figures. It is suggested that males concurrently seek a similar form of individual therapy, and that as soon as it is logical and if indicated, the couple begin conjoint sessions in which the specific interaction patterns that maintain the abuse can be addressed.

Space does not permit an in-depth review of Gestalt therapy theory that can be found elsewhere in original works by Frederick Perls (1969; Perls, Hefferline, & Goodman 1951) and summations of his works (Harman, 1974, 1984; Passons, 1975). This chapter defines "Gestalt," presents Gestalt therapy theory in terms of the major goals of Gestalt therapy, relates these goals to the female victims of abuse, and presents action-oriented therapeutic techniques to aid clinicians in their work with battered women.

GESTALT DEFINED

Central to the Gestalt approach is the premise that humans can choose their existences (Yontef, 1969). Conceived by Frederick S. Perls (1969; Perls, Hefferline, & Goodman, 1951), Gestalt therapy attempts to alter client behaviors by altering present awarenesses. Perls (1969) described the human organism as fragmented, aware of only parts of itself, not accepting and denying some of its parts, and needing to accept itself as an integrated whole. The concept of Gestalt is a German one and was borrowed by Perls from the earlier Gestalt psychologists (Goldstein, Lewin, and Wertheimer) to normalize his therapeutic philosophies and practices. Translated, "Gestalt" means "a form, a configuration or a totality that has as a unified whole, properties which can not be derived from the summation of the parts and their relationships" (English & English, 1958, p. 225).

From a Gestalt therapy perspective, abuse cannot be looked at in isolation. Nor can the implications of the abuse be divided into physical, emotional, and social realms. The totality of the victim's existence is of primary concern.

Research and writings attesting to the effectiveness of Gestalt therapy in individual, group, couples, and family modes are available (Bauer, 1979; Hale, 1978; Harman, 1984; Hatcher, 1978). No articles were found in the available literature on the specific application of Gestalt therapy to victims of family violence.

GOALS OF GESTALT THERAPY

A goal that permeates all of Gestalt therapy is acceptance of reality (Yontef, 1983). Additional goals identified by Harman (1974) include awareness of self in the present, integration of opposites that exist within the person, self-responsibility, maturity, authenticity, self-regulation, and behavior change. Elaborations of these goals as they relate to battered women, along with intervention techniques, follow.

Acceptance of Reality

Perls (1969) believed that humans keep themselves from achieving holism by not attending to the obvious: by tying up energy through avoidance rather than achieving closure. Before change can occur, persons need to attend to and acknowledge their current existence.

Victims of abuse often deny the reality of their situations. They deny the seriousness of the abuse, the dangerousness of their partners, their fears, insecurities, and often the actual source of the injuries. They rationalize behaviors in such fashions as to make the batterer incapable of being responsible for his abusing behaviors (Hendricks-Matthews, 1982):

> Client: He really is a kind and gentle person.
> He loves the kids and doesn't mean to hurt them.
> I love him and couldn't live without him.
> I know he cares about me deeply.
> He promised he won't do it again and I believe him.

By encouraging the client to focus on the "here and now" of her experience, a more balanced picture of her reality is achieved:

> Therapist: *Right now* you are bruised and sore because he hit you.
> *Right now* you are very angry at him.
> *Right now* you fear for your safety.
> *At times* he can be cruel and abusing. *At times* your husband is kind and gentle to you; *at other times* he hurts you.

Victims of abuse often live in a fantasy land of illusions of how they want their lives to be. Parts of life that are believed to be destructive, evil or nonproductive are projected onto others or blocked from awareness. Facilitation of the victim's attending to reality is often painful and threatening. It is also necessary if change is to be facilitated:

> Therapist: Make some statements about your current reality. Complete the following sentence, This is my existence right now.

Client: My husband says he loves me and can't live
           without me, and he beats me when he drinks.
           This is my existence right now.
           I feel trapped and helpless in a marriage that is
           more hurtful than it is fulfilling. This is my
           existence right now.

Increased Awareness

In the process of accepting reality, the client's current awarenesses
of self and others are facilitated. The Gestalt therapist focuses on
increasing the client's awareness of what she is doing, thinking,
feeling, sensing, and wanting in the present. The therapist views the
client as a whole and points out discrepancies that emerge in the
realms of awareness that the client might not recognize and that
carry information for the client that is of great value for her functioning. The client who, while speaking in a harsh voice and clench-
ing and unclenching her fist, describes herself as a warm and loving
wife is aided by the therapist in becoming more aware of her total
experience when she is encouraged to also attend to the tone of her
voice and the anger that is demonstrated in her hands. The therapist
can help her (a) clarify that she wants to be warm and loving and (b)
acknowledge that part of her feels harsh and is angry when talking
about her spouse.

   Gestalt therapy is present-oriented. It is not primarily concerned
with establishing the historical precipitates that cause a woman to
remain in a toxic environment. Gestalt therapy assumes that dysfunctional patterns of behavior learned at an earlier stage of life will
emerge in the present if they are unresolved. Instead of focusing on
gathering a detailed history, Gestalt therapy attempts to increase
awareness of the client's current processes by focusing on the
present situation. Unfinished Gestalts emerge as they are relevant to
current reality, and thus are addressed. This is done by allowing the
client to set the agenda and by careful probing so that parts of the
client's functioning that are outside her awareness are brought into
focus:

Therapist: You say that you are miserable with your hus-
             band right now. How are you contributing to
             your misery?
             How are you stopping yourself from being what
             you want?

> When do you feel like striking out at your husband?
>
> What can be changed so that you will be able to meet your needs?
>
> What parts of you are you avoiding right now?

Awareness of where the client is focusing in the present, whether the client is getting what she wants from her current existence, and how she can change to be better satisfied in the present are foci of Gestalt therapy.

Client:	(with a smile on her face and speaking in a soft voice) I am so mad at my husband that I could scream.
Therapist:	Are you aware of what you are doing with your mouth and your voice? Just continue what you are doing and say your words again.
Client:	I am smiling and talking very softly. There is a part of me who says, "Please don't be mad at me for getting angry. Don't take me very seriously."

Integration of Opposites

"It is important to clarify the ambivalent feelings of battered women. They center around issues of love/hate, anger/passivity, rage/terror, depression/anxiety, staying/leaving, omnipotence/impotence, security/panic, and others" (Walker 1978, p. 199). The ambivalent feelings demonstrate the extremes of opposing wants and forces with which victims of abuse deal. Victims are either loved dearly by their spouses and put on pedestals, or they are deemed unworthy of human kindness and subjected to abuse. Victims see their options as either staying or leaving, their husbands as either good or bad, themselves as either good enough or inadequate. Their whole existence is characterized by this either-or stance.

A goal of Gestalt therapy is to aid the client in moving toward the acknowledgment of polar wants that exist and toward acceptance of opposing forces. Until the person can acknowledge both poles of the personality (anger/love; dependence/independence), her existence is a flip-flop affair of emotional highs and lows. She then experiences herself as immobile and passive or fragmented and attending only to those wants that are congruent with what is seen as the desirable pole of behavior (Perls, 1969).

The nonintegrated person develops a rigid, stereotyped view of herself. She cuts off parts of her personality. Victims of abuse often learn to be quiet and respectful of others. They learn to acquiesce and to see their role as rescuer. The angry, aggressive, deserving, assertive parts are often pushed out of awareness and not integrated into the personality. Integration focuses on bringing the opposites together (at times I want to leave and at times I want to stay) so that the person is more balanced, centered, and can make choices.

Polarization of the personality is encouraged at early ages with many victims of spouse abuse. Estimates suggest that as many as 50% of all battered women have been abused as children or have watched their mothers being battered (McG Mullen & Carroll 1983, p. 32). Living in such environments, children learn which feelings to express and which to keep quiet. They learn to deny wants and to assume roles that will, to the best of their abilities, keep them out of trouble. When these people grow into adults they have *holes* in their personalities and have rid themselves of valuable emotions and responses that contribute to their emotional health. By focusing on integration of opposites, the Gestalt therapist encourages the abuse victim to reclaim missing parts of the personality so that she may become more whole in her functioning. The past merges with the present, and behaviors, attitudes, and thoughts that once contributed to the person's survival are challenged for their current relevance. This integration is facilitated by asking such questions as:

> Therapist: How is your anger good for you?
> What do you deserve?
> Who told you not to cry?
> How old were you when you were told to say something nice or keep your mouth shut? How old are you now?
> When is it good to be selfish?
> What do your tears do for you that is positive?

When the victim of abuse allows herself to explore the parts of her personality that she has deemed bad and discovers that there really isn't a monster lurking underneath her thin exterior, she is often extremely relieved and more self-accepting.

Responsibility

Descriptors of battered women include dependent, helpless, passive, fearful, immature in established identities, other-directed, low self-concepts, paranoid, manipulative, and gullible (Bowen, 1982; Walker, 1978; Weitzman & Dreen, 1982). The totality of the image is not of a person with high levels of self-responsibility. Assumption of the victim role attests to the lack of control abused women experience in their lives. Victims of abuse tend to attribute power over their functioning to others in their environments. More specifically, all that they experience that is pleasing to them personally is seen as originating with others—as outside their control—while all that they experience that is negative is somehow construed as self-inflicted (Hendricks-Matthews, 1982). Again, this demonstrates the conflict of omnipotence/impotence described by Walker (1978).

The relinquishing of power by battered women—of responsibility for their lives—is experienced often by clinicians who work with them. Victims turn over their lives (at least in the sessions) to the therapist who becomes the expert on what they should do, how they should feel, and whom they should become. The therapist who falls into accepting this trap becomes just one more person who reinforces the victims' lack of control and responsibility. A goal of therapy is for victims of abuse to learn that they are responsible for themselves. Not guilty, but responsible.

In Gestalt therapy, statements that give away responsibility are challenged, and a repeated emphasis is kept on reclaiming power over oneself:

> Client: He *makes* me so mad.
> Therapist: How do you allow him to do that? . . . Teach me to make you mad at me.
> Client: I have no choices.
> Therapist: How do you cage yourself in?
> Client: I shouldn't feel this way?
> Therapist: Where does the *should* come from? Whose *should* is that?

Often women know the sequence of events that lead to abuse and don't take action for self-protection:

> Client: First he drinks, then he starts picking on me verbally, then I get mad and verbally defend myself, then he hits me.

They do not see how they contribute to the abuse by playing their "roles" in the unfolding drama of abuse.

Therapist: How do you contribute to your abuse? What could you do instead?

Responsibility is also given away by the use of depersonalized language:

Client: People shouldn't be beaten.
Therapist: Say the same sentence and say I.
Client: We deserve better.
Therapist: Again, say I.

Responsibility is given up when questions are asked, rather than statements made:

Client: Don't you think that women should not be beaten?
Therapist: I think you have a statement behind that question. Please rephrase your question so that you are making a statement about yourself.

When wants are in conflict, rather than recognizing both wants, battered women often confuse themselves and make themselves helpless:

Client: John wants an answer right now but I don't know. I just don't know.
Therapist: Substitute *and* for *but* and restate what you just said.
Client: He wants an answer and I'm not ready to give him one.

All of the above language techniques are used throughout the course of therapy to emphasize constantly the power each individual has over her functioning. Gestalt therapists, more than therapists from many other schools, emphasize how one conveys his/her message rather than the meaning being conveyed. Words are seen as powerful, and increasing clients' awareness of how they use language to empower or make themselves powerless is an ongoing process in Gestalt therapy.

Maturity

Relinquishing responsibility for one's existence keeps the person immature in interactions with others. Immature people are dependent on others to take control of their lives.

Perls (1969) described the unhealthy personality as one who seeks to manipulate the environment so that she can be supported and have no need to learn to support herself. Immature behavior—behavior that is manipulative, indirect, passive, and helpless—is very typical of the abused woman. Many abused women learned in childhood that asking directly for what they wanted was a sure way not to get their wants met. Carry this over to adulthood and all other relationships, and you find a woman who is really in a no-win situation. If she does not get her wants met, she perceives that she did not manipulate successfully. If she does get her wants met, it's because, in her belief, she has manipulated, planned, schemed, and plotted so that others are doing what is pleasing to her. There is no victory—no gift of love, no meaning behind the benevolent acts. Getting what is wanted is still losing, originating with her power, not the free will of others.

The immature person is also characterized by helplessness—by dependency on others to make everything "right" and to see that their lives are put back together again. This is a very dangerous therapeutic situation. Battered women are very willing to see the therapist as a benevolent despot who has all of the answers and who can set their lives straight again. By their indirectness, through dropping hints as to what they need and playing dumb and not knowing, battered women set the therapist up to rescue them. They often believe that they want the therapist to give them what they want without their needing to assert themselves to get their needs met. This relinquishing of power is so normal that battered women don't perceive that they have options. A goal of Gestalt therapy is encouraging, through the taking of self-responsibility, maturity of behavior. Maturity means that rather than trying to manipulate others so that needs are met, the woman becomes self-supporting. She learns not to lean so close to other people that her weight is supported by them and not to lean so far away that no support from others is forthcoming.

A mature person is balanced; she is capable of standing on her own two feet, of making decisions, and of asking for what she wants.

In the therapy session per se the Gestalt therapist facilitates mature behavior by insisting that the client be the person who sets the agenda to be worked on and the goals of the individual therapy session and by insisting that she does know what is best for her functioning. The therapist is unwilling to rescue the client—to support the neurotic helplessness, dependency, and immaturity syndrome of getting what one wants through manipulation.

Warning signals for the therapist that she/he is being seduced into treating the client as a child can be observed (a) when the therapist experiences that she/he is doing most of the work and the client is extending little effort, (b) when the therapist discovers she/he feels the responsibility for solving the presenting problems, and (c) when the client is seen as helpless, without resources, and in need of being protected.

Immature people also hold to the belief that those around them are capable of reading minds (Perls, 1969): If another person really does care, that person will know what the battered woman wants without having to be told.

> Client: What do you think I ought to do about going
>   back to Johnny?
> Therapist: I don't have any *oughts* for you. I know what
>   my limits are in terms of what behaviors I will
>   and won't live with. I have heard you predict
>   what you can expect were you to return. You
>   want me to tell you what I think you *should* do.
>   How will that help?
> Client: I value your opinion. I want to know what to
>   do.
> Therapist: Let me make sure I'm hearing you right. If I tell
>   you what I would do if I were you, I'm telling
>   you what you should do about going back with
>   Johnny. You give me a lot of power and I feel
>   uncomfortable with that. You're putting your
>   whole future in my hands. How is that for you?

Authenticity

Mature persons are capable of authenticity. Being authentic—saying what one wants, acknowledging how one feels and what one is really thinking—is risky. It is often feared that others will reject the real person, so a pseudo-person is presented who is conceived to be more acceptable and less threatening to others. Thus, a myth is perpetuated that it is better to pretend, monitor oneself, and maintain one's self-control than to be the "who" who flows naturally.

Growth and change demand risks. When a risk is taken and the goal is achieved, self-confidence is enhanced. Therapy for victims of abuse encourages risks in being authentic, and provides a setting where feared parts of the self can be explored and seen as less to be feared than previously. Appropriate anger is encouraged. Saying what is wanted is responded to. Tears are interpreted as warmth and caring, and relabeled as a beautiful part of the person rather than something to be hidden or cut off. The fear that "if I am really known I would be hated," or "a monster exists inside" diminishes with each successful risk at self-disclosing. Anger emitted without the feared loss of control or brutality that has long been suspected is celebrated, and the myth of "totally falling to pieces" is challenged with each authentic expression.

Self-Regulation

Acceptance, awareness, responsibility, maturity, and authenticity lead to self-regulation—the ability to know and trust oneself—and to the belief that "I am the best judge of what I need right now. I can trust my experiences. I might at times be confused and have opposite wants—wants that are in conflict—but I can acknowledge my conflict. I can care for myself today in such a way that my life is enhanced tomorrow." The goal becomes one of enhancing the client's total well-being. That Gestalt therapy encourages clients to "let it all hang out" is a myth held over from the 1960s. Gestalt therapy also focuses on containment—learning when, where, and how to reveal the self so that the total person is enhanced. For example, recent literature suggests that battered women trained in assertion reported dissatisfaction and disillusionment with therapy. The act of assertion served, in many cases, as the catalyst for additional battering (O'Leary et al., 1985). To train women to assert indiscriminately without consideration of past patterns of behaviors that led to abuse, or without warning of potential consequences of confrontation, does not model or support self-regulation.

Behavior Change

The above goals of Gestalt therapy result in behavior change. Behavior can be overt or internal. One can change thoughts, actions, and interactions with others—one's relationships.

The female client is told that were she to leave her relationship she would take her problems with her. This at first might seem threatening because of her belief that she has caused all that has occurred in the spousal relationship. Through the process of therapy, however, she learns to distinguish what is her and what is not her. She learns that whereas she can be responsible for what is her, she cannot control that which is not. This defining of the contact boundary, the me and the other, is a vital focus in Gestalt therapy (Harman 1988). When the client reclaims the me and disassociates from the non-me, a major step has been taken to extricate herself from her role in the abusive relationship.

Place the Individual Behavior into a Larger Gestalt

Battered women often despair that they *chose* this debilitating relationship. They question themselves about how they could have been so stupid, how they allowed themselves to care for someone capable of such cruelty and violence. It is important at this time to educate women about known characteristics of male abusers and the larger cultural milieu that allows men to behave in abusive ways toward the women in their lives. Knowing that male batterers have a whole set of adjustment issues with which they must deal and that there are identified stages in abusive relationships helps the victim to have some distance from which to view her own experiences.

Bernard and Bernard (1984) described the typical batterer with whom they dealt in over two years of intervention groups as having a "Jekyll and Hyde" (p. 543) personality. He was seen as initially ingratiating, pleasing, and easy to like. In successful interventions, the likable facade was replaced by one that blamed the victim, exploded into angry outbursts, expressed extreme jealousy, underestimated the use and abuse of substances, and was incapable of having meaningful heterosexual relationships. Their clinical work and Minnesota Multiphasic Personality Inventory (MMPI) profiles of the male participants indicated a group of males with severe psychological problems who fluctuate from "excessive insensitivity to the consequences of their actions and overconcern about the effect they have on others" (p. 545).

Knowledge of such predictable behavior from male batterers clarifies for the victim the extremes of behavior that she could not reconcile. It is not uncommon for abused women to report feeling more loved and supported during the honeymoon stage of their relationships than any time previously. It is after this commitment—when boundaries are lowered and the women dare to be intimate—that the tables are turned. Traits that were once loved by the abusers are now rejected. Stories told in faith and innocence are retold as weapons used to lower the women's self-esteem and convince them of their powerlessness in the relationships. Vulnerability, helplessness, fearfulness, and weakness often are used as justification for abuse by the batterers when in the abusive mode, and thus an ever escalating spiral of abusive behaviors on the part of the male and self-diminishing behaviors on the part of the female stoke the fire necessary for the abusive relationship to continue.

Knowing that the perpetrator has separate issues—his issues—that must be worked through prior to his focusing on and committing to the relationship provides the woman some freedom. It no longer is her sole responsibility to determine whether the relationship is going to exist. It no longer is her responsibility to make everything right. If he needs time, so too can she allow herself time to heal and to learn more functional coping strategies.

Self-Protection

The issue of self-protection is one that needs to be dealt with directly in therapy. Walker (1989) reports data on family homicides analyzed by Browne (1988) and Browne and Williams (1989) from the Centers for Disease Control. "Two thirds of family violence deaths are women killed by their male partners, often at the point of separation. Over half of all women homicide victims are killed by current or former partners" (Browne, p. 697). As long as the female feels that it is *not* her life that is being threatened by the abuse, little movement is likely to occur. She can continue to deny the escalation of episodes and can even learn to adapt to the physical harm inflicted. She didn't die the last time, and can easily assure herself that she can survive additional attacks. To counter this attitude of tolerance, females need to come to terms with what steps they are willing to take in order to protect themselves.

Because of the insidiousness of abuse, the fact that it is a killing act is diminished in the minds of the participants. The death might not actually be a physical one, but small deaths occur with each abusive episode. There is the death of pride, of feeling valued, of trust, of respect, and of loyalty. The game of abuse, initially at least, prevents the female from actually being killed, because then the game would end and there would be no outlet for the rage of the abuser. Though with each successive act the violence escalates and the fear of death might become more real, the denial that actual death could happen and that symbolic deaths are happening occurs with both the perpetrator and the victim.

Abused women are most traditionally told by well-meaning, helping professionals, "You have to get out of that relationship." Often they resist. "I love him," "I am afraid of him," "He will kill me if I leave," and "I can't make it on my own" are typical polar responses supporting the woman's position of "I can't—won't leave this relationship; at least not now." The first task of the therapist is to hear and honor the *Gestalt* of the woman. Only by first accepting this world view and the choices that surround it can any movement occur. A brief case example using this approach follows.

Barbara had been the recipient of repeated physical beatings by her live-in boyfriend of 12 years. Most recently the threats of abuse were accompanied by the presence of a large hunting knife. The knife had been held at Barbara's throat, and Bill had pricked her chest with it on more than one occasion. The abuse repeatedly occurred when Bill had been drinking, and was always preceded by Bill's declaration that Barbara didn't love him and was going to leave him. Her solution was to try to reassure him of her love and her loyalty. As she became more affectionate and solicitous, the battering would start. Bill would call her names, insults would escalate to physical shovings or holdings to demonstrate superior power by Bill. This would be followed by Barbara expressing sorrow, and continued attempts of reassurance.

Barbara convinced herself and attempted to convince her therapist that were she to leave Bill she would be fulfilling his long-term expectations of her behavior. He would be right—his anger would have been justified.

The therapist chose to accept Barbara's perception of her fate. She asked her to predict what her life would be like in three months, six months, one year, and five years. Barbara saw nothing but more of the same. She acknowledged, given the recent introduction of a weapon into the abuse, that her physical symptoms would most likely become severe. She even verbalized that their relationship might end with her death. Barbara began mourning for her fate. The therapist acknowledged her belief that she loved Bill, was unwilling to leave him, could not change his behavior, and was helpless to make a difference in her future with Bill. Barbara was encouraged to do nothing different for at least a week. Instead, she was to focus on her reality, which was agreed to be a very bleak one.

Barbara entered the next therapy session with a huge smile. She reported to the therapist that Bill had again begun to accuse her of not loving him and she had recognized the first stage of yet another abusive episode. She had been riding in the car with Bill at the time, holding a large carry-out cola. Barbara reported to the therapist that she took the cola, and "dumped it into Bill's lap." "I was damned if I was going to play that game again, and I told him so." Barbara reported that Bill was so shocked that they focused on her behavior rather than continuing the typical abusive pattern. Barbara had moved to the other pole of behavior—initiating a shift in the interaction between the two.

Barbara expressed to the therapist that although for the remainder of the week Bill had been more respectful in his actions toward her, she still did not trust him. The opportunity was again presented to the therapist to go with the client's *Gestalt*. They could focus on both the part of herself who was hopeful and encouraged that she had, at least for once, found a way to be heard by Bill, and the part who needed to take precautions for her physical safety.

In dealing with the issue of self-protection the female has a minimum of two tasks. First, she must become convinced of the seriousness of the abusive acts. Second, she must come to grips with the consequences of ending or attempting to end the relationship. The process of dealing with the issue challenges many of the beliefs that contribute to women's roles in abusive relationships. The timing of the interventions concerned with self-protection is critical, the relationship between therapist and client must be well established, and progress should have been made on many of the other goals of therapy prior to this work beginning.

At this stage in therapy several women have been encouraged to enroll in self-protection courses. This information is not to be shared with the spouse or used as a threat, but is to be savored by the woman as she feels her body in space, gains confidence in her movements, claims her physical power, and learns that she potentially could be responsible for her physical safety. The therapist is working on changing an attitude about the self: I am worthy of self-protection, I can do something about my self-protection, and if I need to always be cautious, do I wish to stay in this relationship?

A caveat is introduced with the above suggestion. The dangers of assertive training as a solution to abuse have already been introduced (O'Leary et al., 1985). The client might protest to the therapist that if she were to no longer tolerate abuse or attempt to avert abuse by self-defensive actions, she would fear being injured even more severely. *She should be encouraged to listen to her fears.* The therapist acknowledges with her client that it might well be that if she stays in the relationship no behaviors on her part could extricate her from further abuse. Passivity did not help. Assertiveness is feared. The focus in therapy shifts to how she can negotiate with her partner so that her behaviors have an impact on the couple's interactions or to how the woman can maximally protect herself while she ends this relationship.

If similar individual therapy has been simultaneously occurring for the male, this is a possible juncture in therapy where conjoint therapy can begin. The focus centers on how the couple can win by being together or by moving apart in the absence of abuse.

CONCLUSIONS

Abusive relationships often mask and distract from other serious relationship problems that impede day-by-day functioning as a couple. Removal of the abuse as a threat to the relationship can precipitate false confidence in the ease with which the couple will resume interacting. Just as there is often a honeymoon period after an episode of physical violence, the therapist could predict a honeymoon phase as progress is made in therapy. It is during this period, when each partner is gaining skills, confidence, and demonstrating behavior change, that the work of couple's therapy begins. The goals of Gestalt therapy are applicable for couple's work. Accepting what is, increasing awareness of self, integrating opposites, and learning responsibility, maturity, authenticity, self-regulation, and behavior change define the context for couple interactions within the therapy sessions.

REFERENCES

Bauer, R. (1979). Gestalt approaches to family therapy. *The American Journal of Family Therapy*, 7(3), 41–45.

Bernard, J. L., & Bernard, M. L. (1984). The abusive male seeking treatment: Jekyll and Hyde. *Family Relations*, 33, 543–547.

Bowen, N. (1982). Guidelines for career counseling with abused women. *The Vocational Guidance Quarterly*, 31(2), 123–127.

Browne, A. (1988, August). *Battered women who kill: Policy implications*. Symposium conducted at the annual meeting of the American Psychological Association, Atlanta.

Browne, A., & Williams, K. (1989). Exploring the effect of resource availability and the likelihood of female-perpetuated homicides. *Law and Society Review*, 23(1), 75–94.

Cook, D., & Frantz-Cook, A. (1984). A systemic treatment approach to wife battering. *Journal of Marital and Family Therapy*, 10(1), 83–93.

English, H., & English, A. (1958). *A comprehensive dictionary of psychological and psychoanalytical terms*. New York: David McKay Company.

Gondolf, E. (1985). *Men who batter: An integrated approach for stopping wife abuse*. New York: Learning Publications, Inc.

Gullatte, A. (1979). Spousal abuse. *Journal of the National Medical Association*, 71, 127–129.

Hale, B. (1978). Gestalt techniques in marriage counseling. *Social Casework*, 59, 428–433.

Harman, R. (1974). Goals of Gestalt therapy. *Professional Psychology*, 4, 178–184.

Harman, R. (1984). Gestalt therapy research. *The Gestalt Journal*, 7(2), 29–38.

Harman, R. (1988). *Gestalt therapy with groups, couples, sexually dysfunctional men, and dreams*. Springfield, IL: Charles C Thomas.

Hatcher, C. (1978). Intrapersonal and interpersonal models: Blending Gestalt and family therapies. *The Journal of Marriage and Family Counseling*, 7(2), 61–69.

Hendricks-Matthews, M. (1982). The battered women: Is she ready for help? *Social Casework*, 63(5), 131–137.

McG Mullen, R., & Carroll, M. (1983). The battered-woman syndrome: Contributing factors and remedial interventions. *American Mental Health Counselors Association Journal*, 5(1), 31–38.

Neidig, P., & Freidman, D. (1984). *Spouse abuse: A treatment program for couples*. Champaign, IL: Research Press.

O'Leary, K. D., Curley, A., Rosenbaum, A., & Clarke, C. (1985). Assertion training for abused wives: A potentially hazardous treatment. *Journal of Marital and Family Therapy*, 11(3), 319–322.

Passons, W. (1975). *Gestalt approaches to counseling*. New York: Holt, Rinehart & Winston.

Perls, F. (1969). *Gestalt therapy verbatim*. Lafayette, CA: Real People's Press.

Perls, F., Hefferline, R., & Goodman, P. (1951). *Gestalt therapy: Excitement and growth in the human personality*. New York: Dell Publishing Company.

Straus, M. (1978). Wife beating: How common and why? *Victimology: An International Journal*, 2, 443–458.

Straus, M., Gelles, R., & Steinmetz, S. (1980). *Behind closed doors: Violence in the American family*. Garden City, NY: Doubleday.

U.S. Department of Justice (1983). *Report to the nation on crime and justice: The data*. Washington, DC: Government Printing Office.

Walker, L. (1978). Treatment alternatives for battered women. In J. Chapman & M. Gates (Eds.), *The victimization of women* (Vol. 3, pp. 168–173). Beverly Hills, CA: Sage Publications.

Walker, L. (1989). Psychology and violence against women. *American Psychologist*, 44(4), 695–702.

Weitzman, J., & Dreen, K. (1982). Wife beating: A view of the marital dyad. *Social Casework*, 63(5), 259–265.

Yontef, G. (1969). *A review of the practice of Gestalt therapy*. Los Angeles: Trident Shop, California State College.

Yontef, G. (1983). The self in Gestalt therapy: Reply to Tobin. *The Gestalt Journal*, 6(1), 55–70.

Zinker, J. (1977). *Creative process in Gestalt therapy*. New York: Brunner/Mazel.

4 Treatment for Spouse-Abusive Males

Daniel R. Clow
David E. Hutchins
Daniel E. Vogler

Men from every region of our country, from every socioeconomic level, and from every race, religion, and creed do violence to their wives, ex-wives, cohabiting partners, girlfriends, or dates. Men victimize their intimate partners at a rate of 15 to 28 million incidents each year, involving a conservatively estimated 1.8 million women (Straus, Gelles, & Steinmetz, 1980).

Each victim cries out for someone to make the abuser stop. In the case study below, we can observe Walker's (1979) three-phase cycle of violence. Tensions build (phase one), he strikes (phase two), he repents (phase three). The treatment model described in this chapter emphasizes the previolent phase of the cycle of violence and the abusers: unique thoughts (T), feelings (F), and actions (A) in order to prevent future violence from happening.

> Bill is a 25-year-old truck driver. He is married and has three children. His wife, Marie, secured child care and found a responsible job in a professional business office. Bill watched Marie prepare for work in her new clothes, bought with her money. He accused her of flirting with the men at work. She complained about the money he wastes on alcohol. The morning argument stayed with him as he grumbled to himself over the course of the day. Feeling angry and jealous, he convinced himself that something had to be done. He met her at the door as she came home from work. Bill says he can't remember what happened next, but Marie suffered a fractured cheek and black eyes. He says he's sorry and that it will never happen again.

The TFA System, developed by Hutchins (1979), have been refined to equip clinicians, clients, and others with a methodology to assess thinking, feeling. and acting in specific problem situations (Hutchins & Vogler, 1988). These refinements make it possible, for the first time, to teach individuals the skills necessary to assess their levels of TFA and make needed adjustments. This methodology has been effectively applied to a population of spouse abusers (Clow, 1989).

Using TFA Systems, it is now possible to illustrate the interactions of an abusive man's TFA behavior as he moves through a cycle of violence. Let's return to our case study and concentrate on Bill's experience as tensions were mounting. In phase one, Bill was experiencing frustrations within himself and within his intimate relationship. The closer he approached being out of control, the greater the number of negative thoughts of great intensity he experienced ("I'm losing my wife"). More of his feelings became unpleasant (jealousy, anger), and their intensity drove him to find relief. His actions lacked productiveness and efficiency (drinking, harping, ambush). There was an atmosphere of desperation, and feelings began to take over. In phase two, Bill is out of control. In phase three, he is repentant, but tensions inevitably rise again. In many cases like Bill's, the violence repeats.

Stopping the Cycle

Abusers learn violence. They also live in a violent society that appears to tolerate spousal abuse. Though being exposed to violence and living in a violent society are contributing factors to the use of violence, these (and numerous other variables) don't explain why some men are batterers and others are not. Men are not forced to abuse, but their choices are influenced by factors on many levels. Insight into what actualizes violence comes from an examination of thoughts, feelings, and actions experienced by an abuser prior to loss of control.

A variety of factors allow violence to continue in relationships. Violence continues because the battering man has acquired a repertoire of maladaptive thoughts, feelings, and actions in response to the demands of being in an intimate relationship. The tension-building phase of the violence cycle is the point of intervention in the treatment described in this chapter. If new and more adaptive thoughts, feelings, and actions to specific sources of tension can be learned, anger and rage can be more controlled and less destructive (Clow, 1989).

Examining the Context

Chapter 1 of this book presents an ecological model of domestic violence. The situational factors (including cultural, family, and individual) have the potential of contributing to a man's ultimate use of violence. The numerous associated variables could become overwhelming to the treatment provider simply because it is difficult to determine which factors from the ecological model directly contributed to a particular man's use of violence. The clinician's problem is one of determining which factors actually led to the reported incident. To manage the complexity, this treatment for abusers functions on a case-by-case basis, looking for specific situational (context) variables and idiosyncratic behavior in terms of thoughts, feelings, and actions.

TABLE 4.1 Thought Behaviors of Abusive Men in Situations of Mounting Tension

Variable	Citation	Year
Cognitive Distortions		
Exaggerate minor conflict	Glasser	1986
Hold unrealistic and high expectations	Star	1983
Rationalizations		
Maintain that behaviors aren't seriously violent	Ganley	1981
Justifications		
Maintain that wife's behavior caused crisis	Ganley	1981
Believe violence is excusable	Hornung et al.	1981
	Stahly	1978
Learned Thinking Errors		
Believe man is boss	Walker	1977
	Glasser	1986
Think wife should submit without question	Walker	1977
	Hornung et al.	1981
	Goode	1971
Believe religion permits vengeance	Brutz & Allen	1986
Believe God made women inferior to men	Brutz & Allen	1986
Presume women aren't equal	Walker	1977
	Glasser	1986

TABLE 4.2 Feeling Behavior of Abusive Men in Situations of Mounting Tension

Variable	Citation	Year
Suppressed anger	Deschner	1984
Low self-esteem	Star	1983
Hostility	Gil	1986
Frustration	Gil	1986
Depression	Gil	1986
Escapism	Gil	1986
Exploited	Gil	1986
Inner pain masked by minimizing	Ganley	1981
Embarrassment	Ganley	1981
Anxiety	Ganley	1981
	Walker	1984
Sadness	Ganley	1981
Guilt	Ganley	1981
Helpless	Ganley	1981
Vulnerable	Ganley	1981
Fear	Ganley	1981
Unsatisfied with relationship	Ganley	1981
	Walker	1984
Jealous	Walker	1984
Emotional scars, damage	Deschner	1984
	Seligman & Rosellin	1975
Loneliness, impaired intimacy	McCall & Shields	1986
Powerless to change life	Star	1983
	Walker	1984

Thoughts, Feelings, and Actions

Typically, people use their cognitive process to accurately interpret sensory information. The abuser tends to misinterpret events around him. The erroneous thoughts of an abuser often allow him to carry out the abuse and avoid ultimate responsibility. It is clear that cognitive distortions, rationalizations, and justifications abound. Indications are that a number of learned thinking errors also plague the abuser. Researchers have described the dysfunctional thoughts of abusers (summarized in Table 4.1).

Abusive men are also known to experience a variety of feelings and emotions. With limited self-awareness, abusive men tend to suppress and mask what they feel. A summary of the research on abusers' feelings is presented in Table 4.2.

Not surprisingly, the actions of abusive men are better known than their thoughts or feelings. We know that they hit, punch, slap, and beat, often with fatal results. But as Table 4.3 illustrates, there are other actions represented in the repertoire of abusive men. Their interactions tend to be self-centered, they can be controlling and manipulative, and they often appear self-destructive.

While the latent factors of consort violence may seem complicated and unwieldy, a systematic review of thought, feeling, and action behaviors clearly limits the scope of possibilities to manageable dimensions. Thus, the parameters for describing abuse and planning treatment are in realistic reach of the trained therapist.

TABLE 4.3 Acting Behavior of Abusive Men in Situations of Mounting Tension

Variable	Citation	Year
Act impulsively (change jobs, friends, move)	Glasser	1986
Isolated from others	Star	1983
Excessively possessive and dependent on		
partner	Hilberman & Munson	1978
	Giles-Sims	1983
	Pagelow	1981
	Frieze	1980
Express most emotions as anger outbursts	Ganley	1981
Control and dominate others	Straus et al.	1980
	Walker	1979
		1984
	Deschner	1984
Poorly communicating	Star	1983
Rigid, unbending	Star	1983
High ratio of negative interactions	Patterson	1982
Make decisions unilaterally	Giles-Sims	1983
	Pagelow	1981
	Walker	1984
Sexual assault and marital rape	Finkelhor & Yllo	1983
	Giles-Sims	1983
	Pagelow	1980
	Walker	1984
Abusive of drugs and/or alcohol	Bayles	1978
	Gelles	1974
	Prescott & Letko	1977

TABLE 4.3 (Continued)

Variable	Citation	Year
	Roy	1977
	Straus et al.	1980
Abusive of children	Johnson & Morse	1968
	American Humane Association	1974
	Gil	1970
	Straus et al.	1980
Hostile, dominant	Brekke	1987
Suicidal/self-destructive	Ganley	1981
High ingestion of food additives, sweets	Adams	1981
	Prinz et al.	1980
	Stare et al.	1980
	Reed	1983
Insulting, sulking, stomping out of room or house, crying, being spiteful, threatening to hit or throw things, throwing, smashing, hitting, or kicking	Straus	1986
Throw things at partner, pushing, grabbing, shoving partner; slapping; kicking, biting, or hitting with fist; hitting or trying to hit with objects	Straus	1986
Beating up female partner; threatening her with knife or gun; using a knife or firing a gun	Straus	1986

Implications for Treatment

Research indicates that treatment programs tend to be moving in the direction of using situationally specific interventions (i.e., anger logs, incident analysis, anger cue awareness). Many programs have cognitive, affective, and behavioral components, though level of emphasis varies. Treatment programs seem to be looking for a way to consolidate the various treatment methodologies (Clow, 1989).

Several implications for treatment can be drawn from the Thinking, Feeling, Acting model. First, the possible combinations of context plus thoughts, feelings, and actions are definable and manageable. Second, while abusers share many factors in common, each man's particular experience is unique. Third, an irrational belief, an intense feeling, or a self-centered action does not by itself cause abuse. It is the combination of factors/variables that precipitates an abusive behavior. Fourth, since the actual occurrence of consort violence is idiosyncratic, a treatment strategy aimed at a man's specific context and individual TFA experience, not generalizations, is required. These authors have found that fitting the treatment to match the man rather than asking the man to meet abstract preconceptions of partner violence is the preferred methodology. Fifth, our experience is that the best clinical question is "What intervention will work for this client in this situation given these individual factors?" Finally, to be most effective, the therapist needs deliberately and systematically to incorporate the abuser's specific situation and his unique thoughts, feelings, and actions into a treatment program designed specifically for him. The TFA Treatment methodology is briefly described below, beginning with the intake process.

THE TFA TREATMENT METHODOLOGY

Intake

The intake and initial assessment process is conducted in two parts. The first part is written and consists of completing (a) a client data sheet, (b) a self-report of known cues/signals of approaching loss of control, (c) a report of known nonviolent alternatives, and (d) the Conflict Tactic Scale (CTS) (Straus 1980). The second part of the intake process is the TFA assessment. This is partly for the leader's benefit in preparing an individualized treatment plan, but it also assists the abuser to begin to be accurately aware of his TFA anger pattern. The intake process concludes by explaining the group treatment contract and getting permission to contact the abuser's victim in order to collect data about the level and frequency of violence using the CTS.

TFA Assessment

Each court-referred man is assessed by the counselor during intake in the following manner:

STEP ONE. The counselor asks the subject to concentrate on the recent incident leading to his arrest and subsequent appearance in court (What happened? When did it happen? What led up to it? How much force was used?). Typically wordy, the counselor digests the subject account into two or three sentences. It is read back to the client to verify accuracy.

STEP TWO. The counselor asks the client questions regarding his thoughts during the moments prior to the critical incident (What were you thinking? What was going through your mind?). Responses are recorded on the TFA Assessment Worksheet above the Thoughts (T) angle of the TFA Triangle. Frequently, the subject responds with descriptions of feelings. The counselor responds, saying, "That is a feeling. Before we go on to explore your feelings, I want to get an idea about what you were thinking. Before you lost control, what were you thinking?"

STEP THREE. The counselor inquires about the subject's feelings in the moments prior to loss of control. The identified feelings are recorded on the counselor's TFA Assessment Worksheet. To clarify the range of feelings experienced, the counselor asks, "What other feelings did you experience?" The intensity of emotions is also explored by asking questions such as "How angry were you? How deep was your resentment?" The counselor notes nonverbal communicators (facial expressions, clenched fists, etc.).

STEP FOUR. The counselor asks the subject to consider the actions he took in the moments prior to abusing his partner. To clarify, the counselor asks, "What did you do next?" The counselor inquires about voice pitch and volume, movements, and chains of behavior. Also included in this assessment of action are the subject's involuntary actions (e.g., respiration rate, pulse). These actions were recorded alongside the action (A) angle.

STEP FIVE. The counselor asks the client to judge his own behavior on the Thinking–Feeling, Feeling–Acting, and Acting–Thinking continua. To illustrate, let's return to our case study.

With the specific problem situation in mind, the counselor asked Bill to look at the partially completed TFA Assessment Worksheet. He then asked, "In the moments prior to the abuse, were you (a) more thinking, (c) more feeling, or (b) about in the middle (doing both in equal amounts)?" In Bill's case, he had indicated he was feeling jealousy, anger, and resentment. In his response to the counselor's question, Bill indicated he was more feeling. The counselor marked the "(c) more feeling" response on the Thinking–Feeling (left) side of the Triangle.

The assessment continued in the same manner for the Feeling–Acting (bottom) side of the Triangle. The counselor asked Bill, "Were you (a) more feeling, (c) more acting, or (b) in the middle?" Bill answered that he was "more feeling," telling the counselor that he had felt angry all day. The counselor marked the feeling response.

Next, the counselor asked Bill, "Were you more (a) action-oriented, (c) more thinking, or (b) about in the middle?" Bill's answer was "a" (more acting), and told the counselor, "I was so damn mad I just hit her, and when she yelled, I hit her again." The counselor connected all the marks on the TFA Triangle, forming an inner triangle, known as the TFA Triad (see Figure 4.1).

STEP SIX. The final step in the TFA Assessment process is to discuss the resulting TFA Triad with the client. Bill was asked what his TFA Triad meant. He said, "I guess my emotions are getting the best of me. When I should be thinking, I'm not thinking—I'm just emotional. It wasn't something I thought about."

Clinical Observations of the TFA Assessment Process

A number of observations are made during the course of the TFA Assessments. First, subjects tend to experience difficulty identifying

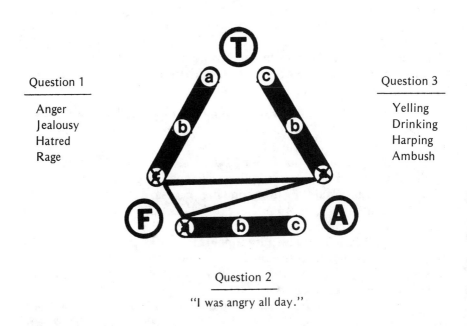

FIGURE 4.1 **TFA Assessment Worksheet illustrating results of counselor-client interactions generated at intake.**

their thoughts as the violent incident occurs. Second. in their initial responses to the question about thoughts versus feelings, abusers tend to identify "thoughts" as their dominant orientation. This may be due to their low comfort level with feelings, and underscores the difficulty abusive men have identifying and reporting feelings. Third, they give evidence of being unable to differentiate between thoughts and feelings. When asked to report what thoughts they have during the incident, they frequently answer, "I was angry." The therapist processes their responses in order to provide clarity, often teaching them the difference between thoughts and feelings. Fourth, the results of the TFA Assessment make it possible for each client to interpret his TFA Triad with little assistance. Finally, the TFA Assessment of each man's abusive incident tends to result in similar F–A Triads, in spite of the fact that their critical incidents are different. It is possible that all abusers can be described using the F–A Triad.

The F–A Triad Interpreted

The F–A Triad illustrates the dynamic interaction of thoughts, feelings, and actions in the situation just prior to abuse. Actions appear to be taken without the moderating influence of thoughts. Without restraining themselves from brutish action, men (like Bill in our case study) behave impulsively. Their swift actions occur with minimal, if any, cognitive awareness of all that was taking place inside themselves. They are not likely to fully consider the consequences of their behavior. Thoughts are conspicuously absent in the F–A Triads emerging from intake assessments with abusive men.

Formulating Individualized Group Treatment Plans

The therapist compiles all the information gathered in the intake process. Five pieces of data allow a thorough and individualized group therapy plan. First, the therapist knows the pattern of each man's dysfunctional thoughts, feelings, and actions leading to their offense. This TFA pattern is illustrated by a Triad, typically the F–A Triad. Second, the therapist has an objective assessment of each man's previolence cue awareness, expressed in TFA terms. Intervention strategies will be aimed at raising the client's awareness of cues (signals) of approaching loss of control. Third, the therapist considers possible nonviolent alternatives for each man's problem situation. These alternatives may need to be taught as nonviolent skills. Fourth, the therapist has reports of the extent and frequency of violence. The client's CTS self-report is compared against his victim's CTS results. Her report is used as an objective validator. Finally, the therapist considers the client's subjective reports. The self-report of cues and alternatives give an indication of the resources the abuser brings to treatment. Individualized treatment strategies are formulated with the aim of raising awareness of previolence anger cues and knowledge of nonviolent alternatives. The therapist is able to illustrate this nonviolent pattern of behavior with the midpoint TFA Triad, a relative balance of thoughts, feelings, and actions. The therapist seeks to be sensitive to the needs of each abusive man. In this way, group treatment is individualized.

TFA GROUP TREATMENT PLAN

The TFA treatment plan presented here calls for six court-referred men to complete a twelve-week program. (Length of program will vary according to size of group.) The program is divided into two parts.

Part One—The Presenting Problem

This part of treatment addresses previolent experiences marked by rising tensions leading to the abusive man's use of violence and subsequently his arrest. The specific context and the specific thoughts, feelings, and actions interacting in the moments just prior to the abusive man's behavior are examined in detail.

Week One

Leader and participant introductions; review of group contract; subjects describe their offense; the TFA System is introduced: a volunteer is taken through a group TFA Assessment (probing the subject's behavior just as the therapist did in the intake interview) resulting in a group assessment of the volunteer subject's previolence experience; denial and rationalizations of behavior are confronted; cues of loss of control are isolated and a discussion of possible alternatives takes place (e.g., "time-out"); group assignment: use the TFA Triangle to analyze their most recent or worst incident of abuse.

Week Two

A second man is taken through the TFA group assessment; his TFA behavior is probed, raising his awareness of his previolence experience; cues and nonviolent alternatives are discussed; minimizations of violence are confronted with CTS results (subject's and spouse's); group assignment: use TFA Triangle to complete an analysis of most recent or worst incident of abuse (whichever was not chosen for week one).

Weeks Three Through Six

The same format is followed until all participants have benefited from the group process. When Part One is completed, all men have a personalized TFA Triad that illustrates their presenting problem situation. Group assignments include describing three frequently encountered problems with wife/partner.

Part Two—The Predicted Problem

The attention of the group process turns toward preparing each man to nonviolently handle their most frustrating problem situation, which was known to be prone to loss of control.

Weeks Seven through Twelve

Each week, the counselor asks for a volunteer to present his most tense situation and work with the group toward being able to handle the situation nonviolently. The TFA group process begins again. During Part Two of treatment, the group helping process probes for new options, challenges mistaken interpretations of events, and helps the subject to finalize goals for nonviolence. The end result of this process is that the man develops a strategy for his TFA behavior that enables him to be nonviolent when that problem occurs. He is able to describe his plan using a more productive TFA Triad. His pre-violence cues and nonviolent alternatives are reviewed. The group works with the volunteer until it is satisfied that he can remain in control. During the last week of court-ordered treatment. assessments of cue awareness and knowledge of nonviolent alternatives are read-ministered. Feedback discussions and treatment evaluations are conducted.

Characteristic Results of the TFA Treatment Method

Due to the individualized format of treatment, group participation is typically active and lively. Subjects quickly acquire the skill to use

TFA concepts in problem situations, and many report using the TFA problem solving method in areas outside their intimate relationship. Subjects identify the changes needed to be nonviolent in terms of their total personality—thoughts, feelings, and actions. Following treatment, abusers identify the midpoint TFA Triad (t=f=a) as illustrative of their strategy for nonviolence (see Figure 4.2). In the t=f=a Triad, thoughts (T) take a new and influential role in moderating feelings and actions. Previolence awareness increases, measured by gains in awareness of violence cues (signals), and knowledge of nonviolent alternatives. A distinctive result of this treatment is that nonviolent strategies are individualized and relevant to the particular needs of the abuser. Each man leaves treatment with a workable strategy for preventing relapse. Tentative assess-

"I can control myself."
"It's good she likes her job."
"I know my anger pattern."
"I've got options to abuse."

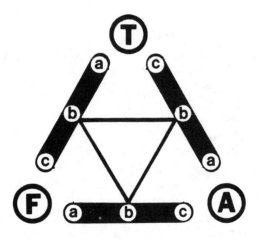

Disappointment	Time Out
Let down	Relax
Love	Calmly talk
Concern (About men)	Stop drinking
Eager to talk	Get marital counseling

FIGURE 4.2   The Midpoint (t=f=a) Triad illustrating posttreatment nonviolent strategies for control.

ments of the abuser's use of violence can be made immediately following treatment by readministrations of the CTS to both the abuser and his partner. The individualized treatment methodology can be followed in making follow-up referrals that are unique to the client.

Recommendations for Treatment

Therapeutic intervention with male spouse abusers is by no means an established art, nor has it developed to the point of a science. However, we can consolidate literature, research, and practical experience to develop guidelines to help in the therapeutic treatment of the male abuser. Our recommendations follow:

1. *TFA.* The TFA experience of the male abuser must be dealt with in treatment. Any treatment approach that excludes the cognitive, affective, and "behavioral'" dimensions of the abuser is likely to be incomplete.

2. *Integration.* It is the integration of the man's thoughts, feelings, and actions that determines his pattern of response, whether positive or negative. The therapist must determine how thoughts, feelings, and actions interact and mutually affect each other. This sequence has major implications for treatment strategies.

3. *Context.* A man's behavior must be assessed in light of his unique situation. Generalizations have limited value in promoting change. Specific contextual cues can provide guidelines for what behavior to change, and how it can be changed. As such, treatment must fit the individual rather than trying to force the client into some predetermined therapeutic mold.

4. *Group treatment.* The developers of TFA Treatment think that a group approach to therapeutic intervention is the treatment of choice. Gathered with other abusive men, each man's behavior can be examined by a group of "experts" on the topic. Because they know all the tricks for resisting therapy and minimizing problems, they can as a group confront counterproductive behavior and offer concrete suggestions for change. Furthermore, group members can model desired behavior for others. Accurate awareness, clear thinking, positive feelings, and constructive actions are reinforced in therapy groups.

5. *Client involvement.* If treatment methods are understood by the abusive man, his ability to participate actively in therapy is enhanced. This almost seems too simple. Mental health practitioners

80   Treatment of Spousal Abuse

have hidden too long behind the cloak of mystical-sounding psychological "mumbo-jumbo." Parsimonious, straightforward, and understandable strategies improve chances that the client can actively participate in changing his own behavior both inside and outside the therapeutic situation. The TFA treatment method presented in this chapter encourages individuals to work together in groups toward the goal of stopping their abuse of their partners.

REFERENCES

Adams, W. (1981). Lack of behavioral effects from Feingold diet violations. *Perceptual and Math Skills*, 52(1), 307–313.

American Humane Association. (1978). *National analysis of official child neglect and abuse reporting*. Denver: American Humane Association.

Bayles, J. A. (1978). Violence, alcohol problems and other problems in disintegrating families. *Journal of Studies on Alcohol*, 39(3), 551–563.

Brekke, J. S. (1987). Detecting wife and child abuse in clinical settings. *Social Casework: The Journal of Contemporary Social Work*, 68, 332–338.

Brutz, J. L., & Allen C. M. (1986). Religious commitment, peace activism, and marital violence in Quaker families. *Journal of Marriage and the Family*, 48, 491–502.

Clow, D. R. (1989). Group psychotherapy for male spouse abusers using TFA Systems (tm). PhD. diss., Virginia Polytechnic Institute and State University, Blacksburg, Virginia.

Deschner, J. (1984). *The hitting habit*. New York: Free Press.

Deschner, J., Geddes, C., Grimes, V., & Stancukas, E. (1980). *Battered women: Factors associated with abuse*. Arlington, TX: University of Texas at Arlington, Graduate School of Social Work.

Finkelhor, D., & Yllo, K. (1983). Forced sex in marriage: A sociological view. In D. Finkelhor, R. Gelles, G. Hotaling, & M. Straus (Eds.), *The dark side of families*. Beverly Hills, CA: Sage.

Frieze, I. H. (1980). *Causes and consequences of marital rape*. Paper presented at the American Psychological Association Annual Convention, Montreal.

Ganley, A. (1981). *Participant and trainer's manual for working with men who batter*. Washington, DC: Center for Women Policy Studies.

Gelles, R. J. (1974). The violent home. Beverly Hills, CA: Sage.

Gil, D. (1970). *Violence against children: Physical child abuse in the United States*. Cambridge, MA: Harvard University Press.

Giles-Sims, J. (1983). *Wife beating: A systems theory approach*. New York: Guilford Press.

Glasser, D. G. (1986). Violence in the society. In M. Lystad (Ed.), *Violence in the homes: Interdisciplinary perspectives*. New York: Brunner/Mazel.

Goode, W. (1971). Force and violence in the family. *Journal of Marriage and the Family*, 33, 624–636.

Hilberman, E., & Munson, L. (1978). Sixty battered women. *Victimology: An International Journal*, 2(3–4), 460–471.

Hornung, C. A., McCullough, B. C., & Sugimoto, T. (1981). Status relationships in marriage: Risk factors in spouse abuse. *Journal of Marriage and the Family*, 43(3), 675–692.

Hutchins, D. E. (1979). Systematic counseling: The T-F-A model for counselor intervention. *Personnel and Guidance Journal*, 57, 529–531.

Hutchins, D. E. (1984). Hutchins behavior inventory interpretation guide. Unpublished manuscript, Virginia Polytechnic Institute and State University, Blacksburg, Virginia.

Hutchins, D. E., & Vogler, D. E. (1988). TFA systems (tm). Unpublished manuscript, Virginia Polytechnic Institute and State University, Blacksburg, Virginia.

Johnson B., & Morse, H. A. (1968). Injured children and their parents. *Children*, 15, 147–152.

McCall, G. J., & Shields, N. M. (1986). Social and structural factors in family violence. In M. Lystad (Ed.), *Violence in the home: Interdisciplinary perspectives*. New York: Brunner/Mazel.

Pagelow, M. (1981). *Does the law help battered wives? Some research notes* Madison, WI: Law and Society Association.

Pagelow, M. (1981). *Women battering: Victims and their experience*. Beverly Hills, CA: Sage.

Patterson, G. (1982). *Coercive family process*. Eugene, OR: Castiglia Press.

Prescott, S., & Letko, C. (1977). Battered: A social psychological perspective. In M. Roy (Ed.), *Battered women: A psychosociological study of domestic violence*. New York: Van Nostrand Reinhold.

Prinz, R. J., Roberts, W. A., & Hantman, E. (1980). Dietary correlates of hyperactive behavior in children. *Consulting and Clinical Psychology*, 48(6), 760–769.

Reed, B. (1983)., *Food, teens, and behavior.* Manitowoc, WI: Natural Press.

Roy, M. (1977). A current survey of 150 cases. In M. Roy (Ed.), *Battered women: A psychosociological study of domestic violence*. New York: Van Nostrand Reinhold.

Seligman, M. E., & Rosellin, R. A. (1975). Frustration and learned helplessness. *Journal of Experimental Psychology: Animal Behavior Processes*, 104(1), 149–157.

Stahly, G. B. (1978). A review of select literature of spousal violence. *Victimology, An International Journal*, 2(3–4), 591–607.

Star, B. (1983). *Helping the abuser: Intervening effectively in family violence*. New York: Family Service Association of America.

Stare, F. J., Whelan, E., & Sheridan, M. (1980). Diet and hyperactivity: Is there a relationship? *Pediatrics*, 66(4), 521–525.

Straus, M. A. (1980). Victims and aggressors in marital violence. *American Behavioral Scientist*, 23, 681–704.

Straus, M. A., & Gelles, R. J. (1986). Societal change and change in family violence from 1975 to 1985 as revealed by two national surveys. *Journal of Marriage and the Family*, 48, 465–479.

Straus, M. A., Gelles, R. J., & Steinmetz, S. K. (1980). *Behind closed doors: Violence in the American family.* Garden City, NY: Doubleday.

Walker, L. E. (1977). Battered women and learned helplessness. *Victimology: An International Journal*, 2(3–4), 535–544.

Walker, L. E. (1979). New York: Harper & Row.

Walker, L. E. (1984). *The battered woman syndrome.* New York: Springer Publishing Co.

5 Family Therapy for Spouse Abuse

Sandra M. Stith
Karen H. Rosen

Jack, a 28-year-old technician who recently moved to the area from another state, called for an appointment. His wife had moved out of the house and would not see him until he sought help to control his violent temper. Jack reported a long history of abuse toward his 24-year-old wife, his mother, his first wife, and, as a child, his sister. He had never sought counseling before because he had not recognized the connection between his violent behavior and the losses of significant relationships in his life, that is, his first wife and their child and contact with his family of origin. Jack had always assumed that his behavior was justified because he was surrounded by infuriating women who "didn't know their place."

His second wife, "Mary," had confronted him with a different perspective and an ultimatum. She took the position that she did not deserve to be hit and that she was not going to remain in a marriage where her husband was physically abusive to her. Their relationship was going to have to change if she was going to stay with him. Jack came alone to the first sessions to confront and begin to deal with his violence. After the seventh session Mary came to the clinic with Jack. This session was one of many in the next twelve months in which Jack and Mary were first seen individually, then conjointly. With the help of their therapist, the couple renegotiated their marital contract to eliminate violence from their relationship. Jack learned to deal differently with his anger and began to view women, and especially Mary, in a new way.

For many years, family therapists believed that spouse abuse was a relatively isolated problem, affecting only very pathological families. However, recent research by Murray Straus and his colleagues (1986; 1980) has caused therapists to take a second look at the families they treat. Straus' latest work (1986) suggests that in the United States 1.6 million wives are severely assaulted by their husbands each year.

Although spouse abuse is a significant problem with extensive impact on American families, clinicians in community settings often find the families they treat unwilling to reveal that violence. Often they discover, after several therapy sessions focused on presenting problems other than violence (e.g., parent–child conflict or ineffective marital communication), that spouse abuse is occurring. Even then, the importance of violence and its contribution to the presenting problem is often minimized (Little, 1986).

Therapists who lack understanding of the complex cultural factors that maintain violence and the devastating effects of any form of violence against women may collude in minimizing the importance of the violence (Pressman, 1989). They may continue treating the initial problem and ignore the violence or they may view the violence as a problem in which each member of the couple shares equal responsibility, thus minimizing the batterer's responsibility for his behavior and ultimately confirming his belief that "she made me do it."

This chapter presents an integrated family therapy approach to marital violence informed by a feminist perspective. This approach is based on family systems theory and is influenced by empirical research findings delineating individual and familial variables related to marital violence. First, a brief review of literature pertinent to the treatment of spouse abuse is provided. This review is followed by a brief overview of spouse abuse treatment models and issues. Finally, the treatment program is delineated as a series of stages with case examples to add clarity.

FACTORS RELATED TO SPOUSE ABUSE

To develop the treatment program presented in this chapter, empirical and theoretical literature on spouse abuse was examined. The following factors are among those incorporated into the treatment model:

1. stereotypical sex-role attitudes
2. attitudes that support the use of violence to maintain power in the family
3. poor impulse control

4. abuse or exposure to abuse as a child
5. intense stress in present day-to-day life
6. poor relationship skills
7. isolation

A number of studies have examined the relationship between marital violence and stereotypical sex role attitudes. Coleman (1980), Bernard and Bernard (1984), Sonkin, Martin, and Walker (1985), and Stith (in press) reported that men who abuse their spouses tend to have more traditional gender-role orientation than do nonbatterers. Pressman (1989) suggests that abusive men tend to be controlling, dominating, and aggressive in order to get their needs met. She indicates that the wife is commonly demoted in the executive hierarchy and relegated to the level of a child.

> Because of this hierarchical structure and the socialized inequities between men and women, women unconsciously accept their role of deferring to their husbands and caretaking of others. Patriarchy insures the enormous likelihood that an abused wife experiences herself as powerless and helpless in relationship to her husband while at the same time believing she is responsible for his well-being. (p. 28)

Dibble and Straus (1981), Stith (in press), and Saunders et al. (1987) have established a link between the approval of marital violence and violent behavior. These researchers found that abusers were more likely than nonabusers to believe that wife beating is not only justified but acceptable. The belief that violence is justified to maintain power may explain why men may choose not to use newly learned anger-management skills.

Empirical evidence suggests that poor impulse control is a characteristic of men who batter their wives. In their comprehensive review of the literature, Hotaling and Sugarman (1986) reported a consistent link between men's use of violence against their partners and their use of violence in other relationships. Rouse (1984) found that batterers were more likely to be violent in nonfamily situations than were men who did not batter their wives. This evidence suggests that men who abuse their partners often have ineffective anger-management skills.

Hotaling and Sugarman (1986) also found that witnessing marital violence as a child was consistently related to abuse in adult relationships. Other studies support these findings (Kempe et al., 1962; Steele & Pollock, 1974). Straus and his colleagues (1980) have asserted that being a member of a violent family is how each generation learns to be violent. Exposure to family violence during childhood leads to the development of the belief that violence is an acceptable way to deal with anger and frustration and to cope with stress.

Research data also suggest that marital violence increases as stress increases (Neidig et al., 1984; Rouse, 1984; Straus et al., 1980). Neidig (1985), who investigated the effect of stress on domestic violence in the military community, concluded that "domestic violence within the military can be understood as a result of high levels of stress affecting couples who do not have the ability to resolve difficulty through appropriate means" (p. 5). However, Ganley (1981) ascertains that although some people resort to violence as a response to stress, it is important to recognize that the cause of the violence is not the stressful event, but the individual's learned response to stress. Thus, stress does not cause violence, but the individual who is under stress may choose to use violence to deal with that stress rather than use more appropriate stress-management techniques.

Hotaling and Sugarman (1986) also examined relationship risk markers of spouse abuse. These researchers reported that physical violence was positively related to verbal aggression and marital conflict in nine studies. Men who hit their wives seem also to yell at them and to report high levels of conflict. Men who resort to physical violence may not have developed other ways to resolve conflicts or to communicate.

TREATMENT OF MARITAL VIOLENCE

Although Gelles and Maynard (1987) reported that current research and theory construction has moved beyond thinking about marital violence from an individual/psychopathological model to a multidimensional model that includes the individual, family, and society, they suggested that treatment tends to lag behind theory. "The individual as victim or offender is still the major focus of treatment efforts" (p. 270). Separate group work for men and women is generally recommended (Pressman, 1989).

Controversy continues to surround the use of a systemic perspective in the treatment of domestic violence (Taggart, 1985; Hare-Mustin, 1978; 1980; Westurland, 1983). Some professionals have suggested that systems theory implies the blurring of boundaries between batterer and battered spouse, thereby calling for the victim to be "co-responsible" for the assault. Taggart (1985) maintains that the idea of co-responsibility permits conclusions altogether too compatible with the dominant culture's sexist views on the causes of violence against women.

Giles-Sims (1983) has responded to such criticisms by suggesting that a systems theory explanation is not a unicausal explanation:

> Systems theory explains violence as the product of interdependent
> causal processes including the preexisting behavior patterns of system
> members and the system processes that lead to stability or change in
> the patterns of behavior over time. This does not, however, remove any
> individual from responsibility for his/her own behavior. What it does is
> to provide new and important insights into how to deal with this
> problem. (p. 143)

These insights include not only ideas on how interactions between spouses contribute to the maintenance of the abuse but also
how feedback from society contributes. For example, systems theory
would suggest that a message that a battered woman might get from
her local magistrate, such as "take time to cool down; do not press
charges," may contribute substantially to the maintenance of the
abusive pattern in the relationship.

Approaching treatment from a systems theoretical framework
does not mean taking the responsibility for the abusive behavior
from the abuser. This framework, however, does allow for consideration of the role that society plays in contributing to the abuse.
Marianne Walters, quoted in a recent article on family-therapy approaches to working with domestic violence (Mathias, 1986) suggests
that

> It's a tremendous help to therapists to understand the larger context of
> violence instead of thinking in terms of victims and victimizers or
> figuring out how she got him to hit her. The fact is, both partners in a
> relationship are caught in a cultural context that historically has said
> that wife beating . . . is an acceptable way to keep order in the family.
> When you understand that as a therapist, you don't have to pathologize
> the couple or get lost in their unique patterns of interaction. Instead,
> you can help them see the cultural mandates that shape their behavior.

A system's perspective suggests a variety of appropriate points
to intervene in a violent system. For example, the choice could be to
enter the abusive system through the court, which has traditionally
not supported the battered woman in her effort to change her situation. Or the entrance could be through the economic system, which
has maintained women's salaries at a fraction of their male counterparts', thereby making it financially difficult for women to leave
their abusive husbands. The treatment program described in this
chapter enters the abusive system at the level of the individuals in
the abusive relationship. It has been implemented in a university-
based family therapy clinic that provides low-cost family therapy for
individuals and couples.

A SPOUSE ABUSE TREATMENT PROGRAM

The treatment program presented begins to bridge the gap between research and practice. It is based on an integrated family therapy model that incorporates the findings of current research on risk markers for spouse abuse. The rigid hierarchical structures frequently present in abusive marriages are modified by a structural-strategic approach that includes careful planning and specific strategies to encourage rapid changes in couples.

A cornerstone of this approach is that violent behavior is inappropriate and destructive to *all* participants. It is emphasized that violence is different from anger, misunderstanding, and frustration, which are part of the "human condition."

A first step is to assist clients in developing a clear "bottom line" that does not permit violence. For example, when couples come to treatment, they frequently minimize the seriousness and inherent danger of the abusive behavior. To a wife who says that her husband "just slapped" her but it wasn't that serious, the therapist may say, "Would you be willing to call the police or call the shelter if he slugs you? What if he threatens you with a gun? How far can he go before you will know that you've reached your bottom line?"

At the same time, it is important that the therapist join with the couple in appreciating and normalizing the anger and frustration that accompanies daily living in a family and working in this society. Another crucial point in gaining entrance to the family and as a base from which to build is the emphasis on the competencies of each partner and on the strengths of the relationship. Noticing and pointing out what each partner does well at home and on the job is an important way to empower clients to make changes. Asking the couple choosing to remain together to talk about what is going well in their relationship often helps remind both' partners what is at stake and that they have something together worth saving.

Other key areas of work include modifying stereotypical gender-role attitudes and behaviors and developing communication and conflict-management skills. Clients become aware of their gender-role attitudes and behaviors and how they are influenced by society and their family of origin. They are encouraged to broaden their repertoire of appropriate behaviors so that they can appreciate and respect their own and their partners' expressive and instrumental sides. Couples are coached to build communication skills as well as anger and conflict-management skills.

Structure of Treatment

The specific structure of treatment is determined by the client's wishes. For example, if the initial telephone call is from a woman who is thinking of ending an abusive relationship and who does not want her partner involved in treatment, the therapist works with her individually to help her understand her options and their consequences. She may then be connected with local shelters for battered women and encouraged to contact support groups available in the community. Individual counseling, such as that presented in Chapter 3 by Little, may be recommended. She is not encouraged to involve her husband in treatment unless she needs help negotiating a divorce or she is considering remaining in the marriage.

In contrast, if one partner calls requesting marital therapy and reports that he or she is in a violent relationship, or if marital violence is reported after treatment has begun, the therapist may work with both partners. Often there is a strong emotional bond keeping the couple together. Therefore, when couples choose to remain together, working with both partners at some time during the treatment process is preferred.

However, therapists should use caution before beginning conjoint couples therapy during the initial stages of treatment for spouse abuse. As Gelles and Maynard (1987) have suggested, beginning with conjoint therapy in cases of life-threatening violence is clearly inappropriate and extremely dangerous. Cook and Frantz-Cook (1984) also recommend that couples therapy begin only after partners are sufficiently differentiated so that relationship issues can be worked on in tandem without escalating the violence. If the therapist believes the risk for further violence is high, individual work with the partners would continue until a convincing commitment to nonviolence is made by both spouses. When the batterer has not taken responsibility for the abuse, when the wife lacks a sense of her own worth and her right to assert her own views, and when the violence or the fear of violence still permeates the relationship, individual and/or group work such as that proposed in Chapters 3 and 4 of this book by Little and Clow et al. would be recommended before beginning *any* conjoint work.

Stage One: Contracting for Nonviolence

Although questions are asked about marital violence early in family treatment, often violence is not revealed until the couple develops trust in the therapeutic relationship. When it is learned that marital violence is part of the couple relationship after several weeks of treatment, even if the presenting problem concerns a child, this new information is considered vital to treatment. The therapist responds by directing attention away from the initial problem and escalating the family's concern about the violence. The seriousness of the violence is never minimized.

In the initial stages of treatment for marital violence, both partners are seen separately to assess the lethality of the violence and the commitment of each partner to ending the violence. The primary concern is for the safety of the battered wife and the children. Therefore, the initial assessment is conducted with the partners individually rather than conjointly. If the couple were to be seen conjointly during the assessment stage, the wife might fear being honest about her experiences. If she minimizes her experience, the therapist may not be able to assess accurately the lethality of the situation. On the other hand, if she does not minimize the abuse, her responses to the therapist may put her at increased risk of further abuse after the session.

The assessment of the lethality of the violence includes questions about the first incidence of marital violence, the most serious incident, and the most recent incident. The therapist is particularly interested in how frequently the violence occurs. Other areas that are assessed include the possession of weapons in the house and whether the violence is a part of a larger pattern of antisocial events or violent acts by the batterer (see Neidig et al., 1984). The battered wife is helped to develop a safety plan to ensure her safety during the work to follow (see Appendix A, this chapter).

If each spouse agrees on the level of violence in the marriage and expresses a desire to end the violence, and if the couple has chosen to remain together as they restructure their relationship, a conjoint session may be held to punctuate the seriousness of the violence, to emphasize that violence is an unacceptable way to cope with the stresses in life, and to discuss ways to decrease the risk of further violence. At this point, the couple is required to dispose of any guns in the house and do other concrete things to reduce the lethality of the situation. The recommendation may be that the couple separate temporarily to decrease the risk of increased violence.

A goal of therapy is to empower both partners by helping them obtain a sense of control in their life. The abused wife is empowered to develop a clear sense of her "bottom line" with regard to the abuse. The husband is encouraged to recognize that he too is a victim of his own rage and that controlling his rage would put him in a stronger position. Both partners are helped to consider ways to increase the safety of the home. The wife may be urged to contact local shelter programs and make psychological as well as physical preparations to leave if the need arises. The husband may be urged to eliminate drug or alcohol use and to prepare to leave the house if he should begin to feel enraged.

Both partners are asked to sign a contract to end the violence in their family and to contribute to the development of contingencies should the abuse recur (see Appendix B, this chapter). Contingencies that clients have used in their contracts include commitments that the wife go to the local shelter for battered women, that she call the police to file a complaint or restraining order, that she call a relative to protect her, and/or that her husband leave the home temporarily while therapy continues. These contingencies are presented as crucial to the relationship and to each as individuals if they are to have the nonviolent marriage they both want. Throughout therapy the couple is asked to renew their commitment to the contract and to follow through with the contingencies should abuse recur.

Case Example

Mr. and Mrs. Johnson had been coming to therapy for two months for assistance with their thirteen-year-old daughter, who was encopretic, academically unmotivated, and fought with her brothers verbally and physically. When discussing an intervention to stop the sibling violence, Mrs. Johnson revealed that she had been threatened and physically assaulted by her husband intermittently during their marriage.

At this point, all efforts to focus on the children were stopped in order to emphasize the seriousness of the spouse abuse. The therapist reframed the children's behavior as "protective" because they were concerned about both parents. The children were frightened that their dad would hurt their mom and kept the attention on themselves in order to redirect the tension between the couple. The children were congratulated for their hard work and were told that the therapist would work with their parents to end the violence and that they could have a vacation from their role of keeping things stirred up.

Mr. and Mrs. Johnson each met individually with the therapist and reported that they wanted to remain in the marriage and to stop the violence. When the couple met conjointly, they were asked to sign a nonviolence contract and to develop contingencies to which they could both commit. The therapist used information obtained previously to emphasize the competencies of both Mr. and Mrs. Johnson and their joint commitment to ending the violence. Strengths such as their willingness to work with their daughter to help her with her problems and to make her needs a priority in their life and their commitment to attend therapy regularly at great financial sacrifice were framed as helpful to them in their greater struggle to eliminate violence in their own relationship.

The contingencies which they developed included Mrs. Johnson's leaving and taking the children to a local shelter if abuse occurred or threatened as well as Mr. Johnson's leaving the family temporarily. Both Mr. and Mrs. Johnson were encouraged to make nonviolence the "bottom line" in their relationship. Following through on the contingencies was framed as a "sacrifice" Mrs. Johnson would be making to take care of herself, her children, her husband, and her marriage. For Mr. Johnson, following through was framed as a demonstration of courage and a caring way to show how much his family meant to him.

Second Stage: Teaching Anger-Management Skills

After both partners have agreed to a nonviolence contract, basic anger-management skills and time-out techniques are discussed and practiced. These skills and techniques are described thoroughly elsewhere by Sonkin and Durphy (1982) and Deschner (1984). Both the batterer and the battered wife are taught to recognize the signs that they are becoming angry and that tension is escalating. They are given information about the cycle of violence, first explained by Walker (1979). Violence often proceeds from normal everyday tensions, to a tension-building stage, to an explosion, and finally to a honeymoon stage. The therapist emphasizes that these cycles usually become more frequent and that violence normally escalates with time. Couples usually recognize this cycle in their own relationship.

Couples are also taught a structured time-out technique that involves an agreement to separate, to refrain from drinking or driving, and to engage in relaxation or physical activities that will alleviate their anger or fear (see Appendix C, this chapter). They are directed to practice taking a time-out several times each week in order to make it a normal part of their life experience.

Both partners are strongly urged to participate in group treatment programs conducted by local domestic violence programs. Groups for abusing men serve to help them to take responsibility for their violent behavior and teach basic anger management skills (Pressman, 1989). Supportive group treatment for women in abusive relationships helps them see that they are not alone, reduces isolation, and helps them develop identities apart from their spouses.

Reconnecting clients with their own resources for controlling anger has been an effective and self-reinforcing process for a number of clients. Abusive clients are sometimes trained to use an "anchor" to recapture past periods of calm and stability as a substitute for present feelings of anger and violence (Cameron-Bandler, 1985). By touching a preconditioned spot, clients can become conditioned to activate healthy, calming memories to replace current out-of-control feelings.

Case Study

Mr. Renwick, who was initially in therapy for abusing his step-daughter, had successfully developed an appropriate relationship with the child but continued to have difficulty in controlling his anger with his wife and his co-workers. For example, on several occasions Mr. Renwick lost his temper and threatened or resorted to physical violence with fellow employees at work. He was in danger of losing his job.

The therapist asked Mr. Renwick to think about times in the past when he had been calm and successful; when he had felt free of ego-threatening thoughts; when he had felt "laid back" and in a mood to laugh at himself. Mr. Renwick was able to remember several situations in detail: how his face looked, his voice sounded, his body felt; how others reacted to him positively; how he acted and what he thought when others responded positively. These pleasant situations were "anchored" by having Mr. Renwick press the middle finger of his right hand as he vividly recalled these experiences. The anchoring process was reinforced several times over the next several weeks as part of his regular therapy sessions.

Mr. Renwick reported very favorable results from using his "anchor" to activate calming memories. On one occasion he reported experiencing instant relief after using his "anchor" in response to his growing rage at being given conflicting orders from two different supervisors. He was able to envision himself as the comedian Richard Pryor, humming and dancing around in the face of imminent threat. Several months later, Mr. Renwick noted the development of a new extension of his anchor: when aroused to violent feelings, he would notice his wedding ring on the finger next to the anchored finger. The wedding ring had become the surrogate anchor. Simply looking at it evoked a feeling of calm and well-being. Mr. Renwick was also successful in using the anchor (and the wedding ring) imagery during arguments with his wife. The couple could take a time-out and then calmly and productively discuss the problem. Six months later Mr. Renwick was still using the anchor effectively both at home and at work.

Unlike many treatment programs that end their work at this point, the program presented here moves to a new phase. When couples successfully rework their relationship to exclude violence and batterers learn techniques to manage their anger, they can then begin the more sensitive process of refining relationship skills and individual flexibility.

Stage Three: Enhancing the Marital Relationship

During this phase of the work, the focus is on enhancing personal and relationship flexibility, beginning with the development of a plan to cope more effectively with and/or to reduce the level of stress. Clients are also encouraged to understand and change stereotypical sex-role attitudes that not only support the use of violence but also limit the options for both men and women. Specific problems unique to the couple provide the context for the couple to learn new ways to communicate and to manage conflict.

While it is emphasized that stress is not an excuse for violence, couples explore ways that they can begin to take control of their own lives to reduce stress levels. Couples are directed to list the sources of stress for the family and the resources to meet demands, and to prioritize areas that require immediate attention. The therapist assists the couple as they select stressors that can be eliminated and develop options for handling their priority areas. Couples are given permission to take time for themselves as individuals and as a couple to "refill their cup" so that they will have the energy to meet the high demands. Stress management work provides an excellent opportunity to assist clients in developing effective communication and negotiation skills.

Therapeutic reframing is used freely to help couples perceive stressful events in new ways. For example, when the battered wife, "Alice," reported feeling depressed and unable to complete her chores, her behavior was reframed as an important step in her recovery and that it was an appropriate time for her to slow down and allow herself to rebuild. She had been experiencing a great deal of change in her life, and her body knew that it was time for her to relax and to heal. When she was able to view her behavior as appropriate and healthy rather than lazy or pathological, she was able to get beyond this period of discouragement. A constant goal is to aid family members to see stressors as challenges rather than barriers.

While our therapeutic approach is present-focused, intergenerational information is gathered to determine what couples have learned from their family of origin about male–female relationships and the use of violence in these relationships. Anger-management skill training alone is ineffective in combating strong intergenerational patterns and cultural messages justifying the appropriateness of using violence to maintain power in relationships. As Walters (cited in Mathias 1986) suggested, recognizing intergenerational and cultural influences on behavior frees the therapist and clients from taking a blaming position, making room for change and growth.

Case Example

Mr. and Mrs. Cricket began treatment with spouse abuse as the presenting problem. Although the physical violence was eliminated, tension remained high in the family. It became clear that Mr. Cricket was concerned about problems related to the small business that he owned and operated. He was worried that his business was failing and his family's financial security was in jeopardy. At this point the therapist focused treatment on these stressors. Particular attention was given to Mr. Cricket's concern for his family's welfare, his long history of successfully providing for his family, and his business competencies. Areas that were in his control were identified, and a financial recovery plan was developed that began with a visit to a financial consultant.

Next, the therapist began to look at the intergenerational patterns that may have been a barrier to the family's ability to find alternatives to their financial stress. The therapist helped the couple to understand the role financial security played in each spouse's family of origin. Mrs. Cricket had never worked outside the home, as was true for both her mother and her mother-in-law. Mr. Cricket had inherited a strong legacy of the males in the family being the sole providers and protectors of the family. They discussed how and why family work patterns have changed in the 1970s and 1980s. It was discovered that Mrs. Cricket had wanted to be more of a contributor to the family financial coffer but had not pursued the issue with her husband. The therapist helped Mr. and Mrs. Cricket negotiate an agreement whereby Mrs. Cricket could assist her husband in the bookkeeping aspects of his business to free him to do more marketing. Their collaboration helped relieve some of the financial stress. More importantly, their new partnership helped to create a more balanced couple relationship and helped the couple gain confidence in their ability to negotiate and work together.

Each partner's world view with regard to violence and sex roles is considered when creating in-session experiences in which the couple learns to appreciate other parts of him/herself (both nurturer and nurtured, both instrumental and expressive). As men begin to appreciate their expressive, nurturant parts, they seem to be able to respect and appreciate those parts of their spouses. As the abusive partner learns new ways to deal with anger and both partners begin to appreciate their spouses in new ways, the therapeutic work can begin to focus on creating experiences in the session that are based on and reinforce inherent strengths.

Case Example

When Mr. Jackson, who, like his father, used violence to enforce his dominant position in the family, recognized that Mrs. Jackson would actually leave if things did not change in their relationship, he began to take a more active part in the treatment process. In a session that included the couple's two young children (ages two and four), the therapist noticed and commented on how much his children seemed to enjoy sitting on his lap and how gentle he was with them. The therapist noted how lovely it was that the children had both the strong arms of their father to hold them as well as the soft arms of their mother. The therapist talked about how special and unique each of their gifts were to their children. When asked about his experiences with his father's gentleness, Mr. Jackson came close to tears because he did not remember his father ever holding him or being gentle with him. Mr. Jackson's experience of being nurturing, and being affirmed for his nurturing, seemed to be a real turning point in both Mr. and Mrs. Jackson's ability to view him as a nonviolent contributor to the family.

Finally, the dynamics unique to each couple's relationship are the guide to creating experiences within the sessions to help couples learn new ways of dealing with each other that empower and enhance self-esteem. Taking responsibility for one's position and speaking for oneself are a part of learning effective conflict-management skills. Discussion is focused on the present and toward finding a solution to a specific problem that can be behaviorally described. Each partner clarifies what he or she wants to happen and what he or she is willing to concede to the other.

SUMMARY

An important difference between this program and many other treatment programs is that this program goes beyond teaching anger-management techniques for batterers and developing shelter programs for victims. Although both men's programs and shelter programs are vital components in the treatment of spouse abuse, if the family's goal is reunification, it is imperative that the entire family be involved in treatment. Long-term success in the treatment of spouse abuse will involve not only changing behaviors in the short run, but also changing the ways males and females are valued in families. Risk markers for spouse abuse that have been elucidated in research findings must be considered in the development of comprehensive treatment programs. The ultimate goal of spouse-abuse treatment is, of course, to end the physical and emotional abuse. An essential corollary to this goal is to enhance the flexibility and competency of all family members, not by supporting wives over husbands or husbands over wives, but by empowering all; by empowering the husband to find new ways to deal with angry and frightened feelings and to appreciate his ability to be affectionate with his family; by empowering the wife to be strong in her resolve not to live with violence.

REFERENCES

Bernard, J., & Bernard J. (1984). The abusive male seeking treatment: Jekyll and Hyde. *Family Relations, 33*, 543–547.

Cameron-Bandler, L. (1985). *Solutions: Practical and effective antidotes for sexual and relationship problems.* San Rafael, CA: Future Pace, Inc.

Coleman, K. (1980). Conjugal violence: What 33 men report. *Journal of Marital and Family Therapy, 6*, 207–213.

Cook, D., & Frantz-Cook, A. (1984). A systemic treatment approach to wife battering. *Journal of Marital and Family Therapy, 10*(1), 83–93.

Deschner, J. (1984). *The hitting habit: Anger control for battering couples.* New York: The Free Press.

Dibble, V., & Straus, M. (1981). Some social structure determinants of inconsistency between attitudes and behavior: The case of family violence. *Journal of Marriage and the Family, 42*(1), 71–80.

Ganley, A. (1981). *Court mandated counseling for men who batter: A three-day workshop for mental health professionals (participants manual).* Washington, DC: Government Printing Office.

Gelles, R., & Maynard, P. (1987). A structural family systems approach to intervention in cases of family violence. *Family Relations, 36*(3), 270–275.

Giles-Sims, J. (1983). *Wife battering: A systems approach.* New York: Guilford Press.

Hare-Mustin, R. (1978). A feminist approach to family therapy. *Family Process, 17*, 181–194.

Hare-Mustin, R. (1980). Family therapy may be dangerous for your health. *Professional Psychology, 11*, 935–938.

Hotaling, G., & Sugarman, D. (1986). An analysis of risk markers in husband to wife violence: The current state of knowledge. *Violence and Victims*, 1, 101–124.

Kempe, C., et al. (1962). The battered child syndrome. *Journal of the American Medical Association*, 181, 17–24.

Little, L. (1986, May). *Gestalt therapy with females involved in intimate violence*. Paper presented at the National Symposium on Building Family Strength, Lincoln, NE.

Mathas, B. (1986). Lifting the shade on family violence. *The Family Therapy Networker*, 10(4), 20–29.

Neidig, P. (1985). Domestic violence in the military: The impact of high levels of work-related stress on family functioning. *Military Family*, 5(4), 3–5

Neidig, P., Freidman, D., & Collins, B. (1984). *Attitudinal characteristics of males who have engaged in spouse abuse*. Paper presented at Second National Conference for Family Violence Researchers, University of New Hampshire, Durham, NH.

Pressman, B. (1989). Wife abused couples: The need for comprehensive theoretical perspectives and integrated treatment models. *Journal of Feminist Therapy*, 1, 23–43

Rouse, L. (1984). Models, self-esteem, and locus of control as factors contributing to spouse abuse. *Victimology: An International Journal* 9(1), 130–141.

Saunders, D., Lynch A., Grayson, M., & Linz, D. (1987). The inventory of beliefs about wife beating: The construction and initial validation of a measure of beliefs and attitudes. *Violence and Victims*, 2, 39–57.

Sonkin, D., & Durphy, M. (1982). *Learning to live without violence: A handbook for men*. San Francisco, CA: Volcano Press.

Sonkin, D., Martin, D., & Walker, L. (1985). The male batterer: A treatment approach. New York: Springer Publishing Co.

Steele, B., & Pollock, C. (1974). A psychiatric study of parents who abuse infants and small children. In R. Helfer & C. Kempe (Eds.), *The battered child* (pp. 89–134). Chicago: University of Chicago Press.

Stith, S. (in press). The relationship between the male police officer's response to victims of domestic violence and his personal and family experiences. *The victimology research handbook*. New York: Garland Publishing Co.

Straus, M., Gelles, R., & Steinmetz, S. (1980). *Behind closed doors: Violence in the family*. Garden City, NY: Anchor Press.

Straus, M., & Gelles, R. (1986). Societal change in family violence from 1975–1985 as revealed by two national surveys. *Journal of Marriage and the Family*, 48, 465–479.

Taggart, M. (1985). The feminist critique in epistemological perspective: Questions of context in family therapy. *Journal of Marital and Family Therapy* 11(2), 113–126.

Walker, L. (1979). *The battered woman*. New York: Harper Colophon Books.

Westurland, E. (1983). Counseling women with histories of incest. *Women and Therapy*, 2, 17–31.

APPENDIX A: SAFETY PLAN

A safety plan is designed to help keep you and your children as safe as possible from physical abuse. Now, before your partner becomes violent, consider the following things:

1. Practice "time-out" technique.
2. Observe physical cues in partner (before abusive incident).
3. Be aware of rooms to avoid (during/before anger episode).
4. How would you get help?
5. Where would you go in an emergency situation?
6. How would you get there? Where could you keep extra keys?
7. What papers would you need? Where can you keep them?

IMPORTANT: Now that you are in counseling, you may believe that the abuse will end. Please do not believe that your partner's agreement to enter counseling will assure your safety and guarantee that violence will end. Many men continue to be violent or relapse back into violence after they have made a commitment to end the violence. Nothing will be hurt by having planned for your safety and the safety of your children. When women have a clear plan for protecting themselves and leaving the violent situation, couples' work is able to proceed more safely, and men are often more willing to commit to their work when they know that their partners have clear alternatives to living in an abusive marriage.

APPENDIX B: THE NO-VIOLENCE PLEDGE

I pledge never to allow my anger to go to the point where I force-fully touch another family member, no matter how right I feel I am.

I pledge to use time-out procedures instead, and to cooperate when-ever my partner initiates time-out.

If I am unable to keep this contract, I pledge to:

1.

2.

3.

Name _____   Date _____

Name _____   Date _____

APPENDIX C: TIME OUT

Time out is a way to manage anger safely. It can be used when either partner feels threatened by the intensity of a discussion, or either person feels his or her own level of anger escalating. "Time out" means: (1) to leave the scene of conflict, (2) to think about what has transpired and one's own feelings, and (3) to return to the partner after calming down.

Steps

1. *Make a prior agreement.* Plan together how and when to use Time Out. Time Out is not a means of escaping or an easy way out. It is a technique that is used cooperatively before feelings have escalated to the point of becoming unmanagea-ble.
2. *Use a prearranged cue.* Agree to use a word, phrase, or ges-ture that signals time is needed for a Time Out.

3. Take a Time Out.
    (a) Talk to yourself about what is really going on.
    (b) Use some kind of activity to help slow down the adrenalin. Aggressive activity, like pumping iron or punching a bag, may only keep the tension high. Do not drink or drive while very angry.
4. Return to the discussion, if possible. Check in: "I'm OK—how about you?"
5. Share feelings and thoughts about why a Time Out was needed, what was going wrong. Accept your share.
6. Plan the next step.

II Treatment of Child Abuse

6 The Multidisciplinary Team Approach to Child Abuse and Neglect

Meriam S. Rogan

Child abuse and spouse abuse are often intimately related. Spouse abusers are often also child abusers. Spouses who have been abused may take out their rage and frustration on their children. Violence as a means of problem resolution becomes an intergenerational way of life as children who are abused, in later life, abuse their spouses and/or children.

Families in which child abuse occurs are usually multiproblem families. Many community agencies, for example, schools, courts, mental health services and social services, become involved with the same families. It is essential that these agencies coordinate their efforts and services to provide an effective program to stop the abuse and help families learn and practice positive, nurturing ways of relating.

One of the ways this can be accomplished is through the use of multidisciplinary child abuse teams. This chapter explains how a team concept can be utilized effectively to coordinate expertise and services among community agencies that share the goals of protecting children and empowering them and the members of their families to become positive, caring individuals.

HISTORY OF MULTIDISCIPLINARY TEAM DEVELOPMENT

The Child Abuse Prevention and Treatment Act (Public Law 93-247) of 1974 created the National Center on Child Abuse and Neglect, and charged the Center to provide technical assistance to public and nonprofit private agencies and organizations to assist them in planning, improving, developing and carrying out programs and activities relating to the prevention, identification, and treatment of child abuse and neglect.

As states assessed their own needs in light of this legislation, many identified the need for coordinating the many services offered to abusing and neglectful families. The multidisciplinary team approach to this coordination was chosen in some instances as the logical solution to this problem.

In Virginia, a 1975 addition to the Code (63.1-248.6) reads: "The local department shall foster, when practicable, the creation, maintenance and coordination of hospital and community-based multidisciplinary teams." However, multidisciplinary teams, used in hospitals since the 1950s, had a slow start in the area of child abuse and neglect. Kempe and Helfer (1972) wrote:

> Our social system is not geared to a rapid exchange of knowledge and information between its various disciplines. In fact, many of the subdivisions of this system often compete with or duplicate the work of each other; all too often even a degree of distrust develops between them. (p. 177)

Progress in team building spread slowly but surely as more and more communities realized the complexity of working with abusive, dysfunctional families and the increased need for interprofessional cooperation in finding viable solutions.

By 1982 Sgroi (1982) noted, "Nowadays it is practically 'un-American' for a community to lack a multidisciplinary team of professionals to review cases of child maltreatment" (p. 355).

PURPOSE OF MULTIDISCIPLINARY TEAMS

Multidisciplinary teams have been developed for several different purposes in the field of child abuse. The Public Social Service Laws of Virginia (Kepler, 1986) suggest that they be used for

> helping to develop innovative programs for detection and prevention of child abuse, promoting community concern and action in the area of child abuse and neglect, and disseminating information to the general public with respect to the problem of child abuse and neglect, and the facilities and prevention and treatment methods available to child abuse and neglect. (p. 123)

The Guidelines for Multidisciplinary Child Protection Teams for the State of Washington (Cramer, 1987) state:

The most important elements that determine the function of effective teams appear to be three-fold:

1) team members understand and accept the function of the team as defined by the team

2) a strong positive bond is established with Child, Youth, and Family Services and

3) the function the team has adopted is relevant to the protective services process. Within the context of these elements, teams can assume a diagnostic function, a case management function, or a case consultation function. (p. 3)

Teams have been very successfully utilized in investigations of allegations of abuse and in the determination of which of these cases should be pursued for prosecution.

Both of these functions were combined in a model developed in Huntsville, Madison County, Alabama. The moving force behind this program was Madison County District Attorney, Robert E. Cramer, Jr. (1985), who said

In Madison County/Huntsville, Alabama, we looked at our system and saw how it was damaging child victims. Recognizing that "we are the system and we can change it," professionals in our community developed the Children's Advocacy Center Program, a multidisciplinary approach that involves law enforcement, child protective services, prosecution, mental health, and other resources in a response to child sexual abuse. The program focuses on the needs of the victims, while also meeting the needs of the professionals who handle their cases and holding offenders accountable for their crimes.

. . . The route a case takes is determined by the team review process from initial interview to case retirement. This ensures a comprehensive approach which maximizes the quality of services to the child and family. It also provides a constant support system for the professionals serving the child. (p. 4)

Another program of note was developed in Middlesex County, Massachusetts. This program was motivated by the 1983 Massachusetts Law known as Chapter 288, The Child Abuse Reporting Law, which mandates interdisciplinary communication and cooperation among those who are involved in the most severe cases of child abuse and child sexual assault. Karen Kepler, J.D. (1986), states:

Since 1983, when Chapter 288 (The Child Abuse Reporting Law) was enacted, serious cases of child abuse no longer are the responsibility of any one state agency or department. Rather, as recognized by the legislature, effective treatment of these cases requires a multidisciplinary approach involving law enforcement and social service agencies.

. . . Chapter 288 also created multidisciplinary teams which meet
to discuss each case reported to the District Attorney. As they presently
exist, these teams are composed of at least three members: the DSS
caseworker, a representative of the district attorney's office, and a third
party who is experienced with either criminal justice or children. The
purpose of the team is to evaluate the DSS service plan and make
recommendations as to whether or not the case should be prosecuted.
(p. 5)

The purpose of multidisciplinary teams as discussed in
this chapter is to provide a structured format for the sharing of
professional knowledge and resources to help prevent or remediate child abuse and neglect. This sharing improves the quality
of services to the family and at the same time prevents both duplication of services and gaps in services provided. Teams also
give much-needed recognition and support to casework staff
and other service providers who work with abusive and
neglectful families. They also help to resolve misunderstandings
and misconceptions that may develop over service delivery
issues.

MEMBERSHIP

Multidisciplinary child protection teams are composed of members
of agencies or professions, or their alternates, who work with child
abuse or neglect.

Optimum functioning of a multidisciplinary team results when
the team represents all of the community agencies that are mandated
reporters of abuse/neglect and all those that provide services to families to either prevent or remediate these problems. It is essential, however, that social services, mental health, the court, and law
enforcement agencies have active, cooperative members on the
team.

All team members have an equal voice in the making of recommendations. Recommendations by consensus are desirable, but minority recommendations are acceptable. Recommendations are advisory in nature; the final decision rests with the case manager. Since,
however, recommendations represent the best thinking of the professionals most closely associated with the case, they are usually followed.

A multidisciplinary team's effectiveness will be largely determined by the ability and desire of team members to work together
with mutual concern for the protection of and services to abused

and neglected children and their families. There must be mutual respect for and by all members with a willingness to listen and a willingness to present. Members must believe in teamwork in general and their own team in particular.

TEAM COORDINATOR

In many communities multidisciplinary teams are coordinated by members of social service agencies because it is these agencies that are mandated to investigate child abuse/neglect and that are aware of the family's needs for extended multiagency services. Referrals are made to mental health and medical providers, and close cooperation with law enforcement is routine. Therefore, it is appropriate that social services staff coordinate the multidisciplinary team. Other alternatives are for the team to hire or appoint a coordinator who has broad knowledge of the dynamics of abuse/neglect or to choose a coordinator from one of the other agencies represented on the team.

Typically, the team coordinator is responsible for arranging the schedule of meetings as well as for notifying members of the time and place of meetings and being attentive to time limits and group process. Coordinators also keep the official record of members in attendance, cases reviewed, and recommendations made on a case-by-case basis.

CONFIDENTIALITY

Information is readily shared among the members of the team so that lines of communication are open among the professionals. It is absolutely essential, however, that team members, upon appointment, sign confidentiality statements in which they, as members of a multidisciplinary team, acknowledge their responsibilities to keep confidential all information that comes to them through their roles as members of the team.

All written materials, including agenda and case information, are collected and destroyed at the end of each meeting in the interest of confidentiality. The official copy of the agenda, members present, cases presented, and recommendations are kept for the record.

CASE REFERRAL CRITERIA

Any case in which team input would be helpful to the resolution of the presenting problems or to the servicing of the family is considered to be appropriate for presentation to a multidisciplinary team. Each team prioritizes cases based on criteria established by the team. Very often, cases presented are those in which numerous community agencies are involved and services to the family must be coordinated. Other appropriate referrals include those in which there are specific questions regarding diagnosis or treatment for the child or parents, agencies are in disagreement on recommendations, or cases previously presented need review as the family dynamics change. Many cases are originally presented by child protective service workers and later brought back to the team by foster care or ongoing treatment social workers. Any member of the team may present a case about which there are concerns after requesting that the team coordinator place the case on the agenda.

EVALUATION

Self-evaluation of the team and its effectiveness is ongoing. Some of the following issues are considered:

1. Are all the agencies essential to service coordination represented on the team? If not, how can this be remedied?
2. Are recommendations made by the team bringing about the desired results? If not, why not? Are they unrealistic or otherwise inappropriate?
3. Are communications among members flowing smoothly so that services are well coordinated?
4. Is there a good sense of team rapport and mutual support?

CHILD SEXUAL ABUSE INTERVENTION TEAM

Child protective services programs that deal with sexual abuse are particularly concerned that victims and their families are not further damaged and overwhelmed by the often uncoordinated, usually very extensive, multiagency social services delivery system involved in these cases.

While believing strongly in the multidisciplinary team concept, Sgroi (1982) writes:

... most child-protection teams are ill-equipped to deal with child sexual abuse. At the risk of sounding elitist, I submit that in most communities it is unrealistic to expect that the local child-protection team will be able to address this problem. Instead it may be preferable for a second group of professionals to work with child sexual abuse cases. (p. 355)

In many communities there are public agency social workers, mental health professionals, medical personnel, and members of support groups such as Victim's Assistance Network and Victims/ Witness programs who work almost exclusively with sexual abuse victims and their families. In these communities, the creation of a child sexual abuse multidisciplinary team is particularly appropriate.

Child sexual abuse multidisciplinary team members should have knowledge of or be willing to learn the particular dynamics of incestuous families and the unique therapeutic needs of each family member—the child victim, the sibling nonvictim, the sexually abusive parent, and the nonabusive parent—who often has been sexually abused as a child but has never dealt with that abuse. Members should be aware that these families often also need parenting classes, substance abuse counseling, and financial counseling.

Case Illustration

The following scenario illustrates a typical child sexual abuse team meeting.

The setting is a large, comfortable room. It is nine o'clock Thursday morning. Representatives from local agencies gather to listen to a case presentation of the H. family. Social services, juvenile court intake, probation, mental health, public schools, county attorney, police, and public health agencies are represented. The rotating team coordinator, one of two social workers who share this responsibility, greets the team and then introduces the case manager who will present the first case. Background information is distributed on the victim (Jane H., born 1/2/71), the perpetrator (Joe H., born 5/10/ 51, stepfather to the victim, salesman), and other household members (mother, Mary H., born 7/18/53, and half-sister, Susan H., born 8/16/74).

The previous investigation findings (medically confirmed long-term anal and vaginal intercourse) and those concerning mental health and court involvement are distributed as well.

Issue for the Team

Should Mr. H. be allowed to reenter the home, as he is requesting? If he returns, what is the risk of future abuse, and what court restrictions need to be requested?

Process

Initially, the case manager reviews the facts of the case as they were when originally staffed with the Team four years ago. Jane, 13 years old when she revealed the abuse, had always been a very attractive child with a loving disposition. She had never known her birth father. She and her mother, Mary, lived alone for the first three years of Jane's life until Joe came to live with them. Eventually, Joe and Mary married. Mary soon became pregnant with Susan and had a very difficult pregnancy. Joe and Jane became very close at that time, and even as a little child, Jane talked about growing up and marrying Joe. The sexual abuse began with fondling when Jane was six years old and had progressed to full sexual intercourse by the time she was eleven. Jane's mother was aware of what was happening, but both because she was sickly and because she was intimidated by Joe, she did nothing about it. She was much closer to Susan than she was to Jane and guarded Susan to the best of her ability. Susan was not abused.

The abuse came to light when Jane, at 13, decided she wanted to date, and Joe refused to allow her to do so. Jane told her school guidance counselor of the sexual abuse, and the counselor contacted social services. A joint police/social services investigation was conducted. Jane stood by her story and testified against Joe, who was sentenced to serve 10 years, all but 2 of which were suspended.

Jane was removed from her home and placed in foster care at her own request because of her intense anger at her mother for allowing the abuse to occur and continue. Susan, who had a good relationship with her mother, remained in the home.

With her entry into foster care, Jane received both individual and group counseling. Jane had originally been very resistant to treatment but had gradually lowered her defenses and eventually participated actively in therapy. She also had family therapy with her mother, where she was able to work through her feelings, as well as some sessions with both her mother and Susan.

At the same time, a strong, coordinated service support system was put in place for Mary and Susan that included home-based services to help Mary with her parenting skills. In addition, both Mary and Susan received individual counseling.

The team is reminded that they had participated in a second staffing on this case when Jane's foster care worker considered Jane's return home after Jane had been in foster care for 18 months. At that time the team recommended Jane's return home as long as the strong, ongoing coordinated service support system in place for Mary and the girls continued. In this way, Mary could be helped to provide a nurturing home life. The court agreed to Jane's return home, with continued supervision by social services. This placement at home has gone quite well.

The case manager also reviews the intensive services still being provided for Mary and her daughters by agencies represented on the team. These include individual mental health counseling for Mary and Jane and group therapy for both Jane and Susan. Mary also receives physical therapy for a degenerative illness and participates in a self-help group for incestuous families. The major concern centers around Mary's deteriorating physical condition in spite of her cooperative participation in physical therapy. How long she will be physically capable of caring for the girls is uncertain.

The update on Joe is that he continues to be on parole after serving two years in prison. He is receiving court-ordered individual and group counseling. In addition, he and Jane have biweekly counseling sessions together. During these sessions Joe has accepted responsibility for the abuse and has apologized to Jane. She accepted the apology. Since this occurred, Joe has been allowed monthly supervised visitation with Jane. Joe now wants to return home.

Mary, Jane, and Susan are willing to consider Joe's return to the home, particularly in view of Mary's deteriorating physical condition.

During the team meeting, therapists for each of the parents and for Jane, a doctor who knows Mary's physical condition, and Joe's probation officer update the team on the current status of their clients. After all the reports are presented, the case is discussed and recommendations made.

The recommendations from this team meeting could contain any or all of the following:

1. Social, psychological, and/or psychiatric evaluations, as needed, of Joe, with particular emphasis on the degree of risk of reabuse.
2. A determination, based on the above, of the conditions to be met by Joe before any reunification can be considered.
3. Evaluations of the social interactions of the other three fam-

ily members, Jane, Susan, and Mary, and their individual and collective readiness for the reentry of Joe.

4. Continued supervision of the home by social services.

5. Review of the case in 60 days.

SUMMARY

Child abuse and neglect are complex phenomena with causative factors as diverse as childhood victimization, lack of support systems, life crises, or poor impulse control. Successful remediation of these phenomena can best be accomplished by the coordinated efforts of community professionals and child advocates skilled in these areas. The use of multidisciplinary teams to this end is strongly recommended.

As a result of the team approach, services to families are better coordinated; there is a higher level of communication among the agencies involved; team members are supportive of each other, thus lessening burnout; professionals in related fields both give and gain insight from discussing cases of mutual interest and involvement.

Multidisciplinary teams do not have magic solutions to complex child-abuse problems, but they have proven to be one of the most effective means we have found to date to intervene and heal the wounds left by child physical, emotional, and sexual abuse and neglect, and to prevent further damage.

REFERENCES

Cramer R. E. (1985). *Madison County Alabama News, 4. Guidelines for multidisciplinary child protective teams.* Developed by Department of Social Services of Washington State.

Kempe, C. H., & Helfer, R. E. (1972). *Helping the battered child and his family.* Philadelphia: Lippincott.

Kepler, K. (1986). *Public social service laws and related statutes of Virginia.* Issued by the Department of Social Services. Charlottesville, VA: Michie.

Sgroi, S. M. (1982). *Handbook of clinical intervention in child sexual abuse.* Lexington, MA: Heath.

Swagerty, E. L., & Marcus, B. (1986). In S. Harshbarga (Ed.), *The child abuse reporting law: The Middlesex County experience.* Multidisciplinary perspectives on child abuse interventions under Chapter 288. Middlesex County, MA: Child Abuse Project.

7 Working with the Unmotivated Client

Martha L. Jones

It had been a difficult and frustrating day for Sara. She wanted to work in child welfare so that she could help families overcome the problems that lead to child abuse, but her efforts did not seem to be having much impact. Her first home visit of the day was to the home of a single mother, Ms. Anderson, who was suspected of abusing her two-year-old. Although she allowed Sara into her trailer this morning, Ms. Anderson continued to watch TV during the whole visit and had made no progress on the plans that had been outlined the previous week. At her second stop, the Bird family was not home for their scheduled appointment, a typical reaction of this very resistant family. Her third stop was with a mother of six children. The Carols have been known to the agency for years. The current referral related to possible abuse of a 12-year-old who was often truant from school. Sara found Mrs. Carol to be very angry and threatening. She told Sara that the agency has caused her nothing but trouble in the past, hurting her reputation in the neighborhood and turning her children against her. She talked of getting a lawyer or finding some other way to protect her rights. It was now midafternoon on a Monday, and Sara was not sure how she would get through another week with her various unmotivated clients.

Working with the unmotivated client can take its toll on even the most experienced and best-trained professionals. The accumulated frustration that results from working with these families often leads to burnout, cynicism, and high worker turnover. Unfortunately, little has been written about effective techniques for working with the client who is highly unmotivated. This article presents a structure to help professionals assess and deal with these clients. Specific intervention strategies for this special population are discussed along with brief examples of how they may be used.

RESISTANCE AND THE UNMOTIVATED CLIENT

In looking at resistance and lack of motivation, it is helpful to think in terms of three major categories of client: voluntary, nonvoluntary, and involuntary. The voluntary client recognizes a problem and actively seeks help. Voluntary clients, no matter how motivated, will exhibit various forms of resistance once counseling begins. This is a natural part of the helping process since change is a frightening and difficult thing. There are specific techniques that the professional can use in overcoming the client's resistance. Anderson and Stewart (1983) provide a comprehensive discussion of some of these techniques. Resistance in the voluntary client is a subject for study in most programs that train counselors and therapists. Working with the nonvoluntary and involuntary client requires some different approaches and is the primary focus of this article.

The nonvoluntary client is one who does not actively seek help but who is willing to accept it once it is offered. This is the person whose behavior might appropriately be referred to as a "cry for help." For example, a mother who has been under great stress and abuses her child for the first time may not actively seek help. However, once reported to the child welfare authorities, she may be willing to accept help for the problems that precipitated the abusive incident. Likewise, an abusive husband may respond to outreach services of a women's center staff when his wife seeks help for herself. There are many situations in which family members are drawn into treatment via residential facilities, schools, and hospitals treating the identified patient. These family members have not asked for help themselves; thus, they are nonvoluntary. They also have the option of refusing help, but when approached appropriately many will accept it.

In the area of domestic violence we often see individuals who are aware that they have a problem but are unable to ask for help because they are not knowledgeable about what is available. Women in abusive relationships, for example, often need help in learning about shelters and other services that could protect them. Parents who abuse their children may want to change their behaviors but not know how. Programs that offer concrete help with child care while teaching these parents new and more effective parenting skills can do much to reach the nonvoluntary client. Many children referred to professionals for help are really nonvoluntary clients. They frequently are exhibiting behavioral problems at school or at home and may feel that they have problems. Seldom, however, would they choose to come to a strange adult for regular counseling. Likewise, the parents of such children often see the child as the problem and are frequently not asking for help themselves.

The third type, the involuntary client, is often the most difficult to engage in treatment. These are individuals who did not ask for and do not want help. These clients are usually mandated for treatment by social service agencies such as child welfare, juvenile probation, or public mental health programs. An involuntary client may be a child abuser who is required by the court to seek treatment. Another client may be the wife of a child abuser who is required by the child welfare agency to get help for herself as a parent. Perpetrators of child abuse often come into this category of involuntary client. The involuntary client frequently denies the problem and may actively resist treatment efforts to the point of being hostile and even violent. This type of client differs significantly from both the voluntary and nonvoluntary client in the nature and tractability of their resistance to change.

THE DILEMMA OF MANDATED SERVICES

We generally assume some level of motivation for clients entering into contracts for change. The idea that there are groups of clients who are involuntary seems contrary to some fundamental assumptions in social service. Some background about mandated social services puts this dilemma in perspective.

The growing professional concern with domestic violence issues, especially child abuse, has led to an increase in mandatory social services. Such services require families to receive some type of service because the larger community has determined that the clients are in need of help. As a society we are saying more and more clearly that child abuse is not acceptable. When child abuse is reported to a child welfare agency, that agency is required by law to intervene. The agency in such a situation is acting as an agent of social control for the larger community. This social control function is often unwelcome in the family, where the abusive behavior may be considered an acceptable form of discipline. The professional who attempts to "help" such a family is faced with a challenge— how to help someone who not only does not want to be helped but may even see the intervention as a violation of individual and family rights.

It is essential that professionals who face this challenge be clear about the authority they are using when intervening in the lives of these unmotivated clients. Hutchison (1987) stresses that professionals should not use authority to impose a personal standard of conduct but instead should use only the authority delegated by governmental or administrative structures. When a professional moves to impose unwanted changes on others, he/she runs a serious risk of violating clients' rights. Therefore, the professional should move cautiously when intervening in the lives of clients. Intervention should come either by invitation or in an official capacity as required through the formal authority of the larger society. For example, the child welfare worker is required by law to investigate child abuse and to provide various services to protect children at risk in their own home. Even though not invited into such a family, this worker has a legal mandate to intervene.

The first phase of work with unmotivated clients focuses on the reason for the dilemma. Does this client want help? If not, by what authority is the professional delivering it? For example, is the professional a child protective service worker with legal authority to intervene in families where children are at risk? A good question to ask of both client and worker at this point is why am I here? The exploration of those questions leads naturally into the next phase—contracting and relationship building.

CONTRACTING AND BUILDING A RELATIONSHIP

Relationship is the foundation of any counseling or therapeutic intervention. Oxley (1981) points out that clients who actively seek help demonstrate greater competence and ability to form relationships than those who do not. Voluntary clients have a strong base for building a relationship in that the client has recognized a problem and sought help. The move to seek help indicates a client's ability to use community services and to trust that others will be of assistance.

Developing a relationship with the involuntary client begins with honest contracting. The professional needs to acknowledge openly the authority that he/she has over the client, the limits of that authority, and the feelings of powerlessness that this evokes in the client (Hutchison, 1987). Through openness and clear communication of these issues, the social worker demonstrates the respect for the client that is crucial if a relationship is to develop. However, social workers and others in the helping professions frequently feel uncomfortable with the use of authority (Koerin, 1979).

Unmotivated clients have not sought help and may not even recognize their problems. Some may have great difficulty in forming and maintaining relationships. Their prior experiences in relationships may have been damaging to them in a variety of ways, particularly if they come from violent family situations. Help based on a relationship of caring may be a foreign concept to these families. Caring and empathetic concern will need to be demonstrated to them over and over before it is accepted. The honest contract between professional and involuntary client is often one where the professional acknowledges that the client wants the professional out of his or her life. Frequently, the clinician agrees that she would like to leave the client alone but is unable to do so because of her responsibility. The following example will illustrate how a therapeutic explanation of authority can bring about change in a family.

> The Carol family had been known to a particular child welfare agency for six years. Their youngest child had been in foster care for three years due to abuse and serious neglect. The family was hostile, uncooperative, and threatening to all the social workers who had attempted to help them during this time. The family continued to deny their neglect and abuse. They complained to the judge, county officials, and others that their child was wrongly removed, and the family even kidnapped him from the child welfare office during a routine visit.
>
> The new social worker assigned to the case found that there was clear, solid evidence of the neglect and abuse at the time of the child's removal from the home. The family's failure to admit to the allegations was a primary barrier to considering the child's return to the home. The agency's position was that the child would only be safe in the home after he was able to talk and take care of some of his own basic needs. The first several home visits were as previous social workers had described. The family was sullen and uncooperative. On the third visit, the father confronted the social worker about the agency's stalling in returning the child. The social worker responded by telling the parents that she and the agency did not believe their story about the child's condition at the time of placement. She stressed that all the indications were that he had been abused and neglected and that the family's continued denial made it very hard to trust that he would be safe at home. It was made clear to the family that the social worker, as a representative of the agency, had a legal responsibility to protect their son. This protective responsibility took precedence over meeting their stated need to have him home.
>
> This encounter proved to be a significant turning point in the case. By making the authority of the social worker explicit, the working contract with this family was more clear. The fam-

ily immediately became cooperative, as they accepted the fact that the role of the social worker was to protect their child. Whereas before the family had fought the agency, they now began to work with the social worker to have their son returned. They even began to refer friends to the agency for help, because they perceived the worker to have been so helpful to them.

The key to the development of this relationship was the honest use of authority. The agency had the power to keep the child in placement as long as the family seemed unsafe. The family knew the social worker represented that authority. Earlier workers had failed to openly address this authority issue. Thus, the old social work adage "start where the client is," is most true in working with the involuntary client. Where the client often is, at least in the beginning, is that he or she does not want help and it is being forced on him or her.

Relationship building with a nonvoluntary client is equally challenging. In working with the nonvoluntary client the social worker may not have any strong authority for involvement with the client. Often the worker must convince the client that he or she has something useful to offer. The nonvoluntary client may recognize that there is a problem but may not believe that there is anything that can be done about it—at least by the social worker. The social worker is therefore in the position of proving to the client that he or she can be helpful.

In this early stage of relationship building it is important for the worker to remember that actions speak louder than words. Clients may be presenting behaviors that are perceived by professionals as a way of asking for help. Such requests, when responded to with care, empathy, understanding, and concrete assistance, may lead to the development of strong, long-term relationships.

Oxley (1981) suggests a variety of professional roles that can be effective with these clients. The social worker may need to provide concrete resources, to function as an advocate with other organizations or family members, or to serve as teacher and role model. Thus, as the worker demonstrates that help really is possible, the nonvoluntary client begins to trust the relationship and moves into a voluntary role.

Jack, age 15, had recently moved in with his mother and stepfather after his father had been sent to jail for sexually abusing Jack's stepsister. His mother brought Jack for counseling because of concerns about his inappropriate touching of his 12-year-old sister. Jack continued to believe that his father was innocent and totally denied that his dad had done anything wrong. The worker recognized Jack as a nonvoluntary client and began by finding ways to develop a relationship with him. She started by listening to his version of things and encouraged him to talk about how difficult all the recent changes had been for him. She was nonjudgmental and supportive. Gradually, Jack saw that he really did feel better having a social worker to talk with and that she did not attack his beliefs. She next began to teach him about the nature of sexual abuse. He responded by asking hypothetical questions about perpetrators. She continued to allow distance between him and the subject matter and treated the sessions as educational discussions. As he began to feel safe in this relationship, he moved from being a nonvoluntary client in the beginning to asking for help for himself. At this point the social worker was able to put more responsibility on Jack to bring up issues for discussion and to make changes.

The urgency of violent situations sometimes creates a feeling of pressure for professionals who want people to change quickly. As previously noted, many of these clients do not voluntarily seek help and may be less proficient at relationship building. The first stage of relationship building is crucial. The professional has the responsibility to attempt to develop a clear contract and honest relationship. However, if the worker does not have the necessary official authority, effectiveness may be limited with involuntary clients. Nonvoluntary clients, on the other hand, can be reached through concrete services and demonstrations of real help.

In the entry phase, questions focus on "Why are we here?" In the relationship-building phase the focus of the questions becomes "What do I as a social worker have to offer the involuntary and nonvoluntary client?" The professional outlines helpful services that are available as well as consequences if changes are not made. In the latter phase, the social worker provides direct, helpful interventions and encourages the client to avail him or herself of other resources.

GAMES AND PASSIVITY

Game theory, as developed in Transactional Analysis, defines games as a series of transactions in which there is the illusion of problem-solving but where interactions are, in fact, working against productive communications. Unmotivated clients are frequently excellent game players. Professionals must constantly be aware of and avoid being hooked into games by and with their clients. Game theory provides some guidelines for recognizing these potential pitfalls. Schiff (1975) suggests that games begin with passive behaviors: clients move into passivity by discounting some part of the problem. They may discount (1) the problem itself, (2) the significance of the problem, (3) the options/solutions, or (4) people's ability to behave differently. In games, behaviors are considered passive because energy is used not to solve the problem but to "hook" others into solving the problem for them. A resultant unhealthy, symbiotic relationship often traps professionals into the role of Rescuer or Persecutor as they take on client problems in a gamelike way.

In the Schiff paradigm there are four passive game behaviors: Doing Nothing, Overadapting, Agitation, Incapacitation or Violence. A mother of four preschoolers, for example, does nothing about discipline and control of the children. A visiting caseworker may be tempted to take over this function because the children's behavior causes the worker so much discomfort. The mother then moves to the stage of overadapting. In response, the caseworker is likely to take on the Rescuer role and give the mother specific guidelines to control her children. For example, a caseworker suggested to a client that she confine her young children for part of the day. The caseworker was thinking of a playpen, but the mother locked the children in a closet for long hours. When confronted, she said she was only doing what the worker had said to do. This client— overadapting—shifted the discomfort and responsibility for thinking onto others (i.e., the social worker).

This same mother may later move to the agitation phase of game playing, complaining and pacing and working up feelings about how the children are getting on her nerves. The worker may find it easier to move in and solve the problem than to stay close to the agitation.

The final stage of passive game playing is violence or incapacitation. Violence is considered passive because, again, the energy is not used to solve the problem but invites others to do something about it. The mother who has worked herself up into a frenzy about her children lashes out at them, forcing the agency to intervene and possibly take the children into foster care. The mother has not really addressed her issues and may become so depressed and incapacitated that she may require hospitalization or other professional intervention into her own life.

Staying out of games may be a significant challenge. Professionals need to recognize and redirect ownership of problems to clients, allowing and encouraging them freedom to feel their own discomfort. It is ineffective to work with clients on possible solutions until they have owned their own problem. Why would anyone put energy into changing something if it is not a recognized or owned problem? One of the most common ways professionals become involved in games with clients is to try to contract for change in client behaviors when clients are not convinced that a problem exists, let alone that it needs to be worked on.

Many clients discount options, as well as their own ability or others' ability to change. They may say that they have tried "everything" to help control their temper. Parents may say that no matter what they do their child will never clean his room. Their grandiose statements stop them from considering other options. Social workers may be helpful in this situation by helping to brainstorm about options. By listing many, many options—especially some very far-out ideas—the worker helps to break the denial cycle. The client then begins to consider other options.

Game theory also illustrates the need for professionals to maintain appropriate boundaries between themselves and their clients' problems. Working with an unmotivated client can by very frustrating because the worker may not only see the problem but often knows that it could easily be solved. Frequently, the social worker "crosses over" the boundary and begins taking on the client's problems as his/her own. This causes the client to become increasingly passive. Thus, the professional will try harder and harder to "fix" things and get less and less help. Both client and professional become trapped in a game in which both become more frustrated and the problem remains unsolved. To reiterate, it is crucial to recognize who "owns" the problem and to maintain appropriate boundaries.

SARA'S MORNING

This chapter began with a description of Sara's work with several unmotivated clients. Let's revisit those situations using this framework. First, Sara works for the public child welfare agency, which means that she is intervening with families as a legal representative of the larger community. She brings great authority to her home visits, including the responsibility to protect children from abuse and neglect.

All of her families are either involuntary or nonvoluntary. Her first stop is with Ms. Anderson. Ms. Anderson let Sara in the trailer but kept the TV on; she had not done anything she had previously agreed to do. Ms. Anderson was overadapting to Sara's interventions—agreeing to do them but not actually taking any action. Ms. Anderson further discounted Sara by keeping on the TV when they were to have been talking about a very serious concern, the abuse of her two-year-old. In this case Sara may begin by assuming Ms. Anderson is an involuntary client. Sara needs to outline to Ms. Anderson the serious charges against her and Sara's responsibility and options to protect this child. To stay out of a game, Sara needs to recognize that Ms. Anderson may choose not to work with her and to point out the consequences for such a decision. While she can let Ms. Anderson know that she doesn't want to remove the child, Sara represents an official authority and must use that to protect the child if necessary.

Sara's second family, the Bird family, also appears to be involuntary. They do nothing and have been successfully avoiding the agency's caseworkers for some time. Again, an intervention needs to involve the clear use of authority to protect the children. The family does not have to want to work with Sara. They must, however, cooperate enough to insure that the children are safe. Sara may need to rely on court action to bring the Bird family into compliance with court orders to produce the children for services.

Finally, Mrs. Carol has abused her 12-year-old, who is frequently truant from school. Although she appears hostile and angry, she also seems to be asking for help. Sara may assume that Mrs. Anderson is a nonvoluntary client who will respond if Sara can offer concrete assistance. Sara might intervene by working with school officials to work out a plan to get and keep Mrs. Carol's son in school. Sara might listen supportively as Mrs. Carol describes how difficult it is to control the child. Supportive listening might lead to Mrs. Carol's becoming more open to suggestions for new discipline techniques. While Sara cannot ignore the abuse, one way to get Mrs. Carol to make changes is to make use of school issues to develop a relationship. The long history of involvement with the agency suggests that if Sara is able to build a supportive relationship with Mrs. Carol, she will have made great progress.

SUMMARY

There are few areas of social service in which professionals do not, at some point, deal with unmotivated clients. It is important to recognize that there are different types of unmotivated client. Even the voluntary client will demonstrate some resistance during the course of therapy. The more challenging clients are those who are either involuntary or nonvoluntary. Successful interventions with them begin with clear assessments of their interests in obtaining help.

The client-helper relationship, so crucial in any therapy, is even more important with these clients. Relationship building with the involuntary client begins with a caring, yet clear, use of formal authority. The nonvoluntary client needs to be "won over" by the worker's demonstration that he or she has something that will be of use to the client. Through outreach efforts of advocacy, teaching, or supportive counseling, the nonvoluntary client frequently becomes motivated to make changes.

In all interventions with unmotivated clients, professional social workers are particularly at risk for being drawn into games. A knowledge of problem boundaries and game theory may help workers to get out and stay out of this most destructive set of interactions. Clients must be allowed to feel some discomfort for, and ownership of, their problems if they are to generate energy for change. Allowing clients to take responsibility for their own problems allows them also to take the credit for their later growth and change. However, professionals need to be realistic about their abilities as helpers. At best they are facilitators of change in others. Work with unmotivated clients requires special skills in relationship building, the creative use of authority, and the ability to respect individual differences.

REFERENCES

Anderson, C. M., & Stewart, S. (1983). *Mastering resistance: A practical guide to family therapy*. New York: The Guilford Press.

Hutchison, E. D. (1987). Use of authority in direct social work practice with mandated clients. *Social Services Review*, 61(4), 581–598.

Koerin, B. (1979). Authority in child protective services. *Child Welfare*, (10), 650–657.

Oxley, G. B. (1981). Promoting competence in involuntary clients. In A. N. Maluccio (Ed.), *Promoting competence in clients: A new/old approach to social work practice* (pp. 290–316). New York: The Free Press.

Schiff, J. L. (1975). *Cathexis reader: Transactional analysis treatment of psychosis*. New York: Harper & Row.

8 Families Who Physically Abuse Adolescents

Anthony P. Jurich

It was two o'clock in the morning and the phone rang. I dragged myself across the bed, picked up the phone, and heard a faint female voice whisper, "Dr. J., I mean Dr. Jurich, is that you?" With cracked voice I replied, "Yes, this is Tony Jurich." "Did I wake you up?" The voice inquired. "Oh, no, I was up anyway," I lied. "I need help. I'm running away from home." With that introduction, I became part of the case of Emily.

Emily was a 13-year-old girl, oldest of three children. She had a brother named Mark, who was 10, and a sister Theresa, age 8. Her father, Phil, was 37, and her mother, Sarah, was 35. Phil was a banker, and Sarah worked as a department manager in a local store. Socioeconomically, they were upper middle class. By all outward appearances, they were an all-American, middle-class family. They belonged to a church, had never had any trouble with the law, and participated in volunteer charitable activities.

Emily appeared to have no obvious personal deficiencies or problems. She was cute but not glamorous, participated in several school clubs, and received mostly A's and B's in school. She wasn't the most popular girl in school, but she had lots of friends, was well liked by her peers, and seemed to have no enemies. Learning all of this, I couldn't figure why this girl wanted to run away from home.

She explained that her mom and dad had always been very good to her and she thought that they had loved her. However, in the last six months everything had changed. Her dad had changed from being loving and understanding to being cruel and filled with hate. No, he hadn't been drinking, and his job seemed to pose no problem. He just seemed to "turn mean." Emily explained that, after never having been struck or even spanked as a child, her father had hit her in the face three times in the past half year, twice with an open hand and once with a closed fist. Emily said that although it did hurt she was much more hurt inside to think her dad would treat her that way. She was also hurt that her mother, with whom she had always been so close, did nothing to intervene and did not comfort her afterward. Emily felt more and more angry at her parents and felt worse and worse about herself.

The event that precipitated her running away happened earlier that night. Mark had teased her that "Ricky Sanders was her boyfriend," and she told him to "shut up." Her mom had yelled at them to "stop fighting," and her dad had burst into the room and demanded to know "who the hell is Ricky Sanders?" When Emily tried to explain that Ricky Sanders was not her boyfriend and she didn't even like him, her father called her a liar and left the room. He returned waving his pistol and pointed it at Emily, screaming, "I'm going to get the truth out of you or you'll never leave this house alive!" Her mother yelled, "Phil, what's got into you?" and told Emily to leave the house. Emily wasn't sure the gun was even loaded, but she wasn't staying around to find out. She ended her story by saying, "I'm never going back to them!"

I asked her if she had a safe place to stay for the night and she said yes. I then asked her permission to call her parents and try to set up a time when we could all meet to talk. After a little convincing she said, "O.K."

When I phoned Emily's house, her mother answered. I introduced myself and explained that I had gotten a phone call from Emily. Sarah cried in relief and wanted to see Emily right away. I suggested that it was better to wait until tomorrow to let things cool down and give everybody time to reflect on what had happened. Sarah said that Phil had calmed down and felt bad about what he had done and wanted to apologize. I suggested that I meet with the whole family the next day after school to talk everything over. She agreed. The therapeutic process now had begun.

The next day we embarked upon the first therapy session as an information exchange session. Emily told her story. Nobody disputed anything she said. Mark apologized to Emily for starting everything and said he felt guilty. Theresa kept her head in her mother's lap and cried occasionally. Phil kept his head down and said he was sorry. Sarah's predominant feeling was desperate frustration. I asked Phil to talk about why he thought that things had gotten out of hand. Phil reported that Emily had always been a good girl and that they had always been rather close. However, in recent months, Emily

had become disobedient and rebellious. When I asked him to elaborate, he explained that Emily became disrespectful, defiant, and,
worst of all, "boy-crazy." He explained that each of the previous
times he had slapped her she was exhibiting some "boy-crazy" behavior and, when he had confronted her with this "unacceptable
behavior for his daughter," she had sassed him back. Emily burst out
that her dad was being unfair and that one time he had scolded her
"just because a boy carried my books home for me." Phil yelled
back, "That's the way it starts!" I wanted to ask Phil what "it" was,
but before I could get the question out, Sarah explained that Phil
and Emily had always been very close. Early in Phil's career, when
he was having some trouble getting established, Phil would come
home and play with Emily, which would "give him perspective on
his job problems." She fretted, "I don't know what's going on. Emily's changed, and Phil is acting just like his father did towards his
mother." Emily looked puzzled, and Phil put his face in his hands.
For a poignant moment of silence, the family sat, frozen in time, an
almost archetypal case of physical abuse of an adolescent child.

WHAT IS THE NATURE OF ADOLESCENT ABUSE?

There are many patterns of behavior in Western culture that may be
present for quite some time before they are "discovered" by the
scientific community. Adolescent abuse is one of those patterns.
Only since the 1970s have social scientists and providers of human
services noticed the abuse and neglect of adolescents (Garbarino,
1980). Abused adolescents were ignored in the research literature
until the late 1970s (Berdie et al., 1977; Doueck et al., 1987; Fisher &
Berdie, 1978; Garbarino & Jacobsen, 1978; Libbey & Bybee, 1979;
Lourie, 1977, 1979; Morgan, 1978). Despite the relatively recent
emergence of adolescent abuse in the scientific community, adolescent abuse is a large percentage of the behavior that falls under the
heading of "child abuse." Estimates of both child abuse in general
and adolescent abuse in particular vary greatly from study to study,
reaching as much as one-third of the population of all children
(Miller & Miller, 1986). In a study by the National Center on Child
Abuse and Neglect (1981), it was estimated that of the 652,000 children who are victims of abuse and neglect annually, 47% are between the ages of 12 and 18. The officially reported figures for the
years 1976–1979, 1981, and 1982 list adolescents as the victims of
abuse in 25% of all reported cases (Trainor, 1984). Most studies cite

figures between 25 and 50% (Doueck et al., 1987; Libbey & Bybee, 1979). Straus, Gelles, and Steinmetz (1980) have pointed out that there appear to be two ages at which child abuse peaks: ages 3–4 and 15–17.

Why is it that we, as a society, have chosen only to see the abuse that occurs at the younger ages? There are a multitude of reasons why child abuse is treated differently from adolescent abuse. A young child is small in stature, does not have many life skills or coping skills, and is dependent on his or her parents for survival. Therefore, he or she is looked upon by society as relatively defenseless. However, an adolescent may be physically bigger than his parents, have a multitude of life and coping skills, and have access to many alternative resources, both for survival and nurturance, in addition to his or her parents. The teenager is viewed as having much more power and control over life. Consequently, teenagers are viewed as being better able to take care of their own lives and less in need of outside intervention (Garbarino, 1980, 1984; Garbarino & Gilliam, 1980).

Adolescents are often looked upon as exacerbating their own plight by provoking their parents with their behavior by their actions or "sassing back" their parents (Berdie et al., 1977; Garbarino, 1980). In fact, the dynamics of adolescent abuse have been seen as more similar to those of spouse abuse than child abuse (Garbarino, 1984; Garbarino & Gilliam, 1980). Both adolescents and spouses are seen as being more competent than children, able to provoke the abuser with their words and actions, and capable of being responsible for ambivalent feelings toward the abuser. None of these perceptions of the victims of spouse or adolescent abuse tends to elicit sympathetic or helping responses from society as a whole. Therefore, less attention is paid to them by society than is rendered to the younger victims of child abuse.

The abuse suffered by adolescents also tends to be less severe in terms of physical damage than the abuse received by younger children (Garbarino & Gilliam, 1980; Libbey & Bybee, 1979). Typical injuries suffered by adolescents include bruises, contusions, cuts, and scratches (Libbey & Bybee, 1979). Adolescents, having more control of their lives physically and having more alternative resources, are more likely to stop the physical abuse by leaving or striking back than their younger counterparts. They are also less vulnerable to the injuries sustained by children of smaller stature. However, it is because these injuries are less severe than many of the injuries suffered by children who are victims of child abuse that they may be overlooked by the legal and social welfare authorities as

being minor (Lourie, 1977). Some adolescents make a point of telling
their therapists that the physical injury did not bother them as much
as the emotional and psychological trauma (Libbey & Bybee, 1979).
Adolescents have been found to be more likely to be psychologically
or sexually abused than children (Garbarino & Gilliam, 1980). Therefore, the adolescent may be more damaged by the psychological and
emotional trauma surrounding the physical abuse than the abuse
itself (Doueck et al., 1987).

A compounding factor in the lack of recognition of adolescent
abuse is the fact that many abusing parents attempt to justify their
physical abuse by labeling it as discipline (Libbey & Bybee, 1979).
This labeling is condoned by the society at large and by many
communities as being a part of "good parenting" (Parke, 1977).
When the physical injury is not severe, this view of discipline is
more likely to be accepted (Lourie, 1977). In fact, 20 states require
only that "serious injuries" be reported to the authorities for investigation of child abuse (Fraser, 1974). If the parent also blames the
victim, perceiving the adolescent as deliberately provoking the abuse
through his or her actions or words, the abuse can be labeled "discipline" without causing any alarm to the community in general or
the child abuse authorities in particular (Libbey & Bybee, 1979). If a
parent believes that he or she is not abusing an adolescent but is,
instead, disciplining the teenager, the adolescent will also be reluctant to report any injury to the authorities. Therefore, the case goes
unreported. This is a major reason why cases of adolescent physical
abuse typically come to the attention of the juvenile court as cases
of "acting-out" or delinquent behavior (Fisher & Berdie, 1978; Garbarino & Gilliam, 1980). It is only upon further investigation that the
physical abuse is uncovered. Thus, the physical abuse of adolescents
is illuminated to the society only from the glow of the spotlight that
focuses upon child abuse.

PATTERNS OF ADOLESCENT PHYSICAL ABUSE

When child abuse in general first came to the focus of public attention in the 1980s, the first assumption was that it was the result of
psychopathology within the individuals in the family (Steele & Pollock, 1968). Causation was associated with a defective personality of
the abusive parent, who was assumed to be mentally or emotionally
ill. Treatment regimens focused on the psychological or psychiatric
treatment modalities of the disturbed parent who was identified as
the abuser.

As researchers started to study the characteristics of child-abusing families, the focus was shifted to a sociological or social–environmental view of child abuse (Gelles, 1973; Gil, 1973; Kempe & Kempe, 1978). The focus of attention was shifted from the individual to the social context in which the family resided. Factors that were linked to child abuse included poverty, loss of job, and social isolation. However, as the research knowledge base grew larger, it was clear that these theories were too simplistic for such a complicated phenomenon as child abuse in general and adolescent abuse in particular (Libbey & Bybee, 1979). Adolescent abuse was found to be less correlated to social class than child abuse (Garbarino, 1984). Libbey and Bybee (1979) found that in only 20% of their cases was there a major influence by outside social factors (such as being on welfare) in the commission of adolescent physical abuse. In most cases, social factors played only a relatively minor role in the abusing family. Family dynamics and developmental forces seemed to play a larger role in precipitating the maltreatment of adolescents (Libbey & Bybee, 1979; Lourie, 1977, 1979).

McCubbin and Patterson (1986) have adapted their "Double ABCX" model of family crisis to the development that takes place in the family during the adolescent years. Key factors in the development of stress within the adolescent's family are

1. Stressors—discrete events that signal change in the biological, psychological, and social spheres of both the adolescent and his or her family.
2. Resources—aids that give strength and energy to the adolescent and his or her family to allow the family to adapt to the stressor involved. Resources may be *personal*, such as financial, educational, health, or psychological resources; *family*, such as protection, boundary maintenance, or family characteristics (e. g., adaptability, cohesion); or *community*, such as emotional support, esteem support, or network (structural) support.
3. Family definition and meaning—the cognitive perception of the situation, which can lend clarity, decrease emotional intensity, or encourage the family to continue the tasks of emotional and social development.
4. Coping—cognitive and behavioral response patterns to the demands experienced that serve to protect the family from the pile-up of demands and their consequences.

If the stressors are reasonable, if the resources are solid (either personal, family, community, or any combination of the three), if the family defines the situation in such a way as to minimize disruption, and if the family has good coping skills, the family will not only weather the crisis but will grow to be stronger than they were previously. This is called "bonadaptation." However, if the stressors are great enough or highly disruptive, if the resources are low, if the family definition of the situation is extreme and exacerbates the situation, and if the coping skills are poor, the family experiences "maladaptation." Their growth is stunted, they experience distress, and they function at a much lower level than they did before the crisis.

The physical maltreatment of adolescents is a perfect example of maladaptation to stress. A multitude of stressors both internal and external to the family system exist (Libbey & Bybee, 1979). One key stressor is the stage of development in which both the adolescent and parent find themselves (Lourie, 1977, 1979). The family is often isolated from social relationships outside the home (Garbarino, 1980) and has few resources within the family on which to draw (Lourie, 1977). Its perception of the situation is extreme (Lourie, 1977, 1979) or unrealistic (Berdie et al., 1983). Coping skills are poor and problematic (Bolacek & Kilpatrick, 1982; Libbey & Bybee, 1979; Lourie, 1977). These conditions are archetypal in adolescent abuse. However, there is not one type of abusive family. Families who physically abuse adolescents form different patterns.

The Maladaptive Normals

In summarizing the literature on child abuse, Kempe and Kempe (1978) found that "difficult" infants and young children, such as those who were hyperactive and colicky, were more subject to child abuse by their parents than "normal" babies. Therefore, they reasoned that "difficult" adolescents might similarly be subject to more abuse. However, one of the problems with adolescence as a time of life is that many adults look upon the typical, developmentally appropriate behavior of an adolescent as deviant (Doueck et al., 1987). If Kempe and Kempe's speculations are correct, many "normal" families with "normal" adolescents might sporadically engage in adolescent abuse, becoming "Maladaptive Normals."

Maladaptive Normal families seldom have engaged in physically abusive behavior before the onset of adolescence (Doueck et al., 1987; Garbarino, 1980; Lourie, 1977). Before the beginning of adolescence, these families have shown no deviant characteristics and, in many cases, report never having used any physical discipline. However, the onset of adolescence brings about many changes (Jurich, 1979). Any time there are changes resulting from transitions from one stage to another in the family life cycle, the family will face high levels of stress (Gelles & Straus, 1979). When such a transition in the life cycle of one family member coincides with a transition of another family member, the stress is enhanced and the family undergoes severe strain (Kidwell et al., 1983). This situation faces the family with an adolescent in the home: The developmental tasks of the adolescent and the developmental tasks of his or her parents collide with each other and increase the tension within the family (Lourie, 1977). At the same time the adolescent is excited about leaving home and striking out on his or her own, the parents are mourning the end of their parenting role (Jurich, 1979). The parents are coping with a loss of physical energy and sexual prowess; the adolescent seems to have unbounded energy and lots of sexual opportunity. As the adolescent tries to choose from a multitude of career possibilities, the parents must face the fact that many of their career dreams will never come to pass. The adolescent's need to individuate is countered by the parents' need to consolidate (Jurich, 1979). The adolescent's central developmental task is to assert himself or herself, while the parent threshold for tolerance of such "rebellion" is lowered (Doueck et al., 1987). It is a recurrence of the dynamics that were present in the "terrible twos" (Garbarino, 1980; Garbarino & Gilliam, 1980). The "ornery adolescent" is, once again, testing boundaries and striving for independence. However, boundary testing and provocative behavior, which may be developmentally appropriate for an adolescent, is not perceived as being positive by the parents (Doueck et al., 1987). Instead, the parental definition and meaning of this type of action and attitude stereotypes the adolescent as irrational, "hard to handle," and unlovable. Such behavior from a teenage female is even less tolerated. This is a major reason why, unlike child abuse, adolescent females are more likely to be abused than adolescent males (Libbey & Bybee, 1979; Lourie, 1977; Miller & Miller 1986; Trainor 1984), especially by fathers (Garbarino & Gilliam, 1980). Utilizing the "Double ABCX" model of McCubbin and Patterson (1986), the family with an adolescent experiences a rather severe set of stressors, defines them in a way that exacerbates the stress, and may have few resources to tap in handling the situation. It is little wonder that it is during the adolescent stage of the family life cycle that families have the highest stress levels (Olson et al., 1983).

A family's coping skills determine whether they cope successfully with this crisis of the adolescent years. Unfortunately, many families try to cope with the adolescent' s attempts at independence with attempts of their own to repress that independence (Jurich, 1987). If the adolescent does not respond to this repression by giving up his or her strivings for independence, the parent will often resort to coercion and violence (Gelles & Straus, 1979; Lourie, 1977, 1979). Maltreatment becomes a punch, tolerance becomes rejection (Garbarino, 1980). Most parents in the Maladaptive Normal pattern are quick to point out that their abusive behavior was preceded by their adolescent's disobeying or arguing with them (Libbey & Bybee, 1979). These arguments may have centered around such mundane issues as cleaning their room, boyfriends, closing a door, staying out too late, and leaving food around the house. Parents report that their discipline simply "went too far" (Doueck et al., 1987). This type of abuse tends to be one time or sporadic and tends to be described by the adolescent as less physically than emotionally damaging (Libbey & Bybee, 1979). This pattern does not fit the cultural image of the parent as the all-powerful, ruthless perpetrator and the child as the innocent, severely damaged victim (Fisher & Berdie, 1978). This pattern is the most frequent pattern of adolescent abuse comprising, as many as 75% of the cases studied (Libbey & Bybee, 1979). In many respects, the physical abuse of the Maladaptive Normals is secondary to the emotional and symbolic maltreatment that it spawns. It is also dangerous because, if the family does not develop the skills to cope with their stress of the adolescent years, the Maladaptive Normals could degenerate into more severe forms of physical abuse.

The Disillusioned Idealists

The Disillusioned Idealists are very similar to the Maladaptive Normals. These are families that, during the childhood years, were very child-oriented and overindulgent of their children (Lourie, 1977). As with the Maladaptive Normals, there was little or no physical discipline, much less physical abuse, during childhood. It is at the onset of adolescence, when the adolescent starts his or her normal assertive boundary testing behavior, that sporadic, even "accidental" abuse takes place. Often this physically abusive episode is triggered by a stressful event having little to do with the parent–adolescent relationship specifically (Libbey & Bybee, 1979). These parents center much of their life around their children. Often they have unrealistic expectations of what the child is developmentally able to do (Purcell, 1979). They become enmeshed with their children, sometimes expecting the children to provide for them the nurturance that would more properly come from an adult. The boundaries between parents and child become diffuse, creating feelings of belonging but leaving little room for independence or autonomy (Jurich, 1983). While the child is still a child, this enmeshment is tolerated by the child, the parents, and the community, in some cases even being labeled as "good parenting." However, once the child reaches adolescence, this degree of enmeshment becomes a problem. The adolescent's natural push for self-differentiation, as described above, becomes even more devastating for the Disillusioned Idealist parent. Not only are the same disruptive stressors present as for the Maladaptive Normal parent, but there is also the tearing of an extremely close bond and the distancing of a major source of nurturance and identity for the parent. While the nonviolent discipline and laissez-faire nature of the Maladaptive Normal parent–child relationship mitigates against the outbreak of violence, the acute sense of loss and desperation may push the Disillusioned Idealist to such an extreme that a violent episode explodes on the normally quiescent family scene. When these families come into therapy, their interpretation of the violent episode seems to be much more emotionally charged than the event seems to warrant. Their extreme sense of disillusionment and loss fuels this perception and pushes them to seek help.

The Dethroned Despots

A third pattern of adolescent abuse also begins with the onset of adolescence. The "Dethroned Despots" are parents who always have used physical, punitive discipline and have been rigid in their approach to child rearing specifically and, in many cases, to their entire lives (Lourie, 1977). The family structure is rigid and is designed to be impervious to problems and stressors. When a problem is anticipated, the family simply closes ranks and expects the stressors to bounce off the family like bullets off Superman's chest. This family may appear to be very strong as the parents take leadership to fend off stress. However, this type of family often has severe problems hidden by the veneer of imperviousness. The family may have many structural resources but few personal resources. Therefore, the family has very little resiliency. As long as the Dethroned Despot family can be impervious to stress, it appears to function normally. However, if a stressor does not "bounce off" the closed ranks of the family and penetrates the family system, the family has no mechanism to employ to reduce the level of stress. Consequently, the Dethroned Despot parents employ maladaptive coping mechanisms, like adolescent abuse, to cope with stressors like the adolescent's bid for independence (Berdie et al., 1983; Trainor, 1984; Ziefert, 1981). These parents are more likely to use more extreme physical force (e. g., more head injuries) and to use physical abuse more frequently than the Maladaptive Normal or Disillusioned Idealist parents (Libbey & Bybee, 1979). They are also more likely to demonstrate other maladaptive coping mechanisms, such as alcoholism, drug abuse, or mental illness (Lourie, 1977). The Dethroned Despots cannot cope, once their impervious shield has been shattered, and adolescent abuse is employed in an effort to regain the control they have had in the past. Seldom will these families come in for therapy on their own. Instead, they will come in for their own problems (e. g., alcoholism) or for their adolescent's problems (e.g., truancy), typically under pressure from the law or the community.

The Chronic Abusers

The most severe cases of adolescent physical abuse, in terms of both frequency and intensity of abuse, are the Chronic Abusers. With these families, the pattern of abuse started in childhood and simply has continued into adolescence (Garbarino, 1980; Lourie, 1977). This type of family comprises 20 to 25% of the cases studied (Libbey & Bybee, 1979). Chronic Abuser parents are most likely to cause severe injury and head injuries to the adolescent. Their discipline is both verbally and physically abusive. Both the parents and the adolescents describe the Chronic Abuser parents as being disorganized, inadequate, and incompetent (Lourie, 1977). They are subject to multiple problems (e. g., divorce, money strain, family conflict, and alcoholism) (Berdie et al., 1983). Much of the more severe abuse occurred when the parents were using alcohol or drugs (Garbarino & Gilliam, 1980). There are no special reasons, for the adolescent's abuse. It is just a continuation of a pattern of abuse that, for the teenager, started when he or she was very young, often in infancy. Chronic Abuser parents are most likely to have been abused when they were children (Berdie et al., 1983; Rathbone-McCuan & Pierce, 1978). Berdie et al. (1983) reported that 50% of their sample of adolescent abusers were abused as children, and almost 50% had witnessed parental violence as a child. Seldom do Chronic Abusers seek therapy for their maltreatment of their adolescents. Both the parents and the adolescent justify the abuse as deserved because of the behavior exhibited by the adolescent, even though the behavior in question might be considered quite normal by societal standards

(Libbey & Bybee, 1979). Both the parents and the adolescent have grown so used to their skewed way of life that they define the abuse as normal. It is only after several sessions and a great deal of rapport building that a therapist will even get an admission of abuse from an abused teenager of a Chronic Abuser family. These are the most difficult cases to treat therapeutically because the pattern of abuse has been so ingrained (Berdie et al., 1983).

COPING WITH ADOLESCENT PHYSICAL ABUSE

Once adolescent physical abuse occurs, it becomes a potential stressor for further crises. The family as a whole and the family members as individuals must employ their coping strategies to deal with this situation. Because the family is in turmoil over the original stressor and the subsequent adolescent abuse, it is seldom that the family members can band together to arrive at a unified coping strategy for the entire family to pursue actively and overtly. Families in this situation are more likely to cooperate covertly or pursue individual coping strategies. There are four typical coping strategies employed by families who have just experienced an episode of adolescent abuse: (1) avoidance, (2) intrapunitive measures, (3) extrapunitive measures, and (4) help seeking.

Avoidance

The most typical response to an abusive incident is avoidance. In many families, the family members conspire covertly to pretend that "nothing is wrong" and "everything is back to normal." It is easy to understand why the parents would want to conceal the abuse. They either were the perpetrators of the abuse or they tacitly condoned it by letting it happen. It would seem logical that they would, therefore, want to conceal or minimize the abuse. In fact, chronic child and adolescent abuser parents will often isolate themselves socially to avoid detection (Young, 1964). It also seems logical that siblings of the abused adolescent would avoid dealing with the incident because they fear reprisals from their parents similar to the ones perpetrated on the adolescent victim or because they find themselves isolated by their parents' actions to cut off the whole family from the prying eyes of the outside world. However, it is also the adolescent victim of the abuse who cuts himself or herself off from social interactions and relationships with others and, in doing so, separates himself or herself from important resources for handling stress (Garbarino, 1980). Even when pressed into a therapeutic relationship, many victims of adolescent abuse conceal their injuries, do not seek help, and are highly resistant to therapy (Kempe & Kempe, 1978). They want to avoid the entire episode.

In some cases, avoidance takes on even more dramatic consequences. Many adolescents turn to alcohol (Dembo et al. 1987) or drugs (Wright, 1985) to avoid confronting the physical abuse, remaining physically present while mentally dropping out. Other adolescents attempt to isolate themselves physically from social relationships that might push them to actively cope with the abuse. They become truant (Garbarino, 1980; Jenkins, 1986) or drop out of school (Harris, 1983). It is as if they see no reason to invest in the "adult world," which for them includes school, if the adult world will not understand and protect them. Other adolescents run away from home (Konopka, 1975). One of the most consistent factors in the backgrounds of adolescents who continually run away from home is the continued use of violence by their parents in maltreating them (Fisher & Berdie, 1978; Hartman, et al., 1987). The added tragedy of these runaway adolescents is that, if they're caught and returned to their homes, they often become victimized once again, and if they remain on the streets, they have a good chance of becoming vagrants, drug dealers, or prostitutes (Garbarino, 1980). Either way, they lose.

Intrapunitive Measures

In this coping scenario, family members may try to punish themselves. Typically, the only parents who tend to be very intrapunitive are the Disillusioned Idealists. Some Maladaptive Normals may get pretty hard on themselves, but for the most part, they will put a reasonable boundary on their self-recriminations. The adolescent victim of physical abuse, however, is much more likely to be intrapunitive than the other family members (Garbarino, 1980). Abused adolescents are more prone to generalize anxiety, emotional problems, thought disturbances, feelings of helplessness and overdependency, and depression (Farber & Joseph, 1985). Such self-feelings, created by physical abuse, lend themselves to lower self-esteem and a self-defeatist attitude toward one's future (Kazdin et al., 1985) and are an integral part of the etiology of alcohol and drug abuse (Dembo et al., 1987). It is because of these negative self-messages that physically abused adolescents are more likely to have longer stays when they are placed in psychiatric hospitals (Mills et al., 1984). When an adolescent who has been physically abused internalizes those negative sanctions, he or she has a good possibility of entertaining suicidal thoughts (Wright, 1985). In that way the adolescent seeks to be loyal to his or her parents, punish himself or herself, and end the misery of his or her existence all with one act. Tragically, adolescent physical abuse may lead to the ultimate in intrapunitive behavior: suicide attempts (Connell, 1972; Jacobs, 1971) or suicide (Garbarino, 1980; Konopka, 1975).

Extrapunitive Measures

A third method of coping with adolescent physical abuse is by further aggression. This is the typical coping technique used by the Dethroned Despots and the Chronic Abusers. Parents who have been dethroned as despots often escalate the violence in their "discipline" in order to regain their lost throne. Such parents often exhibit a sense of desperation about their violence that should alert the therapist to the insecurity of the parents' position as they see it. For the Chronic Abuser parents, violence is simply a way of life. "If an obstacle is in the road, push it out of the way!" "If an adolescent won't do what you want, hit him and he'll respond!" These attitudes only serve to further exacerbate an already violent situation. If the adolescent also uses extrapunitive coping mechanisms, the violence can easily spiral out of control at the drop of a hat. Physically abused adolescents are more likely to be aggressive and angry (Mills et al., 1984; Moane et al., 1984). This level of aggression makes them very hard to work with in therapy and hard to place (Kagan & Reid, 1986). Some physically abused adolescents turn their aggressive behavior outside the family through extreme acting-out behavior (Farber & Joseph, 1985), delinquent behavior (Libbey & Bybee, 1979; Wright, 1985), or violent delinquency (Lewis et al., 1980) such as arson (Bradford & Dimock, 1986). Of 14 juveniles incarcerated and condemned to death for murder, 12 suffered brutal physical abuse and five were sodomized by family members (Lewis, 1985; Lewis et al., 1987). Often that degree of violence is turned back to the family from which it originated (Kratcoski & Kratcoski, 1982). This may lead to the adolescent's assaulting his or her parents (Garbarino & Gilliam, 1980), physically abusing them (Ney & Mulvihill, 1982), or even killing them (Garbarino, 1980). As the old adage notes: "Violence begets violence." There is, however, an extrapunitive response by some abused adolescents that may actually serve to break the cycle of violence. Some adolescents assert themselves and seek to "get even" with their parents for their abuse by reporting the abuse to the authorities (Libbey & Bybee, 1979). Regardless of the motivation, this coping strategy may have the result of getting the family help from the professional community.

Help Seeking

Help seeking is by far the best method of coping after an abusive episode. By going beyond the coping strategies and solutions the family has heretofore had to offer, the individual or family may find a way to lessen the original stressor. The adolescent whose bad grades were the original stressor that spawned the abuse may find, upon professional consultation and testing, that he or she is in need of glasses. Once the glasses are fitted, the original reason for the abuse is eliminated. Help seeking might provide the family some perspective on their problems. In our original case study, Phil might better understand the normality of his 13-year-old daughter's interest in boys. Emily might see how her father is trying, although not very successfully, to express his fear over her safety. Finally, help seeking can open new resources to the family. There may be professionals to shore up the structure of the family, interpersonal resources to validate the family's goals, or community support networks. There could even be family therapy for the family to utilize.

However, before a family is able to seek help from a family therapist, several barriers must be overcome. It is difficult for a family under stress to seek solutions beyond their typical means of coping. They are often trapped in the inertia of their own system. Their perception is bound by the urgency of their crisis. There are also a multitude of external barriers. Because parents often don't seek help and the adolescent engages in avoidance, interpunitive, or extrapunitive coping strategies, the family therapist is not typically the first professional the family sees. Abusive families most often have their first contact with physicians who are treating the adolescent's injuries, social workers who have been alerted to the case, or law enforcement and juvenile authorities investigating adolescent misconduct (Boszormenyi-Nagy & Spark, 1973). Schools are often the first in the community to identify problems within the family (Libbey & Bybee, 1979). However, many of these professionals are not trained or equipped to deal with the physical abuse of adolescents (Fisher & Berdie, 1978; Garbarino, 1980). Sometimes when cases of adolescent abuse are brought to the attention of a professional, the case is not reported to Child Welfare because the initial professional despaired that anything constructive could be accomplished (National Center on Child Abuse & Neglect, 1981). Protective service workers are often reluctant to take adolescent abuse cases because they may believe that it would be difficult to prove maltreatment to a judge (Fisher & Berdie, 1978; Garbarino & Gilliam, 1980). This is reasonable when one considers that the adolescent often appears irrational, unlovable, and hard to handle, while the parent puts on the face of the pained martyr or concerned parent (Doueck et al., 1987). These stereotypical roles hinder both the identification and treatment of adolescent abuse. There are simply too many abused children, where the case is much more clear-cut on the caseload of an overworked child protection worker, for that worker to be overconcerned with an abused adolescent, who is better able to take care of himself or herself or probably deserved to be hit for his or her snotty attitude (Doueck et al., 1987). Even if the family does get some help from an agency or professional, the professional community is vulnerable to manipulation by the parents, who may go from agency to agency, playing one off against the other (Libbey & Bybee, 1979). This manipulation by the "sick but slick" abusive parents (Wright, 1976) is but another barrier to the very frightening process of confronting oneself in therapy. If these barriers are cleared, the family may be able to participate in the process of family therapy.

FAMILY THERAPY WITH FAMILIES WHO PHYSICALLY ABUSE ADOLESCENTS

As in the case of Emily and her family at the beginning of this chapter, most adolescent physical abuse cases come to the family therapist labeled as another type of case. Emily's case ostensibly dealt with an adolescent status offense—running away from home. Because Emily's running away was so immediately connected to the abuse, the case was easily identified as an abuse case. However, the reader will notice that, while the precipitating incident was highly symbolic and potentially lethal, no physical harm was done to the adolescent at that time. Such an incident could easily be passed over by the authorities as having caused no physical harm. The reader will also notice that Emily had been struck in the face on several occasions by her father without anyone labeling it as abuse and without Emily reporting it to anyone in authority. As pointed out by Kempe and Kempe (1978), adolescents often conceal injuries that they have received in an abusive family. Sometimes this is out of a misguided family loyalty. Other adolescents find it incongruous to strive for independence on one hand while asking for professional help on the other. Therefore, they are resistive to therapeutic intervention. This is why many therapists discover the abuse of an adolescent only after a therapeutic relationship has been established (Libbey & Bybee, 1979). Therefore, the first rule of therapy is to expect resistance from the family, including the abused adolescent, and take time in establishing an empathic therapeutic relationship with each family member.

One of the main problems in establishing rapport is the fact that child abuse, even when the adolescent is the victim, is illegal and must be reported in most states. For all the reasons stated previously, it is often difficult to determine where discipline ends and abuse begins. For instance, some readers of this chapter may have serious questions as to when Emily, in our case study, was abused or whether she was ever abused at all. Was she abused when she was slapped in the face, when she was hit with a closed fist, or when she was threatened with a gun? What circumstances surrounded each incident? When we speak of gross physical abuse of young preschool children, we are more likely to see "abuse." However, what is the abuse of an adolescent? In the National Center on Child Abuse and Neglect national survey, only 24% of the adolescent maltreatment cases were reported to protective services (1981). This was the lowest percentage reported of any age group. In this survey, many professionals cited the ambiguity of the law concerning adolescents, the feeling that little could be done with the family, and the feeling that the professional or his or her agency could better handle the case as reasons for nonreporting. Other professionals routinely tell the client family that they are mandated to report all cases of child or adolescent abuse and do so after the first session. Still other therapists encourage the abusing parents to report themselves to Child Welfare in order to enhance the therapeutic alliance, restore self-esteem to the parent, and reestablish the hierarchical position of the parents as the responsible adults (Trad & Pfetter, 1988). There are no hard and fast rules to deal with this problem. Each therapist must decide the ethics, legality, and commitment to his or her clients, weighing the individual merits of each case. The key is to minimize the damage this decision will have on the rapport established with the family, which is no easy matter.

It is crucial for the family therapist to begin therapy by being very client-centered, letting each family member, including the siblings who may be "innocent bystanders," tell the story of what is happening in the family in his or her own words. This gives the therapist a multiple perspective of the precipitating sequence of events and any recursive family patterns that seem to be fueling the cycle of violence. There is an excellent chance that the other family members have never heard the adolescent's story or the views of each parent, or if they have heard it, they listened with only half of their attention while simultaneously planning a response in the "great debates" that pass as family discussions. To truly hear each other may be a new experience. This process also allows the therapist to get a better picture of the dynamics of the family interactions. The therapist can then assess which type of family is coming in for therapy: Maladaptive Normals, Disillusioned Idealists, Dethroned Despots, or Chronic Abusers. Therapy is quite different with each.

In treating Maladaptive Normals or Disillusioned Idealists, an educational component is emphasized first. Many of their problems stem from the fact that both parents and adolescents are unfamiliar with the basic information about adolescent development, family development, and the transitions associated with the middle years of adulthood. Focusing on the developmental tasks of both parents and adolescent helps to normalize the behaviors each family member assumed to be aberrant (Doueck et al., 1987). Therapists may explain to parents that when their adolescent rebels against a rule, he or she is not rebelling against the parent but instead against his or her own childhood image of himself or herself (Jurich, 1987). This normalizes the behavior while removing the parent from being the object of rebellion. As the therapist helps the family to understand the nature of their development, points of similarity that they may not see are emphasized and explained for the family (Barton & Alexander, 1981). An adolescent who is grounded sees himself or herself as the prisoner and the parents as the jailers. However, if the therapist can ask the parents how they feel when one or both of them has to stay home in order to make sure the adolescent stays on restriction, they might talk about how restricted they feel. The jailor becomes a prisoner in his or her own jail. It can be pointed out to both the parents and the adolescent that they are all prisoners of their dysfunctional family pattern. In this way, the family system is redefined, and similarities are pointed out to people who had previously defined themselves as adversaries. The dysfunctional family patterns are made the "bad guy" against whom they can join forces to defeat.

At this point in therapy it is crucial to strategize a plan of action with the entire family. Not only are the parents consulted but so is the adolescent in almost equal partnership. The adolescent's participation in the planning of interventions in therapy is of crucial importance (Garbarino 1980; Libbey & Bybee, 1979). If the therapist is behavioral in his or her approach, Garbarino's (1980) suggestion of the use of a Teaching Parent Model of parent–adolescent interactions may be used. However, it is imperative that the adolescent be considered as a near-equal partner in the establishment of rules, the formulations of punishments, and the possibilities of exceptions to these rules. This is a much longer process than simply giving the adolescent a set of rules to follow. However, if the adolescent has some input into the rules and their reinforcement, he or she will be more likely to follow them. Pointing out dysfunctional patterns and establishing new patterns will reestablish the hierarchy of the parental executive system on one hand while recognizing the incipient adult who is the adolescent on the other. This enables the family to shift patterns to form a more functional family system. Such cases can employ structural or strategic methods of therapy depending on the style of the therapist (Jenkins, 1986), and the Maladaptive Normals and Disillusioned Idealists will make great strides in therapy. However, these are not always the cases that show up at the door of the family therapist.

It is often the most severe cases of adolescent maltreatment that wind up in family therapy (Libbey & Bybee, 1979). When the family seeking therapy is a Dethroned Despot or Chronic Abuser family, the rules change. First, they are seldom self-referred. As such, the therapist takes on the additional role of policing this family for the societal system. Establishing rapport is ten times harder, and the family is much more resistant to any offer of help from anyone. It is still important to let each family member tell his or her story his or her own way, but the same amount of "empathic listening" may not take place. It is still important to try to teach about "normal" development in the family, but the therapist must realize that "normal" may be a foreign concept to some members of these families. Therefore, the differences between the norms of the community and the abuse that has taken place in the family must be more forcefully emphasized (Libbey & Bybee, 1979). Many of the Chronic Abuser families have had maladaptive patterns that have been entrenched for so long that they are extremely difficult to dislodge and change to more functional patterns (Doueck et al., 1987). With these families, family therapy may have to be conducted in conjunction with financial counseling, treatment for chemical dependency, and individual psychotherapy as well.

Therapy with these more extreme cases begins the same way that therapy with a Maladaptive Normal or Disillusioned Idealist family begins. However, as soon as they are diagnosed as a Dethroned Despot or Chronic Abuser family, the therapist should immediately look for the family's resistance and switch into a very heavy strategic modality (Jurich, 1986). This consists of a series of stances taken by the therapist to appear to agree with a family member's view of the situation while maneuvering himself or herself into a position to strategically challenge that same family member's view. In this way the therapist creates cognitive dissonance within the person or family system, thereby disrupting the maladaptive pattern and forcing the family to change its behavior. That is a not-so-simple explanation of a complicated process that is very hard to explain because it is reactive to the family system and therefore shifts with every family and every situation.

For example, in the case study of Emily's family, Emily's dad labeled his daughter's behavior as "boy-crazy" and said that he was afraid that a boy carrying his daughter's books was unacceptable for his daughter because "That's the way it starts!" In this situation the therapist might "track with him" by agreeing that his daughter could have problems with her reputation if she were too "boy-crazy" and ask him if he feared anything else. Ultimately, he might admit that he was scared that she might have sex with a boy. While always agreeing with him that this was a "difficult situation," the therapist would hope to accomplish two things: (1) to relax his defenses and lower his resistance and (2) to try to gather enough information so that he or she could point out some flaw in his logic to cause him cognitive dissonance.

In the case presented at the beginning of this chapter, as Phil went on about the horrors of his daughter's possibly having sex with a boy, I realized how absolute he was in his condemnation of his daughter's sexuality. I said to him, "Phil, it must be difficult for a man like you, who has three children and obviously loves his wife, to explain to your daughter how much you like sex and how sex is a wonderful gift which must be shared with the right person. It isn't all black or white but a complicated situation with goods and bads and lots of shades of gray. That must be a difficult message to get across to your daughter who is becoming a woman so fast." I was trying to cause cognitive dissonance between his view of sex as totally wrong for his daughter but all right for him and his wife. My leverage point was his degree of emotion around "sex being wrong for his daughter." At that point I was trying to disrupt the recursive cycle, but I didn't know where he would take my strategic push. Somewhat to my surprise, he started to cry, looked at his wife and apologized, and then looked at his daughter saying, "Don't make the same mistake I made with your mother. We never dated anyone else, and sex has never been as good as it should have been. I'm afraid for you and I'm jealous of you and I'm sorry for the way I've treated you." Emily said to her dad, "I'm sorry for you and Mom. I guess I always knew something was wrong."

Not all cases turn this dramatically. Not all cases have one quick intervention that works. Not all interventions are that gentle. For example, when a Dethroned Despot attempts to justify his or her abuse by "dehumanizing the victim" (Parke & Collmer, 1975) by saying that the adolescent "deserved it because he or she was bad," I ask the parent, "So you're telling me that when people are bad they should be hit?" I have to say this with a sincere voice and with no hint of sarcasm in either my voice or manner. This lets the parent think that I am agreeing or "tracking" with him. I then ask, very sincerely, "Then who hits you when you're bad?" In this way I am not confronting the parent but am confronting him or her with the logical conclusion of his or her own beliefs. The pattern is disrupted. If a father says that his parent punished him when he was an adolescent, I will ask him to explain to the adolescent how it felt and how he felt about it. I will tell him that they, parent and adolescent together, are engaging in an almost heroic struggle to stem the tide of tradition from previous generations. That may sound corny, but I truly believe that, dynamically, that is what is happening. If the resistance breaks down, family of origin work may begin (Rathbone-McCuan & Pierce, 1978). If the family is still resistant to change, the loyalty to previous generations can be used as a means of confronting their maladaptive pattern without their feeling as if the therapist is confronting them. It is simply pointed out the way that their present circumstances are confronting the maladaptive family patterns that they have learned from generations before.

One last note to the therapist is necessary. Not all families can or should be kept intact (Garbarino, 1980). Forcing an adolescent back into a dysfunctional, chaotic, brutal family for the sake of reuniting the family unit may do more harm than good. In some families, the disengagement process has already begun (Doueck et al., 1987). Sending the child back into the home is like trying to turn back the hands on the clock. When family therapy with families who physically abuse their adolescents is successful, the adolescent, the family, and society receive a great service. When it fails, and it will in some cases, we as therapists admonish ourselves for our failure. We must stop and ask ourselves if the price of temporary success, pushing the family back together, would have been more expensive than the price of our failure to keep the family together.

REFERENCES

Barton, C., & Alexander, J. F. (1981). Functional family therapy. In A. S. Gurman & D. P. Kniskern (Eds.), Handbook of family therapy. New York: Brunner/Mazel.

Berdie, J., Berdie, M., Wexler, S., & Fisher, B. (1983). An imperial study of families involved in adolescent maltreatment: Final report (Grant No. 90-CA-837/01). Washington, DC: National Center on Child Abuse and Neglect, Department of Health and Human services.

Berdie, J., Braizerman, M., & Lourie, I. S. (1977). Violence towards youth: Themes from a workshop. Children Today 6(2), 7–10, 35.

Bolacek, J. F., & Kilpatrick, A. C. (1982). Abused adolescents: Whose responsibility? Social Work Education 42, 6–16.

Boszormenyi-Nagy, I., & Spark, G. M. (1973). Invisible loyalties. New York: Harper & Row.

Bradford, J., & Dimock, J. (1986). A comparative study of adolescents and adults who willfully set fires. Psychiatric Journal of the University of Ottawa 11, 228–234.

Connell, H. M. (1972). Attempted suicide in school children. The Medical Journal of Australia 1, 686–690.

Dembo, R., Dertke, M., la-Voie, L., & Borders, S. (1987). Physical abuse, sexual victimization, and illicit drug use: A structural analysis among high risk adolescents. Journal of Adolescence 10, 13–34.

Doueck, H. J., Ishisaka, A. H., Sweany, S. L., & Gilchrist, L. D. (1987). Adolescent maltreatment: Themes from the empirical literature. Journal of Interpersonal Violence 2, 139–153.

Farber, E. D., & Joseph, J. A. (1985). The maltreated adolescent: Patterns of physical abuse. Child Abuse and Neglect 9, 201–206.

Fisher, B., & Berdie, J. (1978). Adolescent abuse and neglect: Issues of incidence, intervention, and service delivery. Child Abuse and Neglect 2, 178–192.

Fraser, B. A. (1974). A summary of child abuse legislation, 1973. In R. Helfer & C. H. Kempe (Eds.), The battered child. Chicago: University of Chicago Press.

Garbarino, J. (1980). Meeting the needs of mistreated youths. Social Work, 25, 122–126.

Garbarino, J. (1984). Adolescent maltreatment: A guide for practice and policy. Practice Applications (2), 1–11.

Garbarino, J., & Gilliam, G. (1980). Understanding abusive families. Lexington, MA: Lexington Books.

Garbarino, J., & Jacobsen, N. (1978). Youth helping youth in cases of maltreatment of adolescents. Child Welfare 57, 505–510.

Gelles, R. J. (1973). Child abuse as psychopathology: A sociological critique and reformulation. American Journal of Orthopsychiatry 43, 611–621.

Gelles, R. J., & Straus, M. A. (1979). Determinants of violence in the family: Towards a theoretical integration. In W. R. Burr, R. Hill, F. I. Nye, & I.

C. Reiss (Eds.), *Contemporary theories about the family* (Vol. 1). New York: Free Press.

Gil, D. (1973). *Violence against children*. Cambridge, MA: Harvard University Press.

Harris, L. H. (1983). Role of trauma in the lives of high school dropouts. *Social Work in Education* 5, 77–88.

Hartman, C. R., Burgess, A. W., & McCormack, A. (1987). Pathways and cycles of runaways: A model for understanding repetitive runaway behavior. *Hospital and Community Psychiatry* 38, 292–299.

Jacobs, J. (1971). *Adolescent suicide*. New York: Wiley-Interscience.

Jenkins, H. (1986). A family and other systems: Treatment within a structural-strategic framework. *Maladjustment and Therapeutic Education* 4, 33–41.

Jurich, A. P. (1979). The challenge of adolescence for youth and parents. *Family Perspective, 13*, 93–99.

Jurich, A. P. (1983). The Saigon of the family's mind: Family therapy with families of Vietnam veterans. *Journal of Marital and Family Therapy* 9, 355–363.

Jurich, A. P. (1986, October). Family therapy with adolescents: *Confronting without confrontation*. Paper presented at the American Association for Marriage and Family Therapy Annual Conference, Orlando, FL.

Jurich, A. P. (1987). Adolescents and family dynamics. In H. G. Lingren et al. (Eds.), *Family strengths*: Vols. 8–9. *Pathways to well-being*. Lincoln, NE: University of Nebraska.

Kagan, R. M., & Reid W. J. (1986). Critical factors in the adoption of emotionally disturbed youths. *Child Welfare* 65, 63–73.

Kazdin, A. E., Moser, J., Colbus, D., & Bell, R. (1985). Depressive symptoms among physically abused and psychiatrically disturbed children. *Journal of Abnormal Psychology* 94, 298–307.

Kempe, R., & Kempe, C. H. (1978). *Child abuse*. Cambridge, MA: Harvard University Press.

Kidwell, J., Fisher, J., Dunham, R., & Baranowski, M. (1983). Parents and adolescents: Push and pull of change. In H. I. McCubbin & C. R. Figley (Eds.), *Stress and the family*: Vol. 1. *Coping with normative transitions*. New York: Brunner/Mazel.

Konopka, G. (1975). *Young girls: A portrait of adolescents*. Englewood Cliffs, NJ: Prentice-Hall.

Kratcoski, P. C., & Kratcoski, L. D. (1982). The relationship of victimization through child abuse to aggressive delinquent behavior. *Victimology* 7, 199–203.

Lewis, D. O. (1985). Biopsychosocial characteristics of children who later murder: A prospective study. *American Journal of Psychiatry* 142, 1161–1167.

Lewis, D. O., Pinons, J. H., Bard, B., & Richardson, E. (1987). Neuropsychiatric, psychoeducational, and family characteristics of 14 juveniles condemned to death in the United States. Paper presented at the Annual Meeting of the American Academy of Child and Adolescent Psychiatry, Washington, DC.

Lewis, D. O., Shaneck, S. S., Pincus, J. H., & Glasser, G. H. (1980). Violent juvenile delinquents: Psychiatric, neurological, psychological, and abuse factors. *Annual Progress in Child Psychiatry and Child Development*, 591–603.

Libbey, P., & Bybee, R. (1979). The physical abuse of adolescents. *Journal of Social Issues* 35, 101–126.

Lourie, I. S. (1977). The phenomenon of the abused adolescent: A clinical study. *Victimology* 2, 268–276.

Lourie, I. S. (1979). Family dynamics and the abuse of adolescents: A case for a developmental phase specific model of child abuse. *Child Abuse and Neglect* 3, 967–974.

McCubbin, H. I., & Patterson, J. M. (1986). Adolescent stress, coping, and adaptation: A normative family perspective. In G. K. Leigh & G. W. Patterson (Eds.), *Adolescents in families*. Cincinnati: South-Western.

Miller, E. K., & Miller, K. A. (1986). Abusive histories in youth/young adult students. *International Journal for the Advancement of Counseling* 9, 159–165.

Mills, T., Ricker, P. P., & Carmen, E. H. (1984). Hospitalization experiences of victims of abuse. *Victimology* 9, 436–449.

Moane, M., Leichter, D., & Lewis, S. O. (1984). Physical abuse in psychiatrically hospitalized children and adolescents. *Journal of the American Academy of Child Psychiatry* 23, 653–658.

Morgan, R. (1978). The battered adolescent: A developmental approach to identification and intervention. In M. L. Landerdale, R. N. Anderson, & S. E. Cramer (Eds.). *Child abuse and neglect: Issues in innovation and implementation*. Austin, TX: Region VI Resource Center on Child Abuse and Neglect.

National Center on Child Abuse and Neglect, Office of Human Development Service, DHHS. (1981). *Executive summary: National study of the incidence and severity of child abuse and neglect*. Washington, DC: Government Printing Office.

Ney, P., & Mulvihill, D. (1982). Case report on parent abuse. *Victimology* 7, 194–198.

Olson, D. H., McCubbin, H. I., Barnes, H., Larsen, A., Muxen, M., & Wilson, M. (1983). *Families: What makes them work?* Newbury Park, CA: Sage.

Parke, R. D. (1977). Socialization into child abuse: A social interactional perspective. In J. Tapp & F. Levine (Eds.), *Law, justice and the individual in society*. New York: Holt, Rinehart, & Winston.

Parke, R. D., & Collmer C. W. (1975). Child abuse: An interdisciplinary analysis. In Heatherington, M. E., Hagen, J. W., & Kron, R. (Eds.), *Review of child development research* (Vol. 5). Chicago: University of Chicago Press.

Purcell, E. I. (1979). *Child abuse: A controlled study of demographic data and family interaction patterns*. Ph.D. diss., Kansas State University, Manhattan, KS.

Rathbone-McCuan, E., & Pierce, R. (1978). Intergenerational treatment approach: An alternative model of working with abusive/neglectful and delinquent prone families. *Family Therapy* 5, 121–141.

Steele, B. F., & Pollock, D. (1988). A psychiatric study of parents who abuse infants and small children. In R. E. Helfer & C. H. Kempe (Eds.), *The battered child*. Chicago: University of Chicago Press.

Straus, M. A., Gelles, R. J., & Steinmetz, S. K. (1980). *Behind closed doors: Violence in the American family*. Garden City, NY: Doubleday.

Trad, P. V., & Pfetter, C. R. (1988). Treatment of an abused preadolescent and the role of parental self-reporting. *American Journal of Psychotherapy* 42, 124–134.

Trainor, C. (1984). *A description of officially reported adolescent maltreatment and its implications for policy and practice*. Denver: American Humane Association.

Wright, L. (1976). The "sick but slick" syndrome as a personality component of parents of battered children. *Journal of Clinical Psychology* 32, 41–45.

Wright, L. S. (1985). High school pot drug users and abusers. *Adolescence* 20, 853–861.

Young, L. (1964). *Wednesday's children: A study of child neglect and abuse*. New York: McGraw-Hill.

Ziefert, M. (1981). Abuse and neglect: The adolescent as the hidden victim. In K. C. Fuller (Ed.), *Social work with abused and neglected children: A manual of interdisciplinary practice*. New York: Free Press.

9 Models of Community Coordination in the Treatment of Abused and Neglected Children

Robert S. Nevin
Albert R. Roberts

Child abuse was the cause of death for 6-year-old Lisa Steinberg, who died in New York City on November 1, 1987. Her father, Joel Steinberg, was tried and convicted for her murder. It was a heartwrenching tragedy that became a major news story across the United States. Why did this particular case receive so much media attention? In large part, it was because this was a middle-class family; the father was an attorney, and the mother had been a children's book editor for a major publishing company. And while Lisa Steinberg's horrible murder is no longer a big news story, child abuse and neglect are stark realities for millions of children every single day—children whose tragic stories never made it to the evening news. Sadly, the Lisa Steinberg case is not an unusual or isolated occurrence.

The National Committee for Prevention of Child Abuse (NCPCA) (1989) has reported that fatalities from child abuse have numbered in the thousands during the latter part of the 1980s. In 1988, 1,225 child abuse and neglect fatalities were reported. Concurrent with the high child fatalities statistic is an enormously high incidence of child abuse. NCPCA states that over 2.2 million child abuse reports were filed in 1988, an increase of more than 3% from the year before. It is widely acknowledged than these figures are underestimates because so many instances of child abuse go unreported.

In the NCPCA report, the majority of the states reported increases in the number of multiproblem families in their caseloads. Parental substance abuse was cited as a dominant characteristic among the child protective services caseloads. In addition to alcohol abuse, cocaine and crack abuse were reported as being increasingly prevalent. With the increased complexity and severity of reported child protective cases, communities will need to develop a multi-treatment and multidisciplinary endeavor to treat these children and their families in a more coordinated and comprehensive manner. A related development is the greater need for out-of-home placements, which requires even more careful community delivery of treatment services.

In many communities, the treatment of children in instances of child abuse and neglect is not being addressed sufficiently. Due to the lack of communication and absence of formal coordinating mechanisms between the representatives of law, child protection services, medicine, education, mental health, substance abuse treatment, and essential community agencies, a very uneven delivery of services is provided to these children and their families in stress. Greater attention by professionals and communities will need to be placed on comprehensive treatment for both the child and the family.

This chapter examines (1) the influence of legislation for community cooperation, (2) the alternate choices communities have made to more adequately address the treatment needs of children, (3) the various conceptual models for community action, and (4) the expanding role of the criminal justice system in advocating treatment interventions that are in the best interests of the child victim. Special emphasis is placed in this chapter on the vulnerable populations in communities and the nature and responsiveness of the child protection, medical, and criminal justice systems.

LEGISLATION'S INFLUENCE ON THE DEVELOPMENT OF COMMUNITY SERVICES

In 1963, no state legislation existed to require the reporting of suspected child abuse. Today, each state has passed a reporting law. Many more reports are being made, and local communities have set up their own specialized child protection services (CPS). Despite these improvements, numerous professionals—physicians, nurses, teachers, social workers, child care workers, and police officers—fail to report more than half of the incidences of child maltreatment that they encounter (Besharov, 1985, pp. 21–22). The laws, in many instances, are very clear regarding the penalty for failure to report. But many of the state laws are vague about their purpose, such as when the child's "environment is injurious to his welfare," when the child "lacks proper parental care," or when the parents are "unfit to properly care for such child." Besharov notes:

Other statutes are blatantly tautological, calling for intervention when a child has been "abandoned or physically, mentally, or emotionally abused or neglected or sexually abused" without further defining these terms. In an attempt to be more specific, some recent statutes address the failure to provide "adequate" or "necessary" or "proper" food, clothing, shelter, medical care, education, supervision, or guardianship. But, again, these statutes do not define the key—but ambiguous—words: "adequate," "necessary," or "proper." (p. 23)

Besharov (1985, pp. 24–27) recommends that laws be changed to recognize two categories of seriously harmful parental behaviors: *immediately* harmful behavior and *cumulatively* harmful behavior. He identifies and provides definitions for 11 seriously harmful parental behaviors. These are (1) physical battering, (2) physical endangerment, (3) physical neglect, (4) medical neglect, (5) sexual neglect, (6) sexual exploitation, (7) emotional abuse, (8) developmental neglect, (9) improper ethical supervision, (10) educational neglect, and (11) abandonment. Laws should be redrafted so that the two major child protective interventions are authorized only when the parents have already engaged in abusive or neglectful behavior (Besharov, 1985). The most common child protective intervention is involuntary supervision of the home situation and provision of treatment services. Over the past 20 years, foster care, as the second major child protection intervention, has seen a dramatic increase. Besharov states that in utilizing the legal processes, far too many children have been removed from their homes and placed in foster care arrangements. CPS workers have often used this intervention, but have had no legal standards to guide their foster care decisions. Besharov recommends that

child protective laws should prohibit the removal of children from cumulatively harmful situations unless: the parents refuse to accept or cooperate with efforts to provide needed compensatory services; the child needs specific diagnostic or remedial services that are available only through residential care; foster care is used in response to an otherwise irreconcilable conflict between the parent and an adolescent child; or foster care is a planned precursor to the termination of parental rights and a subsequent adoption. (p. 27)

These recommended changes could minimize unreasonable expectations about what social workers and judges can accomplish. The result would be more manageable caseloads due to fewer unfounded reports being made, smaller numbers of children being placed in foster care (which may place them in a less desirable environment), and improvement of the reporting of and services to children in serious danger.

Koerin (1980) believes that the history of the child abuse laws over the past 20 years has reflected punishment versus treatment themes.

> The first child abuse reporting laws were protective of the professionals reporting suspected incidents and punitive in the measures dealing with abusive and neglecting families. The new laws included provisions for reporting incidents to law enforcement bodies, with an underlying stress on removal of children and prosecution of parents . . . between 1967–1970, most state laws were revised on the basis of research related to therapeutic work with families, on the recognition that a large majority of abuse and neglect cases are handled successfully by agencies without court action, and on the understanding of the increased damage to child and family that a punitive approach often has (especially when prosecution of parents fails and a child suffers from the parents' heightened hostility). (p. 546)

Koerin urges that more preventive programs be established to maintain family integrity by treating, rather than punishing, such families.

Gottesman (1981, pp. 42–43) has summarized the five key provisions of many state statutes:

1. A list of designated professionals who are required to report suspected abuse or neglect to the police department or Protective Services.
2. A section encouraging all other citizens to report suspected incidents of abuse and/or neglect.
3. A statement that all records maintained in accordance with the statute will be confidential.
4. Establishment of a central registry of names of child abusers.
5. A section that ensures that those who report in good faith cannot be successfully sued for libel and/or slander by the accused parent.

These reporting provisions are designed to make professionals more willing to perform their duty in reporting. As can be seen, the state laws have included various legal safeguards designed to protect the reporter from potential liability for filing a child abuse report.

Expanding on this analysis of state laws is Bremner's listing (1974, pp. 881–889) of 13 basic elements in the laws: (1) statement of purpose, (2) age limits for reportable children, (3) definition of reportable abuse, (4) nature of report, (5) who reports, (6) how reports are made, (7) to whom reports are made, (8) mandate to agency receiving report, (9) immunity, (10) waivers, (11) the penalty clause, (12) central registry, and (13) special clauses, such as those related to child abuse as a crime and those exempting cases of children receiving religious healing. As states have enacted reporting laws, the nature of the legislation largely influences and determines a community's response to a victim of child abuse and neglect. The clarity of these laws helps professionals cooperate more readily, whereas the lack of clarity in these laws impedes this process.

COLLABORATIVE STRATEGIES AND COMMUNITY PREVENTION PROGRAMS

Problems occur when the community's services do not seem to be as coordinated as they should. The characteristics of problems that occur in communities are identified by Cohen (1983, p. 84) as including unclear rules of interaction, lack of agreement on the system's purpose, ambiguous roles of professionals, an unclear and changing arena of action, and lack of mechanism for surfacing or resolving any of these dilemmas.

Model Programs

The multidisciplinary management of child abuse and neglect, especially the obtaining the mutual cooperation of various professionals and disciplines in a community, is very difficult to achieve. Numerous problems exist, according to Newberger (1975, pp. 16–18), and include

  lack of understanding by the members of one discipline of the objectives, standards, conceptual bases, and ethics of the others

  lack of effective communication from members of one discipline to members of another

  confusion as to which personnel can take what management responsibilities at what times

  kind of professional chauvinism about the domain of services to the child and the family

  too much work for everybody and a sense of hopelessness and despair in the face of overwhelming problems and unsympathetic colleagues

  institutional relationships that limit effective interprofessional contact

prevailing punitive attitudes and public policies about child
abuse

a lack of confidence and trust on the part of personnel from one
profession toward colleagues in the others

In many communities, effective interagency cooperation is a
very large challenge to address. The development of the public child
welfare system has resulted in a bureaucratization of the services.
What has resulted is a highly organized system of agencies of multi-
level authority, extremely specialized functions, elaborate rules gov-
erning eligibility, and rigid jurisdictional divisions.

In the development of model systems for the prevention and
control of child abuse and neglect, Newberger (1975, pp. 24–25) has
identified these essential attributes:

Underlying support through public policies that strengthen family life.

Incorporation of child advocacy and child development education.

Commitment of adequate resources to assure that a successful
program is possible.

A model program in a community needs to (1) see child abuse
as a symptom of family crisis, (2) recognize the values and traditions
of child rearing in its community, (3) maintain protection of information about people, (4) include citizen supervision of professional
policies and practices, (5) evaluate the outcomes of the services
provided, (6) maintain the family as the unit of practice and not
fragment health, social, and psychological problems into separately
provided services, (7) provide 24-hour services, (8) assure adequate
legal representation for all parties in any court proceeding relating to
child abuse, and (9) respond creatively to individual families problems with services suited to their needs (Newberger, 1975, pp. 24–25).

In a slightly different manner, Schmitt (1978, pp. 268–275) has
identified the needs in a community as a range of treatment options
that are essential for case management. A carefully planned combination of treatment options is the most useful means of intervening with
parents and children. These include (1) treatment interventions for
the parents (individual psychotherapy, lay therapy, marital therapy,
group therapy, and crisis hotlines), (2) treatment interventions for
children (therapeutic play schools, individual play therapy, and
group therapy), and (3) treatment interventions for families (crisis
nurseries, family therapy, family residential treatment, and parent–
child intervention).

Collaborative Strategies

Trohanis (1980, pp. 367–372) has presented an effective framework for designing a communications campaign and planning guide for building acceptance for a interagency cooperative child abuse and neglect program within a community. His guidelines to encourage community acceptance of efforts to build support and increase participation within the community collaborative planning and services include

> solidifying support for the communication effort within the program staff and agency before going public
>
> collaborating with other local programs
>
> building community awareness as a long-term proposition
>
> building up a community awareness program over time and not having it "shot all at once"
>
> identifying and using people with credibility in communications efforts to serve as spokespersons or chairpersons
>
> being straightforward in approaching controversial topics or issues
>
> striving for active participation and avoiding passivity wherever and whenever possible
>
> using a mix of delivery methods
>
> communicating the message simply, honestly, and concisely, with sensitivity to audiences; being positive in your approach and prompt in delivering services

The process by which interagency cooperation occurs is very complex. Factors that *facilitate* the occurrence include an interest in cooperation in one agency, a history of cooperation between the agencies, a mutual desire to decrease overlap in services, a scarcity of resources crucial to adequate delivery of services, funding reductions necessitating a more efficient operation, consumer or public demand for new services or improvements in old ones, and a gap in services. Various factors that *hinder* interagency cooperation include fears of changes in the level of funds or a loss of funds, lack of information about the other agency, a great distance between the agency and the project, ideological differences, competition for clients or other resources, incompatible goals, and a legal structure that may prevent changes needed for cooperation. Resources are available for developing a structure to build better cooperation through initial contact preparation, gaining access to and establishing the contact, maintaining and directing the interaction, interpersonal techniques, getting the commitment and expediting contacts, relating to role behavior needs, and keeping one's perspective. Key thoughts to keep in mind are cooperation doesn't happen overnight, your first effort may not work out, expect the unexpected, timing is important, and don't expect to reform your entire community!

CONCEPTUAL MODELS FOR COMMUNITY ACTION ON CHILD ABUSE AND NEGLECT

Four key conceptual models for community action on child abuse and neglect reports have been identified in the literature: child protection, medical, legal, and interdisciplinary models. Each of these approaches has a unique orientation to investigation, case planning, treatment, use of court action, and level of involvement in prevention activities.

Child Protection Model

Bremner (1974, p. 851) quotes the rationale for CPS work, provided by the American Humane Association, as an obligation of society to assure to every child the standard of care and protection below which the state does not wish its children to live. CPS should stand ready to act on behalf of children who are abused or neglected and should take suitable action in regard to those causing such neglect or abuse, or contributing to delinquency.

DeFrancis (1975) sees the need for CPS to do more work in prevention, casefinding, and examination and assessment of practices in dealing with an identified case of child abuse. He has succinctly expressed the CPS orientation as

> attempts to rehabilitate the home. . . for the most part, we are dealing . . . with acts resulting from parental incapacities and parental inabilities. These are situations where parents need to be helped to do a better job; they need to be helped to understand their responsibilities; they need to be taught to resolve the many difficulties which they find too difficult to cope with. . . . We are frequently dealing with parents who are so overwhelmed that they become unmotivated to seek help voluntarily. They become immobilized; and do not, themselves, voluntarily seek help. Help has to be brought to them. . . . This is the focus of child protective services! It reaches out to the family to offer services to remedy the situation; to offer the services which will make a good home out of a "bad home" and make "responsible" parents out of "less than responsible people." (pp. 6–7)

In order for CPS workers to function, Carroll (1978, pp. 83–85) states that appropriate professional qualities need to be present: knowledge of child development, understanding of abuse and neglect dynamics, knowledge of pertinent legal process and skill in court procedure, ability to take referral information, ability to communicate through writing, competence in interviewing techniques, and the ability to integrate areas of knowledge and skill.

In a critique of the child protection model, researchers (Powell et al., 1985) have found that "those who work most closely with children in care, especially the children with the most serious problems, are often the staff members with the least training." They recommend more diversified and specialized training and education in the practice and administration of programs for children and youth. Fryer et al. (1988) agree and state that "child protection has in this country been entrusted to a system staffed by dedicated, but seriously overworked personnel."

Medical Model

Newberger and Bourne (1978, 597) have seen medicine's expansion, after the formulation of the "battered child syndrome" and the related laws that were passed requiring the syndrome to be reported, as a basis for a new proper and legitimate concern. They define this process as "medicalization" of child abuse so that it is seen

> as the perception of behavior as a medical problem or illness and the mandating or licensing of the medical profession to provide some type of treatment for it. (p. 597)

Schmitt et al. (1978) developed a manual of guidelines for hospitals and clinics and identified the objectives of the health care facility in addressing child abuse and neglect (CA/N) as the following:

1. *Identify* those children seen in the hospital setting who have been abused and neglected.
2. Provide adequate *medical care* for the injuries sustained . . .
3. Carry out the legal obligations of *reporting* CA/N cases according to State Law.
4. Collect data in a comprehensive manner so that if these data are needed later in court as evidence, they will be adequate to *document the diagnosis* of CA/N.
5. *Remain therapeutic and helpful* to the parents of the abused child so that parents will remain receptive to long-term treatment. (I-1)

This manual (Schmitt et al., 1978, pp. I-1–IX-8) spells out very clearly for health care facilities the requirements for personnel, laboratory and x-ray facilities, policies, and procedures; responsibilities of nonmedical CA/N personnel; legal policies and procedures; emergency room protocols, hospitalized cases of physical abuse (physician's guidelines to management); incest and other family-related sexual abuse cases (physician's guidelines to management); failure to thrive secondary to nutritional deprivation (physician's guidelines to management); newborn nursery: identification of and intervention with high-risk families; child protection team protocols; and physical and behavioral indicators of child abuse and neglect.

Heindl et al. (1979, pp. 7–8) have articulated the reasons for nurses, as well as doctors, being involved with child abuse and neglect as (1) nurses work with and for children and their families, (2) the law mandates nurses' involvement and professional responsibility dictates it, and (3) nurses have a personal commitment to the health and well-being of children and their families. Some of the reasons that nurses have encountered difficulties in reporting or continuing to be involved in child abuse and neglect (pp. 38–40) are personal feelings (i.e., people don't want to get involved or parents have a right to treat children in any way they wish), relationship with the parents (i.e., fear that they may betray someone's trust in them), problems internal to the employing organization (i.e., a doctor or school principal may discourage reports), and difficulties with child protection services (i.e., they feel nothing will be done or they had a previous unfortunate experience when reporting). However, all health professionals need to report what they observe, for if no report is made, a child may continue to be in danger.

Legal Model

Newberger and Bourne (1978) have identified the "legalization" of child abuse and neglect cases as follows:

> . . . the legal response to child abuse was triggered by its medicalization. Child abuse reporting statutes codified a medical diagnosis into a legal framework which in many states defined official functions for courts. Immunity from civil liability was given to mandated reporters so long as reports were made in good faith; monetary penalties for failure to report were established; and familial and professional–client confidentiality privileges, except those involving attorneys, were abrogated. Professional autonomy for lawyers was established, and status and power accrued to legal institutions. (pp. 598–599)

The role of law enforcement has been developed in all of the 50 states. Each has identified for the police department some role in the investigation of child abuse and neglect cases.

Sometimes the law enforcement efforts may be complicated by jurisdictional issues, such as the variety of arrangements existing about the appropriateness of action in dealing with reports of child abuse and neglect situations on Indian reservations and military installations (Broadhurst & Knoeller, 1979, p. 8). Law enforcement officers encounter various difficulties in their work on child abuse and neglect complaints: (1) personal feelings of not wanting to get involved or interfering with the parent's rights, (2) distinguishing between appropriate discipline versus abuse in families, and (3) difficulties with CPS workers since they feel nothing will happen or be handled to their satisfaction. For a more detailed discussion of the role of the criminal justice system, see the following section, Child Abuse and the Criminal Justice System.

Interdisciplinary Model

Jenkins et al. (1979) see that a broad community response is necessary for child abuse and neglect situations because "no single individual, agency, or professional discipline has the necessary knowledge, skills or resources to provide all the services needed by families" (pp. 1–14). A coordinated community is better equipped to intervene with the most appropriate services and minimize duplication of services. A formal community coordinating committee should fulfill the following functions (p. 3):

> Encourage policies on the part of community agencies that demonstrate a capacity and willingness to work together.
> Survey and analyze needs and resources.
> Determine community awareness of needs and resources.
> Make program recommendations.
> Develop new community resources as needed.
> Review service delivery.
> Establish and/or facilitate multidisciplinary child abuse and neglect case consultation teams.
> Serve as advocates for children and families.

Representation on this committee will vary widely, depending upon the community. According to Osborn (1981), San Mateo County is one of the California counties that has a multidisciplinary team (MDT) to review all serious cases of abuse and neglect. This San Mateo MDT operates in the following manner:

> The MDT (within a Health and Welfare Department) meets on a regular basis to review new and ongoing cases of physical, sexual, and emotional abuse of children. The team includes a pediatrician, child psychiatrist, clinical psychologist, district attorney, public health nurse, day care and foster care placement specialist, and representatives of Children's Protective Services. Mandatory referrals for discussion and review include all cases of physical abuse to children under 2 years of age, serious physical abuse of a child of any age, sexual abuse and serious neglect, such as failure to thrive, which may endanger a child's life, safety, or health. (p. 291)

Key issues the MDT looks at include (1) the type of injury or neglect a child has sustained, (2) distress and problems of the parents, (3) the resources that could be used to allow the child to remain safely in the home, and/or (4) the factors that would safely allow a child to return to his home. The MDT process can bring to bear a collaborative influence on cases that can be influential, especially in the juvenile court.

All too often the role of mental health professionals and educators are overlooked. Lauer et al. (1979, pp. 29–31) report that a number of mental health facilities have established policies and procedures regarding child abuse and neglect as well as appointed a staff member to act as a liaison to the local CPS program. Some of the difficulties mental health professionals may have relate to personal and professional feelings about jeopardizing their therapist–client relationship, procedural problems internal to the agency, and their belief that nothing will be done even if they report. Many of these issues can be addressed and resolved as mental health professionals collaborate with the community CPS program.

Likewise, Broadhurst (1979, p. 6) states that the reasons educators get involved in child abuse and neglect are that they work with and for children, law and policy command educator involvement, professional responsibility demands it, and they have a deep sense of personal commitment to the children in their care. Some of the difficulties that schools need to overcome (pp. 38–39) include principals who may discourage teacher involvement by refusing to take teachers' reports seriously, central administrative staff who provide no backup to line staff, and superintendents who fail to provide to staff in-service training that informs them of their legal obligations. Barth (1985) has identified additional difficulties that private schools may have:

Most private schools are inexperienced in helping children who are economically disadvantaged, and these schools are largely unprepared to work with foster children and identify child abuse. At times, because of the pressures to please their paying customers, private schools may fail to report abuse to public authorities and instead attempt to handle such cases on their own. Similar pressures from educational consumers operate in all alternative schools and may block unpopular but needed assistance to children. (pp. 42–44)

Thus, the professionals in both mental health and education need to be included in the community's plan to provide comprehensive services.

CHILD ABUSE AND THE CRIMINAL JUSTICE SYSTEM

Personnel from the social service, medical, law enforcement, and legal professions need to develop mutual respect and work cooperatively to help victims of child abuse and child sexual abuse. Individuals who work with abused children can gain greater understanding of the responsibilities of the other disciplines through participation in multidisciplinary training sessions. It is also important for social workers, law enforcement officers, and prosecutors to conduct a joint investigation of child abuse cases.

Children who have been abused (physically and/or sexually) may be subjected to a double trauma: the victimization itself and a secondary victimization brought on by inexperience, insensitivity, and a lack of coordinated efforts from individuals in the criminal justice system. But contact with the justice system does not necessarily have to be traumatic. In this section the interaction between the child victim and the criminal justice system will be discussed, with emphasis on the ways in which interdisciplinary cooperation can and should be utilized to serve the best interests of the child.

Role of the Police

In every community, law enforcement is the agency most likely to be available—at any hour of the day, seven days a week—to respond to a report of child abuse or neglect. Therefore, it is vital that all police officers (not just juvenile officers) receive extensive training in identifying children who have been abused and in referring them to the appropriate agency (e.g., Child Protective Services). A police officer may be called to a home for a reason unrelated to child abuse, but if properly trained, the officer may be able to detect signs of previously unreported abuse.

Police departments should have a specialized child abuse or family abuse unit that is alerted to and investigates every reported abuse case in that community. It is particularly important that the police exhibit sensitivity when investigating a case of suspected child sexual abuse. To help them acquire the knowledge and skills to be effective interviewers, specialized training workshops on child sexual abuse should be developed that include the following components:

A film which describes the physical and psychological effects of sexual abuse on children and adolescents

Lecture and discussion, including the opportunity for small group discussion

Case studies that depict the different dynamics of sexual abuse, including an examination of different methods for interacting with the child and the family (Stone et al. 1984)

Some police specialists advocate using audiotapes and videotapes of actual interviews for the training sessions. If this technique is used, it is recommended that confidentiality be protected by disguising the identities of the involved parties.

In addition to receiving information on the dynamics of child abuse, police officers need training (including role playing) in interviewing children who have been sexually and/or physically abused (Graves & Sgroi, 1982; Stone et al., 1984). The location of the interview is an important factor in helping the child feel less anxious. Graves and Sgroi (1982) suggest conducting the interview in a quiet room in a neutral setting with comfortable chairs and no interruptions. The interview should not be conducted in the home if there is reason to suspect that the assault took place there or that a family member was involved in the abuse.

The child may feel more comfortable if the police interview is conducted in the presence of a person the child trusts, preferably a social worker or counselor. The third party should not be a family member, even if that individual is not suspected of being involved in the assault. Some relatives might attempt to suppress information (through verbal or nonverbal cues) that might incriminate another member of the family or a close friend. It is suggested that prior to the interview the police officer contact the supportive and trusted adult to gather background information regarding the abuse of the child. The officer can advise the other adult about the way in which the interview will be handled and establish ground rules for when the officer elicits comments or clarification from the adult during the interview (Graves & Sgroi, 1982).

Many communities have developed child abuse teams and task forces in an effort to create a coordinated service delivery system. One example of a successful coordinated approach was established in Tucson, Arizona, in the mid-1970s. Sadly, the impetus for creating the coordinated system was the death of a young boy. The boy was taken to a hospital emergency room after being beaten into a coma.

> He was treated and sent home with his mother. But a few days later . . . he was back, again severely battered. This time, the social workers released him to his grandparents. But a judge allowed the mother to take the little boy home as long as the mother's boyfriend, who had been doing the beating, was not allowed to be alone with him.
>
> The next day . . . the mother left the house, and the boyfriend killed the child. The boyfriend was charged with murder but contended that the child fell out of his high chair. At the trial, the judge instructed the jury to acquit the boyfriend because the prosecution could not prove the child died from a beating. Had there been a more complete investigation, which could have been accomplished through better coordination among different agencies, a conviction would have resulted. (Bernstein. 1978, p. 59)

Before the development of a coordinated approach in Tucson, the police, social workers, and physicians were distrustful of one another. Rather than sharing information and coordinating services, each group maintained its own records using "confidentiality" as an excuse for refusing to work together. The obvious tragedy of the above-cited case and numerous others is that innocent children may be killed when professionals, who should be maintaining open lines of communication, refuse to work cooperatively.

The Tucson police department began its child abuse unit in 1976 with one specially trained law enforcement officer. Following the development of the coordinated system, physicians who suspected that a child had been abused contacted the police child abuse unit and the social worker simultaneously, and both became involved in the case. A police officer from the child abuse unit trains other police officers in the proper way to respond and communicate in suspected child abuse cases. He also speaks to medical and nursing students about the need for a coordinated approach (Bernstein, 1978).

One reason for social workers' reluctance to share information on abuse cases with the police was their belief that the police were mainly interested in arresting the parents rather than being concerned about the welfare of the child. In Tucson during an 18-month period (after the coordinated system was underway) there were nearly 400 abuse cases and only 15 prosecutions. In most of the cases the abuser agreed to participate in counseling as an alternative to arrest (Bernstein, 1978). Thus, if the situation in Tucson is representative of other cities, social workers need not be concerned that coordination with the police will result in too many abusive parents being prosecuted while too few parents receive counseling.

Guardians Ad Litem

Most cases of child abuse that go to court are heard in the juvenile court. Generally, the judge appoints a guardian ad litem to represent the best interests of the child. (The Child Abuse Prevention and Treatment Act of 1974 requires states to assign a guardian ad litem in order to receive federal monies.) This individual's responsibilities include counseling the child, providing information on legal procedures, and accompanying him or her to court and to a medical examination (if it is needed). The guardian ad litem is also expected to evaluate the case and may offer recommendations to the court. Opinions vary on whether this role should be filled by an attorney or a layperson. The obvious advantage of using attorneys is their knowledge of the legal process. But there are drawbacks as well, the most significant being (1) prosecutors who serve in this capacity may be insensitive to the needs of the abused children and place emphasis on obtaining a conviction and harsh sentence at the expense of the children's feelings and needs and (2) many attorneys are too busy to devote sufficient time to working with child victims (Whitcomb et al. 1985).

A productive arrangement has been established in Des Moines, Iowa, and Orlando, Florida, in which guardian ad litem attorneys are paired with lay advocates. The lay assistant may be a professional social worker (as occurs in Des Moines) or a trained volunteer (as in Orlando). In these two cities, the attorney's attention is devoted solely to legal issues, while the advocate's efforts are spent in the more time-consuming role of becoming a friend to the child, explaining the procedures, and doing case investigation (Whitcomb et al., 1985).

Prosecuting Attorneys

There is a need for improved collaboration between attorneys and personnel working in the child protective services field. Child protective workers are testifying in court with greater frequency and with less time for preparation. Attorneys can be of assistance in advising child protective workers on collecting and presenting to the court "competent evidence" to justify their recommended interventions. Barth and Sullivan (1985) use the term "competent evidence" to refer to "evidence that is court admissible, reasonably reliable and valid, and convincing" (p. 130).

Child protective services workers may also need to consult with an attorney regarding the following types of issues:

> whether a child can legally be removed from home
> the use of voluntary parent–agency service agreements
> whether a court proceeding should be initiated
> relations with the other attorneys in the proceedings
> (Horowitz & Davidson, 1981, p. 396)

There are also areas in which prosecutors need to seek the advice of social workers and other mental health professionals, for example, conducting interviews with child victims, choosing potential jurors, and preparing statements of introduction and summation to the court (Whitcomb, 1986). Finally, all attorneys who prosecute cases of child abuse should receive training in such areas as child psychology and family dynamics as well as case precedent and state law (Whitcomb et al., 1985).

Reducing the Stress of Multiple Interviews

The Attorney General's Task Force on Family Violence (1984) has reported that, during the course of criminal justice proceedings, a child who has been sexually abused has an average of 12 investigative interviews. Therapists, attorneys, judges, and police officers agree that being required to discuss the events so many times may be one of the most upsetting aspects of the entire ordeal (Whitcomb et al., 1985). There are several ways in which the lengthy interview process can be consolidated:

1. By conducting some form of "joint" interview among two or more of the agencies involved.
2. By assigning specialists within each agency, so there is only one interviewer per agency.
3. By videotaping the child's first statement.
4. By eliminating the need for the child to appear at one or more of the formal proceedings.

  5. By coordinating the juvenile and criminal court proceedings
      (Whitcomb et al., 1985, p. 100).

The following are two examples of interagency cooperation that
have been successful in reducing the number of times a child needs
to be interviewed. In Seattle, Washington, staff from all involved
agencies have weekly meetings to examine the status of their cases.
To reduce the number of interviews, one person is selected to interview the child; the others view the interaction from behind a one-
way mirror (Whitcomb, 1982). In Huntsville, Alabama, all cases of
child sexual abuse are acted on in one building, known as the Children's Advocacy Center, which has offices for representatives from
the involved agencies. Interviews are handled by a team consisting
of a prosecutor, a police officer, and a child protective worker (Whitcomb et al., 1985).

Court Proceedings

Efforts are underway in all parts of the United States to alleviate
stress for child victims when the case against the abuser goes to
court. Changes in the proceedings focus on ways in which victims
can be spared the stress of testifying personally in court. Two of the
primary areas in which statutory reforms are being made are reducing
the number of times a child provides testimony (e.g., permitting
hearsay) and recording the child's recollections on videotape.

In addition to the above-mentioned reforms, there are techniques to reduce children's anxiety prior to giving testimony that do
not require statutory reform, such as

> enhancing the child's communication skills through dolls, artwork,
> and simplified vocabulary
> modifying the physical environment—providing a small chair for
> the child, having the judge sit on a level with the child and
> wear business clothes instead of a judicial robe
> preparing child victims before their courtroom appearances—
> briefing them on the roles of people in the courtroom, intro-
> ducing them to the judge, taking them for a tour of the
> courtroom, and allowing them to sit in the witness chair and
> speak into the microphone (Whitcomb, 1986, p. 5)

Judges should take on a more active role when hearing a child's
testimony. Whitcomb et al. (1985) offer the following recommendations to enhance the involvement of judges:

  1. Advise the attorneys before the trial on appropriate behavior, e.g.,

caution them to maintain a specific distance from the witness chair; instruct them not to talk in a loud or angry tone of voice.

2. Be prepared for questions that may be intimidating to the victim.
3. Be observant of a child becoming embarrassed or upset and if the child's emotional state appears to be distorting the testimony, be prepared to call a recess to enable the victim to calm down.
4. Grant a continuance only if it is urgently needed.
5. Ensure that every child is accompanied by a supportive adult friend.

The above-mentioned issue of a child having a supportive adult nearby in court would seem to be a matter of common sense, but in fact, it may be difficult to carry out. In an effort to lessen the trauma of the court proceeding, the juvenile court may prevent anyone who has not witnessed the crime from being in court. Although the intentions are good, the result may be increased stress for the child, who must endure the proceeding without the benefit of reassurance from a supportive adult (Rogers, 1982).

In cases of child sexual abuse, the National Legal Resource Center for Child Advocacy and Protection (1981) recommends coordination of the proceedings scheduled by the criminal and juvenile courts. The child may become confused if the two courts hear the case at the same time and make conflicting rulings. It is not uncommon for the judge in the criminal court to be unaware that the same case is simultaneously being heard in the juvenile court and vice versa. Testimony being provided by the child victim should be made available to both courts.

To expedite scheduling of trials involving victims of child abuse, the Attorney General's Task Force on Family Violence (1984) has recommended having a special docket for cases of domestic violence (which would also handle elder and spouse abuse). The defendant's lawyer may try to delay the proceedings in the hope that the child will forget the details of the victimization. Numerous postponements are very stressful for the child and should be avoided.

The stressfulness of requiring a child to repeatedly describe the events surrounding the victimization has already been discussed. In some jurisdictions, the child is required to testify at the preliminary hearing, the grand jury proceeding, and the trial. A child's anxiety at testifying during all of these proceedings could be alleviated if judges permitted hearsay evidence prior to the trial. Allowing hearsay at the pretrial stages would result in fewer children being required to give formal testimony because a considerable number of cases never come to trial; many cases are dismissed or handled through pleas (Rogers, 1982).

Videotaping

Videotaping a sexually abused child's recollections soon after the assault has been endorsed by victim advocates as an effective means of lessening the trauma of testifying in court. This technique has been approved by the Attorney General's Task Force on Family Violence (1984) and by the National Conference of the Judiciary on the Rights of Victims of Crime (U.S. Department of Justice, 1983). In at least 14 states, videotaped testimony is admissible in court. It is recommended that all videotapes of children's statements be placed under "protective orders" to ensure privacy (Whitcomb et al., 1985).

There are many advantages to videotaping the child's first formal statement following the victimization.

> The child's memory may fade over time.
>
> In intrafamilial cases, family members often pressure children to retract their stories, thereby sapping their strength and weakening their testimony as their cases progress.
>
> Videotaping can help to reduce the number of interviews children must give, thereby allowing them to get on with their lives and minimizing the prospect of testimony that is so well-rehearsed that it loses credibility.
>
> In states that permit hearsay evidence at the preliminary hearing or before the grand jury, the video could preclude the need for the child's live testimony at these proceedings.
>
> Many prosecutors have observed an unanticipated, yet welcome side effect of videotaping: . . . it tends to prompt a guilty plea when viewed by defendants and their attorneys. (Whitcomb et al., 1985)

It should be pointed out, however, that a videotaped statement does not take the place of the victim's being cross-examined during the trial. In addition, the judge may determine that the video is not admissible in court. The skill of the interviewer appears to be the key element in the decision on admissibility. Interviewers need training in eliciting the facts of the case without resorting to using leading questions or being too encouraging (Whitcomb et al., 1985).

It is important to distinguish between videotaping of the first formal statement (as described above), which is generally recommended, and videotaping a deposition, which is considered to have too many drawbacks. In taping a deposition, the victim and the defendant are brought together in a small room—a much more confined space than in a courtroom. Furthermore, "the judge may not be there to monitor the behavior of the defendant or his counsel, and victim advocates may not be permitted to attend" (Whitcomb, 1986,

p. 4). In some jurisdictions, a finding of "emotional trauma" is necessary before the judge will permit a videotape to substitute for live testimony. Thus, the victim may be required to undergo a series of medical and/or psychiatric tests (Whitcomb et al., 1985; Whitcomb, 1986).

CONCLUSION

There has been an increased awareness among professionals of the need for early intervention, treatment planning, and provision of services to physically and sexually abused children. Cohn and Daro (1987), in their critique of the treatment approaches of the last decade, said these approaches could have been more successful had they emphasized collaborative interagency longstanding treatment relationships rather than time-limited singular agency interaction. An improvement in child welfare services has occurred with the growing emphasis on diagnosis and consultation by multidisciplinary teams, law enforcement agencies, prosecutor's offices, and the courts. Many of the problems of the past—lack of planning, lack of interagency coordination, fragmentation, duplication of services, and failure to effectively intervene on behalf of the abused child—are gradually being remedied. In this regard, model collaborative interagency efforts, including community strategies, multidisciplinary teams, specialized training models, interagency consultation and collaboration, and improved coordination between social workers and criminal justice professionals, offer much promise for successfully intervening on behalf of abused children.

REFERENCES

Attorney General's Task Force on Family Violence (1984). *Final report.* Washington, DC: US Department of Justice.

Barth, R. P. (1985). Collaboration between child welfare and school social work services. *Social Work in Education,* 8(1), 32–47.

Barth, R. F., Ash, J. R., & Hacking, S. (1986). Identifying, screening and engaging high-risk clients in private non-profit child abuse prevention programs. *Child Abuse and Neglect,* 10, 99–109.

Barth, R. P., & Sullivan, R. (1985). Collecting competent evidence in behalf of children. *Social Work,* 30(2), 130–136.

Bassuk, E. L., Fox, S. S., & Prendergast, K. J. (1983). *Behavioral emergencies: A field guide for EMTS and paramedics.* Boston: Little, Brown and Company.

Baxter, A. (1985). *Techniques for dealing with child abuse*. Springfield, IL: Charles C Thomas.

Bernstein, D. (1978, November). Police vs. child abuse: Protecting the victim comes first. *Police Magazine*, 59-63.

Besharov, D. (1978). *Child sexual abuse: Incest, assault and sexual exploitation*. In Kirschner Associates, Inc. (eds.), *Child abuse and neglect: The user manual series*. Washington, DC: National Center on Child Abuse and Neglect, USDHEW.

Besharov, D. J. (1985). Right versus rights: The dilemma of child protection. *Public Welfare*, 19-27.

Billingsley, A., & Giovannoni, J. M. (1972). *Children of the storm: Black children and American child welfare*. New York: Harcourt, Brace, Jovanovich.

Bockman, H. R., & Carroll, C. A. (1978). The law enforcement's role in evaluation. In B. D. Schmitt, (Eds.), *The child protection team handbook: A multidisciplinary approach to managing child abuse and neglect*. New York: Garland STPM Press.

Borgman, R., Edmunds, M., & MacDicken, R. (1979). Crisis intervention: A manual for child protective workers. In Kirschner Associates, Inc. (Eds.), *Child abuse and neglect: The user manual series*. Washington, DC: National Center on Child Abuse and Neglect, USDHEW.

Bremner, R. H. (Ed.). (1974). *Children and youth in America: A documentary history* (Vol. 3). Cambridge, MA: Harvard University Press.

Broadhurst, D. (1979). The educator's role in the prevention and treatment of child abuse and neglect. In Kirschner Associates, Inc. (Eds.), *Child abuse and neglect: The user manual series*. Washington, DC: National Center on Child Abuse and Neglect, USDHEW.

Broadhurst, D., & Knoeller, J. (1979). The role of law enforcement in the prevention and treatment of child abuse and neglect. In Kirschner Associates, Inc. (Eds.), *Child abuse and neglect: The user manual series*. Washington, DC: National Center on Child Abuse and Neglect, USDHEW.

Byles, J. (1985). Problems in interagency collaboration: Lessons from a project that failed. *Child Abuse and Neglect*, 9, 549–554.

Carroll, C. A. (1978a). The protective service social worker's role in treatment. In B. D. Schmitt (Ed.), *The child protection team handbook: A multidisciplinary approach to managing child abuse and neglect*. New York: Garland STPM Press.

Carroll, C. A. (1978b). The social worker's evaluation. In B. D. Schmitt (Ed.), *The child protection team handbook: A multidisciplinary approach to managing child abuse and neglect*. New York: Garland STPM Press.

Carroll, C. A., & Schmitt, B. D. (1978). Improving community treatment services. In B. D. Schmitt (Ed.), *The child protection team handbook: A multidisciplinary approach to managing child abuse and neglect*. New York: Garland STPM Press.

Child Abuse Prevention and Treatment Act (1974). P.L. 93-247.

Close, M. M. (1983). Child welfare and people of color: Denial of equal access. *Social Research & Abstracts*, 19(4), 13–20.

Cohen, B. J. (1983). Coordination strategies in complex service delivery systems. *Administration in Social Work*, 4(3), 83–87.

Cohn, A. H., & Daro, D. (1987). Is treatment too late: What ten years of evaluative research tells us. *Child Abuse & Neglect*, 2, 433–442.

Compher, J. V. (1984). The case conference revisited: A systems view. *Child Welfare*, 63(5), 411–417.

Craft, J. L., & Clarkson, C. D. (1985)). Case disposition recommendations of attorneys and social workers in child abuse investigations. *Child Abuse & Neglect*, 9, 165–174.

DeFrancis, V. (1975). Child protection—a comprehensive, coordinated process. In The American Humane Association, Children's Divison (Eds.), *Fourth national symposium on child abuse*. Denver: AHA.

Deutsch, F. (1983). *Child services on behalf of children*. Monterrey, CA: Brooks/Cole Publishing Company.

Duquette, D. N. (1981). The expert witness in child abuse and neglect: An interdisciplinary process. *Child Abuse & Neglect*, 5, 325–334.

Etherington, C., & Stephens, K. (1984). The police officer and the sexually abused child: Developing an approach to a critical problem, *The Police Chief*, 1(2), 44–45.

Fisher, N. (1979). Reaching out: The volunteer in child abuse and neglect programs. In Kirschner Associates, Inc. (Eds.), *Child abuse and neglect: The user manual series*. Washington, DC: National Center on Child Abuse and Neglect, USDHEW.

Frank, M. (Ed.). (1983). *Child care: Emerging legal issues*. New York: The Haworth Press.

Fraser, B. G. (1978). The court's role. In B. D. Schmitt (Ed.), *The child protection team handbook: A multidisciplinary approach to managing child abuse and neglect*. New York: Garland STPM Press.

Frederickson, H., & Mulligan, R. A. (1972). *The child and his welfare*. San Francisco: W. H. Freeman and Company.

Fryer, G. E., Poland, J. E., Bross, D. C., & Krugman, R. D. (1988). The child protective service worker: A profile of needs, attitudes, and utilization of professional resources. *Child Abuse & Neglect*, 12, 481–490.

Gabay, G. N. M. (1983). Neither adversaries nor co-conspirators: Creating a dialogue between attorneys and child care professionals. In M. Frank (Ed.), *Child care: Emerging legal issues*. New York: The Haworth Press.

Gottesman, R. (1981). *The child and the law*. St. Paul, MN: West Publishing Co.

Graves, P., & Sgroi, S. (1982). Law enforcement and child sexual abuse. In S. M. Sgroi (Ed.), *Handbook of clinical intervention in child sexual abuse* (pp. 309–333). Lexington, MA: Lexington Books.

Grosz, C. A., & Lenherr, M. R. (1978). The coordinator's role in evaluation, In B. D. Schmitt (Ed.), *The child protection team handbook: A multidisciplinary approach to managing child abuse and neglect*. New York: Garland STPM Press.

Haeuser, A. A. (Ed.). (1978). *Interdisciplinary glossary on child abuse and neglect: Legal, medical, social work teams, Midwest Parent-Child Wel-*

fare Resource Center at the University of Wisconsin-Milwaukee. Washington DC: National Center on Child Abuse and Neglect, OHDS, USDHEW.

Heindl, C., Krall, C., & Salus, M. (1979). The nurse's role in the prevention and treatment of child abuse and neglect. In Kirschner Associates, Inc. (Eds.), *Child abuse and neglect: The user manual series.* Washington, DC: National Center on Child Abuse and Neglect, USDHEW.

Hochstadt, N., & Harwicke, N. (1985). How effective is the multidisciplinary approach? A follow-up study. *Child Abuse & Neglect, 9,* 365–372.

Horowitz, R. (1983). Policy: Child welfare: An evolving legal basis. In M. Frank (Ed.), *Child care: Emerging legal issues.* New York: The Haworth Press.

Horowitz, R., & Davidson, H. (1981). Improving the legal response of child protective agencies, *Vermont Law Review, 6,* 381–402.

Irusete-Montes, A. M., & Montes, F. (1988). Court-ordered vs. voluntary treatment of abusive and neglectful parents. *Child Abuse & Neglect, 12,* 33–39.

Jenkins, J., MacDicken, R., & Ormsby, N. (1979). A community approach: The child protection coordinating committee. In Kirschner Associates, Inc. (Eds.), *Child abuse and neglect: The user manual series.* Washington, DC: National Center on Child Abuse and Neglect, USDHEW.

Kadushin, A. (1980). *Child welfare services* (3rd ed.), New York: Macmillan Publishing Co.

Koerin, B. (1980). Child abuse and neglect: Changing policies and perspectives. *Child Welfare, 59(9),* 542–50.

Krieger, M., & Robbins, J. (1985). The adolescent incest victim and the judicial system. *American Journal of Orthopsychiatry, 55,* 419–425.

Lauer, J., Lourie, I., & Salus, M. (1979). The role of the mental health professional in the prevention and treatment of child abuse and neglect. In Kirschner Associates, Inc. (Eds.), *Child abuse and neglect: The user manual series.* Washington, DC: National Center on Child Abuse and Neglect, USDHEW.

LeBlang, T. (1979). The family stress consultation team: An Illinois approach to protective services. *Child Welfare, 58(9),* 597–603.

Martin, H. (1979). Treatment for abused & neglected children. In Kirschner Associates, Inc. (Eds.), *Child abuse and neglect: The user manual series.* Washington DC: National Center on Child Abuse and Neglect, USDHEW.

Morgan, G. G. (1983). Practical techniques for change. In M. Frank (Ed.), *Child care: Emerging legal issues.* New York: The Haworth Press.

National Committee for Prevention of Child Abuse (1989, April). *NCPCA memorandum.* Chicago: NCPCA.

National Legal Resource Center for Child Advocacy and Protection. (1981). *Innovations in the prosecution of child sexual abuse* (J. Bulkey, Ed.), Washington, DC: American Bar Association.

Newberger, E. H. (1975). Interdisciplinary management of child abuse: Problems and progress. In The American Humane Association, Children's Division. *Fourth National Symposium on Child Abuse.* Denver: AHA.

Newberger, E., & Bourne, R. (1978). The medicalization and legalization of child abuse. *American Journal of Orthopsychiatry*, 48(4), 593–607.

Nightingale, N., & Walker, E. (1986). Identification and reporting of child maltreatment by head start personnel: Attitudes and experiences. *Child Abuse & Neglect*, 10, 191–199.

Osborn, P. (1981). A model plan for coordination and management of child abuse services. *Child Abuse & Neglect*, 5, 287–297.

Palmer, S. E. (1989). Mediation in child protection cases: An alternative to the adversary system. *Child Welfare*, 68(1).

Paul, J. L. (1977). Advocacy program development. In J. Paul, G. Neufeld, & J. Pelosi (Eds.), *Child advocacy within the system*. Syracuse, NY: Syracuse University Press.

Paul, J., Neufeld, G., & Pelosi, J. (Eds.), (1977). *Child advocacy within the system*, Syracuse, NY: Syracuse University Press.

Pelosi, J. W., & Paul, J. L. (1977). Advocacy in home, school, and community: child advocacy system design. In J. Paul, G. Neufeld, & J. Pelosi (Eds.), *Child advocacy within the system*. Syracuse, NY: Syracuse University Press.

Pelosi, J. W., Taylor, D., & Paul, J. L. (1977). Child advocacy in government: a statewide program. In J. Paul, G. Nufeld, & J. Pelosi (Eds.), *Child advocacy within the system*. Syracuse, NY: Syracuse University Press.

Powell, N., Manburg, A., & Peck, J. T. (1985). Professional growth through partnership between a national organization and a university. *Child Welfare*, 64(2), 165–172.

Riddle, J. I., & King, L. (1977). Advocacy in an institution. In J. Paul, G. Neufeld, & J. Pelosi (Eds.), *Child advocacy within the system*. Syracuse, NY: Syracuse University Press.

Rogers, C. (1982). Child sexual abuse and the courts: Preliminary findings. *Journal of Social Work and Human Sexuality*, 1, 145-153.

Schmitt, B. (Ed.), (1978). *The child protection team handbook: A multidisciplinary approach to managing child abuse and neglect*. New York: Garland STPM Press.

Scmitt, B., et al, (1978). Guidelines for the hospital and clinic: Management of child abuse and neglect. In Kirschner Associates, Inc. (Eds.), *Child abuse and neglect: The user manual series*. Washington, DC: National Center on Child Abuse and Neglect. USDHEW.

Selinske, J. (1983). Practice: Models for implementing child abuse and neglect legislation, *Child care: Emerging legal issues*. New York: The Haworth Press.

Selinske, J. (1983). Protecting CPS clients and workers, *Public Welfare*, 4(3), 30–35.

Shay, S. (1980). Community council for child abuse prevention. In C. Henry Kempe & Ray E. Helfer (Eds.), *The battered child* (3rd ed., pp. 330–346). Chicago: University of Chicago Press.

Shireman, J., Miller, B., & Brown, H. (1981). Child welfare workers: Police and child placement. *Child Welfare*, 60(6), 413–422.

Skaff, L. F. (1988). Child maltreatment coordinating committees for effective service delivery. *Child Welfare*, 67(3), 217–230.

Stehno, S. M. (1986). Family-centered child welfare services: New life for a historic idea. *Child Welfare*, 65(3), 231–240.

Stone, L., Tyler, R., & Mead, J. (1984). Law enforcement officers as investigators and therapists in child sexual abuse: A training model. *Child Abuse and Neglect*, 8, 75–82.

Tower, C. C. (Ed.), (1984). *Questions teachers ask about legal aspects of reporting child abuse and neglect*. Washington, DC: National Education Association.

Trohanis, P. (1980). Developing community acceptance of programs for children, *Child Welfare*, 59(6), 365–373.

U.S. Department of Justice, National Institute of Justice. (1983). Statements of recommended judicial practices. Adopted by the National Conference of the Judiciary on the Rights of Victims of Crime. Reno, Nevada.

Valentine, D., Acuff, D., Freeman, M., & Andreas, T. (1984). Defining child maltreatment: A multidisciplinary overview, *Child Welfare*, 63(6), 497–509

Vinokur-Kaplan, D., & Hartman, A. (1986). A national profile of child welfare workers and supervisors. *Child Welfare*, 65(4), 323–335.

Whitcomb, D. (1982). *Assisting child victims of sexual abuse*. Washington, DC: U.S. Department of Justice, National Institute of Justice.

Whitcomb, D. (1986). Prosecuting child sexual abuse: New approaches. *NIJ Reports*, 2–6.

Whitcomb, D., Shapiro, E., & Stellwagen, L. (1985). *When the victim is a child: Issues for judges and prosecutors*. Washington, DC: U.S. Department of Justice, National Institute of Justice.

Wolfe, D., MacPherson, T., Blount, R., & Wolfe, V. (1986). Evaluation of a brief intervention for educating school children in awareness of physical and sexual abuse. *Child Abuse & Neglect*, 10, 85–92.

III Treatment of Child Sexual Abuse

10 A Cognitive-Behavioral Approach to the Treatment of Incestuous Families

Barry W. McCarthy

The topic of incest is highly emotionally charged for both professionals and the lay public. Incest is an immensely complex area, involving legal, social service, educational, and public health concerns as well as mental health issues. For professionals in the field, incest raises profound emotional and personal questions about sexuality, family, and ethics. State reporting laws and community outrage have increased professionals' concerns about malpractice, court testimony, and/or adverse media attention. Dealing with incestuous families requires extra professional time and attention. The net effect is for clinicians to avoid working with the complex problem of incest because of personal and emotional factors, concern over the legal and community complications, and fear that it is an unsolvable problem. Treating incestuous families is difficult and takes special therapeutic training and skill. Still, it can be very rewarding in terms of helping families make significant positive changes in the individual members and family system.

Most of our scientific knowledge about incest and most of what is written in the lay and professional literature concerns adult survivors of incest (Courtois & Sprei, 1988). Adult survivors are typically females in their 20s or 30s who seek therapy for a different mental health problem—alcoholism, eating disorder, agoraphobia, depression, sexual aversion, or inhibited sexual desire. In the course of therapy the incest is uncovered as a "shameful secret." Survivors explore the abuse in individual or couple therapy and, increasingly, in "adult survivors of incest" group therapy or self-help groups.

McCarthy (1986) has observed that confusing, guilt-inducing, negative, and/or traumatic experiences with sexuality are an almost universal experience for both females and males. The category of sexual trauma refers to child sexual abuse, rape, and incest as well as guilt over masturbation, being sexually humiliated or rejected, having a sexually transmitted disease or unwanted pregnancy, being sexually harassed, being exhibited to or peeped on. Incest is perhaps the most negative and traumatic of these sexual experiences.

Finkelhor (1984) estimates that approximately one in three girls and one in seven boys has experienced sexual abuse. A working definition of child sexual abuse is inappropriate sexual contact between a child (up to age 16) and an adult or adolescent at least five years older where the contact is to satisfy the sexual needs of the perpetrator. Most child sexual abuse does not involve intercourse or physical force, and the perpetrator is someone the child knows rather than a stranger.

Perhaps half of the abuse of female children is "hands off," that is, exhibitionism, voyeurism, obscene phone calls, sexual harrassment. "Hands-on" abuse is more traumatic and involves holding, fondling, and/or caressing as well as manual, oral, anal, or vaginal stimulation and/or penetration. The more invasive, the more genitally focused, the more physically forceful, and the more orgasm-oriented the abuse, the greater the trauma (McCarthy, 1986).

Perhaps the best working definition of incest is child sexual abuse with a member of the living-together or close family system. This would include uncles, live-in boyfriends, brothers, grandfathers, stepbrothers, fathers, and stepfathers. Incest does not include family friends, distant cousins, or authority figures, for example, teachers, ministers, or boy scout leaders. Less than 20% of reported incest cases involve father–daughter contact, although this is the most traumatic since it involves such a direct attack on the family bond of trust (Herman, 1981). Stepfather–stepdaughter incest accounts for another 15 to 20%. The remaining 65% of cases involve brothers, uncles, stepbrothers, grandfathers, and live-in boyfriends. Most cases of incest involve neither physical violence nor intercourse. The sexual interaction is often nonverbal and most often involves holding, caressing, exhibiting, viewing, and in some cases manual, rubbing, oral, or anal stimulation. The most traumatic form of incest is ongoing father–daughter intercourse, including physical violence, subjecting the child to emotional blackmail or threats, and burdening the child with carrying the secret and the guilt (Maltz & Holman, 1987).

There is growing evidence that boys as well as girls are the victims of incest (Finkelhor, 1984). Although aunts, older sisters, stepmothers, or biological mothers can act out sexually against boys, the evidence is that in at least 80% of the cases the perpetrator is a male. The greatest trauma occurs when the relationship is between a biological father and son, involves anal or oral stimulation to orgasm, employs force, and burdens the boy with the blame and the secret. When a male child is sexually abused by another male, there is additional trauma because the offense breaks the same-sex (homosexual) taboo. Additionally, the boy feels that the boundary of his control over his body and sense of masculinity has been breached. Male children are more likely to be coerced into more orgasm-oriented activity such as anal intercourse and fellatio, and are more likely to be subjected to physical violence and verbal humiliation. Boys are less likely than girls to report sexual abuse incidents or to use counseling resources, and they cope less well (Finkelhor, 1984).

What allows incest to occur and continue in a family? Although there are many patterns of incest as a multicausal phenomena (Trepper & Barrett, 1986), the central dynamic to its maintenance is secrecy. As long as incest is secret, the perpetrator can deny it and the behavior can and does continue. Breaking secrecy is the central ingredient in the successful therapeutic treatment of the incest family. Maintaining open channels of communication is the reason that the treated incest family has an extremely low recidivism rate (Barrett et al., 1986).

Successful treatment of the incest family is possible and can innoculate against later sexual trauma and other mental health problems. This chapter focuses on a cognitive–behavioral treatment model for the intact incest family when the incest has just come to light. The model borrows heavily from work at the Masters and Johnson Institute (Schwartz & Masters, 1984) and the work of Trepper and Traicoff (1983). It is at major variance with the traditional therapeutic models for treating incest (Meiselman, 1978) and quite different from the legal/prosecutorial approaches (Sgroi, 1982).

A COGNITIVE–BEHAVIORAL TREATMENT FOR INCEST FAMILIES

The major guidelines of the cognitive–behavioral approach to treating incest families are

1. The incest is viewed as a family problem in terms of asssessment and intervention.
2. The decision of whether to keep the marriage and family together is a husband–wife decision, not to be made by the children, a social service agency, or the court system.

3. The approach is therapeutic, not legal or adversarial.
4. The perpetrator leaves the house, not the child.
5. The therapy is time-limited, with sessions lasting 4 to 12 months. The family participates in a 2-year follow-up.
6. There is a specific, yet flexible, therapeutic structure and plan.
7. The preferred mode is a male–female therapy team.
8. The key concept is open channels of communication so that the incest cannot be repeated.
9. Each person in the family needs to assume responsibility for his or her behavior, including sexual behavior.
10. Restoring the husband–wife bond of respect, trust, and intimacy is a major goal of therapy.
11. The family system is to be restructured to prevent inappropriate sexual behavior and to promote the well-being of each family member.

The cognitive–behavioral approach to sexuality (Leiblum & Rosen, 1989) involves a present and future time orientation, adopting positive and appropriate cognitions concerning sexuality, a psychoeducational model for teaching communication and assertiveness skills, developing clear and specific agreements among family members, positive motivation and reinforcement for behavior change, negative contingencies for inappropriate behavior, and a commitment to try to help clients reach their stated goals.

These concepts will be illustrated in a more concrete manner using the following extensive clinical case example.

The Jones Family

A family does not come into treatment declaring themselves an incest family. Typically, a family crisis occurs, and as part of the crisis reaction, the incest is revealed to someone outside the family.

Sixteen-year-old Michelle was arrested for driving a car used by two older males in committing a felony robbery. When Michelle was questioned by her high school guidance counselor, Michelle revealed that she had a sexually abusive relationship with her father, Mr. Jones, that included intercourse. The incest had ended four months earlier when Michelle became involved with the young man with whom she was arrested. The guidance counselor called Michelle's mother, Mrs. Jones, a 38-year-old housewife, to report the accusation and also reported it to the protective service section of the county social service department. Protective services began an immediate investigation, as is required by law. Mr. Jones, a 43-year-old alcoholic airline mechanic, denied the charge. Mrs. Jones, who was both depressed and agoraphobic, seemed paralyzed and unable to act. There were two other children in the home, 14-year-old Arthur and 12-year-old Samantha.

The social service worker said that unless the Jones family agreed to immediate treatment she would request a court hearing to remove the children from the home. Since Mr. Jones had health insurance that covered mental health and alcoholism services, the family was referred to a psychological clinic.

If at all possible, it is strongly recommended that the whole family attend the first therapy session to frame the incest as a family problem. This sets the stage for the family to be more amenable to therapeutic interventions as treatment progresses. It is important that the clinicians be both respectful and empathic with all family members during the sessions. Many clinicians find incest work with families to be untenable because of anger at the perpetrator, disrespect for the mother, the need to sympathize with the children, or inability to deal with explicit sexuality. Incest therapy is not for all clinicians, but if it is to be done effectively, clinicians must be genuinely empathic and respectful to all family members and able to deal explicitly with sexual communications and behavior.

The traditional protective service approach with incest families is to remove the child from the home in "the best interest of the child." This is viewed by the children as punitive. The father has urged the child to keep the sexual contacts secret, warning that revealing them will break up the family, involve so many social service and court workers that they will stumble over each other and stigmatize the child and family, and that the mother will not be able to handle the disclosure or keep the family together and that things will be worse than they were before. One of the real tragedies is that these threats and dire warnings often turn out to be true. The typical intervention model is confused and ineffective. It is inadvertently iatrogenic, causing more severe problems for the family and its individual members.

In the Jones's initial family meeting, the first focus was to intervene in the crisis and restructure the family environment. The Joneses were assured that the clinicians were aware how painful a revelation of incest is. The clinicians committed themselves to help and support each family member. Mr. Jones denied and

minimized the problems (the normal response). He was confronted by the male therapist with two options: he could cooperate with the initial assessment and treatment plan, signing
himself into a 28-day inpatient alcoholism treatment unit, or the
case would have to be turned over to the district attorney's
office for prosecution and the social service worker would remove Michelle and Samantha from the home.

Alcoholism is a good prognostic sign for treatment of incest
families. Both alcohol and incest programs emphasize an abstinence
approach and acknowledge wrongdoing from the past. Additionally,
an inpatient program gives the father a place to go when he temporarily leaves the family, i.e., a hospital treatment program covered by
health insurance. When he is discharged from the hospital, he is
able to return to work full-time, has the support of the AA group,
and is able to stay temporarily with a sponsor or another AA member in a relatively inexpensive living arrangement while he is gradually being reintegrated into the family.

The initial crisis intervention caused the Jones family much
stress, but was an opportunity for individual and family change.
Mrs. Jones became the person in charge of the house and children. Mr. Jones temporarily left the home, eliminating the opportunity for further abuse, and the children remained at home
and in school. Mr. Jones began treatment for his alcoholism.
Mrs. Jones had the opportunity to rebuild her self-esteem and
reassert her power in the family. Additionally, she was referred
to a group-oriented agoraphobia program in which she was assigned a companion to help her practice anxiety-reduction tasks
in the real-world setting. Michelle was strongly encouraged to
establish a working relationship with her probation officer and
to take personal responsibility for dealing with the felony
charge.

Each family member had an individual sex history/
assessment session with a clinician. Mr. Jones was given es-
corted leave from the hospital to attend that session and later
attended couple therapy sessions. The decision about whether
the marriage and family should remain intact is an adult decision, not a child or agency decision. The Jones's marital bond
was in disarray, with marked disrespect, a badly damaged trust
bond, and little emotional or sexual intimacy. They had intercourse once or twice a month, but it was always male-dominated
and initiated when Mr. Jones was drinking. Mrs. Jones felt very
negative about her body and sexuality, although in reality she
was an attractive woman who did not attend to her clothing or
appearance. During the sexual history interview, she revealed for
the first time that she had a sexually abusive 3-year relationship

with a young adult cousin when she was between ages 8 and 11. Mr. Jones had not been sexually abused but had been physically abused by his father and emotionally neglected by his alcoholic stepmother (his biological mother died in a car accident, driving while intoxicated). There was a good deal of symbiotic dependency in the Jones's marriage. Mr. Jones claimed the family needed to stay together for financial reasons, but, in fact, he was a lonely and isolated man whose only real emotional bond was his family. Mr. Jones's view of family was patriarchal, rigid, and authoritarian. Under his thin veneer of control and domination lay an emotionally inadequate, defensive, and scared person. Mrs. Jones did not work and did not think she could survive without the marriage. She felt controlled by her agoraphobia, had poor self-esteem, and was afraid she could not manage financially or emotionally on her own. She had an associate degree in accounting and possessed a number of life skills that had been allowed to atrophy as she became more handicapped by the agoraphobia. She viewed herself as helpless, hopeless, and unable to contribute to the family.

A major therapeutic question was whether Mr. and Mrs. Jones could revitalize their marital bond. They were told that although financial and practical matters were important and their fears of living independently had a realistic basis, negative motivation does not promote positive behavior. The clinicians asked if they had positive motivation to rebuild self-respect and respect for each other, trust that the incest would not reoccur, and trust that the other would not do something to hurt or undercut the marriage and family. Could they build an emotionally close and sexually expressive relationship? After three conjoint sessions, Mr. and Mrs. Jones made a commitment to try to rebuild their marital bond and keep their family intact.

During individual sessions with Mr. Jones, the male therapist confronted him with the inappropriateness of the incest activity and the need to increase his commitment to total abstinence from any sexual touching with his children. In addition, covert sensitization, an aversive imagery technique, was utilized to reduce sexual arousal to his daughters. Mr. Jones was not a pedophile and had not acted out against other children. Mr. Jones read *Male Sexual Awareness* (McCarthy, 1988) to increase his awareness and acceptance of appropriate masculine, husband, and father behavior. In addition, Mr. Jones was strongly encouraged to continue his 12-step alcoholism program.

The focus of individual sessions with the female therapist and Mrs. Jones was on rebuilding self-esteem as a person, wife, and mother. Mrs. Jones explored the impact of her own sexual abuse and began to see herself as well as act like a survivor rather than a victim. She read *Female Sexual Awareness* (Mc-

Carthy & McCarthy, 1989) to increase her knowledge of and
comfort with positive sexual expression. She learned cognitive–
behavioral techniques to deal with her depression and to be
more assertive in personal expression. Her progress in overcoming agoraphobia was reinforced.

Couple sessions focused on rebuilding the marital bond and
learning new ways to relate as a sexual couple. Concepts such
as nondemand touching, being sexual in a sober state, both people initiating, verbalizing sexual thoughts and feelings, and utilizing sexuality to strengthen emotional intimacy were
developed and reinforced.

Michelle reported that sexually abusive touching began at
age 12 with Mr. Jones holding her close and fondling her breasts
when he put her to bed at night. Over the ensuing four years,
the sexual interactions were intermittent but became increasingly erotic (a typical pattern). These sexual incidents were
highly correlated with Mr. Jones's drinking with almost no verbal
exchange. By age 14 the pattern was set where he would rub his
penis against her breast to ejaculation while she pretended to be
asleep. For the last six months of the sexual abuse, intercourse
occurred on occasion, but less than one-third of the time. The
sexual abuse ended in a nonverbal manner. Michelle had started
the relationship with her boyfriend and had a picture of him on
her nightstand. One night when Mr. Jones came into her room
after drinking, she surprised him by turning on the light and
holding up the picture. Mr. Jones was stunned and left the
room. He came back once more several weeks later, and Michelle turned on the light and again father left.

Michelle had a number of confused, ambivalent cognitions and
emotions about the incest experience. In her individual therapy sessions the prime therapeutic intervention was to have her write her
own book about the experience. Writing a book about sexuality and
sexual abuse is the basic intervention used with sexually abused
children whether age 4, 8, 12, or 16. It is the focus of the individual
session, and, at the termination of formal therapy, the child keeps
the book as a reference source when he or she thinks about the
incest. The book is divided into four chapters: (1) a positive view of
sexuality and appropriate sex education for a child at that age; (2) a
review of the incest experience, with clear descriptions of the behavior, cognitions, and emotions—a description of both positive and
negative components; (3) a new set of cognitions and understanding
of the incest, which allows the person to see him- or herself as a
survivor, not a victim, and realize that the responsibility for incest
lies with the adult, not the child; (4) future plans for his or her

sexual self-esteem and how sexuality will be expressed in a positive manner in his or her life.

Another therapeutic issue was Michelle's having too much power in the family. Hence, Michelle found it difficult to return to being an adolescent. She was particularly angry about having to deal with the court and probation system. Michelle was relieved to have the incest behind her and to be done with the destructive boyfriend relationship. However, it seemed strange and awkward for her to return to adolescent dating, rules and curfews, and responsibility for tasks at home.

There were two individual sessions with the son, Arthur, who had not been abused. The focus with Arthur was on increasing his understanding and empathy with his sisters and on preventive counseling by presenting relationships between men and women in a positive, nonexploitive light. Arthur's experience with masturbation was discussed, as was his relationship with Mr. Jones. A differentiation was made between respecting Mr. Jones but not respecting his alcoholic or incestuous behavior.

When an older daughter is sexually abused, it is probable the younger daughter has also been victimized. The older daughter hopes and believes that her sexual activity with the father will prevent him from being sexual with the younger daughter, which usually is not the case. Samantha reported abuse beginning at age 10. She did not engage in sexual intercourse with Mr. Jones but did experience the same pattern of nonverbal genital abuse over a two-year period. Samantha's reaction differed from Michelle's in that Samantha wanted the family to remain together and wanted to reestablish a relationship with both father and mother. While Michelle was angry and blaming, Samantha was confused and tearful and felt guilty. It was especially important in doing the sexuality book with Samantha that she realize that the responsibility for the incest lay with her father, not with her. Samantha had a strong desire to return to being a child and to be taken care of. Samantha wanted to be accepted and listened to by Michelle, Arthur, and her mother.

A crucial session was the first family meeting after Mr. Jones was discharged from the inpatient alcoholism program. The issue was whether he could reintegrate into the family. The first step was coming to dinner twice a week, observing clear rules and open channels of communication so that inappropriate sexual behavior could not reoccur. In this meeting, Mrs. Jones's role as a strong member of the family was clearly asserted. She stated she would confront Mr. Jones and demand that he leave the home if there was any drinking or inappropriate sexual touching.

The first channel of communication for an incest family is for the children to confront the father; the second, to be able to tell the mother; the third, to talk to each other; the fourth, to call the therapist; and the fifth, to call the social service worker or the police. Incest thrives on secrecy. As long as the lines of communication are opened and remain open, incest will not reoccur. The father has to be committed to total abstinence from alcohol and sexual touching with his children. He typically minimizes the incestuous activity and blames it on the alcoholism. This rationalization must be confronted. The rate of incest is two and a half times greater in alcoholic or chemically abusive families. However, alcoholism and sexual abuse are two different problems, and both must be confronted and treated (Maltz & Holman, 1987).

> Whenever Mr. Jones came home for dinner, there was a clear agreement that he would not go into the children's bedrooms but that he could go into the couple's bedroom with Mrs. Jones. In this case there was no affectionate touching with the children, but it was agreed that if there were to be affectionate touching it would be in a public area with someone else present.
>   Another important issue in the family session is to make it clear that the decision regarding the marriage is between the husband and wife and is not for the children to make— particularly Michelle, who wanted a vote in the marital decision. Michelle was told firmly that she had a right to live in a house free of the fear of sexual abuse but that she had to resume the role of an adolescent, not a decision-making adult.

A couple cannot stay together just for the sake of the children, nor can they be controlled by the wishes of the children (whether the pressure is for the father to return or for him to stay separate). A marital decision is an adult, not a child, decision. If a couple is to remain together, they need to reestablish a viable marital bond.

The decision to stay in the house and neighborhood is another difficult issue. Incest families feel stigmatized, or at least gossiped about, by neighbors and schoolchildren. They feel embarrassed about contact with police and social service agencies. The children's feelings in the situation must be discussed and considered, but ultimately it is an adult decision to stay in the house or move to another neighborhood.

As therapy for the Jones family progressed, there were fewer individual sessions and more couple, family, and subgroup (especially mother–daughter(s)) sessions. The focus shifted from the incest incidents to being survivors and reorganizing self-esteem and family relationships. The prime relationships that needed to be rebuilt were the husband–wife relationship and the mother–daughter relationship.

The Jones family was aware that their progress would be monitored for two years after the formal termination of treatment. The final session was a formal apology session, which was scheduled as a double session. This is usually a very emotional, highly impactful experience. The structure was that Mr. Jones apologize to each child in turn. He would say specifically what he did and why he did it, take responsibility for it, apologize, and express any other feelings he wished. Each child was able to ask any question and say whatever he or she wanted, but Michelle and Samantha were told that when they accepted the apology they could no longer use incest as a way of asserting power, control, or blame in the family. Mr. Jones's apology to Michelle was very emotional. He clearly stated that the abuse, and especially the intercourse, was to meet his needs and was not her fault. Michelle said she could accept the apology but would always resent that he made her keep the secret for so many years. Michelle opted to stay at home, but her relationship with Mr. Jones was distant. Mr. Jones's apology to Arthur centered on his not being a very concerned or interested father, and Arthur vowed to be a better father to his children and to treat the women he would date with more respect. Arthur asked for his father's help and support in his soccer activities. Samantha was very accepting of Mr. Jones's apology, and at the end she asked for an "affectionate hug," which is unusual with incest families but seemed acceptable and appropriate in this case.

Mrs. Jones's apology to each child focused on her letting them down because she felt controlled by her agoraphobia and low self-esteem. She promised to be there for them and assured them she was strong enough to prevent any reoccurence of the alcohol or sexual acting-out. Michelle and Arthur were more angry at Mrs. Jones than at Mr. Jones. They felt she had let them down by not doing what mothers are supposed to do—"take care of children and protect them." It is hard to apologize and still maintain one's self-esteem. However, that is what is needed. Mrs. Jones regretted the incest but couldn't let those incidents control her present self-esteem, marriage, and family. She could not undo the past but could commit herself to being an active, involved mother in the present and in the future. She made the point—especially to Michelle—that mothers are people with strengths and weaknesses and that if you don't take care of yourself it is hard to take care of others.

The Joneses were told that they could call the clinic either individually or as a family if they felt the need for support or individual or family therapy. They did not need the "calling card" of incest or a crisis to resume therapeutic contact. Regular six-month follow-up family sessions were scheduled for the next two years.

At the two-year follow-up the Jones family remained free of incest. Mr. and Mrs. Jones maintained a regular rhythm of affectionate and/or sensual contact three to four times per week that culminated in intercourse one to three times per week. Mrs. Jones reported quite good progress with her agoraphobia. She felt comfortable moving around the community and resumed driving by herself but did not feel comfortable about going on airplane trips or leaving the state. Her self-esteem greatly improved after she was hired for a 30-hour-per-week job in data processing. She reported greater parental involvement and more satisfaction with Arthur and Samantha, although she continued to have difficulty with Michelle. Mr. Jones remained abstinent from alcohol (with two lapses—during which he left the house as agreed) and no sexual acting out against his daughters. He was still somewhat rigid and authoritarian in his marriage and parenting but was not abusive. Interestingly, he had channeled some of his energy into being a volunteer in local politics. His best parenting was with Arthur, and he kept emotional distance from Michelle. Although he was not a particularly nurturing parent with Samantha, he was responsible and dutiful. Of all the members of the family, Mr. Jones felt least good about the therapy. He felt more accepted and supported in his AA program, whereas he felt more confronted in this therapy. Michelle turned 18, had successfully completed high school and her court probation, and planned to attend college with a major in social science. She had a steady boyfriend with whom she was sexually involved and was using contraception. Arthur was active in athletics, was a B student, and seemed the most stable member of the family. He was most supportive of continued family meetings and had a closer relationship with his sisters than most brothers have. Samantha entered adolescence with a reasonably good psychological attitude and had an excellent relationship with Mrs. Jones, Michelle, and Arthur. At that point, Samantha had no interest in dating but was very involved with her field hockey team.

GUIDELINES FOR TREATING INCEST FAMILIES

Each incest family has its own uniqueness and its own therapeutic issues. While father–daughter incest causes the most trauma and is most likely to involve therapy, brother–sister, uncle–niece, and stepfather–stepdaughter incest are more common. A central theme in therapy with incest families is to avoid the iatrogenic effects of intervention (more guilt, confusion, stigma, and victimization). Good psychotherapy involves teaching all family members, especially the children, to see themselves as survivors, not victims. The incest survivor is aware of and responsible for his or her sexuality, has a clear cognition that responsibility for the incest lies with the perpetrator and not him- or herself, is assertive and has open channels of communication so that the incest cannot reoccur, acknowledges that he or she is a strong person and did survive the incest, and focuses his or her psychological energy on the present and future rather than allowing his or her life to be controlled by the past sexual trauma.

A person's or family's self-esteem should not be defined by a negative event, whether it involves incest, rape, alcoholism, family violence, or bankruptcy. It is important to help the person and family confront and accept the reality of the incest but not allow them to use incest as their primary self-definition. The appropriate cognition is to be a survivor of incest, not a victim of incest.

It is difficult for a single clinician practicing alone to deal with an incest family. Doing individual sex histories, seeing subsystems of the family, and coordinating with court and social service agencies demand much time and energy. The major area of difficulty is maintaining clinical objectivity and facilitating therapeutic goals where there are so many demands and conflicting needs. The co-therapy model is much preferred. It is crucial that the male–female co-therapy team model the concepts they are teaching. Specifically, the co-therapy team needs to have equity in terms of power, to communicate with each other in a clear, respectful manner, and to trust each other's judgment and clinical skills. They can have complementary skills; for example, one may be more expert in dealing with child issues and the other more expert dealing with court matters. Both need to be competent in individual, couple, and family therapy. The goals of therapy are to confront and stop the incest and to help each family member develop cognitive and behavioral skills that allow each to be a more competent and emotionally healthy human being.

The clinician needs to guard against falling into the trap of viewing the family that stays together as a success and the family that separates as a failure. Some families must be separated in order to halt the incest pattern. The husband–wife bond is not viable in other families, where, for example, the stepfather marries because he is a pedophile attracted to the children and has no attraction to his wife. Families remain intact when the marital bond is restored, when the parental roles can be applied appropriately, when the children are able to see themselves as survivors, and, most importantly, when the family is safe from sexual abuse. Staying together because of negative motivation or where incest might continue is iatrogenic.

Because the clinician's task is primarily therapeutic, he or she should not become a legal advocate for the family. The clinician needs to work cooperatively with the court system and to use the legal system as a backup if the perpetrator acts out.

SUMMARY

Treatment of incest families is a subspecialty skill that is a difficult but very rewarding therapeutic challenge. This chapter and case example do not argue that it is the only way to conceptualize and treat incest families or that this model works with all incest families. This model attends to the typical goals of the family: that the incest ceases, that the family stay together, that each member change his or her behavior, that the family function better, that there be better communication—especially open channels regarding inappropriate sexuality—and that they not feel shameful and stigmatized by the incest. Furthermore, this model provides strategies and techniques to enhance individual and family functioning. At a minimum, it is crucial that the intervention be effective in stopping the incest. It is of great importance to help the child or children see themselves as survivors rather than stigmatized victims.

Whether or not a family stays together, subsystems and individuals have practical and psychological needs that must be attended to. Incest is a major insult to the family system and to the individual family members. It must be dealt with therapeutically in a respectful, concerned, and helpful manner to facilitate the process of being a survivor rather than a victim of incest.

REFERENCES

Barrett, M. J., Sykes, C., & Bynes, W. (1986). A systemic model for the treatment of intrafamily child sexual abuse. In T. Trepper (Ed.), *Treating incest*. New York: Haworth Press.

Courtois, C. A., & Sprei, J. E. (1988). Retrospective incest therapy for women. In L. Walker (Ed.), *Handbook on sexual abuse of children*. New York: Springer.

Finkelhor, D. (1984). *Child sexual abuse*. New York: Free Press.

Herman, J. L. (1981). *Father-daughter incest*. Cambridge, MA: Harvard University Press.

Leiblum, S., & Rosen, R. (1989). *Principles and practice of sex therapy.* New York: Guilford Press.

Maltz, W., & Holman B. (1987). *Incest and sexuality.* Lexington, MA: Lexington Books.

McCarthy, B. (1986). A cognitive-behavioral approach to understanding and treating sexual trauma. *Journal of Sex and Marital Therapy* 12, 322–329.

McCarthy, B. (1988). *Male sexual awareness.* New York: Carroll and Graf.

McCarthy, B., & McCarthy, E. (1989). *Female sexual awareness.* New York: Carroll and Graf.

Meiselman, K. C. (1978). *Incest.* San Francisco: Jossey-Bass.

Schwartz, M. F., & Masters, W. H. (1984). Treatment of paraphiliacs, pedophiles, and incest families. In A. Holstrom (Ed.), *Research handbook of rape.* New York: Haworth Press.

Sgroi, S. (1982). *Handbook of clinical intervention in child sexual abuse.* Boston: Lexington Books.

Trepper, T. S., & Traicoff, E. M. (1983). Treatment of intrafamily sexuality. *Journal of Sex Education and Therapy* 9, 14–18.

Trepper, T. S., & Barrett, M. J. (1986). Vulnerability to incest: A framework for assessment. In T. Trepper (Ed.), *Treating incest: A multiple systems perspective.* New York: Haworth Press.

11 The Multidimensional Role of the Therapist Treating Child Victims of Sexual Abuse

Shelley Kramer-Dover

For the mental health practitioner who works therapeutically with children, the traditional office session actually comprises only a portion of the therapeutic work. A substantial amount of time generally is devoted to consultation with other persons who have a significant impact on the child's development. Consultation and cooperation among the significant people in a child's life make it more probable that action taken on the child's behalf will truly be in the best interest of that child.

When the issue of sexual abuse is introduced into therapy, the number of issues the therapist needs to address increases exponentially. The therapist who works with child victims of sexual abuse should try to assess the complex dynamics involved in the abuse situation and address therapeutically the many ways in which the abuse may affect the child. As therapists may be subpoenaed to give testimony in related civil and criminal court proceedings, the therapist should also be prepared to participate in legal sequelae that may follow disclosure of the abuse.

The therapist should be prepared to support the child through what can be a long series of events that have the potential to compound the trauma of the abuse. The investigative and medical procedures following a disclosure, the reaction of family members, changes in living situation that may occur when the abuser is a family member, and involvement in court proceedings may all serve to add new trauma to the life of the child victim. It is therefore essential that a therapist who works with child victims be aware of these events in order to offer emotional support to the child and, when appropriate, recommend actions that are consistent with the best interests of the child. Such efforts will likely involve work with the child's parents and other family members and may involve consultations with Child Protective Services workers, police, attorneys, teachers, physicians, foster parents, and court-appointed special advocates.

This chapter describes various roles a mental health therapist may be called upon to play when treating child victims of sexual abuse and presents practical suggestions regarding this type of work. These suggestions are based on the author's clinical experience with a range of child sexual abuse cases in an outpatient, private practice clinical setting. These cases involved forced exposure to inappropriate sexual materials or activities, involvement in pornography, and experiences between a child and an adult or between a child and another, older child that included a range of sexually abusive acts such as fondling, coitus, fellatio, and sodomy. These cases involved children from two years of age through the teenage years; children who measure across the spectrum of intellectual functioning, including children who measure as learning-disabled or mentally retarded; children who were abused by close family members, other relatives, other caretakers, neighbors, acquaintances, and leaders of specialized children's activities or programs; children who disclosed the abuse immediately and children who disclose the abuse years later; children who were unable to directly disclose the abuse themselves but whose abuse was revealed by witnesses; children who were believed when they disclosed the abuse and children who were accused of being liars; children who remained in the family home and children who were removed from the home; and children who were involved in criminal and civil court proceedings.

Therapeutic work with adults who were victims of child sexual abuse has also significantly influenced the clinical approaches described in this chapter. Listening to these adults describe the specific acts of abuse and the feelings connected with those acts has been of immeasurable value in helping the author understand the experiences of the recently abused child. Hearing adults describe the need to cut off those memories and feelings has enhanced the author's understanding of the intensity of the pain. The issues addressed in the adult therapy demonstrate firsthand the potential, long-term effects of child sexual abuse.

CASE EXAMPLE

While the following case involves several elements that may be found in sexual abuse cases, each case a therapist sees is unique. To build a body of knowledge and understanding of this field and to develop skills as therapists, it is important to look for the common elements among cases. However, each case brings with it special features and an individual configuration of factors and circumstances that must be considered by the therapist to address adequately the patient's needs. Therefore, in clinical practice, flexibility and creativity are essential therapeutic tools.

Mary is a 23-year-old mother who dropped out of high school when she became pregnant at age 16 and 2 years later gave birth to a second child. Mary lived in a small apartment with her two children, Susan, age 7, and Frank, age 5. The fathers of Susan and Frank were unaware of their paternity, and Mary had no knowledge of their whereabouts.

Mary had a day job as a store clerk and had recently met 27-year-old Joe when he came into the store as a customer. Mary and Joe began to go out at night, and as he had no place to live, Mary offered that he could move in with her. His employment was sporadic, and he was often home watching Susan and Frank during the day while their mother was at work.

Three months after his arrival, Susan's physical education teacher noticed a change in Susan's movements. Susan's walk changed in a way that suggested physical discomfort, and on two occasions the teacher saw Susan rubbing herself in her vaginal area. The teacher became concerned and met with the principal and the school social worker. The principal and social worker then met with Susan, and she began to tell them that Joe had hurt her and pointed to her vaginal area. The principal then called Child Protective Services to report their suspicions, and later that afternoon a social worker from CPS came to the school to talk with Susan. During the conversation Susan described to the CPS worker details of ongoing sexual abuse by Joe.

The CPS worker then met with Mary to discuss with her what Susan was reporting. During that same afternoon, with Mary's permission, the CPS worker met with Susan's brother Frank, age 5. Frank revealed that he and Joe had a special secret game they played together in which they would take off their clothes and wrestle with each other. Frank also reported that Joe would sometimes take pictures of Susan and him with no clothes on. Frank said that Joe had told them that if he or Susan ever told anyone about this, he and Susan would get in big trouble and be punished.

The CPS worker informed Mary about what both children were reporting. Mary's first response was that she loved Joe, that he would never do such things, that she would not make him leave the house, and that the children must be making all of this up. When Joe was questioned about these allegations, he denied it all and refused to leave the house while the investigation was being conducted. The CPS worker said the children's safety and welfare needed to be protected and asked if there were family members available who could take in the children while the investigation was proceeding. Mary said that she had not spoken to her parents since leaving home at age 16, but the children could stay with her sister.

Arrangements were then made for both children to be evaluated by a mental health professional to assess their emotional status and secure recommendations about the treatment needs of the children. During the evaluation the children each revealed further information about the sexual abuse, describing in words and pictures and demonstrating with dolls what had happened with Joe. They both manifested symptoms of emotional distress over the abuse and the upheaval following disclosure of the abuse, and the therapist recommended that each child be seen in psychotherapy. The therapist met with the children's aunt to assist her in working with them at home around issues and behaviors related to the abuse. The therapist also consulted with the children's teachers about how they should handle inappropriate behaviors exhibited in the classroom. The therapist also met with Mary and recommended that she be seen individually by a different therapist, with family work to be arranged as therapy progressed.

The result of the police investigation led to criminal charges against Joe. The two children, Susan and Frank, were to be subpoenaed as witnesses, and the children's therapist was to be subpoenaed as an expert witness. However, shortly before the court date, Joe confessed and was court-ordered into a treatment program for sexual offenders.

Susan and Frank made good progress in their individual treatment. Joe's confession helped Mary acknowledge the reality of the abuse, and in therapy she began to deal with her own sexual abuse at age 6, perpetrated by her grandfather. Family sessions with Susan, Frank, and Mary were very productive and the children soon returned home.

SOURCES AND STAGES OF REFERRAL

North American studies of child sexual abuse report prevalence rates of 6 to 62% for females and 3 to 31% for males (Peters et al. 1986). These numbers suggest that treatment of victims of child sexual abuse will almost inevitably become a part of the practice of a mental health therapist. Some therapists may make a deliberate choice to focus a portion of their clinical practice in this area by seeking out specialized training and by indicating to referral sources an interest in working with sexual abuse victims. Many therapists may find themselves specializing in this area by necessity, in response to the demands of the clinical population served.

Therapists may become involved in cases at various stages. Referral of a child from Child Protective Services agencies to the therapist occurs after the suspicion of abuse has been officially reported and is either in the process of being investigated or after the investigation has been completed and a finding made. The child would ordinarily be referred for further evaluation and treatment. The therapist may also be asked to provide services related to family work. In some cases, the agency's own investigation may be inconclusive, but the investigating caseworker or the parents may feel that further evaluation of the child around the question of sexual abuse is warranted.

Patients may also be referred to a therapist for reasons other than identified sexual abuse and, during the evaluation period, may disclose previous or ongoing sexual abuse. Disclosure of the abuse may also take place after the patient has been in psychotherapy for a while. The patient may feel sufficient trust in the therapist to confide this information. Sometimes there are circumstances in the patient's life external to the therapy that prompt such a disclosure. For other patients, aspects of the therapeutic process may contribute to a weakening of the walls that have surrounded the memories of abuse.

DISCLOSURE TO THE THERAPIST

There are mandatory reporting laws that govern the reporting responsibilities of therapists. Therapists should consult state codes for current and precise information regarding the reporting of sexual abuse. The value of reporting sexual abuse is multifaceted. If abuse is found, then positive intervention on behalf of the child is possible. The victim and the victim's family may be made aware of the availability of needed treatment and support services. Reporting also allows concerned persons and agencies to work toward prevention of further abuse, either of the original victim or of other potential victims.

When a child discloses information about nonfamilial sexual abuse to the therapist, the therapist needs to inform the child's parents about the abuse and in certain cases may work with other professionals in informing the parents. When a child discloses ongoing familial abuse to the therapist, it is particularly important to work with Child Protective Services in informing the parents so that the protection of the child is ensured. If possible, the therapist should keep the child in the office until appropriate authorities are contacted and arrangements are made for their intervention in the situation. The therapist would then recommend and arrange for appropriate follow-up sessions with individual or various combinations of family members, as fit the particular situation. During this process it is imperative for the therapist to consult with the child and keep the child appropriately informed about what is happening. Inclusion encourages the child to maintain trust in the therapist.

AUTHORIZATION TO PROVIDE SERVICES

Before the therapist meets with the child, the therapist should determine who has custody of the child and who may therefore authorize evaluation or treatment. It is not unusual to work with situations in which only one parent has custody or in which the child has been removed from the home and custody rests with another individual or with an agency such as the Department of Social Services. It is wise to request copies of relevant court orders or other papers that indicate who currently has the authority both to permit work with the child and to obtain or release information about the child. The therapist should maintain copies of such documents in the files, updating them as necessary.

INITIAL ASSESSMENT TASKS

When a child initially discloses abuse to the therapist or when a child who has already partially disclosed the abuse is referred to the therapist for evaluation and treatment, that therapist needs to conduct an initial assessment with the child. In this stage of assessment it is essential that the therapist and the child establish a good rapport, not only to accomplish the evaluation but also to set a foundation for future work together in treatment. How the therapist handles those first moments with the child is critical to the success of future interactions.

The child victim may enter the assessment situation wary of the therapist. Under ideal circumstances the child will have been brought to see the therapist by an adult the child trusts and who has conveyed to the child positive feelings about the therapist. However, even in this situation, the degree of caution exercised by the child depends on a number of factors. How the disclosure was previously received by others, whether the child was believed, whether the child was blamed, who perpetrated the abuse, and what threats kept the child from previously disclosing may all contribute to the way in which the child approaches the meeting with the therapist.

At the outset it is important for the therapist to convey to the child a clear sense of what that therapist's role will be. (When the therapist has the title of "Doctor," it may be necessary to clarify immediately that this is a doctor who does not give shots, as this can be a fear of some children when they are told they are going to see a doctor.) The therapist may explain to the child that he or she is a special person who works a great deal with children who have been in similar situations. The therapist may explain that, when meeting with children, the therapist and child talk together about what has happened. The therapist conveys to the child that he or she wants to understand what has happened in order to help the child.

Ordinarily, the therapist will have already obtained background information about the child and will want to see the child alone first as a means of enhancing the child's ability to speak openly. The therapist should try to receive the child's information in a warm, supportive way. However, no sense of judgment should be conveyed, as this might influence the amount and kind of information disclosed by the child. Explanations about what the therapist already knows about the child and about what the child has disclosed will depend on individual circumstances. How the referral was made and the stage of the investigative or treatment process will also be taken into consideration. However, generally, the therapist generally conveys to the child enough information to give permission to the child to discuss the sexual abuse but refrains from providing specific details to the child already given to the therapist. This allows the child freedom to disclose information without a sense that a particular path must be followed or that disclosure must be limited only to what has been previously disclosed. Children who have been sexually abused may relate details of events in a piecemeal fashion or, over time, disclose information about additional instances of abuse. Thus, the therapist's approach should allow openings for the revelation of further information.

It is important that the therapist understand that, unless the perpetrator confesses, the credibility of the child's disclosure may become highly contested (particularly if there is litigation around the abuse). Contested credibility generally impedes the child's healing process. Therefore, it is important for the therapist to conduct a thorough evaluation early on. The methods of working with the child should be structured so that, without having any adverse impact on the child, they would hold up under the potential scrutiny of family members, other professionals, and the courts. The therapist may be subpoenaed to testify in civil or criminal proceedings as to what the child has said and as to whether evaluation findings are consistent with sexual abuse.

GREETING THE CHILD

When greeting a young child, the therapist will naturally want to be kind, caring, and patient. The therapist may want to kneel down to be at eye level with the child so as not to appear intimidating. The therapist should initially refrain from gestures that involve physical contact with the child, such as touching the shoulder, as it may not be known at the outset how the child would interpret those contacts. Even extending a hand to the child to walk to the meeting room should be done with caution and careful attention to the child's verbal and nonverbal reactions.

SETTING AND MATERIALS

The meeting room should be comfortable and have toys and other play materials evident. The child will perceive that children are welcome at this office and that other children have been here before—with this therapist, in this situation. Materials useful in the evaluation and treatment of sexually abused children include the following: play and dollhouses; dolls (regular and anatomical, representing various ages), puppets, stuffed animals, figures, and small objects that may relate to the specific circumstances of the abuse (which may be used to describe the events or to work through the events); art materials such as paper, crayons, paints, scissors, glue, and clay; a play medical kit; and books of therapeutic stories.

MODES OF EXPRESSION

Many children feel most comfortable expressing themselves through play or art. For others, verbal expression and communication with the therapist can provide a substantial amount of information. Some children will be able to describe in words the events and their feelings, with only minimal therapist encouragement. Phrases such as "I want to be able to understand exactly what happened" and "I need your help" encourage the child to speak by showing interest, by allying with the child, and by stressing the importance of the child's participation in the process.

Following verbal disclosures, it may be helpful to have the child demonstrate what has happened by using a set of anatomical dolls. It is also very useful to have the child make drawings of what has just been described. Drawings and doll demonstrations help ensure that the child's words are in fact describing what the child intends to describe. While questions about the child's individualized terms for body parts or actions will help clarify the child's meaning, drawings of the body parts and the acts will add further clarification. Discussion of these pictures with the child often paves the way for the therapeutic discussions of feelings. The drawings will also support what the child is saying and provide a record. Use of the Forensic Mental Health Associates *Anatomical Drawings* (Groth & Stevenson, 1984) is also useful in this way. They may aid parents and professionals (including court personnel) in understanding what has happened to the child.

PSYCHOLOGICAL TESTING

Psychological testing is often helpful as part of the assessment process. In certain cases the administration of a full battery of psychological tests may be in order for a better understanding of both the cognitive and emotional functioning of the child. In other cases, particular areas of concern may be addressed by specific psychological tests. When the child will be involved in court testimony or the therapist will likely be subpoenaed to testify about the child, presentation of test data may be helpful to support the therapist's statements.

In certain cases, the results of the psychological testing may indicate the presence of a significantly low level of intellectual functioning or of specific learning disabilities. When there is a question of cognitive deficits, it is essential that the therapist be aware of the level and quality of the cognitive functioning of the child to properly interpret the evaluation findings and to work therapeutically with the child on an appropriate level.

NOTES AND RECORDS

While therapists should always take careful notes and maintain organized case files, particular care should be taken when working with child victims of sexual abuse. Therapists frequently are asked to document what the child said to them, the behaviors they observed, and the approaches and methods they used in much greater detail than might ordinarily be required in other kinds of cases. Furthermore, therapists may be asked to present this information months and even years after the sessions. Therapists' notes and records may also be subpoenaed. A prudent therapist will maintain files and document work with child sexual abuse victims in such a way that those files could be clearly understood by another professional working in the field of sexual abuse treatment.

Notes on what was actually said, done, or drawn during clinical sessions must be carefully recorded. These notes should be labeled with the names of who was present at the session and the date and time of the session. Any direct quotes should be denoted by the use of quotation marks. It may be important, at times, to indicate the exact wording of the therapist's question and who was the actual source of the information. For example, parents often report to the therapist something that has allegedly been said or done by the child. The therapist, however, needs to be able to distinguish, now and in the future, what the child actually reported to them and what the parent or another party reported the child as having said or done.

When taking notes while meeting with adults involved in the case, the therapist should inform the speaker why those notes are being recorded. Notes help to ensure accuracy and serve as a backup, rather than relying on memory alone. In fact, it may be useful for the therapist to read back quotes to the speaker to verify accuracy. A brief query as to whether the speaker has any objections to the notetaking process should also open up any concerns about confidentiality and disclosure of information. The therapist can then explain how information secured from all parties will be treated. The therapist should then attempt to arrive at an understanding of or, if possible, come to an agreement as to what is workable, within legal limits, regarding the sharing of information and distribution of written reports. Before the speaker leaves that session, he or she should sign proper release forms clearly listing with whom the therapist may share information. This securing of written release forms, rather than relying on verbal authorization alone, will help protect the therapist.

When meeting with the child, the therapist should always keep pen and paper accessible. Sometimes the therapist will take down notes in a way that is obvious to the child. The reason for notetaking should be explained to the child in much the same way it was explained to the adults. The therapist may, at times, need to write down detailed descriptions of what the child is saying regarding the sexual abuse. The therapist should allow the child to finish descriptions even if the therapist is tempted to interrupt the initial flow. After the child has completed his or her thought, the therapist might say, "Now I want to be sure that I wrote it down just right. I am going to read back to you what I heard you say, and I want you to tell me if that is exactly what you said and if that is what you mean." At other times, especially with very young children, notes may be jotted down unobtrusively. Direct quotes or specific details of what the child is disclosing, again, may be verified with the child. When children make drawings related to the abuse, it is useful to review the content of the drawings and related information with the child, marking this information on the drawing itself, in order to avoid later confusion as to what the child was referring. It is also useful to have the child sign his or her name to the drawing, no matter how primitive the signature, as the drawings might potentially be submitted into evidence in court proceedings.

THE CHILD'S PARENTS

Evaluation of a child sexual abuse victim, whenever possible, also involves sessions with the parents and foster parents to review the child's history and thus gain a base of information from which to measure the child's present status. Information gathered from consultation with parents, teachers, and other significant adults includes, among other things, any unusual aspects of the pregnancy, birth, and early development of the child; a history of language acquisition and motor development; a history of peer relationships and rapport with adults; any identified learning issues and special school placement (and copies of relevant school assessments); a history of trauma or special fears or nightmares; any disturbances in eating, sleeping, or toilet training; and the presence of bedwetting or other conditions such as sexually transmitted diseases. Parents should also be queried as to the child's moods and behavior, especially in terms of observed changes in general behavior and an increase in or special focus on sexually related behaviors.

The parents' reaction to the child's disclosure is very important to the child. The initial session with the parents, in addition to obtaining the developmental history of the child, addresses the parents' understanding of the situation (what they believe has happened to their child) and how they have handled disclosure with their child. It is essential for the therapist to be aware of how the child's information was received, in order to help the child if the parents reacted in a nonsupportive way. The parents must also be able to express how they feel about what has happened, in a setting where they feel supported. Their feelings may include anger, guilt, helplessness, and sadness, or denial and disbelief. Expression helps them begin to come to terms with those feelings and opens them to be more able to address their child's feelings and needs.

The therapist also needs to address parental attitudes and values about sexual issues in general and those aspects of their own childhood, such as their own sexual abuse (if that is the case), that may greatly influence the way in which they handle their child in this situation. Clearly, the identity of the abuser—father, mother, other relative, friend of the family, stranger—greatly affects how the family therapy is handled. Common to many treatment situations is the identification of any marital problems. Depending on the situation, the therapist may offer to work on those issues or may need to refer the couple for further counseling. Even when the abuser is not a parent, parents who must deal with abuse issues may experience a great deal of strain in their relationship. The therapist should endeavor to help those parents explore and channel their feelings in ways that minimize the risk of their turning those negative feelings against the child or against each other. Parents may also have questions about how and why the sexual abuse occurred and what the likely psychological and physical effects may be, including how the abuse will shape their child's sexual identity and relationships.

When a parent does not believe the child, despite independent corroboration, other issues arise that may complicate family work. For example, the family may refuse to cooperate with efforts to remove the familial offender. Furthermore, the parent's disbelief may not only challenge the child's sense of reality but may also preclude that parent from taking action to protect the child from further abuse by the original offender or others.

When the child's safety from further abuse and physical and emotional well-being cannot be ensured, the question of removal of the child from the home will be raised by Child Protective Services. When a child is removed from the home and decisions regarding foster care placement and visitation come to the fore, the therapist may be called on to advise CPS workers as to the best interests of the child. In addition, the therapist should continue to be available to the child during this delicate juncture to lend emotional support.

In some cases a parent may be found guilty of criminal charges pertaining to the sexual abuse and receive a prison sentence. When this occurs, additional critical therapeutic issues may arise. Not only will the child and his or her family need to continue to work through feelings about the victim and the abuser, but they may also need to deal with a number of very concrete, stressful disruptions to their previous lifestyle. Repercussions may include a lowering of financial status, a move to a new neighborhood and school, and a need to make new friends, as well as the tremendous pressures felt by the caretaking parent.

The therapist will need to support the child's efforts to cope with these changes occurring in the child's life. If the family requires additional special services, the therapist may be asked to function in a consultative role. For example, if school problems erupt, the therapist may need to consult with the child's teacher.

COURT

Work with sexual abuse victims frequently means working within highly charged situations that may become particularly volatile if court-related issues of custody, visitation, removal of the child from the home, or criminal proceedings are involved. In such situations it is essential that the therapist respond, not to pressures and demands made by family members, attorneys, or agency officials who may be displeased with what the therapist is saying, but to professional standards of ethical conduct and solid clinical judgment. The therapist should try to protect the child as much as possible from the whirlwind that often surrounds such cases.

When a child will be testifying in court, the therapist should devote some time during the sessions to addressing the child's emotional needs in preparation for the courtroom experience. Before informing the child that he or she will be testifying in court, it should first be determined that the court date is a relatively firm one. Court dates are frequently changed or cases resolved prior to the actual court date. As the firm court date approaches, the therapist should endeavor to strike a practical balance between addressing the child's emotional preparation for court and the child's daily emotional needs, perhaps focusing more on the courtroom experience as that date draws near.

In a civil case the therapist might explain to the child that a judge is going to make a decision about an issue concerning the child. The therapist might ask the child to think about what the child would want the judge to know prior to the judge's decision.

The child should, understand that, under certain circumstances, he or she may spend time at court but not be called to testify. Sometimes the therapist will be able to testify as to what the child is saying. At other times, certain testimony from the therapist will be prohibited and the child must speak directly to the court. It is important that the child understand that any decision about the civil or criminal issues, and the ultimate responsibility for the aftermath of the decision, rests with the judge. This may help the child focus on the issues in a constructive and realistic way, relieving him or her of an inappropriate burden of responsibility. The child needs to understand that he or she has one job in court and that job is to tell the truth.

It is important to take the child to the courthouse to become familiar with the courtroom setting ahead of time (preferably the one in which the child will actually testify). Familiarization helps reduce the scariness and mystique of the court. A visit to the courthouse snack bar or cafeteria may also be helpful. On the day of court, the child should have a comfortable place to wait. It is best if the child waits in a private area, to be able to relax and perhaps even lie down if fatigue sets in while waiting to testify. The day can be a long one, so the adult waiting with the child should come equipped with snacks and a variety of play materials.

The therapist should also make the child aware of the number of people who will be in the courtroom, their roles, and whether there will be a jury. In many jurisdictions the child will be required to testify in front of the abuser. It is imperative that the feelings connected with that confrontation be thoroughly discussed ahead of time. The process of being sworn in should be explained, as well as the stages of a possible evaluation of competency. The child should be informed about the number of people who will be asking questions and about the general format of that questioning. It should be emphasized that the other people in the courtroom want to hear what the child has to say, even if they may not always act as if they believe the child. The child should be made to feel comfortable about asking to have a question repeated or clarified if feeling confused, and about saying "I don't know" or "I don't remember" if that is the case. The overall goal of the therapist is to try to prepare the child to withstand the stress that might accompany court proceedings, so that the child emerges feeling intact and good about him- or herself and proud about having told the truth.

THERAPY

During therapy with the child victim, a wide range of issues will ordinarily need to be addressed. Usually, before the child leaves the first meeting with the therapist, the issue of blame or fault is addressed. The therapist needs to convey unequivocally to the child that the adult abuser is held responsible for the abuse—that it is never the child's responsibility. It is also important to begin immediately to address feelings of guilt. Other feelings may also emerge during treatment, such as anger, helplessness, fear, shame, and confusion. Positive feelings toward the abuser or the experience may also be expressed, and it is imperative that the therapist accept them, allowing the child the freedom to express a range of feelings. During the therapy, issues centering on the adult's abuse of power and trust, the betrayal, and specific threats that were made to the child will also be dealt with.

Child abuse victims may also express confusion and fear about what has happened physically to them and may need, for example, to have body parts correctly identified. The child may also need some help in determining whether he or she has suffered long-term physical effects from the abuse or whether there exists a risk of pregnancy. An examination by a physician experienced in the area of sexual abuse can often be helpful in determining and, if necessary, treating any medical problems connected with the abuse or in reassuring the child that he or she is physically all right. For the older child, reassurances also may be needed about the child's ability to physically participate in sexual activity as an adult and to bear children.

While certain issues may commonly appear among sexual abuse victims, the impact of the abuse must be individually assessed for each child, and the focus and order of the work must be organized to address the specific needs of the particular child. In addition, because there are a range of life experiences that yet await the child victim and because the impact of the early abuse on those later experiences is unclear, it is wise to impart to the child patient a sense that the door to therapy always remains open. Information about how the early abuse may complicate the traditional issues connected with puberty, adolescence, and the anticipated special social relationships of young adulthood should be conveyed to the parents. An understanding of the possible long-range effects may sensitize them to identify signs in the future that indicate that their child may need some special, perhaps professional, attention and support as the child takes on developmental tasks relating to emotional intimacy, sexuality, marriage, and parenting.

THERAPIST NETWORKS

It is important for therapists working with sexual abuse cases to network with each other through local meetings, conferences, and publications to share information and ideas about current research, therapeutic techniques, laws, and community resources. It is also important for therapists to network to provide peer support. All therapeutic work has the potential to be stressful. However, in child abuse cases the need for immediate interventions and coordinated work among numerous individuals and agencies, coupled with the significant impact of the legal system on the lives of the children and thus on the therapy, makes work in the field of child sexual abuse especially challenging.

REFERENCES

Groth, A. N., & Stevenson, T. M. (1984). *Anatomical drawings.* Newton Center: Forensic Mental Health Associates.

Peters, S. D., Wyatt, G. E., & Finkelhor, D. (1986). Prevalence. In D. Finkelhor et al. (Eds.), *A sourcebook on child sexual abuse* (15–59). Beverly Hills, CA: Sage.

12 Using Nonverbal Methods in the Treatment of Sexual Abuse

Jana Staton

Janie walks into the therapist's office with assurance. She has become accustomed in the past month to meeting these nice new people who keep asking her the same questions: What did your daddy do to you? Where did he do it? Did he tell you to keep it a secret? She knows the answers for each of these questions. She sits down in the chair and puts two fingers in her mouth, waiting to be asked again. She is tired of saying the same things and just wants to go home. She doesn't know how to *say* what if felt like, anyway.

Marcia is retelling the story of her abuse to her therapist for the nth time. This session began with a focus on her adjustment to a new job, and soon Marcia found herself explaining how working around so many men was paralyzing her because she kept remembering. She has a very clear, rational understanding of her oppression and fear, but there is no emotional involvement in this retelling. Her therapist sighs and wonders what to do next.

In working with children and adult survivors in cases such as those just described, therapists often find that words aren't enough. Words can become the barrier instead of the key in treating young children and adult survivors of incest and child abuse. Therapists need to use all the verbal strategies they have, but they also need to go beyond words to incorporate treatment strategies that work directly with and transform the client's visual and kinesthetic modes of experience.

This chapter discusses the practical use of various nonverbal modes of comunication in treating children who have been sexually abused and, by extension, adult survivors who are just beginning therapy. The chapter is intended as a beginning point for the thera-

pist who is unfamiliar with the use of nonverbal modes of communication and suggests how they can be integrated into a family
systems approach to treatment. The references at the end of the
chapter provides additional sources of information for therapeutic
practice.

Historically, children—even victimized children—under the age
of 7 or 8 have not been considered reliable witnesses and therefore
are not always allowed to testify as witnesses in legal proceedings
(Goodman, 1984). The law has reasoned that they are not able to
Children communicate effectively with those around them from
birth, using gestures, actions, and visual images. The use of words to
communicate develops last and probably does not become integrated
with the child's other modes of representation until adolescence.
Bruner (1973) has summarized the development of symbolic communication in children as involving "not a series of stages, but a
successive mastering of three forms of representation, along with
their partial translation each into the other" (p. 317).

Infants from birth to approximately two years of age understand
and represent their experiences best through sensorimotor or kinesthetic means. A lost object is remembered and represented, or asked
for, by gestures of hand and mouth that kinesthetically represent its
use. This is indeed "symbolic" communication but without words.

BACKGROUND AND RATIONALE FOR USING
NONVERBAL MODES OF COMMUNICATION IN
TREATMENT

Children communicate effectively with those around them from
birth, using gestures, actions, and visual images. The use of words to
communicate develops last and probably does not become integrated
with the child's other modes of representation until adolescence.
Bruner (1973) has summarized the development of symbolic communication in children as involving "not a series of stages, but a
successive mastering of three forms of representation, along with
their partial translation each into the other" (p. 317).

Infants from birth to approximately 2 years of age understand
and represent their experiences best through sensorimotor or kinesthetic means. A lost object is remembered and represented, or asked
for, by gestures of hand and mouth that kinesthetically represent its
use. This is indeed "symbolic" communication but without words.
The child's earliest memories of experience remain encoded in the
sensorimotor system as smells, tastes, and actions.

The second representational system for knowing and communicating experience uses visual images and, again, develops from early infancy but appears to predominate after age 2. All memories for the young child, and many memories throughout life, are encoded primarily in images, and unless the therapy works with and transforms these images, they may be retained no matter how much "talk" occurs.

The child's linguistic system for representing experience develops more slowly. At least seven years and probably more are required for minimally competent, independent language production and comprehension to occur. Even though children can participate in conversations with adults by this age, they are still not fully proficient in many adult-level strategies for representing and understanding meaning.

This chapter is written from a child's point of view regarding representation and communication of experience. Rather than following the legal perspective that not much can be done until words are available, the approaches in this chapter assume that even the youngest child has effective means of communication that the therapist can use.

FACTORS SPECIFIC TO INCEST AND SEXUAL ABUSE

Factors specific to incest or other kinds of sexual abuse additionally constrain the young child's ability to use linguistic modalities to process and transform the experience during treatment. First, and most obviously, the abusive experience itself is a physical one and is most likely to be encoded in the child's memory through his or her sensorimotor and visual modes of representation rather than in auditory–linguistic terms. Because of their secretive nature and the regressed psychological nature of most perpetrators, such experiences are not likely to have been accompanied by the normal verbalized explaining and labeling. Adults usually provide young children a rich verbal description of any new experience, such as a trip to the zoo. If little language was used, then there will be little language available later to a very young child to explain and describe what happened. Visual images and actions for representing experience are not dependent on adult input and modeling.

Second, the child may be very frightened, embarrassed, or otherwise traumatized. This results in much of the experience being stored in only one modality, probably either visual or kinesthetic.

Thus, the information may not be readily accessible to the child when asked to tell what happened. Even such linguistic ability as the child possesses will therefore be limited in its usefulness in therapy.

Finally, adult perpetrators involved in sexual abuse often make specific prohibitions against talking about it or telling anyone. Even after police or protective service interviews and court hearings during which the child may have told what happened, the therapist can still be faced with the child's reluctance to break that prohibition again by talking about it, especially when the child is embarrassed and is experiencing the common effects of abuse such as fear, shame, guilt, and helplessness. In this instance, the child's understanding that communication with adults counts only if *words* are used can become an advantage, because drawing, acting out with dolls or play objects, or using puppets to "talk for me" are not understood by the child to be prohibited actions or means of communication.

Thus, the therapist working with a young child victim or an older survivor starts by using those "languages" in which the child or inner child-self of the adult is already proficient—visual images and kinesthetic actions. Rather than viewing the child's thinking and communication as deficient in these early years—"disjointed," "illogical," or "rambling"—as some working with children still do (cf., Waterman, 1986, pp. 25–26), the therapist can treat children as if they were intelligent speakers of other languages who are still learning to translate those nonverbal languages they have already mastered into a new auditory/verbal one that adults all seem to prefer and use so fluently.

Children can accurately represent their world and past experience when given toys, a doll house, or other materials to communicate with. The use of two or three communication modalities simultaneously (even with seemingly "verbal" children) allows the child to switch freely and to combine modalities in order to communicate most comfortably. In this approach, we draw no firm line between nonverbal and verbal communication, nor do we believe there is any justification for restricting the child to only *nonverbal* means.

The use of sensory experiences and creative art in the treatment of incest and abuse elicits a child's emotional and sensory responses and memories. In effect, these modes of communication help the child to reencounter the *experience itself* in small, safe steps, much as in remembering a dream, so that the experience can be objectified and reworked in the free and protected space of the therapeutic encounter.

GOALS FOR INCORPORATING SENSORIMOTOR AND VISUAL COMMUNICATION INTO SYSTEMIC TREATMENT OF CHILD SEX ABUSE

There are five basic goals in using nonverbal communication channels in the treatment of survivors of sexual abuse.

1. Establishing rapport by using the child's preferred modes of communication.
2. Separating the child's self from the abuse by objectifying those experiences, memories, feelings that are hidden and subjective.
3. Creating opportunities to symbolically reenact the abusive situation until the child has mastered it.
4. Regaining symbolic control over self and others by transforming prior situations of powerlessness and bringing in both inner (psychological) and outer resources.
5. Building a new reality around a more competent, powerful self; allowing delayed or blocked functions to resume development.

These five goals go beyond the traditional use of play materials to allow the child simply to express him- or herself. They focus on specific treatment goals essential for healing the survivors of sexual abuse, and follow the treatment focus of Sgroi (1982).

The first goal, *establishing rapport*, is accomplished by creating a common symbolic language in which the child is already proficient and that he or she uses comfortably. This approach stresses communication and validates the child's drawings, puppets, or acting out as meaningful and important to the therapist.

Separating the child's self from the traumatic experience through *objectification* is the second essential step in the treatment of incest. Just talking about an event does not provide the needed externalization and objectification of the traumatic encounter, especially for young children and probably for all trauma survivors. Making a drawing, working with clay, or having a puppet or doll act out a "bad" event elicits and makes concrete that which has been hidden and experienced only subjectively (Naitove, 1982). If the "bad" experience can be safely objectified outside the child (in the therapy room dolls, in a drawing or sandtray, in some concrete action), then the self-protecting mechanisms of denial, blaming, and forgetting are no longer needed.

Providing ample opportunities to replay or symbolically *reenact* the abusive situation and its common effects (angry reactions of family members, guilt, court experiences, etc.) is a crucial next step. This step uses the child's normal instinct to play and replay events until the feelings are "mastered" (Schaefer & O'Connor, 1983). One explanation of the psychological purpose of the child's symbolic reenactment of past events is that such play endows "transitional objects" (dolls, clay figures, etc.) with meaning and allows the child to predict and experience control over distressing or harmful experience.

But a traumatic experience requires going beyond just its reenactment if healing and renewed growth are to occur. Nonverbal methods help to *transform* the old experience so that its power is gone. This step of transformation requires the active participation of the therapist to help the child create visual or physical representations of resources that can then come to the child's aid and protection. These might be inner resources, such as a lion or a cartoon character to give the courage to tell if it happens again. Or the child may need to represent actual persons (parent, teacher, new caretaker, social worker/therapist, or the adult survivor) who are now able to help the child.

Finally, the use of a variety of nonverbal methods and materials contributes to the final goal of therapy, the *construction of a new reality* in the child's present life, and it *generates new growth* of delayed or blocked cognitive and functional behaviors.

DESCRIPTION OF BASIC TECHNIQUES

This section outlines the use of various techniques for symbolic communication that a therapist might use in working with children in treatment. The last section briefly illustrates how these straightforward and commonsense techniques are used within the framework of the major issues in treating victims of sexual abuse.

The emphasis in this chapter is on using nonverbal techniques as a means of straightforward communication, without reference to classical psychoanalytic interpretation. A victimized child who uses physical materials or actions to communicate is most likely representing specific aspects of the traumatic experience directly. The therapist does not need an a priori list of symbols (i.e., a house in flames means sexuality) to understand the child's meaning. The therapist who has some knowledge of the events, the family context, and the child's other communications will be able to enter into meaningful therapeutic communication with a child using drawings, clay, or play activities. In this competency-based perspective, the child is recognized as able to provide, over time, any interpretation or explanatory meaning needed.

However, the meaning of any particular nonverbal activity may not be fully apparent to the therapist or even to the child at the time of its production. Each drawing, clay figure, or episode of play with dolls is similar to a single sentence in a story. Only over time does the larger, meaningful pattern become clear. For this reason, the child's work needs to be saved and kept together for the therapist (and eventually the child and therapist together) to review as the therapy progresses. A photograph or a sketch, along with a written description of a clay figure, doll house arrangement, or sandtray creation, can be made after the session ends. Puppet plays and play activities ideally should be audio- or videotaped and a transcript made for the file of important passages, including at minimum a summary of the plot or interactions. Because the meaning of particular figures or actions emerges only over time with this kind of communication, it is particularly important to document each production or creation rather than to rely on memory or general summaries.

Overview of Materials

In order to work with young children, the therapist needs to have simple, versatile materials and toys at hand. Play and art materials should

1. Be versatile in function and usefulness, able to be used in many ways.
2. Require active direction and choices by the child (e.g., not battery operated).
3. Encourage symbolic expression of needs and feelings by their plasticity and lack of defined use (clay or a piece of rope or yarn, for example, rather than a rocket).
4. Encourage feelings that are most central to victimization and abuse and most difficult to deal with, such as anger, fear, and guilt.
5. Be durable, nontoxic, not permanently damaging to clothes, and easily controlled (generally ruling out such media as fingerpaints).

Suggestions for specific kinds of art materials are included in the following discussion of various methods.

Drawing

Because much of the child's first experience and memory of the world is visual, most children like and want to draw. Even when the child is able only to scribble (ages 2–4), the scribbles are usually meaningful to the child and can help the child tell a story or provide a simple verbal description to the therapist.

Visual representation is nonlinear and holistic; it creates a *gestalt*, or whole. As such, it has many advantages to help the child communicate the complex nature of events and family relations. Family or other relationships can be represented simultaneously across time and space, within a meaningful frame. Past, present, and future can be included and the relative psychological salience of different persons can easily be presented.

For example, the drawing in Figure 12.1 by a child who is an incest survivor represents herself, her mother, and her stepfather in a double vision: in the left diagonal half of the house, Mom and Dad are shown as a happy couple, the way the rest of the world saw

FIGURE 12.1   An example of a drawing done by an incest survivor.

them. On the lower right, Dad and a large daughter with a grim face are of equal size, while a very small, ineffectual mom (the daughter's description) is to one side, unable to protect her daughter.

Materials

For therapeutic work with young children, it is important to have available large tablets of paper that are visibly different from "scribble" paper. Because most children like to scribble as part of non-directed play, it is important to communicate to them that this experience is different and is one in which they and the therapist and/or a family member are partners in communicating, A few crayons or nontoxic marking pens are sufficient for drawing, with crayons preferred for preschool children.

Basic Drawing

Any individual or family session can involve drawing the event or experience being discussed. Especially when beginning therapy and establishing trust, the first drawings include drawing oneself and one's family and then (perhaps in the next session) drawing the family doing something together. Older children with some sense of past and present can be asked to draw pictures of the family as it was earlier and as it is now.

These drawing exercises can be repeated throughout therapy, identifying changes in the child's perception of the family and representing feelings caused by changes in family structure. By having the first drawings available to go back to, the therapist also creates continuity across sessions for the younger child. Drawings are especially useful to help parents understand the reality of the child's experience from the child's perspective and can be effectively integrated into family treatment (Landgarten, 1987).

For older children, a natural and important extension of drawing is for the child to imagine or pretend to "become" some aspect of the drawing and act or talk for it—a unhappy cloud, teddy bear, mommy, or "bad" little boy. Oaklander (1978) suggests that children who are initially defensive benefit from more creative directions: "What kind of _____ are you?" . . . "Where are you?" "What's it like to be a _____?" "Who takes care of you?" (pp. 32–33).

Drawing a Feeling

Any experience or feeling or event can become the subject for drawing and for further interaction and discussion. Victims of abuse should be encouraged to draw their bad or angry or frightening feelings as colors, shapes, or perhaps as "awful monsters." Once these are represented on paper, the child can be encouraged to do some action to gain power over them—make them smaller, crumple the paper up, laugh at them, or add a resource figure to the drawing that can "slay the dragon." Such drawings may need to be done many times before the child can distinguish between him- or herself and the feelings. The child is not simply to represent the "bad feeling" but to objectify and take some action toward those feelings within him- or herself that were caused by the abusive event(s).

A child who has drawn or represented a feeling in some way will often want to add words to the picture (orally or, for older children, by writing on the drawing). The therapist can help express the feelings thus represented, assuring the child that this kind of reexperiencing will help master the feeling and put it in its proper place.

Resource Drawing

Mills and Crowley (1986) suggest a very useful and versatile healing technique, the "Resource Drawing," in their book, *Therapeutic Metaphors for Children and the Child Within*. The drawing is really a process that occurs in three steps, using three pieces of paper. First, the child is asked to draw a problem. (The therapist may want to space out each step of the process session by session, depending on the child's responsiveness and degree of engagement with each drawing.) Second, the child is asked to draw what the problem looks like "all better." Third, the child is asked to imagine or create something that "will help picture 1 change into picture 2." Children may bring in a fantasy figure, resurrect a missing parent, or in some other way represent a source of change and healing. Even when the change agent is not a realistic one (e.g., the return of a missing father), the therapist can use the child's representation to explore with the child and with a parent or family the qualities or resources that are missing and are needed, and discuss how these might be provided in some more realistic way. For example, a child who draws an absent father who would make things "all better" needs to know that a strong protecting figure will be available. Through stories, drawings, and work with the available caretaker, the therapist can then help that child construct an alliance with a person who can take on that role.

Mills and Crowley (1986) especially encourage preschool children to imagine how their favorite cartoon characters could help to make a problem situation "all better." Their reasoning is that TV cartoon figures are often sources of strength and power, "living metaphors that can act as a symbolic alternative for working through fears, anxieties and conflicts" (p. 209). They have developed a comic book using Fred Flintstone to help children find the inner resources to talk about abuse (Crowley & Mills, 1986).

Clay

Clay is a versatile medium that requires the child to "make something," create shapes, or express action. Since it involves basic kinesthetic/tactile senses, both children and adults are less able to employ their rational or cognitive defenses when working with clay. Used properly, therefore, it is one of the most useful symbolic media for clients of any age to work with.

Clay is especially useful for children with perceptual and motor coordination problems, as well as for anyone who is "out of touch" with feelings and body experiences—not uncommon for abuse victims. Clay bridges senses and feelings; it can make feelings more conscious and available for sharing and integrating with words. Thus, victims who have coped with abuse by dissociation and splitting into more than one "self" may, by working with clay, be able to regain access to those physical experiences, unpleasant memories, and feelings that have been carefully split off.

Clay is also readily erasable, giving freedom to make something and then "smush" it up. Because clay is not a school-taught art or skill, it carries almost no potential for being done "right" or "wrong." The therapist stresses and models that one "can't make mistakes" with clay.

Materials

While many therapists use commercial Play-Dough or plasticine, there are two other materials that are more durable and easier to work with. For very young children, the best clay is a homemade salt dough, as it is much easier for them to work (Table 12.1). It also keeps well for months in an airtight plastic container.

Because salt dough does not have the resistance or durability of potter's clay, the therapist may also want to have a block of regular clay on hand for older children or adults. Potter's clay withstands pounding and jumping (a good, safe activity for release of anger and aggression). Potter's clay also keeps for a long time if stored properly in an airtight plastic wrap or heavy plastic container. If it gets too

TABLE 12.1 Recipe for Salt-Dough Clay

Two cups regular flour	Two tablespoons vegetable oil
Two cups water	One teaspoon Burnt Siena tempura
One cup salt	paint or other nontoxic paint
Two teaspoons cream of tartar	
(otherwise clay will be pasty white)	

Mix flour, water, and salt carefully to smooth out lumps; add cream of tartar, coloring, and oil. Cook in saucepan over *low* heat for about 10 minutes, STIRRING CONSTANTLY. A solid mass will form, pulling away from the sides. Take out and knead for a few minutes while still warm to create a smooth texture (this is the best part—very soothing). Store in a plastic container with airtight lid.

hard, potter's clay can be "wetted up" in a bowl of water, then allowed to dry to the right pliancy. Neither of these clays will stain clothes or carpet, and they can be worked with on the cardboard backs of writing tablets or drawing pads.

Basic Uses

Clay is a great icebreaker for developing an interactive dialogue with a child. At the first meeting, therapist and child can both take a good-sized chunk of clay to hold onto while getting to know each other. Abused children are often withdrawn, frightened, or hostile (with good reason) and can be suspicious of therapy, especially if they have just been through police interviews or court hearings. Having something to hold onto, without the need to do anything, can provide comfort. No directions are needed; the therapist and child are free to punch or mold the clay while talking.

Durable potter's clay also provides a natural and safe outlet for a child's anger and hostility. Some children like to pound, kick, and stomp on the clay; they can be encouraged to do so as a safe way to let others know how they are feeling. This symbolic communication can be readily integrated into a structured session that explores the child's feelings toward the perpetrator or the nonprotecting parent by using the clay "to show how angry you are."

The Child's Actions with Clay as Metaphors

Oaklander (1978) suggests focusing on the child's physical actions that occur naturally and without thought when shaping clay. This strategy can be used readily with a child or in a family or group setting, by giving everyone a chunk of clay to "play with" and then asking each person what action they enjoyed most. "Pinching," "pounding," "hitting," "smoothing," and other concrete and meta-phorical actions are readily elicited and lead to discussing when/ where/to whom the child would like to do this. The goal is to move beyond polite words to enacting or experiencing feelings in a power-ful but safe way.

Oaklander (1978) also suggests having children talk as if they were the objects they make. For example, a boy might make an ashtray without any particular comment. But when asked to "be-come" the ashtray and speak for it, he is enabled to say, "I am an ashtray, scarred and dirty—my father uses me" (p. 72). Such self-expression is valuable in moving the treatment forward.

These activities with clay can also be used with families in treatment for abuse, both to help parent(s) learn how to play with their children in a constructive, healthy way and to give parents permission to express the feelings and images of their own "inner child." Getting parents in touch with their own "inner child" is an important family therapy goal for incest cases when one or both parents have also experienced similar incestuous abuse.

Play Therapy and Puppets

A variety of play objects provides opportunities for even the young-est child to express concepts and feelings, to communicate with the therapist and family, and to begin to develop coping strategies for mastering trauma and abuse.

The most helpful uses of play therapy are

> initially, to discharge emotions, reducing anxiety levels and pro-viding opportunities for more complex, conscious experi-ence
> to explore and understand boundaries
> to control aggression by finding safe, symbolic actions to ex-press anger and hostility

Materials

Axline (1969), the godmother of art and play therapy, provides a basic list of toys and materials: a doll house with a doll family and some furniture; clay; crayons (and marking pens); drawing paper; toy animals; toy soldiers; toy cars; baby doll and toy nursing bottle; two telephones; hand puppets or dolls representing family members and, if possible, authority figures (especially police and physicians); and some simple building materials.

Simple toy weapons, such as a gun, rope, or rubber knife, are also important to have on hand. Their presence signals that angry, aggressive feelings can be symbolically—and safely—expressed. Guerney (1983) points out that when such representational objects are not provided, children make their own out of sticks or use their fingers. However, they may be more reluctant to act out their aggressive feelings if they do not see objects that are used for that purpose in this society. A structured, time-limited play therapy manual for treating abused/neglected preschoolers is included in the references (Friedrich & Reams, 1985).

Puppets

The primary uses of stuffed animals or puppets in play therapy are to allow "someone else" to use forbidden or dangerous words and to carry out actions the child experiences as "bad" or "not-me." Use of puppets or stuffed animals as actors for the self or others can help achieve the goal of safely objectifying the trauma action and associated feelings. Small hand puppets that are easy for young hands to work or simply ordinary stuffed animals are the most versatile; large, complicated puppets are not as useful. A child can also be asked to bring his or her favorite animal from home, especially the one he or she takes to bed and tells everything that happens. A puppet or favorite animal can also become a symbol of the child's inner resources in the later stages of therapy.

Stuffed animals, dolls, and handmade puppets can all be used to act out experiences and especially to "speak for" the child or others. Because perpetrators of sexual abuse commonly tell their victims not to *tell* or *talk* about what has happened, allowing figures who are visibly and physically "not me" to do the talking is often the only way the secret can be told by a young child. As discussed earlier, preschool children take the meaning of words very literally; thus, if a puppet tells what happened instead of the child telling, from the child's point of view the injunction not to tell has not been violated.

STEPS IN TREATING YOUNG CHILDREN
INTEGRATING THE USE OF NONVERBAL AND
PLAY MATERIALS

Assessment

When initiating treatment of young children who are survivors of
incest or sexual abuse, the therapist will first assess the child's
communication style and preference, the child's level of cognitive
and social-emotional development, the family system and issues,
and the degree of trauma and specific traumatic effects on the child.

Finklehor and Browne (1985) have suggested that the nature and
degree of the sexual abuse and its overt effects can be mapped as a
useful initial guide to the kinds of psychological problems the therapist may encounter. They posit four trauma-causing factors in incest
and sexual abuse: *traumatic sexualization, betrayal, powerlessness,*
and *stigmatization.* These "dynamics" often co-occur in a victim of
sexual abuse. They "alter children's cognitive and emotional orientation to the world, and create trauma by distorting children's self-
concept, world view and affective capacities" (p. 531). Finkelhor and
Browne suggest that each dynamic is associated with some of the
commonly observed effects of child sexual abuse (guilt, withdrawal,
anger, fear, behavioral problems, etc.). The child's initial statements,
actions, and any drawings, clay figures, or doll play may indicate
where the traumatic effects are for this child.

Nondirective Play

Young children or severely traumatized older clients may need a
period of nondirective play before beginning more structured or di-
rective sessions. Such free play sessions can continue the assessment
of the child's concerns and level of development, introduce the child
to play and art materials, and foster rapport. Part of this nondirective play helps establish rituals for opening and closing each session, such as having the child draw a picture to begin each session.

Intentional Therapeutic Communication Process

Phases of therapy with a child and family may not be particularly
linear. However, as a quick guide, the therapist who works with

young incest/sex abuse survivors will probably cover the five goals of treatment already discussed: establishing rapport, objectifying the experience, reenacting the abusive situation to master it, regaining control over self, and building a new reality.

In this therapeutic process, art and play therapy materials can be used to represent family experiences and reactions or feelings, allowing the child to move at his or her own speed toward enacting the abusive experience.

Table 12.2 summarizes how the various kinds of nonverbal communication strategies described in this chapter might be used in connection with specific issues confronting survivors of sexual abuse and incest. [The issues come from the work of Porter et al. (1982); particular goals in relation to each issue, and some nonverbal activities methods for use with children have been added.]

TABLE 12.2 Examples of Specific Treatment Strategies for Major Treatment Issues in Sexual Abuse

Issues	Goals	Media/strategies
Damaged goods	Represent physical defects Represent reaction of others	Draw self or model in clay; "defect" may be represented visually/tactically but not verbally
Guilt	Represent, objectify "bad" actions, feelings	Draw or act out what you think you did wrong
	Help child see that adult initiated, maintained behavior	Represent what other did
Fear	Represent fears of reoccurrence, family change, loss, harm to body, future	Resource drawing; represent past and present as visible/tangible change
		Play out feared future events
Depression	Represent feelings, possible actions	Have child draw self depressed and not-depressed ("when you feel sad/not sad")

(continued)

TABLE 12.2 (Continued)

Issues	Goals	Media/strategies
Poor self-esteem, social skills	Work on size, defects, missing parts of body	Ask child to represent self in relation to others Use puppets, dolls, clay, drawings Represent negative, bad feelings about self
Repressed anger	Represent anger at X---- Express anger symbolically	Use pillows, clay, balloons, puppets, stuffed animals Draw a monster and stab it
Inability to trust	[Group process recommended]	Use mutual/interactive tasks
Role boundaries blurred	Represent "how it was" and "how I'd like it to be"	Draw family structure Puppet play about family interactions, scenes
Pseudomaturity	Help child to express and recover age-appropriate play	Nondirected play recommended with deliberate use of younger age materials
Self-mastery/control	[Group recommended]	Puppet play

The therapist teaches strategies for coping with abuse. As part of building a new reality, drawings of self and other modes of self-representation should be used to focus on the child's wholeness, goodness, and resources. For the future, the child can represent and/ or role-play going to positive helpers in that child's life (teachers, remaining parent, others) for protection. With preschoolers, it is unrealistic to overdo future planning or prevention possibilities; instead, the focus is on starting good habits in the present, such as "talking with my teacher right away if anything happens" (Friedrich & Reams, 1985).

Involvement of Parents/Family Members

This step may occur in parallel, joint, or sequential sessions, depending on the family dynamics. The entire family or the attending member(s) can engage in similar activities to accomplish specific purposes of family therapy—clarifying boundaries, supporting differentiation, rebuilding trust, and removing any stigmatization of the child or family. Simple drawings can be especially effective when working with a family. Each family member is asked to draw the same thing, and then the family discusses the similarities and differences in the way each person perceives a common event or situation.

CONCLUSION

Winnicott (1971) has aptly observed that one cannot do therapy with a child "if there is only one child in the room." While not giving up adult ego-consciousness or strength, the therapist who works with children must be able to interact with them, using *their* language modalities and symbols. In a family systems approach, the therapist must also model and engage some or all of the family members into appropriate ongoing communication with the child.

Many therapists have reservations about their ability to provide direct treatment for young children using materials such as clay, drawings, or play objects. These therapists have forgotten that such activities and materials form the natural, familiar language of the child. By having them available and integrating them into the treatment as a form of communication, the therapist will find the child a willing and eager teacher and guide.

REFERENCES

Axline, V. (1969). *Play therapy.* New York: Ballantine Books.

Bruner, J. (1973). *Beyond the information given.* New York: Norton.

Crowley, R., & Mills, J. (1986). *Fred protects the vegetables.* Woodland Hills, CA: Childhelp USA.

Finkelhor, D., & Browne, A. (1985). The traumatic impact of child sexual abuse: A conceptualization. *American Journal of Orthopsychiatry,* 55(4), 530–541.

Friedrich, W. M., & Reams, R. A. (1985). *A manual for time-limited play therapy with abused/neglected preschoolers.* Unpublished manuscript. Available from first author, Mayo Clinic, Rochester, MN.

Goodman, G. S. (1984). Children's testimony in historical perspective. *Journal of Social Issues,* 40(2), 9–32.

Guerney, L. (1983). Client-centered (nondirective) play therapy. In C. Schaefer (Ed.), *Handbook of play therapy* (21–62). New York: Wiley.

Landgarten, H. B. (1987). Family crisis intervention for a molested child. *Family art psychotherapy.* New York: Brunner/Mazel.

Mills, J., & Crowley, R. (1986). *Therapeutic metaphors for children and the child within.* New York: Brunner/Mazel.

Naitove, C. (1982). Arts therapy with sexually abused children. In S. Sgroi (Ed.), *Handbook of clinical intervention in child sexual abuse.* Lexington, MA: Lexington Books.

Oaklander, V. (1978). *Windows to our children.* Moab, UT: Real People Press.

Porter, F. S., Blick L. C., & Sgroi, S. M. (1982). Treatment of the sexually abused child. In S. Sgroi (Ed.), *Handbook of clinical intervention in child sexual abuse.* Lexington, MA: Lexington Books.

Schaefer, C., & O'Connor, K. J. (Eds.). (1983). *Handbook of play therapy.* New York: Wiley.

Sgroi, S. (Ed.). (1982). *Handbook of clinical intervention in child sexual abuse.* Lexington, MA: Lexington Books.

Waterman, J. (1986). Developmental considerations. In McFarlane, K., & Waterman, J. (Eds.), *Sexual abuse of young children.* New York: Guilford Press.

Winnicott, D. W. (1971). *Therapeutic consultations in child psychiatry.* New York: Basic Books.

IV Treatment of Adults Molested as Children

Incest: A Survivor's Story
and
13 A Therapist's Framework for Healing from Incest

Lana R. Lawrence
Mary L. Froning

I watch a young mother climb into the swimming pool with her 3-year-old daughter. They wrap their arms securely around each other and playfully bob up and down. Not a hint of distrust crosses this child's face; she appears confident of her mother's love and protection.

After a few moments, the mother attempts to place the child into an inflatable toy ring. Protesting, the little girl begins to kick her feet and cling desperately to her mother's neck. The mother tries to assure her daughter that she will not be left adrift, but her efforts fail.

Acknowledging the fear, the mother tosses the ring onto the deck and gently kisses her daughter's cheek. A smile of success and relief appears on the child's face.

The memory of myself as a small child surfaces: My arms are wrapped around my father's neck while swimming in a lake. I see the same joy on my face as I just saw a moment ago on the child's, until my father reaches his hand under my swimsuit to fondle me. My look of joy suddenly turns to one of shame and fear. Today, I am left with an image of horror and betrayal.

I acknowledge another equally painful memory of my mother, who did not protect me from my father. I look at the little girl in the pool and wish that I could have felt the same bond of trust with my mother that she feels with hers. Tears form in my eyes, and I dive into the water so they will go unnoticed.

An earlier version of Lana Lawrence's story appeared in the September 11, 1987, edition of *The Washington Post*.

My vulnerability is difficult to expose to others, but now I can allow myself the relief of crying. For most of my life, the pain was buried under the defenses that I had developed to emotionally survive the incest, physical abuse, and neglect.

My father, a former police officer, began to sexually abuse me at the age of 3 and continued until just prior to my 17th birthday. His assaults ranged from manual stimulation to oral, anal, and vaginal penetration. As a child, I did not understand what my father was doing. It seemed that he was giving me the love and affection that I desperately needed from a parent. He was my father and I trusted him. Only after he began to mention the word "secret" did I question whether what we were doing was right.

My father never physically forced me to participate sexually with him until my midteens. His force was emotional. He often manipulated me by telling me that I was special, granting favors, sparing physical punishment, or bribing me with money.

Between the ages of 13 and 15, I informed four people of the incest: my mother, a physician, a schoolteacher, and my best friend. None of them believed me. Yet my behavior at the time indicated that there was, in fact, something seriously wrong in my home environment.

I was desperately crying for help—through bedwetting, truancy, poor academic performance, attention-seeking behavior, self-destruction/self-mutilation, fatigue, anorexia/bulimia, chronic depression, and eventually drug and alcohol abuse and promiscuity.

Physical indications of sexual abuse were also present, such as chronic upper respiratory, kidney, and bladder infections as well as gynecological problems and rectal bleeding. My entire physical and emotional being screamed for someone to recognize that something was hurting me deeply.

At age 16, no longer willing or able to endure any further abuse, I ran away from home. A week later, my father found and brought me home, only to beat me and throw me physically out onto the sidewalk. My mother's immediate concern was that the neighbors might see what was happening. I walked away knowing that I would never return home, even if it meant ending my own life.

Putting aside my fear that again I would not be believed, I sought the help of a social worker at the county mental health center. Finally, someone believed that I was telling the truth. She looked at the bruises on my face and said that it was her responsibility to report child abuse to the Department of Social Services. She asked me if I would talk to a case worker. I said yes; she dialed the telephone.

As she talked to the case worker, my heart raced. I was terrified of what would happen next. Would my father go to jail? Would I be sent to a foster home?

That telephone call led to my father's indictment and trial. Although I was relieved to be out of my parents' home and in foster care, the thought of testifying against my father in court was horrifying. I was breaking the silence that he demanded I keep—I was betraying him. I thought of recanting my disclosure of the abuse. Telling the court that I had lied felt safer than facing my father in the courtroom.

Although the court was aware that fondling and vaginal intercourse had occurred, I could not tell them of the repeated oral and anal intercourse that my father had inflicted on me. I felt ashamed, as if I were to blame for the abuse and should have been able to stop him.

As I testified, I could see the hate in his eyes. My mother sat next to him; I had been abandoned. Her support of my father strengthened my belief that I was a very bad person.

At the end of the court proceedings, my father was convicted of criminal sexual conduct in the fourth degree. His sentence was a two-year probation, with an order for psychiatric treatment and a $750 fine. My sentence was the emotional aftermath of the abuse.

More than ten years have passed since the trial, and at age 29 I look back on the painful process of recovering. Healing the wounds of my childhood has required more than the passage of time.

In fact, most of this time was spent in a state of emotional denial. On an intellectual level, I knew that I had been a victim of incest, along with physical and emotional abuse. But on an emotional level, I felt numb. When talking about my experiences, it was as though I were speaking about someone totally separate from myself.

I lived from crisis to crisis, was unable to maintain a healthy intimate relationship, and continued to abuse alcohol. I had a brief involvement with prostitution, was financially irresponsible, chronically depressed, a compulsive overeater, and lived in a fantasy world. Yet at times my behavior was the opposite: super-responsible, perfectionist, mature, overachieving, and ambitious—to the point of near exhaustion.

Behavior that I had developed as a child to protect myself from my father was also still present. I would sometimes awaken in the night, screaming for my father to leave me alone. I often locked bathroom and bedroom doors out of fear that someone would attempt to enter and violate me.

I guarded my body with somewhat masculine gestures and clothing. For me, a feminine appearance meant being vulnerable to sexual assault. I rarely allowed anyone to touch me; any form of physical affection was frightening. I also suffered excruciating anxiety in situations where I felt a loss of control, such as a gynecological or dental examination.

The greatest effect of the abuse was the profound sense of guilt and shame that plagued me on a daily basis. I hated myself. No matter how hard I tried to feel good about myself, feelings of shame and worthlessness surfaced. Obsessive feelings of guilt would intrude into my thoughts over some insignificant mistake I had made. I was merciless with myself.

I continuously sought the approval of others. Surely someone would think that I was a good person if only I tried hard enough to please. I would do almost anything for a friend or an employer to gain approval, even if that meant neglecting or overextending myself.

At times, my guilt would overwhelm me to the extent of becoming suicidal. I wanted to end the pain, not my life, but the two were deeply enmeshed. I desperately wanted someone to rescue me from my pain. Turning others into parental figures and expecting to be taken care of was a way of survival. I didn't have to face my losses if I could maintain the fantasy that someday I would have the kind of parents I needed.

Eventually, I recognized my need to return to professional counseling. I had been in psychotherapy during the court proceedings, and again five years later. During my previous work with a therapist, I never allowed myself to cry or become angry. I wanted someone to help me grieve the loss of my family, control over my body, and a normal childhood. I didn't know that crying was a healthy and acceptable expression of pain.

This time, along with therapy, I now sought the help of an incest survivors' support group. Being in the presence of others with similar experiences helped me feel that I was not alone in my quest for recovery. Hearing other victims talk about their sorrow, fear, rage, and confusion allowed me to share my own feelings with them. We supported each other with acceptance and understanding, affirming that it was safe to grieve. Together, we acknowledged our need to learn ways of parenting ourselves. The skills that our parents should have taught us as children were absent. Essentially, we were growing up all over again.

In therapy, my social worker helped me become familiar with the little girl that I still carried within me—the little girl who was hurt by her parents and needed me as the adult to love and accept her. First, we looked at how I treated the part of myself that was still a little girl. When she cried for help, I would usually stifle her as much as my parents had. I learned that my self-abuse was directed at my little girl; I didn't want to acknowledge her existence. I was certain she was a demanding, rebellious, and rotten little kid. After all, wasn't this the message that my parents had given me?

I also learned that I had been treating my little girl as if she were an adult, as though she should have known better than to have been coerced by my father's bribes. I was angry at her for enjoying ths physical closeness and, at times, the sexual stimulation of the abuse.

To help me get to know my little girl, I gave her a name that felt affectionate. "Punky" was a nickname that an aunt called me, so this was my choice. In therapy, I worked on teaching Punky to trust that I would not try to quiet her if she wanted to share her pain with me or my social worker. Learning to listen to her gave me tremendous insight into my own needs, feelings, and behavior. Punky was learning that it was safe to trust—not only me, but also others.

Trust is the foundation of a child's life; my father exploited that trust through incest. Without the ability to trust, it is impossible to develop loving relationships.

Peeling back the layers of defenses to expose the core of my pain was frightening. Only by approaching and then retreating from my feelings could I allow myself to actively grieve. Trusting in my ability to stop when the pain became overwhelming was essential in allowing the grief to surface.

Losing control over my grief was a constant concern. I soon learned, however, that I had the inner strength to control my response to my own emotions, if only I would choose to exercise it.

For the first time, my tears began to flow. I wasn't sure if they would ever stop. My crying lasted, off and on, for several months. Over and over, I needed to recount memories of the abuse in order to accept and let them go. All of my life, the memories had controlled and haunted me. Now, I was gaining control over them.

Underneath the pain lay the rage toward my parents for what they had done. I was afraid of this rage because, as a child, my parents' anger often resulted in violence. The rage that was too threatening to express toward my parents out of fear of violence and rejection became internalized and directed toward myself.

My suppressed anger, the source of my self-destructive behavior, spread into other areas of my life. Often, it was transferred to an authority figure at work. I would overreact to criticism, create conflicts with co-workers, complain constantly, and allow others to take advantage of me.

Through therapy, my anger became apppropriately directed toward my parents. With the support of a friend, I called them on the telephone and screamed about how deeply they had hurt me. I also wrote letters to them in my angriest times. I mailed only one of the letters, but writing helped me to externalize my feelings and place them where they were manageable.

The relief I felt after slowly letting go of much of the pain and anger was great. Tremendous energy had been consumed in keeping it submerged. Now, I could use this energy for taking better care of myself.

In most cases of abuse, there are two people who are abused—the child who is now being abused and the parent who was abused as a child. I suspect that there was sexual abuse in both of my parents' backgrounds. My mother may have been physically abused, and my father's father, who was an alcoholic, apparently was also physically abusive.

Learning about my parents' childhood was helpful in eventually understanding their behavior. They clearly were victims of their own childhoods. This does not excuse them, because ultimately we are all responsible for our own behavior. But now I realize that they abused me because of their own experiences, not because I was "bad" and deserved to be abused.

Families can be successful in recovering from incest through family therapy. Unfortunately, my family was not. My parents' behavior has not changed enough for me to feel comfortable being with them. As painful as letting go is, I am having to break the ties and move toward building a life without them.

Although I am well into recovery, issues remain. Perhaps the most frightening issue is the acknowledgment of my own potential to abuse. Someday, I would like to have a child without being afraid of continuing the cycle of abuse. I know that, in time, I will gain trust in my ability to be a good parent.

Growing up in an environment in which there was little respect for individual privacy has left me with an impaired ability to find appropriate boundaries and balance in my relationships. I am learning to achieve a more delicate balance between dependency and over-self-reliance, and to reclaim my personal boundaries.

Many times when I think that I have resolved an issue, it reappears in my experience. It is not that I haven't dealt with it, but as a fellow incest survivor once said, healing is like a spiral staircase. We approach the same issues again and again, but on a different level in our recovery. From each new level, we gain a different perspective.

Flashbacks, such as the one triggered by the child in the swimming pool still occur. Sometimes they still overwhelm me, but I believe that remembering the horror of my abuse is crucial to my recovery. The incest is not my identity; it was my experience. Fortunately, I am letting that experience lead me to strength, knowledge, and healing.

I've learned that it's important for me to share my experiences with others who can be supportive. For most of my life, I felt as though I was carrying a horrible secret. I had always been certain that, if people knew of my past, I would be rejected. I'm no longer keeping the secret; my friends have helped me validate the fact that, although the secret was horrible, it was not my fault.

Enjoying the closeness in a genuinely loving and nurturing relationship has been my reward in recovery. Gradually, I am learning to give freely of myself, while facing my fears of being victimized or abandoned. I still have fears about closeness, but they no longer interfere with my ability to risk. I am finally learning how it feels to be in a healthy adult sexual relationship.

Most important, I am celebrating a new love of myself. I don't always like my behavior, but I am learning to accept my weaknesses and not expect perfection. My child within, Punky, still grieves, but we are no longer separate. I now know that she was only a little girl. I love Punky and value her softness and sensitivity, no longer believing that she is a "rotten little kid."

A Therapist's Framework for Healing from Incest

Mary L. Froning

As I reread Lana's story, it occurred to me that her anecdotes about parents swimming with children were metaphors for good and bad therapeutic relationships. The first illustrates how to build trust, the second how to destroy it.

When Lana entered into therapy with me, she left what had originally been a warm and helpful therapeutic environment. Unfortunately, that therapy had become unhealthy and frightening. It appeared her therapist not only did not have the specialized training to take Lana through to the end of her treatment, but also had made some dangerous errors by crossing the boundaries of therapy. This triggered the same kind of ambivalent feelings Lana expressed in her anecdote—her joy in her father taking her swimming being ruined when he crossed appropriate physical boundaries. Thus, what Lana had gained from her previous therapist by recapturing her memories and resolving some of her guilt, fear, shame, and rage was in danger as therapist-patient trust was disrupted.

Lana clearly stated, from the beginning, that it was to be my role to help her restore her faith in therapy. Her bravery and dedication to the healing process enabled us to begin this journey toward trust. As we jointly worked at noticing when trust was an issue, therapy began to work. Thus, like the good mother who noticed her child's protestations and put aside the toy ring until another day, I noticed Lana's discomfort and adjusted the pace of therapy. In so doing, I gave her the control she needed to take the necessary risks. Lana has made great strides, and her prognosis is excellent.

The betrayal of trust Lana experienced when her father began to sexually abuse her and her mother did not protect her has been particularly difficult to overcome because of its early childhood occurrence. Erik Erickson writes that the struggle of the developmental stage of Trust versus Mistrust within ourselves and with our environment begins during the earliest childhood years. When trauma interferes with the progression toward trust during the critical period from birth to six years, it is devastating to the child.

The consequences of the interruption of trust are numerous and severe, particularly in parent-child incest situations. The child does not develop a trust in her own instincts and perceptions. Things she felt as wrong, uncomfortable, or even painful were perpetrated continually by someone she was being encouraged to love and obey. This confusion often leads to revictimization, as the victim ignores danger signals and/or is led astray by others older or more powerful than she. Portia Nelson's poem "Autobiography in Five Short Chapters" is an excellent synopsis of the paths of destruction experienced by many survivors of incest who have been robbed of this faith in themselves. It describes the process of staying out of danger (i.e., falling in a hole in a sidewalk) as moving from being lost and helpless to developing the vision and strength to choose another path to avoid the danger. Therapy helps restore and, in some cases, build for the first time a person's trust in her own judgment. The therapist's tools are acknowledgment, validation, and being a trusting and trustworthy role model.

Therapy with survivors of incest requires a special attention to the task of confirming the client's selfhood and feelings. When a survivor asks if she is a worthwhile person, her inquiry is not idle, to be answered only with "I wonder why you are asking that." She needs an affirmative answer, with supporting data. Affirmation allows her to hear the necessary interpretation of transference issues.

When a survivor asks if it is all right for her to be angry with her mother because she told about the abuse and the mother did nothing, it is not sufficient to reply, "What do you think?" Although she might have some intellectual understanding of the issue, she is asking because she does not emotionally trust her belief. The question needs a therapeutic affirmation that a child deserves to be protected by *both* parents. When protection is not a reality, it is not the child's fault but is due to a deficit in the parents. Therapeutic guiding of the client into a review of, for instance, the innocence and helplessness of a small child may help her gain an emotional understanding of the basic premise of her right to parental protection.

For Lana it was particularly important that the therapy session became a safe place to express her anger. She needed to trust that she was not going to hurt anyone with her rage. She needed help to believe that her feelings were controllable and that she did not have to turn out like her parents, who hurt everyone around them with their angry, impulsive actions.

Someone who has been neglected and abused most of her early childhood by parents received the message that she was unworthy of receiving love and affection just for herself. In an incest victim's mind, often her body was her only contribution to the world of her family. This view, unfortunately, leaves her subject to reabuse by other adults. Lana, for instance, suffered physical and sexual abuse at the hands of several perpetrators.

The dynamics of reabuse are complex and varied. Sometimes, in an incest survivor's search for self-worth, she focuses on how it feels to be appreciated—if only for her body—instead of the fact that she is being used by someone. Later acknowledgment of the exploitative part of such a relationship is difficult, because to the client it means giving up the feeling that she was worth something to that person. Exploring the totality of the relationship and putting the abusive part into perspective is complicated and made difficult by the black/white view of many survivors toward their abusers. These all or nothing views are a result of being partially stuck in the concrete views of childhood. When freed to use adult, abstract abilities, survivors begin to unravel the picture of their reabuses and deal with both the abusive and, if present, the loving part of those relationships. This unraveling increases their ability to seek out an intimate relationship that contains no exploitative aspects.

In searching for intimacy, trust becomes central. Closeness feels dangerous and out of the control of the survivor. Cycles of closeness and distance, common in any intimate relationship, often become extreme in her relationships. Obviously, it is helpful for the survivor to work out these cycles at some level in the therapeutic relationship before attempting intimacy with a partner. When the sharing of self that occurs in therapy does not result in rejection or abandonment, the client begins to feel she can take risks to be cared about in an outside relationship. When conflict and distrust occur in the therapy and are resolved, she is encouraged to attempt a similar resolution in her greater world.

Most of the time, however, clients come into therapy with a previous or current history of intimate, nonfamilial relationships. Unfortunately, anguish and even violence frequently have characterized the search for safe intimacy. Almost always there is a confusion between sexuality and affection that makes even the definition of intimacy difficult for these clients.

The solution to difficulties with intimacy must include an appropriate choice of a mate. If the partner also has a limited capacity for intimacy, the client's difficult task is made almost impossible. Therapy often helps to identify the shortcomings of the partner in this area. Unless the partner also is able to use therapy to overcome barriers to intimacy, the relationship often dies a natural death as the client seeks the comfort and health of real intimacy. If the partner starts out or becomes able to be intimate, a relationship with a struggling survivor can be frustrating unless there is an understanding of the cycling she is experiencing. Couples therapy and/or supportive therapy for the partner are extremely helpful in maintaining a healthy relationship during this time of struggle. It is not recommended that the survivor's therapist alone take on the task of doing either couples therapy or individual supportive therapy for the partner. The survivor needs someone all her own, whose alliance will not be in any danger of being swayed. Otherwise, there exists the unnecessary risk that the client would perceive and/or actually experience a recreation of her abusive family and its divided loyalties. This recreation would interfere with both individual and couples treatment.

Another issue of trust is the nature of the therapeutic relationship itself. Above all, the therapist must be a trustworthy person, with appropriate boundaries and limits. It is easy as a "helper" for the therapist to respond to the client's dependency needs and wander across boundaries. However positively reinforcing this may seem for the client, at some level it is frightening as well. The survivor's reality was that people in authority with whom she was close betrayed and abused her. If she becomes afraid that abuse will recur, she will stop trusting and stop making progress in therapy.

The safety of the therapeutic environment is created with caringly given limits and boundaries. These boundaries should never include sexual overtures or behavior. Physical contact should be initiated only by the client. The rules for contact should be made clear at the beginning of therapy and again later, if necessary. If the therapist is not comfortable with appropriate contacts of hugging or holding a hand during a difficult session, the therapist should make her limits clear from the outset to avoid a client's later feelings of rejection. Telephoning between sessions should be limited to actual emergencies. Therapeutic overresponding to requests for more keeps the client from seeking assistance in her greater environment. Also, persistent requests may make the therapist angry and resentful. Seeing a client more than once weekly should also be avoided except, perhaps, in the beginning of therapy or in times of suicidal or other significant crises.

Setting boundaries by providing alternative support systems aids recovery. The therapist should strongly encourage a move toward a group after the client has individually begun the process of memory recovery and identification as a survivor. Self-help support groups such as Survivors of Incest Anonymous and Adults Molested as Children United (a part of Parents United International), as well as more traditional therapy groups for incest survivors, are invaluable therapeutic resources. These groups help clients work through feelings of emotional isolation and allow them to begin to make other friendships and supportive relationships. Groups also provide the client with the opportunity to gauge growth and progress, allowing her to observe new members who are just at the beginning, a place where she used to be. They also give the survivor a chance to learn how to give to others in appropriate ways—instead of their childhood patterns of giving to others always at the expense of themselves.

Lana's involvement in a self-help group was a key factor to her working through the disappointment with her previous therapy, allowing her to make the transition to a new professional. Through her leadership there she seems to gain satisfaction from helping others but is also able to continue to use the group for her own support. The group has also provided her with the challenge of setting appropriate limits—to put her own needs above others when necessary for good mental health.

The issues of survivors of parent-child incest challenge even well-trained therapists. It is imperative that all therapists be trained in this area; whether they plan to or not, they will be treating a survivor eventually. Therapists must be able to recognize the signs that incest may be part of a client's history, feel comfortable enough to ask questions to confirm incest, and be a trustworthy therapist by being competent to help their clients work out the myriad issues needing resolution.

The following short list of books and videotapes are helpful to therapists both at the beginning of their education and beyond. In addition, workshops and conferences, clinical supervision, and co-leading a group of survivors with an experienced therapist will fill in knowledge gaps.

BIBLIOGRAPHY

Bass, E., & Davis, L. (1988). *The courage to heal: A guide for women survivors of child sexual abuse.* New York: Harper & Row. [See page 183 for Portia Nelson's poem, "Autobiography in Five Short Chapters."]

Blume, S. E. (1990). *Secret survivors: Uncovering incest and its after effects in women.* New York: Wiley.

Butler, S. (1985). *Conspiracy of silence: The trauma of incest.* San Francisco: Volcano Press.

Courtois, C. A. (1988). *Healing the incest wound: Adult survivors in therapy.* New York: W. W. Norton & Co.

Daugherty, L. B. (1984). *Why me? Help for victims of child sexual abuse (even if they are adults now).* Racine, WI: Mother Courage Press.

Engel, B. (1989). *The right to innocence: Healing the trauma of child sexual abuse.* Los Angeles: Jeremy P. Tarcher.

Erikson, E. H. (1963). *Childhood and society.* New York: W. W. Norton & Co.

Forward, S., & Buck, C. (1988). *Betrayal of innocence: Incest and its devastation.* New York: Penguin Books.

Fraser, S. (1988). *My father's house: A memoir of incest and of healing.* New York: Ticknor & Fields.

Gelinas, D. J. (1983). The persisting negative effects of incest. *Psychiatry, 46,* 312–332.

Gil, E. (1983). *Outgrowing the pain: A book for and about adults abused as children.* Walnut Creek, CA: Launch Press.

Herman, J. (1981). *Father-daughter incest.* Cambridge, MA: Harvard University Press.

Lew, M. (1988). *Victims no longer: Men recovering from incest and other sexual child abuse.* New York: Nevraumont Publishing Co.

Maltz, W., & Holman, B. (1987). *Incest and sexuality: A guide to understanding and healing.* Lexington, MA: Lexington Books.

Poston, C., & Wilson, K. (1989). *Reclaiming our lives: For adult survivors of incest.* Boston: Little, Brown.

Russell, D. (1986). *The secret trauma: Incest in the lives of girls and women.* New York: Basic Books.

Wisechild, L. (1988). *The obsidian mirror: An adult healing from incest.* Seattle: Seal Press.

Videotapes

Incest: The victim nobody believes. A candid discussion by three incest victims about their experiences as children.

Madeleine. An emotional account of incest and its aftermath by a survivor. Available from Coalition Against the Sexual Abuse of Young Children, 5323 Nebraska Avenue, NW, Washington, DC 20015. Telephone: 202-966-7183. Cost: $25.

To a safer place. AIMS Media, 6901 Woodley Avenue, Van Nuys, CA. 91406-4878. Telephone: 1-800-367-2467.

14 Disguised Presentation of Adult Survivors of Incest and Other Child Molestation

Janet F. Fulmer

> The most important thing I want to say to you is, "Please tell someone about what is happening in your house." You do not have to carry the heavy burden and responsibility for what anyone else has done. Your secret will stop being so painful once it has been revealed. When you share your secret with someone, you join hands with another person and have the strength of two. And that is a start.(Butler, 1985, pp. 188–189)

The incest taboo has been recognized in most societies throughout recorded history. Indeed, the tragedy of Oedipus rests in the dreadful aftermath of his unwitting violation of the taboo, an illustration of the general belief in the strength and effectiveness of the prohibitions against incest. It becomes more and more clear, however, that it is the taboo against *talking* about incest that has in fact been honored; the incidents themselves have occurred and have been accepted, hidden, and denied.

There is increasing agreement that childhood sexual abuse is and has been extremely underreported. Statistics and estimates of incidences of incest are unreliable. Twenty to thirty years ago, incest was viewed as an occurrence as rare as one or two cases among every million people (Weinberg, 1955; Lindzey, 1967, cited in Johns, 1986). Current studies suggest that more than 10% of the female population are incest survivors and that an alarmingly higher percentage have experienced unreported sexual abuse outside the family (Herman, 1981; Johns, 1986; Miller, 1984). As information about early sexual victimization of males emerges, we can expect to find that many more men than previously assumed are also survivors of early abuse.*

The marked increase of reported incidents in recent years is in part attributable to publicity about allegations and investigations of abuse and to dramatizations of the subject. Such media activity helps establish and communicate an atmosphere of societal acceptance that encourages talking about and reporting sexual abuse.

OVERT AND COVERT SEXUAL ABUSE

Sexual molestation is defined as any sexual transaction between an adult and a child, including sexual activity between minors who are more than five years apart in age. The definition of *incest* encompasses sexual contact or interaction between any family members who are not marital partners. Thus, there can be incestuous activity between consenting adults or between minors of approximately the same age without molestation or abuse taking place. For instance, siblings or an uncle and niece one or two years apart in age might engage in nonabusive incest. Whenever the perpetrator is larger, older, more powerful, and therefore someone to whom the child might appropriately look for caretaking, any sexual activity is an abuse.

Fondling, oral/genital contact, masturbation between perpetrator and victim, sexual kissing, and other overt forms of sexual abuse can have lifelong crippling effects on the victim. The same is true for covert forms of sexual abuse, which include lascivious looking at a child, forcing a child to look at an exposed adult, and sexual touching disguised as nurturing. The difference between nurturing or incidental contact versus sexual acts is clearly recognized by the child, no matter how well the perpetrator fools him, or herself (Caruso, 1987; Gil, 1983; Herman, 1981).

Covert incest victims have the same problems as victims of overt incest but to a lesser degree. The differentiating factor seems to be the mother's greater self-respect and socialization. Typically, in the covertly incestuous family the mother is present and healthy, that is, not an invalid. She maintains some self-esteem within the family system; although she may be emotionally abused, she won't

---

*The feminine pronoun is used in this chapter in part for stylistic ease and also in recognition that the preponderance of studies and literature about sexual abuse of children discuss girls' experiences.

let herself be beaten. She has at least one intimate relative or friend outside the nuclear family and will not tolerate being isolated from that person even though she may go along with general isolation of the family from their social milieu. To the extent that she is assertive in her own right, she extends protection to her children, whether or not she gets along well with them (Herman, 1981). Our attention needs to be directed to events and effects of early sexual victimization within broad parameters. Parents who habitually walk around the house nude or exposed; the father who, as a matter of course, goes out to the back porch to finish dressing, in view of the playing children, because "he is too hot inside"; adults who insist on washing a child's genitals even though he is old enough to bathe himself; the family that humiliates a girl at the onset of menses; all are practing covert sexual abuse.

> When Sophie was three, her mother died; she and her dad went to live with his mother and four unmarried brothers. One day soon after Sophie's seventh birthday, her grandmother instructed her to take off all her clothes and get up on the kitchen table to be shaved. Thereafter, this scene was repeated weekly as Grandmother shaved Sophie from waist to ankles, ostensibly in the service of good grooming. This abuse continued until Sophie, at 16, refused any longer to submit and was punished by her father for being rebellious toward her grandmother.
>
> When Sophie entered therapy she deemed herself evil and mean-spirited because (unaccountably to her at the time) she hated the grandmother who took her in and raised her. It was after two years of hard work in treatment that she mentioned the shaving ritual. She had borne intense guilt for her negative feelings toward her grandmother and suffered both body image distortion and dissociation from her body without ever realizing that these feelings might be connected with the shaving ritual, which she accepted as "normal" and "just the way things are."

Mediating Factors

Sexual abuse is always a stressful event, but there are factors that can mediate the severity of its long-term effects, particularly support and acceptance from caring adults. If a child is molested by a stranger and goes home to tell a nurturing and understanding family that cares for her and does whatever is possible to punish the perpetrator, she will have fewer long-term effects from the incident, if any. The greatest ameliorating factor seems to be the child's having someone believe and help him or her. Many persons who survive undamaged remember adults who helped them integrate and overcome their trauma (Tsai et al., 1979, cited in Herman, 1981).

At the other extreme is the child victimized from preschool days into adolescence by someone who is supposed to be a caretaker, a child bound to secrecy about the aggression being visited upon her. The perpetrator threatens her with violence, loss of love, and/or family disaster if she tells. She experiences herself cut off from mother and any other adult. If she tries to tell someone, she is not believed. Unable to find any validation or protection, she suffers not only the original victimization of sexual abuse but betrayal by mother, the chief caretaker. And perhaps worst of all, she is betrayed by a world in which there is nowhere to turn for succor. Thus, the entire emotional environment in which the victim finds herself is part of the stressor.

REASONS FOR DISGUISED PRESENTATION

It has been the rule for incest and other molestation to remain undisclosed even through long therapeutic treatment. Incest victims rarely disclose spontaneously, and professionals do not usually ask about sexual abuse history. Survivors present for treatment in a disguised fashion. If that disguise becomes the focus of treatment, the incest history remains hidden, its negative effects are not available for treatment, and the therapy goes nowhere. Symptoms become repetitive and exacerbated. Treatment is sometimes perceived as yet another betrayal, even though the molestation has not been revealed (Gelinas, 1983).

There are both societal and intrapsychic reasons for this disguised presentation. The taboo against talking about incest or any sexual molestation has been almost inviolate until the past few years. In a society that believed there were only 200 cases of incest in a population of 200 million people, who would be willing to identify himself or herself as one of the few so stigmatized? And stigma there surely would be, for society far too often holds the attitude that the victim has brought it upon herself, that she must somehow have "asked for it."

Families where incest occurs tend to be closed and isolated as well as disorganized. Many cases occur in families where alcohol problems are also present, and where the "no-talk" rule is a strong element in maintaining denial. It is not unusual for the perpetrator to have been a childhood sexual abuse victim. Not infrequently a daughter begins to be abused at the same age her mother was abused, by a father who was himself abused, and thus all three operate under very strong "no-talk" injunctions (Caruso, 1987; Woititz, 1983).

Sometimes clients, like Sophie, believe "that's the way it's supposed to be." There are substrata of society wherein it is accepted that all females in the family are to be available to the sexual needs of any male in the family. In another circumstance, girls seeing sexual abuse endemic around them think about it with a childlike naivete as if it were a plague or unavoidable life difficulty like roaches, rats, or the common cold. Because of such a matter-of-fact view, victims may not deem their experiences of sexual abuse worth mentioning and may not recognize a connection to their current personal problems.

Clients also hide the events out of simple shame. The older the victim was at the time of the abuse the more she is apt to see herself as dysfunctional and at fault. Even in cases where the abuse began during toddlerhood and continued into one's teens, the victim blames herself "because by the time I was ___ years old I should have done something about it," with little understanding of or forgiveness for herself. The victim, already hiding a "bad self," avoids talking about the sexual abuse lest that felt "bad self" be revealed.

Clients may suffer total or partial amnesia about the events. Others may believe they have handled it already. In the case of multiple personality, the personality presenting for treatment may not be aware of the molestation. An individual suffering from Posttraumatic Stress Disorder may be in the repression phase, that is, the denial/numbing phase, with the more obvious symptoms of long-term impact buried (Scurfield, 1985).

The individual may still believe that disclosure can destroy the perpetrator, some other member of the family, or the entire family. She thus lives with the dreadful burden of the (unconscious) knowledge that she has the power to destroy the family just with her words. Or she may understand disclosure to be a threat to herself. A large, menacing adult threatening, "I'll kill you if you ever tell anyone," can terrorize a child so traumatically that the adult cannot speak of the events even though she does not remember why she fears for her life. At another level, it may be that during the sexual abuse the perpetrator offered the only love or gentleness the child experienced during growing up. Under threat of losing that love, she cannot tell.

Some children feel strongly that something is wrong, but, lacking experience and adequate vocabulary, they cannot verbalize it. The feeling, and the inability to talk about it, are not necessarily extinguished simply by growing to adulthood. Some adults present in great distress yet virtually unable to talk about the feelings and thoughts related to their pain.

> I had no vocabulary to express my confusion, my fears, my view. A child has no vocabulary power, so adults rape children thinking the children don't know what's happening. Children *do know*—but children have no language . . . to communicate. It's like being a *prisoner in a foreign country*, and not knowing the language. . . . I cried a lot. (Maltz & Holman, 1987, p. 13)

It can be that the child has no alliance at all with her mother. Victims fear that if they disclose there will be no change, confirming the family's lack of caring for them. This fear is often quite realistic. Nondisclosure can be a child-logic way of maintaining the hope that if disclosure is made, some nameless day in the future, someone will understand and protect. The disappointment of nothing happening or of being punished for disclosing is avoided. The survivor who has already experienced disappointment and even further abuse upon having disclosed in the past may decide to avoid disclosure rather than risk more shame and disappointment.

The victim may not disclose out of fear of mother's anger and jealousy or out of fear that the mother will be crushed, ruined, killed, or driven crazy if forced to view the truth.

Above all, intense control is often a survival mechanism for a child enduring chronic sexual abuse. Disclosure of any kind triggers the experience of loss of that life-sustaining control.

VICTIMS' COPING STRATEGIES

Victims develop coping strategies to protect their sense of well-being and personal integrity. The coping strategies the child uses form the bedrock of the adult's coping style and will strongly influence the adult's presentation of self. Combining with the child's thoughts and feelings about self and world, they serve to delineate the effects of the abuse on the individual's life and psyche.

During sexual abuse, children experience terrible physical sensations, overwhelming discomfort and pain or unusual pleasures, with a flooding of fear, panic, confusion, and anxiety. They may fear for their lives. In chronic abuse, it is an immense strain to find out why this is happening, try to stop or avoid it, all the while surviving and maintaining one's sanity (Maltz & Holman, 1987).

As the child grows to adulthood, the coping strategies solidify, along with some of the beliefs the child has developed to make sense of these confusing events. Abuse victims grow up with no sense of protection or security and little ability to trust. They may believe that all families are like the one in which they grew up. Unconscious processes become established as the ground for lifelong distrust of and denial of the validity of their own feelings and perceptions.

Most coping strategies of sexually abused children are directed toward escape. A chief mechanism is dissociation, which can eventually lead to multiple personality and to mind/body split. In this strategy, the child removes herself from her body. Using intense concentration, the victim hypnotizes herself to "go elsewhere," that is, merge with the wall or the lamp, remove herself to a corner of the ceiling, or become a mouse in the wall and watch the house from there. Another use of self-hypnosis is numbing of parts of the body to the point of losing all feeling. Adult survivors are known who can induce and reinforce anesthesia in their bodies at will, although sometimes they have trouble getting the feeling back (Gelinas, 1983).

Children may pretend to be asleep, sublimating their feelings and reactions during sex. Others use alcohol or drugs, ingesting to be numbed before the perpetrator comes home and begins the night's abuse.

THE DISGUISED PRESENTATION

Survivors present with a spendid variety of lifestyles, complaints, backgrounds, and symptoms and cannot be stereotyped. The effects of early unmitigated sexual abuse, however, generally can be described as comprising negative self-image and low self-esteem, a sense of being different and distant from normal people, a sense of powerful sexuality sometimes expressed in a malignant way, and invariably great difficulty in trusting self or others.

The listing of long-term effects of childhood sexual abuse in Table 14.1 is compiled from careful study of many cases and many detailed discussions with colleagues and culled from the readings listed in the references. Not all victims of childhood sexual abuse present with all the listed symptoms; in fact no one does.

The presence of some or many of these symptoms does not of itself indicate a history of early sexual abuse. This listing is offered as a collection of signals to alert the worker to explore the possibility of past sexual abuse as the genesis of the client's current difficulties.

TABLE 14.1 Long-term Effects of Childhood Sexual Abuse

Hatred of own body
Mistrust of own perceptions
Low self-esteem
Feelings
  Powerlessness and helplessness
  Anger, guilt, depression
  Anxiety attacks, phobias
  Grief, shame
  Feeling different, soiled
  Sense of own badness
  Self-hate, feeling stigmatized
  Feeling isolated, abandoned
  Feeling betrayed
  Imposter syndrome
  Fear of having children
  Dependency/independency conflicts
  Pseudo-maturity
  Overvaluing and/or fearing men
  Control issues
  Denial, dissociation, memory gaps
  Wanting to kill self
  Sexual dysfunction
  Nightmares, flashbacks
  Fear of intimacy
  Paranoia
  Sense of malignant power
Physical problems
  Migraines and backaches
  TMJ; GI problems; genitourinary problems
  Hyperventilation
  Undiagnosed chronic pain
  Epileptic-like seizures
  Sexual dysfunction
Behavioral difficulties
  Passivity
  Substance abuse
  Eating disorders
  Self-defined promiscuity
  Prostitution
  Repeated victimization
  Impulsivity
  Self-multilation
  Suicide attempts
  Hyperalertness, isolation
  Workaholism, overachievement

(continued)

TABLE 14.1 (Continued)

Chronic relationship problems
Perfectionism
Over- and/or underresponsibility
Overprotection of children
Abuse of children
Selflessness
Mistrustfulness
Sexual dysfunction
Suicide thoughts or attempts

Sexual abuse occurs in all strata of society. We can, for instance, contrast the Classic Incestuous Family with the Multiproblem Incestuous Family. The Classic family is not known to social agencies and is well concealed from outsiders. The parents probably married early and stayed married, having many well-behaved children. There are few, if any, extramarital affairs in this group. The father, often a pillar of the community, rules through fear, exercising rigid, restrictive control and limiting family members' contact with the outside world.

> Louise did not enjoy remembering her childhood, hard, bleak and unfashionably Dickensian. . . . Dorothy recalled to Louise one particular foster home where she had been better fed and better dressed than she was used to and far more terrorized, because the father of the household tried to put his hands into her panties whenever he caught her alone. He had been a deacon of the Methodist Church. (Piercy, 1988, p. 111)

The Multiproblem Family is known to social agencies and is identified with physical abuse and neglect. The parents are involved in assault, drugs, drunken driving, financial difficulties, often spotty work records, possibly some criminal activity. The children are involved in truancy, arson, drug dealing, sexual promiscuity, and illegitimate pregnancies. Parents are sexually promiscuous.

Race, financial and social status, geographical location, church affiliation, education, profession, and job are all, in this context, irrelevant data. Sexual abuse of children is a most democratic problem.

Some survivors are extremely functional, genuinely accomplished in their fields, often prize winners and very respected. Work life and nonpersonal functioning proceed at a high level beside a dysfunctional personal life marked by consistently poor relationships, inability to achieve intimacy, characterological depression complicated by atypical impulsive and dissociative behavior such as bulimia, alcohol or drug abuse or compulsive buying, and constant feelings of despair. They live rich and full lives steadily complicated by these "mini-suicides" (Courtois, 1988; Gelinas, 1983; Herman, 1981).

> In the course of two marriages and two divorces, Evelyn moved from a clerical job near her East Coast home through college in the Midwest, founding and owning her own TV production company—which she ultimately sold for a large sum of money—to her present position high in corporate life in New York City. Vice-president of a major corporation, she lives in a ridiculously expensive apartment and spends most of her waking hours negotiating with high-powered people on the international scene.
>
> Both her husbands were alcoholic; one beat her; neither was willing to have children, so she had several abortions during her marriages. She has cut off her relationship with her sister, hates her father, and despises her helpless and now ailing mother. She nearly died in an auto accident caused by her drunken driving. She moves back and forth between anorexic behavior and compulsive eating and is obsessed with shame about her body.
>
> "A dozen times a day," she reports, "I feel a panicky despair. Then I do something that makes things happen. I telephone abroad and change the shape of the world somewhere for somebody, and I feel I've accomplished something, I can be effective, and the hopelessness recedes. If all else fails, I can buy something expensive, but even that doesn't always work. Sometimes I am so lonely that I think the pain of it will kill me. Most of the time I'm not even there for myself."

Some survivors build on their ability to split mind and body and opt for a life of mind (intellectual) or (heart) caretaking. The parentified survivor will choose some kind of caretaking life or work situation, while feeling emotionally needy, low in self-esteem, and driven by a high need for approval from others. The Heroic Caretaker, for example, works literally to exhaustion for the sake of others, uncomplaining and usually unappreciated. Other survivors will be seen as extraordinarily self-effacing, with little ability to express themselves verbally and no capacity for self-assertion—often speaking in very low, soft voices that are quite hard to hear, sometimes so soft that everything must stop around them for their listeners to be able to hear them. They are inwardly fragile and shy, lack self-confidence, and retreat to a world of books, poetry, or art to the exclusion of the social world, much like Laura in *The Glass Menagerie*. When we meet Laura, she is spending her life in a fantasy world she has created around old phonograph records and tiny spun glass animals, hiding and protecting her psychologically crippled self.

The High Flyer presents a contrast to Laura. Intuitive, artistic, often mystical, she runs to all the dangers of love, a chase that may often include compulsive searching for a caring man. Closely related to this style is that of the misfit, whose self-esteem and self-respect are so low that she needs to be adored at all times to feel OK about herself, as exemplified by Marilyn in *After the Fall*. Other variations of the Misfit include the militant lesbian and the Tough Woman, both of whom seem to be operating out of reaction formation. All, however, are living lives of quiet despair (Leonard, 1983).

A major effect of molestation is hatred of one's own body, usually accompanied with persistent body image distortion. Many eating-disordered persons, all of whom suffer from body image distortion, are expressing self-hatred and self-disgust through the punishing and nonnurturing aspects of their eating disorders, acting out a compulsion to self-punishment.

Nonnurturing, self-hating, and punishing components exist in every addiction; it is essential to explore carefully for childhood sexual abuse in any case of compulsive addictive behavior.

Dierdre had been chronically abused by her father from toddlerhood until age 16, when she left home. She joined the army, where she had a successful career for 10 years, during which time she went to college. She then went to graduate school and got her MSW degree and held a responsible position as social worker in a mental hospital. From the time she left home, she never thought about the events of her childhood. She was to all intents and purposes out of touch with her feelings and lived her life from her mind and thoughts. She kept herself as unaware of her body as possible.

She had drunk alcoholically for many years but had joined AA and was in recovery when she was diagnosed as diabetic. In an effort to avoid insulin medication or injections, she was instructed to lose a lot of weight and to feed herself according to a careful, demanding (but not rigid) diet. Her considerable intelligence and fundamental honesty left no room for her to ignore the medical findings or to consciously and willfully harm herself with neglect, so she strove to adhere to the instructions as given and paid attention to her body's needs for nourishment. Thereafter she began to experience nightmares and flashbacks because she could no longer dissociate from her body, feed "it" without conscious awareness, or discount the importance of her physical self.

Victims' dissociation from their bodies is an important component of some eating disorders. The body must be fed, but eating proceeds outside of conscious awareness; in fact all bodily signals remain outside of awareness, since the survivor is unable to tolerate any conscious awareness of her body. Therefore, the discomforts of compulsive overeating or refusal to feed the body are not consciously experienced.

PRESENTATION

Predominant pathologies with which adult survivors present include borderline, hysteric, obsessive-compulsive, narcissistic, paranoid, and mixed personality disorders; a wide variety of anxiety disorders, including dissociative, sexual, and control problems; phobias, substance abuse, and eating disorders; self-mutilation and other self-destructive impulses and behaviors; psychosomatic conditions; characterological depressions and major depressive episodes; and posttraumatic stress disorder (PTSD). PTSD, however, is usually a direct presentation, involving flashbacks and nightmares about the abuse, and is associated with depression, anxiety, impulsive and aggressive characteristics, and suicidal ideation and/or behaviors. PTSD often commences after some change in life circumstances breaches defenses against memories of the abuse, as happened with Dierdre.

There are three basic problematic life positions held by adult survivors. First, the depressive, which encompasses the concepts of absorbing the evil in the world (repeat victims, as well as helping professionals and caretakers) and protecting the parents (protecting the nonabusing parent from punishment along with protecting the abuser). Second, survivors who predominantly experience themselves as "objects," discounting feelings and punishing the self through both vicious superego and self-destructive behaviors, sustain a schizoid life position. They idealize at least parts of the parental figures and at the same time incorporate abusive aspects of the parents. Their "bad self" emerges from the belief that their idealized parents would love them if they were only good enough; they punish themselves, as the abusing parent did, in the unconscious hope of beating themselves into being good enough.

Finally, the paranoid position is based on identification with the aggressor, a choice based on fear. Individuals repeat the damaging parenting they endured, believing that "my parents' strictness made me the honorable person I am today" with a rigid righteousness, thus maintaining the symbiotic attachment between abused and abuser. Inhibition, rather than dissociation, is the primary defense against the parental betrayal in this population, and the primary inhibition may be against the wish and impulse to kill the threatening parent and the betrayer. Children who were both sexually and physically abused, especially if both abuses were perpetrated by the same parent, are most apt to move into the paranoid position (Clarkson, 1988).

Behaviors that can alert the professional to explore the possibility of early sexual abuse include learned helplessness; persistence in keeping oneself in a position of powerlessness; repeated victimization, sometimes combined with compulsive searching for a caring man or woman; chemical dependency in the family; confused family role boundaries; seductive sensual behavior or inappropriate words and talk about sex among young children; early exit from home and early marriage; illegitimate pregnancy; rigid family morals and/or rigid religious beliefs; and repeatedly getting stuck in the same place in therapy.

An over-and-over again aspect to therapeutic impasse is often a sign that undisclosed sexual abuse underlies visible pathology. For example, the on/off attitudinal switch common to survivors contributes to the frequency of borderline diagnosis in this population. Indeed, some adult survivors have borderline personalities, but to treat the personality disorder without addressing the effects of childhood sexual abuse will ultimately turn out iatrogenic; that is, the attempts to be helpful will cause more harm than good. The adult survivor whose molestation issues are not addressed in treatment will most times unconsciously perceive that omission as another betrayal, even if she has never mentioned the sexual abuse to the professional. Her hopelessness about finding health and safety in the world can be reinforced if molestation issues are not addressed.

Some typical cognitive formulations have been noted among adult survivors. Fear and anxiety are sometimes expressed with statements such as "I'm afraid I will be always alone," "I'm afraid I will lose my mind," or "Other people will hurt me" and a general attitude that the world is a dangerous place. Indeed, it is not unusual for a client, when asked if she believes the world is a dangerous place, to respond that it is silly to ask a question to which the answer is so obviously yes.

Anger and frustration are sometimes expressed with the following conflictual emotional and superego messages: "I hate my mother for not protecting me, and I hate my father and want to hurt him for doing that to me" versus "I should not feel so angry and hateful."

"I hate myself [for letting this happen]," "I am responsible for [this]; I believe I caused it," and "I am punished for being a bad person" express guilt and remorse. Infinite sadness lies behind statements expressing grief of a lost childhood and a sense of emptiness or the inability to feel.

Shame and self-disgust are contained in statements such as "I will always be helpless; I don't believe I'll ever be able to control my life," "I have no confidence in myself," "I don't trust myself," and "I cannot trust anyone" (Donaldson, 1983).

Adult survivors present with life problems as varied as any other population. There are, however, a few red flags that should not be overlooked. Adult survivors can live with external crises, but they have a far harder time living with their own feelings, which begin to emerge in consciousness when there is no crisis to deal with.

In one scenario, a woman emerges triumphant from a plethora of life-disrupting problems. She has an acceptable place to live and is not in an abusive relationship, is in compliance with the law down to the stickers on her car, children are all doing well and out of trouble or in recovery programs, and, for the first time in her life, she has a decent job that pays enough money to support her and her obligations. And she tells you she has just quit her job because she realized she ought to be paid more money and they refused her a raise.

"After all, I have to protect myself. I can't go on letting them take advantage of me!" she declaims, explaining indignantly why she took this precipitous, self-destructive action. She treats attempts to inquire how she's going to pay the rent and the other necessaries of her and her family's lives as attacks, replying, "I never thought you would turn against me!" And so she has put at risk all that she worked so long and hard to gain and will, in all likelihood, turn again to that familiar source of "rescue," a man who will sooner or later abuse her in some way.

A milder version of life sabotaging is seen in adult survivors' out-of-character, impulsive, self-destructive acts. Someone who is usually mistrustful will unexpectedly behave in a naively trustful fashion, patently disregarding simple basic self-care principles, and thus get into social, financial, or other trouble. Someone who is usually overly nice will flare out with violent words or actions, sometimes needlessly offending those around her. An overly responsible person's irresponsibility will have lasting consequences. In each instance, some degree of crisis, of external pressures and problems, is created in the survivor's life to provide distraction from inner feelings.

Along the same line, it is prudent to look for childhood sexual abuse in families where any member is chemically addicted, has an eating disorder, or is a compulsive gambler or spender. The procurement of supplies, the addiction itself, and the subsequent crises and feelings serve to keep one's focus outside the self and to escape from memories and feelings.

UNCOVERING SEXUAL ABUSE

The simplest and most efficient way to get at sexual abuse information is to ask for it during intake. Professionals who regularly ask about overt and covert childhood sexual molestation as part of psychosocial history taking report a variety of responses. If there has been no molestation history, the client in most instances simply says so. If she takes umbrage at having been asked the question, the interviewer merely explains that such an inquiry is automatically part of every assessment because of the ubiquitousness of the occurrence. After that explanation, a client's continued disturbance about the questioning can be taken to suggest some undisclosed sexual abuse history.

Sometimes the client's "No" is part of the denial and disguise. More often, however, the client will be relieved, openly or secretly, to hear the question and finally to have met someone who takes the matter seriously. Professionals must train themselves to deal with whatever responses these inquiries elicit, to be ready to seek information just as in any other pertinent area of the client's life.

First and foremost, the professional must deal with his or her own countertransference and molestation issues, lest unresolved personal conflicts lead to unconscious overidentification with or distancing from the victim or from the subject. Furthermore, professionals must overcome their own intense reactions based on the taboo of the abuse and the taboos against talking about it. Adequate education and training is essential. Many of us have been trained to deny the existence and the importance of incest and other childhood sexual abuse. It is still not unusual for a supervisor to advise a worker not to open that subject up because "the client won't be able to handle it." Psychoanalytic traditions, furthermore, mitigate against exploring incestuous events in their own right, teaching that it is not the actual event but "deep unconscious wishes for the father" that shame the child and make her feel guilty. A text in current use maintains that childhood sexual traumas were "provoked by the victims and were compulsive repetitions of preoedipal conflicts" and that the traumas are used as a "masochistic justification for a defense against sexuality" (Blos, 1962, cited in Johns, 1986, p. 39).

The intense rage and helplessness that can accompany the client's disclosure can be frightening and, if care is not taken, can resonate with the professional's own helplessness and anger, sometimes leading to apprehension and debilitating anxiety in the untrained, unskilled worker. Workers can also be hampered in their effectiveness by their sadness for the client's experience and their horror at the realization of what actually happened to the client.

Amid these feelings, however, it is important not to forget reality. Whatever happened, happened; that is not to be minimized but need not be horribilized either.

While guarding against any tendencies toward voyeurism or inapppropriate curiosity, the professional should take an active role in aiding disclosure. A passive tabula rasa position on the part of the worker may inadvertently confirm the victim's belief that her secret is too terrible to share with anyone.

TREATMENT ISSUES

Some guidelines may be useful to help desensitize professionals to the subject of childhood sexual abuse, especially incest. First and foremost, it is important to remember that it is assault that happened, not anything else, no matter how gently or sweetly the sexual approach was couched, for sexual abuse is an act of aggression, not an act of sexuality.

While remaining sensitive to the intense pain that attaches to dealing with this issue for the client, the professional needs to avoid expressions of horror, disbelief, judgment, or denial. Although there is need for special learning and training to treat clients with this particular problem, it is detrimental to treatment to behave as if the adult survivors themselves were special. Once the subject of sexual molestation has been raised, the worker must be careful to keep it in focus and to resist any temptation to avoid it. At the same time, a balance must be struck with other aspects of the client's life, which do not cease to be important as soon as sexual molestation has been disclosed.

Skepticism is best forgotten, for it is better to err on the side of belief than to revictimize a survivor through erroneous disbelief. Trust is the major problem throughout the lives and treatment of adult survivors. It gets in the way of treatment all the time and everywhere, thus making these among the most difficult clients to treat. The professional needs the ego strength to withstand and accept the client's mistrust and anger without taking it personally. Do not ever make the mistake of expecting to be trusted just because you are trustworthy or just because you were trusted in the past by this client!

The hardest part of treatment is to convey to an adult survivor that there is safety in the sessions with the worker and that there can be safety in life. Since trust is the main and constant issue, the therapist absolutely must not use the patient in any way, no matter how innocuous it seems. Get up and get your own cup of coffee!

The major obstacles to forming a good working alliance are the same problems that lead the patient to seek help in the first place: feelings of shame and hopelessness and fear of betrayal in initmate relationships. Once revealing the secret, incest victims have a strong impulse never to see the worker again, so great is their shame. Right at the outset, the professional needs to communicate that he or she has heard of such things before and knows many people who have had the same experience. It is necessary to make it clear that the therapist does not blame or scorn the client. Additionally, it is useful to convey a confident, hopeful attitude about the possibility of resolving the patient's residual problems. The survivor needs to hear that the damage need not be permanent and that she is not indelibly marked or barred from normal social life.

The goal of treatment is to change the client's self-concept from that of victim to that of survivor, teaching the client to protect herself but not the protector. The therapeutic actions of treatment break the cyclical alternations of denial/numbing and intrusive/repetitious thoughts by providing a safe environment to experience, with emotional response and without automatic denial and numbing of the emotions (Donaldson, 1983).

Introducing this subject with clients with whom one has an ongoing relationship presents some sensitive areas. It is important to answer honestly and fully if the client wants to know: "Why do you ask?" and "Why do you ask now?" The survivor will want some assurance that it is not a visible "mark" that had led to the questioning. One possible therapist response might be "The more I study and read about the subject, the more I realize that I see in you some of the dynamics common to adult survivors. Although you have never raised the subject, I also realize that I have never asked, and so I want to remedy my lapse." Or "The more you talk about this, the more my mind has turned to the possibility of your having experienced sexual abuse during your growing up, and so I am asking."

Clients who suffer amnesia about their having been abused often respond to questioning with ongoing anxiety and agitation. They may initially say no but later be open to discussing the possibility that events are hidden in forgotten memories. It is, however, better to go slowly than to precipitate or try to force premature recovery of memories. Remembering and disclosing of the memories can precipitate a desire to leave treatment and sometimes precipitates suicidal ideation or behavior. A client in such a crisis needs protection against self-destructive impulses in order to be able to utilize the safe and welcoming arena the worker presents.

Adult survivors can be treated individually or in groups. Shame is often so great that the client is resistant to groups. Some clients also believe that a group treatment situation exposes one to the danger of mistreatment by more people. After resistance is worked through, however, group therapy is probably the treatment of choice. In the group, the client meets persons who have suffered similar abuse and whom she comes to care for and respect. Her caring and respect for them in time will begin to extend to herself. The issues and struggles of other members of the group will also be her own, and she will be able to do healing work without direct confrontation. And finally, group members are often each others' best therapists. The professional is inevitably an authority figure, a receptable for negative and positive transferences. Other group members are peers, and their words can be heard and sifted through without the compliance/rebellion reactions elicited by authority.

And last but not least, the professional who chooses to work with this population needs to have his or her own issues worked through and to have his or her own support group. Just as parents must not turn to their children for caretaking, so the professional must not turn to clients for support but must find that support elsewhere for him- or herself.

In this world of many problems, we search and research for solutions, trying first this, then that. Answers are not easy, and they are rarely permanent. Solutions are impossible, however, if the problems themselves are not identified and aired. Thus, it may be deemed a hopeful sign of increasing civilization that the sexual molestation of children and the difficulties of adults who were molested during childhood are being addressed. Only a society willing to look at the reality of the problem can offer succor to the survivors and protection to the vulnerable and innocent.

REFERENCES

Butler, S. (1985). *Conspiracy of silence: The trauma of incest.* San Francisco: Volcano Press.

Caruso, B. (1987). *The impact of incest.* Center City, MN: Hazeldon.

Clarkson, P. (1988). Ego state dilemmas of abused children. *Transactional Analysis Journal,* 18(2), 85–93.

Courtois, C.A. (1988). *Healing the incest wound.* New York: W.W. Norton & Company.

Donaldson, M.A. (1983). *Incest victims years after: Methods and techniques for treatment.* Paper presented at the National Association of Social Workers, 1983 National Symposium, Washington, DC.

Gelinas, D. J. (1983). The persisting negative effects of incest. *Psychiatry,* 46, 312–332.

Gil, E. (1983). *Outgrowing the pain.* Walnut Creek, CA: Launch Press.

Herman, J. L. (1981). *Father-daughter incest.* Cambridge, MA: Harvard University Press.

Johns, M. (1986). *Therapists, incest and countertransference: The effects of experience and theoretical orientation on therapists' beliefs and practices.* Master's thesis, Smith College School of Social Work, Northhampton, MA.

Leonard, L.S. (1983). *The wounded woman.* Boulder, CO: Shambhala.

Maltz, W., & Holman, B. (1987). *Incest and sexuality: A guide to understanding and healing.* Lexington, MA: Lexington Books.

Miller, A. (1984). *Thou shalt not be aware.* New York: Farrar, Strauss, Giroux.

Piercy, M. (1988) *Gone to soldiers.* New York: Ballantine Books.

Scurfield, R.M. (1985). Post-trauma stress assessment and treatment overview and formulations. In C.R. Figley (Ed.), *Trauma and its wake: The study and treatment of post-traumatic stress disorder* (pp. 219–256). New York: Brunner/Mazel.

Woititz, J. (1983). *Adult children of alcoholics.* Pompano Beach, FL: North Communications.

15 Treatment of Adult Survivors of Child Sexual Abuse

Eliana Gil

Lydia is a 32-year-old obese Caucasian woman who entered therapy because of a recent incident in which she had been raped during a date. She talked about the rape in a matter-of-fact way, as if she were talking about someone else. She said that this experience had made her painfully aware of a pattern of choosing men who inevitably hurt her. She had been married three times and described her former husbands as "low life." She was emphatic that the rape, which had occurred three months before, was behind her and was not really open to discussion. She wanted to stop choosing the wrong men, and she wanted to lose weight. She proudly announced that she had a good job that she had held for 10 years. She was in a management position and made "decent money."

I was immediately struck with how controlling this client was. She set limits on what she would and would not discuss. She was adamant about the issues that required therapy. She wanted me to know she was competent in her career and yet felt inadequate to lose weight or choose appropriate partners. She talked dispassionately, staying very controlled about her emotions. She claimed to have dealt with the rape and rejected any interest or empathy from me regarding the trauma. She insisted on paying the high end of the fee scale and announced she was only available after 6 P.M. Luckily, I had an evening opening.

During the first interview, I allowed her to speak with few interruptions. It seemed important for her to tell me what she wanted me to know.

Only one question briefly disquieted Lydia. I asked what her current relationship was like with her parents. She seemed speechless for a moment and then stated, "That's also a closed book. . . .

We don't have any contact." I took that opportunity to make a statement: "At some point, I will need to understand what your childhood was like, especially your relationship with your parents. Often the problems of adulthood are connected to early childhood experiences." I noticed she had become very still. "What will it be like for you to talk with me about your childhood?" I asked. "Well, I'm just not sure it's necessary. But maybe I'll feel differently later."

After the fourth visit, I had obtained a great deal of information. Lydia offered generous detail about her young adulthood, her marriages, divorces, and job history. She had lived in about 12 different apartments or houses. She had been in her current condominium for the last four years but now was becoming restless and wanted to move again. She also had a pattern regarding men. She pursued men who showed little interest in her. She described herself as "steam rolling" her chosen "victims" and announced she had never failed to get any man she wanted. She said the men eventually got worn down and agreed to marry her. She felt they married her because she was fun, easy going, and asked little from them. The men had common traits: she perceived them as weak, undemanding, and needing her care and attention. The men were unemployed, and she assumed total financial responsibility in the marriages. She had also drawn up tight premarital agreements and delighted in saying she had made reasonable settlements and was not financially tied to any of them.

Two of the men were alcoholics and under the influence of alcohol became violent and forceful. It appeared that any resentment they may have harbored was unleashed during drinking binges. She would cope with the drinking by staying at work late. She said she had an unspoken limit on the beatings. If any of them beat her more than five times, she would leave the relationship. She reluctantly revealed that her second husband had broken her ribs and arm. She felt sorry for him because once he realized what he had done, the violence caused him a great deal of pain and embarrassment.

The third husband had not beat her, but ironically this man was totally asexual, and this was of greater concern to her. Her previous husbands had repeatedly asked for sexual contact. She had acquiesced. She was quick to add that she never liked sex and basically "shut her eyes and waited for it to be over." When her third husband seemed uninterested, she tried desperately to get his attention by becoming "seductive." She said she could turn seduction on and off at will, and even though she was large, when she "put her mind to it," she could entice any man. When she was not interested in a man, her appearance was of no concern to her. Although she had always been overweight, in the last year she had gained 80 pounds. She commented that it was difficult to move around, and she was often out of breath. She wanted to lose the additional 80 pounds but did not want to become thin. She had never been thin and seemed judgmental about women who were.

In the next four sessions, with her agreement, we explored her childhood. I did a structured history-taking and attempted to obtain her cooperation in giving me additional information about her parents and her early life. Not unexpectedly, she blurted out a history of severe childhood physical and sexual abuse. Her father was an alcoholic who killed himself when she was 12. Her mother was seriously mentally ill and had been in and out of mental institutions while Lydia grew up. When her father committed suicide, Lydia's mother was institutionalized and was released about eight years ago to the care of her sister. Lydia had limited contact with her mother, who had brief periods of stability and usually did not recognize family.

When her mother was at home, she was harsh, punitive, and inconsistent in her care of Lydia. Lydia felt she was the caretaker, frequently having to bathe and feed her mother. She also remembered having to put out fires her mother started and on one occasion taking her mother out of a tub where she was soaking in peroxide. While Lydia slept, her mother frequently was cutting pictures out of magazines. Sometimes when she awakened, her mother was sitting near her holding the scissors. Lydia remembers feeling frightened but mostly angry at her "daffy mother."

Lydia had no friends as a child. She stayed in the house most of the time. She excelled in school and made scholastic achievement her most valued goal. A teacher took interest in her and spent time with her after school going over advanced projects. She did not participate in any social functions or sports.

Her appearance caused other children to ridicule her. She covered herself up with numerous coats. Even in the summer, she wore long sleeves. She picked her eyelashes off, which everyone noticed and laughed about. Her clothes were always out of style, and she had no sense of fashion. She was overweight throughout her childhood. She remembered cooking mashed potatoes and eating it on white bread. "Can you imagine," she remarked, "mashed potato sandwiches for dinner?"

Her affect changed when I asked about her father. "A little demented," she quipped. Her laughter was nervous and unsettling. I commented that they must have spent a lot of time together since mother was at home infrequently. "What was it like to spend time with him, Lydia?" She looked vulnerable, and she became soft-spoken. "You already know, don't you?" "I know what?" "About what he used to do to me." She paused. "I was his wife, not my mother." The next pause seemed interminable, and one tear traced her cheek. "I'm sorry, Lydia. That must have been so painful for you . . . one parent who's not there, and the one who is there is being sexual with you." "I hated it," she said softly. "I don't like to think about those days." She cried quietly and then checked her watch. "I've got to go now. Don't worry, I'll be fine. I'm going out to dinner with friends tonight." I told her I was concerned since it was clear she did not often discuss these childhood experiences, and it was apparent how much pain she was feeling. She canceled the next appointment, and when I called her, she was back to her old self, controlled, upbeat, and in denial. When she returned, it was diffi-cult to discuss the incest, although eventually Lydia was available and willing to explore her childhood feelings and perceptions. The work was underway. The key to lowering her resistance came from her understanding and subsequent belief that her reenactments of abusive or inadequate intimate relationships were directly related to unresolved feelings toward her parents.

ADULT SURVIVORS OF CHILDHOOD ABUSE

Lydia is an adult survivor with many of the long-term psychological problems associated with childhood abuse. Specifically, she had low self-esteem, an eating disorder, difficulty with intimate relationships, issues with trust and dependency, and a history of revictimization. I will offer a brief literature review summarizing the known psycho-logical problems that research shows can be correlated to childhood abuse. The research results are enhanced by clinical observations of clients who seek therapy for childhood abuse problems. In the last 10 years, more and more clients seem able to seek therapy or self-help services for this problem than ever before. This may be a result of increased media attention and public awareness of the problem of child abuse. The literature specific to the subject of adult survivors of childhood abuse has also greatly increased over the last five years. As the attention to this problem has grown, so has the number of available therapeutic and legal resources.

There seems to be congruence between the research findings and the clinical observations. There is also general agreement about the therapeutic goals, whereas the treatment techniques remain var-ied and experimental.

Most of the available data come from research that has been conducted with adult survivors of child sexual abuse. Finkelhor (1986) conceptualizes the impact of child sexual abuse in four levels: traumatic sexualization, stigmatization, betrayal, and powerlessness. Each of these levels has a distinct dynamic, renders a specific psychological impact and has a unique behavioral manifestation.

Finkelhor's conceptual framework is probably the most succinct way to understand and discuss the aftereffects of childhood sexual abuse. The survivors will almost always deal with issues regarding sexuality, self-image and self-esteem, trust and dependency issues, and feelings of learned helplessness. While the framework was developed in consideration of the impact of child sexual abuse, I think it has some applicability to victims of other types of familial childhood abuse, such as physical and emotional abuse or neglect.

It appears that certain child victims with abusive backgrounds are not as damaged and can develop into healthy, well-functioning, productive adults, with few psychological scars. Garbarino et al. (1988) and Anthony and Cohler (1987) speculate that these child victims are "stress resistant." It is virtually impossible at this time to estimate how many victims of childhood abuse escape fully undamaged. The extent of the damage varies based on a wide range of variables.

Most adult survivors of childhood abuse struggle with a negative or undefined self-image; difficulties with self-esteem, trust and dependency; and possible feelings of helplessness or revictimization. The behavioral manifestations of these issues are unique to the child and his or her personality structure. Child victims have been known to exhibit behaviors that can be viewed as externalizing or internalizing (Gil, 1988). Children who internalize behavior may become self-destructive, withdrawn, or depressed; have night terrors; develop phobias; self-mutilate; become addicted to drugs; or attempt suicide. Children with externalized manifestations may become destructive to property, hurt others, or do bizarre things like kill family pets. It is usually impossible to predict how children will respond to acute or chronic trauma. Personality traits, defensive styles, environmental cues, and other variables may predispose a child to behave against the self or against others.

The type of abuse that is experienced may also have a direct link to the type of adult problems that surface. A recent retrospective study of 99 adult survivors (Gil, 1988) found that victims of physical abuse were more likely to have problems with revictimization (experiencing violence in adulthood), whereas sexual abuse survivors were more likely to have sexual dysfunctions. The study also found many other interesting differences related to type of abuse, pointing to the fact that adult emotional problems may differ based on the type of abuse endured and early organizing defenses against the abuse.

It seems that if the sexual abuse occurs within the family, there are common behavioral manifestations, including sexual dysfunctions, isolation, drug and alcohol abuse, criminal involvement, self-mutilation, suicide attempts, revictimization, discomfort in intimate relationships, aggressive behavior, nightmares and phobias, somatic complaints, eating and sleeping disorders, running away, abusive behavior, and depression (Finkelhor, 1986).

In addition, two other psychological disorders have recently been documented as relevant in the diagnosis and treatment of adult survivors. The first is dissociation, which is defined by the *Diagnostic and Statistical Manual of Mental Disorders* [DSM-III-R (1988)] as "a disturbance in the normally integrative functions of identity, memory and consciousness." Simply put, dissociation enables the abused child to be absent during the abuse. In that way it serves as a very effective defense mechanism that helps the victim to survive. A large proportion of clients I have seen in therapy describe the use of dissociation during abuse. This process is frequently first observed when the client is asked to discuss childhood, or childhood abuse specifically. In some cases, dissociating becomes a habit, a reflex response generated by numerous triggers, including emotions, thoughts, or sensory cues. A client who feels afraid may dissociate automatically because that is how the individual learned to cope with the feeling of fear.

Dissociative phenomena can occur on a continuum. The most extreme form of dissociation is multiple personality disorder (MPD). The DSM-III-R defines MPD as follows: "The essential feature of this disorder is the existence within the person of two or more distinct personalities or personality states. Personality is here described as a relatively enduring pattern of perceiving, relating to, and thinking about the environment and one's self that is exhibited in a wide range of important social and personal contexts." This disorder does not occur as rarely as once believed. If a clinician works primarily with childhood abuse, it is important to be aware of the diagnosis and treatment guidelines of MPD. There is convincing evidence of the high correlation between early childhood abuse and multiple personality disorder. Putnam, Post, and Guroff (1983) found that 97 of 100 patients with MPD had a history of early childhood abuse; Schultz et al. (1985) found that 97.4% of 309 MPD clients were abused or neglected. Indeed, Wilbur (1984) believes that "without abuse, we would have few cases of multiple personality disorder."

The second relevant issue pertains to the presence of posttraumatic stress disorder (PTSD) symptoms in adult survivors. Because abuse is a psychic trauma (Eth & Pynoos, 1985), victims of abuse, particularly those who attempt to suppress the experience or have used defensive mechanisms, are susceptible to developing PTSD symptoms. These symptoms seem to represent the unconscious trying to become conscious.

The DSM-III-R defines PTSD as "the development of characteristic symptoms following a psychologically distressing event that is outside the range of usual human experience. . . . The stressor producing this syndrome would be markedly distressing to almost anyone, and is usually experienced with intense fear, terror and helplessness. The characteristic symptoms involve reexperiencing the traumatic event, avoidance of stimuli associated with the event or numbing of general responsiveness, and increased arousal." Many of my clients have entered therapy distressed by PTSD symptoms that can be disorienting and debilitating. One client would experience physical pain in the back and legs as if she were currently being beaten. Another felt throbbing in her vagina as if sexual intercourse had just taken place.

A variety of sensory cues can trigger memory and/or PTSD symptoms. Marjorie came to therapy after her house had been burglarized. When she entered the house and discovered it in disarray with many missing objects, she felt violated. This feeling provoked an immediate memory of being raped 30 years before.

A recent Barbara Streisand film, Nuts, and a previous film with Jane Fonda, Agnes of God, triggered PTSD symptoms in many filmgoers unaware that the films were primarily about incest and abuse. These clients had previously successfully avoided these topics and yet found themselves face to face with many concrete images they could not avoid and that provoked memory and acute distress.

It may also occur that PTSD symptoms develop during therapy. As the client is asked to remember, focus on, and discuss his or her childhood, it is possible that symptoms such as intrusive images, nightmares, and emotionality may surface.

I have always found it useful to alert clients that although by seeking therapy their attempt is to "feel better" right away, therapy can frequently cause pain and confusion, and it takes time for recovery to follow. I let them know that some clients feel worse for awhile and may feel reticent to pursue what appears an overwhelming and painful course of treatment.

TREATMENT OF ADULT SURVIVORS

As I mentioned previously, treatment techniques in working with adult survivors are numerous. However, there appears to be general agreement about the following treatment goals:

1. Broaden self-image and enhance self-esteem. Most adult survivors have either undefined or negative views of who they are or what they have to offer. They need help to recognize strengths, weaknesses, likes, and dislikes and to reclaim their thoughts and feelings. They have rarely been encouraged to explore how they feel and what they need, and one of the first tasks in treatment is to begin to help survivors build a sense of who they are.

2. Powerfulness. Childhood abuse usually rendered the child helpless to escape, fight back, or get out of the confusing, dangerous, or frightening situation. Learned helplessness may have occurred, eliciting in survivors a feeling of "Why try? There's no way out." Because helplessness is one of the keys to feelings of victimization, every effort must be made to encourage the client to block learned helplessness. Blocking efforts include developing options, exploring choices, mobilizing resources, breaking isolation, and fighting feelings of shame.

3. Grief and loss. The abusive childhood is in the past. It is important to grieve for what was not and acknowledge the sense of loss involved in giving up the illusion of a nonabusive background.

4. Pain tolerance. Many adult survivors learned to avoid feelings out of fear. They have little experience with tolerating pain and must be taught to develop coping mechanisms.

5. Depression and anger. Acknowledging childhood abuse naturally causes sadness and possible depression. In addition, most adult surivors can experience anger and resentment at having missed an appropriate childhood. It becomes important to express the range of emotions that may develop regarding childhood abuse. Anger is a healthy emotion. Many adult survivors were exposed to two types of anger expression: an explosion or denial. Anger therefore may be difficult to release in healthy ways. When the anger is denied, it can be turned against the self. Often depression is a symptom of anger turned inward. Expressing anger can be relieving whether it's expressed directly to the person provoking the anger or expressed indirectly. The survivor can choose which mode of expression is more suitable once they know the options.

6. Entitlement. Frequently overlooked, entitlement is an abstract feeling that is enabling. Adult survivors should be helped to feel

they deserve good things. A healthy sense of entitlement may propel the individual toward initiating or sustaining rewarding exchanges with others.

7. Trauma Resolution. If the client is unconsciously reenacting his or her childhood through adult experiences, it will be important to make an in-depth exploration of the childhood abuse. Chances are that the abuse has not been understood or felt. Often, in order to say good-bye to childhood memories of abuse, they must be revisited so that completion or resolution can occur. Otherwise, memories of the abuse remain vague, fragmented, intrusive, and unconsciously perpetuating of victim issues.

Trauma resolution work can be accomplished in a variety of ways. The discharging of emotions is considered helpful and can be accomplished through abreactions or implosive therapy. The individual is carefully guided to remember and describe an abusive incident, perhaps the first or last time the abuse occurred. The importance of this work is to help the client to accurately perceive the experience and reorganize any distortions or distressing fears about the events while discharging feelings. Integrating affect during recall is one of the goals. The client must be encouraged to see the abuse in the past and feel empowered to control his/her present and future.

This procedure may be counterindicated for some clients. Those clients who lack ego strength, decompensate, begin to have psychotic processes, or become dysfunctional and severely depressed are not good candidates for this type of trauma resolution work.

8. Suicide and homicide assessments. Because childhood abuse can be a powerful memory, strong emotions may follow. Suicide and homicide assessments should be conducted periodically. Be sure you are attending to the safety of your client. Childhood abuse memories can elicit regressive and primitive reactions.

9. Breaking isolation. Another characteristic of victimization is isolation and shame. Feelings of worthlessness may encourage isolation. During treatment, clients are encouraged to affiliate with others and take controlled risks in social situations. Referrals to either self-help groups or group therapy may be worthwhile. If clients have a circle of friends that has been neglected, attempts can be made to reengage the client in relationships and interactions with others.

10. Reclaiming the body. Child abuse tends to have an impact on the body. In sexual abuse the body feels invaded. Survivors may feel dirty or damaged. In physical abuse the body experiences pain. The body may be seen as a source of pain rather than pleasure. And in neglect or emotional abuse cases, the child may not have received adequate physical affection and nurturing and may long for, or fear,

physical touch. The body must be reclaimed. The client must learn to have experiences that are pleasurable and nurturing. Massages, swimming, mud baths, and physical exercise are among the options to begin to reclaim the body. Always assess for self-mutilation and assist the client in disengaging from self-inflicted pain.

11. Reclaiming sexuality. In addition, many adult survivors had negative, conflictual, or confusing sexual experiences that may predispose them to having negative associations to sexual thoughts, feelings, or behaviors. Maltz and Holman (1986) describe a process by which adult survivors of incest can reclaim their sexuality and have an increased sense of well-being and empowerment.

These are the basic treatment areas. Simple as it may seem, the therapy with adult survivors can be very slow and fragile because the survivor is unfamiliar with safety, appropriate care and attention, proper boundaries, trust, and affiliation to others.

Probably the single most important aspect of therapy with adult survivors is forming a therapeutic alliance. The therapist's job is to provide a safe, corrective, reparative experience. The transference issues abound as clients enter what may be their first safe and healthy interaction with an adult. Therapists must proceed purposefully and with great sensitivity to the underlying risks of seeking therapy for the adult survivor.

I always follow a few basic rules: I tell clients they can say as much or as little as they want about the childhood abuse (this encourages safety and control); I clearly state I will not hit them, hurt them, or be sexual with them (again, providing them with the parameters of the therapy, which may feel vague or uncertain); I tell them the kind of therapy I do—that is, that I do verbal therapy and may ask them from time to time to draw something, write something, or bring in pictures. (I do this because some clients have had traumatic reenactions of abuse through very dramatic "therapeutic" techniques.) I also tell the clients that whether or not they meet my requests is up to them.

Two questions come up early in treatment: Do I believe their stories, and do I think they are crazy? I usually respond: "I have no reason to disbelieve you. Everything you've told me is quite possible, and I am familiar with these types of abuse." The other response is "I observe no signs of mental illness or craziness in you [if this is true]; if I see anything that concerns me, I will let you know." These responses tend to be more credible early in treatment than an unequivocal "Yes," which may make the client uneasy since they may not trust such definitive statements.

Initially, clients may minimize their abuse or want to avoid discussion. Allow a certain period of denial but tell clients, as I did Lydia, that at some point you will ask about their childhoods. Also ask how they anticipate feeling about that discussion. Resistant clients are allowed to pace themselves, having discussions at tolerable rates. Never, however, collude with the client by avoiding the subject altogether.

Finally, one of the aspects essential to recovery is the client's sense of hope. The therapist has the opportunity to assist by conveying a sense of hope if one is felt.

This work is demanding, challenging, and at times distressing. Probably no other place are countertransference feelings stronger. The therapist is advised to maintain good boundaries, seek consultation and support, and know the limits of assistance that can be provided. The therapist is also encouraged to work in unison with others, since the client's needs will increase over time, and sharing responsibility with others can be helpful to both client and therapist.

REFERENCES

American Psychiatric Association. (1987). *Diagnostic and statistical manual of mental disorders*, 3d ed. (revised). Washington, DC: American Psychiatric Association.

Anthony, J., & Cohler, B. J. (1987). *The invulnerable child*. New York: Guilford Press.

Eth, S., & Pynoos, R. S. (1985). *Post-traumatic stress disorder in children*. Los Angeles: American Psychiatric Association.

Finkelhor, D. (1986). *A sourcebook on child sexual abuse*. Beverly Hills, CA: Sage Publications.

Garbarino, J., Guttman, E., & Seeley, J. W. (1988). *The psychologically battered child*. San Francisco: Jossey-Bass.

Gil, E. (1988). *Treatment of adult survivors of childhood abuse*. Walnut Creek, Ca: Launch Press.

Maltz, W., & Holman, B. (1987). *Incest and sexuality: A guide to understanding and healing*. Lexington, MA: Lexington Press.

Putman, P. W., Post, R. M., & Guroff, J. J. (1983). *100 cases of multiple personality disorder*. Paper presented at the American Psychiatric Association Annual Meeting. (From *New Research Abstracts*, 77.)

Schultz, R., Braun, B. G., & Kluft, R. P. (1985). Creativity and imaginary companion phenomena: Prevalence and phenomenology in MPD. In B .G. Braun (Ed.), *Proceedings of the Second International Conference on Multiple Personality Dissociative States*. Chicago: Chicago Rush University.

Wilbur, C. B. (1984). Multiple personality and child abuse. *Psychiatric Clinics of North America 7*, 3–8.

V | Treatment of Elder Abuse and Neglect

16 Elder Abuse and Neglect: Treatment Issues

Mary Joy Quinn

Elder abuse and neglect are the most recent forms of domestic mal-treatment to emerge as social problems. The 1960s saw the recognition of child abuse and neglect, and in the 1970s the phenomenon of woman battering came out in the open. Beginning in the late 1970s and early 1980s, researchers building on the earlier work on child abuse and neglect and woman battering called attention to the phenomenon of elder abuse and neglect (Block & Sinnott, 1979; Douglass et al., 1980; Lau & Kosberg, 1978; O'Malley et al., 1979; Rathbone-McCuan, 1978, 1980; Steinmetz, 1978). The 1980s have seen more research, Congressional hearings, the passage of reporting laws in most states, the development of assessment tools and intervention strategies, the formation of community coalitions, and the development of multidisciplinary teams to resolve complex cases. Conferences on the subject are common now, and a body of research and literature is forming.

Elder abuse and neglect are difficult for most people to understand, primarily because they think of the phenomenon as occurring only in nursing homes. For many, it is nearly impossible to conceive of older people being mistreated in their own homes. And yet fewer than 5% of people over the age of 65 live in institutions at any given time. This means that the great bulk of older people live in the community, and if help is needed managing activities of daily living, they must rely on those who are closest, usually family members (Quinn & Tomita, 1986). The caregiver may not be capable of being a caregiver or may become stressed, the family may be one where physical violence has always been common, or greed on the part of a family member may result in an elder being financially taken advantage of or literally robbed.

CASE STUDY

The following case example was taken from official court records and illustrates much of what is known about elder abuse and neglect. Several types of abuse and neglect were present, the abuse and/or neglect were ongoing, the profile of the victim and the abuser are fairly common, resolution of the case took several months, and practitioners working with the case experienced a great deal of frustration.

An 85-year-old woman lived with her daughter in her own home in a middle-class neighborhood. The two women had lived together for years. The mother had become impaired physically and mentally, and she relied on her daughter to provide care for her. The police and fire departments became involved and broke into the house after the neighbors, Adult Protective Services, and the Geriatric Home Visiting Team determined that a crisis existed because neither mother nor daughter would leave the house and they had stopped letting practitioners into the house. The home in which the two women were living had been "condemned" and was considered uninhabitable. Utilities had been cut-off due to nonpayment of bills. There was no heat, and neither the stove nor refrigerator was operative. The daughter had apparently cut electrical and telephone wiring and had let the home deteriorate; the house was filthy, and the floors were covered with a large collection of garbage. The daughter, a former Las Vegas showgirl, had a long psychiatric history of paranoid schizophrenia. She had become delusional and had barricaded herself in the house and was keeping her mother locked in the garage. There were indications that the daughter had been abusing and neglecting her mother physically, psychologically, socially, and financially. The daughter was considered gravely disabled and was psychiatrically hospitalized against her will by the police. She was later discharged after agreeing to outpatient treatment, which she promptly refused to obtain once she was back home.

The mother was also admitted to a hospital by the police. At that time, she was found to be dehydrated, malnourished, unreasonably thin, and extremely filthy. She could barely walk—even with assistance—due to the swelling of her lower legs and feet and due to ingrown toenails. It took three baths to clean her due to feces all over her body and due to her ongoing incontinence. She had a prolapsed uterus and required a hysterectomy. She had psychiatric symptoms consisting of depression, extreme mental disorganization, delusional thinking, and lack of interest or initiative in her welfare. She also displayed unusual thinking regarding her daughter. She believed that she was re-

ceiving excellent care from her daughter and worried that something would happen to her daughter to the point that "they"
might execute her. Medical and nursing staff noted that there
was a symbiotic and probably harmful relationship with the
daughter and possibly a shared delusional system. Staff also
noted what they termed a master–slave relationship in that the
mother would do precisely whatever the daughter wanted. Several years prior to the hospital admissions, the daughter induced
her mother to leave her own house for a period of two years.
During that time, the mother lived nearby with a sister and
cooked daily meals for the daughter, sliding the food under the
locked gate so that her daughter would have meals. The daughter was then briefly psychiatrically hospitalized and treated after
neighbors noted bizarre behavior. Upon her discharge, she allowed her mother to return to live with her in the house, which
at that point still legally belonged to the mother.

There were signs of financial abuse. According to the sister,
the elderly woman had signed her house over to her daughter in
order to "keep peace." All cash assets had been dissipated by
the daughter. The mother was receiving Social Security benefits
($250 per month) and was eligible for Supplemental Security
Income but had declined to apply because her daughter thought
it would somehow endanger the benefits she (the daughter) was
receiving.

The elderly woman and her daughter were reunited in the
home following their respective hospitalizations mainly because
they desperately wanted to live together again. The house had
been cleaned and repaired in their absence. Elaborate monitoring arrangements were made involving several agencies. Both
mother and daughter promised to cooperate with inhome services and with having the mother attend a day care center several
times a week. However, they again became reclusive, and approximately a year after the first incident the police were once again
involved and the mother was again hospitalized against her will,
again in a life-threatening state. This time, the physician noted
that the mother was in a badly neglected state with impending
pressure sores. She could not feed herself or walk, was badly
disoriented, was incontinent, and her toenails again badly
needed attention. According to medical staff, the elderly woman
was admitted in a "condition that is completely unacceptable."
Diagnoses included neglect and elder abuse, Alzheimer's disease, dehydration secondary to abandonment, and bilateral con-
junctivitis.

With appropriate nursing care, the elderly woman became
continent and able to feed herself. Her appetite improved, she
gained weight, and she began to walk. She was transferred to a
nursing home, where she seemed to enjoy living in a group
setting. However, she continued to deny that she had ever suf-

fered from any abuse or neglect or even that she had been seriously ill. She said, "Oh, they would have sent me a letter if that were true. I just went to the hospital because I had a case of the sniffles." She continued to believe that she and her daughter could "take care of everything." While at the nursing home her daughter visited constantly and told her mother that "all those people are out to get your money." The elderly woman's sisters were also able to visit; they had stopped visiting at the home out of physical fear of the daughter. It was also easier for the son to visit. He lived in another part of the state, and his sister had made it difficult for him to see their mother at the home. The elderly woman was eventually placed in a board-and-care home once she had become higher functioning, and a neutral conservator was appointed to handle her affairs. The daughter exhibited unusual behavior at the time of the court hearing; she was observed changing her panty hose in the public hall outside the courtroom.

Practitioners involved in the case felt that returning the mother to the house where her daughter lived and which she now legally owned would have amounted to a death sentence for the elderly woman. It was necessary to place a neutral legal authority in charge of the elderly woman; her daughter lacked the capacity and judgment to provide safe care for her mother, and her unrealistic ideas regarding asset management made it unreasonable to allow her to continue to handle her mother's financial affairs.

Discussion

This case history illustrates the complexities of the issues where elder abuse and neglect are concerned. For instance, the mother and daughter were adamant in their desire to live together despite concrete evidence that the home was uninhabitable and that they were having serious problems with basic activities of daily living, including eating, maintaining adequate sanitation, and paying bills. The mother was equally adamant in her belief that her daughter was providing excellent care despite two life-threatening episodes that involved hospitalizations. Practitioners involved in the case attempted to provide care that would help the women remain together, and there was cooperation initially that did not last. Both women literally fought to maintain the status quo; the daughter was physically theatening to practitioners, and when a petition was filed for the appointment of a neutral conservator, she hired an attorney to oppose the conservatorship, and her mother told the court investigator that she wanted only her daughter to handle her affairs.

The length of the case and the seriousness of the mother's condition were of deep concern to practitioners, who were alert to protecting the mother as well as safeguarding her legal rights to freedom from interference. Involvement of the court was used only as a last resort when less restrictive measures had failed, and separation of mother and daughter was done only as a last resort and then only on court order.

The case also illustrates other facets of elder abuse and neglect. For instance, several forms of abuse and neglect were present and they were ongoing. There was certainly physical neglect as manifested by the mother's weight loss, dehydration and malnutrition, and impending pressure sores. It could not be determined if the daughter deliberately withheld food and liquid from her mother or if she did it as the result of her mental illness. It is questionable if outright physical abuse occurred; physical examinations performed in the hospitals never revealed symptoms such as bruises, scratches, or broken bones. The mother may have suffered psychological abuse in the form of fear when her daughter locked her in the garage and thereby isolated her. Certainly her legal rights were violated when her daughter· would not let her live in her own house. There was financial abuse in that the daughter used her mother's assets; she induced her to sign the house over to her, and she deprived her mother of income out of her belief that her own benefits would be threatened if her mother received Supplemental Security Income.

In many ways this case helps to illuminate some of the issues surrounding the phenomenon of elder abuse and neglect. An overview of the subject may bring further understanding.

OVERVIEW OF ELDER ABUSE AND NEGLECT

Responses of Society

The emergence of elder abuse and neglect as a social problem has raised four main responses. These responses are similiar to society's responses to child abuse and neglect and to woman battering when they first became public (Finkelhor, 1983). One of the first responses is to deny or minimize the problem. This reaction gradually shifts to an acknowledgment that the problem does indeed exist, that it is not limited to isolated incidents, and that it is serious. For instance, originally the public thought that all elder abuse and neglect occurred in nursing homes or that it was clearly a rare occurrence if it happened in a private home. Gradually, most people have come to acknowledge that older people are being abused and/or neglected in their own homes or in the homes of relatives. The acknowledgment of elder abuse and neglect is particularly frightening because it is personal; there is still the possibility that it could happen to any of us in the future. Most adults have escaped child abuse and neglect or woman battering, but the realities of elder abuse and neglect still loom as possibilities in the future.

A second response is to view all abusers as pathological. Gradually, with more research, this shifts to seeing the abuser as less deviant from the norm. There is, however, some research to indicate that abusers of the elderly may be more pathological than other abusers (Finkelhor & Pillemer, 1987; Wolf, 1986). The explanation for this may lie in the historical context of family relationships. Traditionally, women and children have been viewed as legal property of the head of the household, and he has been permitted and expected to "discipline" or control them. Elderly parents have not been viewed in the same way. On the contrary, most religious traditions urge adult children to honor and respect their parents. Thus, it is more forbidden to abuse older parents, which could mean that those who do abuse are more troubled or less normal than people who batter women and children.

A third response upon hearing about domestic maltreatment is to blame the victim for the abuse or neglect. This thinking then evolves toward focusing on the actions of the abuser and attempting to devise programs aimed at holding the abuser accountable for his or her actions. With elder abuse and neglect, practitioners are often face to face with the person responsible for the maltreatment because that person is also the main caregiver or the only adult relationship the elder has. Practitioners often find themselves feeling sympathetic with the workload of the caregiver particularly if the elder is verbally abusive, incapable of expressing gratitude, or a total care patient.

There may also be ambivalence about what should be done with people who are found to be abusive or neglectful to older people. Should they be treated? Should they be locked up and the key thrown away? Should they be ignored in favor of focusing on the elder? Should they be prosecuted or forced to make restitution to the victim? To date, no programs have been devised specifically for those who have abused older people and no treatment philosophies have been developed.

A fourth response of society toward domestic maltreatment is bewilderment over defining the bounderies of abuse and neglect. For instance, what is discipline for a child versus what is abusive? What

is normal marital fighting? With regard to old people, is it all right
to spank a demented person who wanders out into the street, or is
that elder abuse? What about the situation of spouse abuse grown
old and reversed, where a wife has been battered by her husband
during the marriage, the husband becomes impaired and dependent,
and the wife becomes the caregiver and is abusive? She retaliates for
the abuse heaped on her in the past. Should that be condoned?
What about financial abuse? Is it all right to help yourself to your
impaired parents' bank accounts if you have access to their funds
and have a personal emergency? Many of these questions are yet to
be resolved or are viewed differently in different communites.

Definitions

There are as yet no commonly agreed upon definitions of elder
abuse and neglect. The research studies use different definitions. For
instance, what one study defines as active neglect, another study
terms abuse. Each state that has a reporting law defines elder abuse
and neglect differently. Basic questions still remain as to what it is
and what it is not. Complicating this picture are the values of individual families and the values of a particular community. Some
communities can tolerate a wider range of behavior than others.
Another confusing aspect of defining elder abuse and neglect is in
the terms themselves. Generally speaking, abuse has been viewed as
more serious and as the result of a deliberate act by an abuser.
Neglect has been seen as resulting from ignorance or stress and
therefore, somehow, less serious. In reality, either abuse or neglect
can have the same results for the elder; it does not matter whether
or not the abuser *meant* to inflict injury; the elder is injured, perhaps seriously, perhaps fatally. Amid all of this confusion regarding
definitions and terms, there is some agreement as to the types of
elder abuse and neglect: physical, psychological, financial, and violation of rights (Quinn & Tomita, 1986).

Physical Abuse and Neglect

This is the type of abuse most people think of when they hear the
words *elder abuse*. Physical abuse and neglect mean that the elder
victim has suffered bodily harm. This harm, which produces pain
and possibly loss of function, can include bruises, sprains, fractured
bones, internal injuries, soft tissue damage, and the formation of
blood clots that press upon vital organs. While it is true that older

people bruise more easily than younger people, inflicted bruises are often bilateral and there commonly are multiple bruises in various stages of healing. Frequently, implausible or conflicting explanations are given by the suspected abuser and/or the elder. For instance, multiple bruises that are obviously in various stages of healing may be ascribed to one fall that took place the day before. Or the elder and the suspected abuser may give completely different accounts of how the injury happened (Quinn & Tomita, 1986).

Signs and symptoms of elder abuse and neglect may include admission to an emergency room under suspicious circumstances: the elder is brought to the hospital emergency room by someone other than the usual caregiver or is brought in by the caregiver who then "disappears." There may be a prolonged interval between the injury or illness and the seeking of medical treatment. There may be evidence that medications are not being administered as prescribed or that several doctors have prescribed medication. There may be "doctor hopping" (Quinn & Tomita, 1986).

FAILURE TO THRIVE SYNDROME.   Those familiar with child abuse and neglect will recognize this term. When applied to elders, it can include dehydration and malnutrition, pressure sores, abnormal chemistry values, hypothermia, poor hygiene, concentrated urine, and infrequent bowel movements. Behavioral indicators include apathy or hypervigilance, expressions of hopelessness and helplessness, gobbling of food and liquid, clinging or whining, and seeking "attention" from practitioners. If extreme enough, failure to thrive can result in death (Quinn & Tomita, 1986). Failure to thrive may occur as the result of self-neglect or other-neglect.

THE NEGLECTED ELDER.   Until recently, there has been very little information with regard to the neglect of the elderly, although these cases comprise the bulk of the caseload of Adult Protective Services practitioners (Salend et al., 1984). There has been confusion over self-neglect and other-neglect. Self-neglect or abuse has been particularly controversial because one man's exercise of personal freedom may be seen as self-neglect by others. In addition, all adults in the United States are deemed competent or capable of caring for themselves and their affairs unless it is determined otherwise by a court of law in connection with a petition to determine legal incompetency or to appoint a guardian or conservator. Other-neglect has been difficult to grasp and define. Adult children do not have a legal responsibility to care for their aged parents. Some other-neglect is surely due to ignorance or stress, and it is not uncommon for practitioners to encounter caregivers who are dreadfully neglectful but who are equally insistent that they are doing an excellent job of caregiving, even in the face of the elder's multiple hospitalizations for life-threatening conditions.

Dubin and her colleagues (1986) are among the first to study the phenomenon of elder neglect. A case study approach was used, taking 84 cases from the records of Adult Protective Service practitioners in one state. According to the study, the neglected elder is one "whose needs are not adequately being met in one or more of the following areas: personal care, nutrition, medical attention or medicating, and condition of the environment" (p. 19). The cases were divided into five general categories without fixing blame as to who was responsible for the neglect: cases where the caregiving system was overwhelmed, cases where the elder refused assistance, cases where there was a self-interested caregiver, cases where the caregiving system was dysfunctional, and finally, cases where the elder was alone.

Overwhelmed caring system. In these situations there was a caregiving system in place; the elder and caregiver were willing to accept help, but still there was neglect. The practitioners were able to help by offering information about service options, actual caregiving techniques, and conditions commonly associated with aging. They also played intermediary between the various family members by offering suggestions from one to the other. They gave practical assistance in seeing to it that a plan was carried out (e.g., the elder was taken to the doctor, household services were instituted, and an appointment was made and kept with legal services). In general, both elders and caregivers were grateful for the assistance.

Elder refuses assistance. In these cases, a caregiving system existed, but the elder refused to take advantage of it. According to the researchers, the elders in this group may have had an awareness of impending death and did not want to be bothered. In some instances they did die. In other cases, they were despairing and wanted to die. Interventions frequently came late in this category and tended to be on an aggressive emergency basis. Practitioners met with some success using friendly visiting and monitoring and sometimes through significant others such as close friends. At times, practitioners threatened elders with coercion, for example, threatening to get a court order to take the elder to the doctor and threatening to call the health department regarding the house when there were problems with vermin infestations, large accumulations of garbage in the house, or animal feces covering furniture and/or floors.

The self-interested caregiver. In these cases, the caregiver was more interested in benefiting from the elder's resources than in taking care of the elder. This was the smallest category. It is interesting to note that some elders prefer these situations even though they know they are being mistreated; being in one's own home is preferable to being placed in a nursing home. Interventions in this category consisted of removing the caregiver from the situation. Caregivers were initially hostile but complied with pressure. Elders received better care consequently, and those who were mentally aware that they had been mistreated expressed appreciation for the intervention.

The dysfunctional caregiving system. In this category, there was a history of difficult family relationships, and the existing caregiving system was not working. The best solution was to find someone other than family members to provide the direct care while family members remained involved. Some of the adult children of elders in this group had been mistreated by their parents when they were children. At times the elders in this category had difficult personalities, which made it hard to help them; they literally ran the help off. Practitioners had to work harder with little help or cooperation from either the elder or the family.

Elder alone. Elders in this category were at a loss as to how to cope with their situation. They tended to be grateful for guidance and assistance, and therefore interventions were quite successful. Because there were no family or friends to help, numerous tasks fell to the practitioner. On the other hand, there was no one to interfere. In less successful cases, the elder never accepted intervention. The researchers noted that for those elderly with no significant others but who were still functional although living in a deteriorated environment, intervention generally had little impact (Dubin et al., 1986).

Psychological Abuse and Neglect

Most likely, this form of abuse and neglect is present with all other forms of elder abuse and neglect. Psychological abuse and neglect result in the elder feeling mentally anguished (Johnson, 1986). The elder may express feelings of shame or complain of ridicule, harrassment, manipulation, name-calling, or being threatened with abandonment by the caregiver. The elder may be evasive when interviewed or overly passive. There may be deference or ambivalence with regard to the suspected abuser. Other indicators include confusion and disorientation in the absence of a diagnosed dementia, trembling and fidgeting when talking about certain subjects, changing the subject frequently, cowering in the presence of the caregiver, or deferring to the caregiver.

Unlike physical abuse, psychological abuse and neglect may be difficult to measure. But the effects may be just as serious. In one study of over 400 battered women, it was reported by the women that the psychological abuse caused more distress and mental anguish than the physical abuse (Walker, 1984). In some instances, psychological abuse and neglect fit the definitions of psychological torture as used by Amnesty International in understanding the psychological profiles of prisoners of war and hostages. That definition includes isolation of the victim, induced mental and physical weakness by limiting food and sleep, threats of death against the victim and other family members perhaps to the point of including sham executions, administration of drugs or alcohol, controlling the perceptions of the victim using obsessiveness and possessiveness, degradation including humiliation and name calling, and occasional kindnesses or indulgences that are given randomly and that keep the victim's hope alive that the mistreatment will stop (Walker, 1984) Practitioners working with elder abuse victims will recognize these elements of psychological torture.

Financial Abuse

Financial abuse means that the legally owned assets of the elder are misappropriated. It can range from being chronically shortchanged by the corner grocer or by grandchildren who run errands to being induced to sign over real property and liquid assets to the point of becoming impoverished. Financial abuse is more common with older people than with other age groups simply because most older people have some type of assets, perhaps a house if nothing else. Also, many older people value relationships over their belongings or assets, and some can be easily induced to make "gifts." Lonely or isolated older people can be more vulnerable to this type of abuse.

Some of the signs and symptoms of financial abuse are confusion over who owns the house or over who has control of the bank accounts; activity on bank accounts that is abnormal for that particular older person, for example, multiple withdrawals in a single week or excessive use of the automatic teller machine. Other indicators include recent acquaintances expressing gushy, undying affection for an older person; disappearance of valuables from the household such as furs, jewelry, and silverware; signatures on checks and other documents that do not resemble the signature of the older person; and implausible explanations as to the handling of the elder's money. If someone has been designated the surrogate decision maker under a durable power of attorney or by appointment as guardian or conservator in a court of law, the signs and symptoms may differ. For instance, there may be a reluctance to spend money on the care of the elder, or the surrogate may focus more on money matters than on the care of the elder (Quinn & Tomita, 1986).

Accurate statistics regarding financial abuse may be hard to obtain, even with meticulous reporting laws. In some instances financial abuse may be viewed as white collar crime and, in some respects, condoned. For instance, if the financial abuser is an only child who has been appointed guardian of his mother and would stand to inherit everything upon her death, some people feel that he should not be held accountable or have to pay back assets he took from his mother. This value system ignores the reality that the elder has had assets illegally appropriated without her knowledge and certainly without her consent.

Accurate statistics may also be hard to obtain because the reports may be made to the criminal justice system and not to agencies mandated to accept the reports. In many states, those traditionally aware of financial abuse, such as banks, lawyers, and judges, are not mandated to report financial abuse to the appropriate agency (Salend et al., 1984).

Violation of Rights

All adult Americans have certain inalienable rights under the Constitution as well as under federal and state laws. These rights include the right to be free from forced labor, the right to assembly, speech, and religion, the right to appropriate medical treatment, the right not to be declared incompetent without due process of law, the right to vote, and the right to be treated with courtesy, dignity, and respect (U.S. House Select Committee on Aging, 1981). Violations of rights can include not being able to see personal friends, open mail, attend the church of choice, or being confined to one room.

Most cases of elder abuse and neglect involve some violation of rights. In the case example cited earlier, the elderly woman's rights to freedom from abuse and neglect and proper medical care were violated, as were her freedoms of speech, the right to a safe, clean environment, and the right not to have property taken without due process of law. She also lost the right to associate with others by the actions of her daughter, and she was confined to an unsafe environment.

Prevalence of Elder Abuse and Neglect

Accurate and detailed statistics regarding elder abuse and neglect do not exist. In part this is due to the lack of commonly agreed upon definitions and methodology in research studies and to the lack of uniformity in state reporting laws and record keeping. It is also due to the underreporting of cases and to the hidden nature of elder maltreatment.

The estimates of the prevalence of elder abuse and neglect vary between 1 and 10% of all elders. The most commonly used figure is 4%, which means that elder abuse and neglect are at least as common as child abuse and neglect (Hudson, 1986). In the first random survey of elder abuse and neglect, Pillemer and Finkelhor (1988) found that that the prevalence rate of elder maltreatment (physical violence, verbal aggression, and other-neglect) was 3.2% of all elderly or 32 per 1,000. The researchers found 63 cases in their sample of 2,020, 40 of which involved physical abuse, 26 of which were connected with verbal aggression, and 7 of which involved neglect. Financial abuse and violation of rights were not measured in this study.

The hidden nature of elder abuse and neglect was well demonstrated in this study. In comparing the prevalence rate of elder abuse and neglect found in the research study with actual cases reported to state authorities in the same state, the researchers found that only 1 in 14 cases of elder abuse and neglect came to the public attention. This means that state statistics most likely grossly underrepresent the true prevalence of elder abuse and neglect (Pillemer & Finkelhor, 1988).

Profiles

Studies in the late 1970s and early 1980s tended to identify the victim of elder abuse and neglect as an impaired, dependent woman over the age of 75 who was widowed and living with relatives, one of whom was her abuser. Most often, the abuser was identified as an adult child, usually a son, who was also the caregiver (Block & Sinnott, 1979; Douglass & Hickey, 1983; Lau & Kosberg, 1978; O'Malley et al., 1979; Wolf, 1984).

Later studies have found different profiles. Pillemer and Finkelhor (1988) found that elderly men were just as likely to be abused as elderly women. However, the women sustained more severe damage both physically and psychologically. Most often the abuser was a spouse (58%), although a son was the abuser in 16% of the cases, with daughters responsible for 8% of the cases. Those at high risk for abuse were those who lived with a spouse and one other person and who were in poor health. No particular age group within the population over 65 years of age was found to be more vulnerable.

The abusers were found to show signs of serious maladjustment. They had a high rate of having been arrested, having been hospitalized for a psychiatric condition, having been involved in other violent behavior, or being limited by some health problem. They were also found to be heavily dependent on the victim, especially financially. They were also more likely than those in a comparison group to have suffered recent life stress (Finkelhor & Pillemer, 1987).

A study focusing solely on adult offspring as the abusers outlined three major categories of abusers: those who were hostile, those who who were authoritarian, and those who were dependent (Anetzberger, 1986). The first group, those who were hostile, had long-term relationship problems with their parent and considered the the parent to be a "mental case." They seemed to prefer that the elder parent be passive or even dead. In this group, there was a history of the abuser having been abused by the parent when the abuser was a child. The abusers in the hostile group were the best educated but saw themselves as underachievers and blamed their lack of success on the parent. They found caring for the parent extremely burdensome and were the most abusive of the groups of abusers. But they felt they had to take care of the parent, that it was expected by others in the family.

The second group was the authoritarian group. These abusers tended to be married and living lives that would be well accepted in the community. However, they were rigid, punitive, intolerant of ambiguity, domineering to subordinates, and servile to superiors. They had a need for control and were inflexible with respect to household routines and other standards. They were not mentally ill, but they were rigid in their expectations of their parent, sometimes to the point of disregarding the impairments that the elder parent was suffering. They punished the elder and described the elder as having been authoritarian with them when they were children. In fact, they tended to infantilize the elder and were particularly resentful if the elder spoke to "outsiders" about "family business."

The last category of abusers was described as being dependent. These abusers were financially dependent on their elder parents and in most cases had lived with the parent for the entirety of the last two years. They seemed to represent the "losers" in life; they were poorly groomed, seemed quite immature, and had never achieved the emotional, economic, or social status expected of American adults. They were very attached to their parent in a "childlike dependency" and seemed to have no desire to alter their circumstances. They were unmarried, poorly educated, did not work, and had low incomes. Of the three groups, they were the most isolated and the least likely to admit to inflicting harm on their elderly parent (Anetzberger, 1986).

SUMMARY

The growing societal awareness of the prevalence and destructive consequences of elder abuse has been a catalyst for continued research studies, the passage of reporting laws, and developing assessment and intervention strategies. Although a body of information is forming, it is clear there are still many unanswered questions surrounding the phenomenon of elder abuse, including what is and is not abuse and how to intervene in the caregiving system. It is hoped that the review of the literature and the case study presented in this chapter will help the practitioner have a better understanding of the issues surrounding this multifaceted, complex problem.

REFERENCES

Anetzberger, G. J. (1986). *The etiology of elder abuse by adult offspring.* Springfield, IL: Charles C Thomas.

Block, M. R., & Sinnott, J. D. (Eds.). (1979). *The battered elder syndrome: An exploratory study.* College Park, MD: University of Maryland Center on Aging.

Douglass, R. L., & Hickey, T. (1983). Domestic neglect and abuse of the elderly: Research findings and systems perspective for service delivery planning. In J. I. Kosberg (Ed.), *Abuse and maltreatment of the elderly: Causes and interventions.* Littleton, MA: John Wright PSG.

Douglass, R. L., Hickey, T., & Noel, C. (1980). *A study of maltreatment of the elderly and other vulnerable adults.* Ann Arbor: Institute of Gerontology, University of Michigan.

Dubin, T. A., Garcia, R., LeLong, J., & Mowsesian, R. (1986). *Family neglect and self-neglect of the elderly: Normative characteristics and a design for intervention.* Austin, TX: Hogg Foundation for Mental Health, Family Eldercare Inc.

Finkelhor, D. (1983). Common features of family abuse. In D. Finkelhor, R. J.

Gelles, G. Hotaling, & M. Straus (Eds.), *The dark side of families: Current family violence research.* Beverly Hills, CA: Sage.

Finkelhor, D., & Pillemer, K. (1987). *Correlates of elder abuse: A case-control study.* Durham: Family Research Laboratory, University of New Hampshire.

Hudson, M. R. (1986). Elder mistreatment: Current research. In K. Pillemer & R. Wolf (Eds.), *Elder abuse: Conflict in the family.* Dover, MA: Auburn Publishing Company.

Johnson, T. (1986). Critical issues in the definition of elder mistreatment. In K. Pillemer & R. Wolf (Eds.), *Elder abuse: Conflict in the family.* Dover, MA: Auburn Publishing Company.

Lau, E. A., & Kosberg, J. I. (1978, November). *Abuse of the elderly by informal care providers: Practice and research issues.* Paper presented at the 31st Annual Meeting of the Gerontological Society, Dallas, TX.

O'Malley, H. C., Segars, H., Perez, R., Mitchell, V., & Knuepel, G. M. (1979). *Elder abuse in Massachusetts: A survey of professionals and paraprofessionals.* Boston: Legal Research and Services for the Elderly.

Pillemer, K., & Finkelhor, D. (1988). The prevalence of elder abuse: A random sample survey. *The Gerontologist, 28*(1), 51–57.

Quinn, M. J., & Tomita, S. K. (1986). *Elder abuse and neglect: Causes, diagnosis, and intervention strategies,* New York: Springer Publishing Co.

Rathbone-McCuan, E. (1978, November). *Inter-generational family violence and neglect: The aged as victims of reactivated and reverse neglect.* Paper presented at the International Conference of Gerontology, Japan.

Rathbone-McCuan, E. (1980). Elderly victims of family violence and neglect. *Social Casework, 61*(5), 296–304.

Salend, E., Kane, R. A. M., & Pynoos, J. (1984). Elder abuse reporting: Limitations of statutes. *The Gerontologist, 24*(1), 61–69.

Steinmetz, S. K. (1978). Battered parents. *Society, 15*(15), 54–55.

U.S. House of Representatives Select Committee on Aging. (1981). *Elder abuse: An examination of a hidden problem.* 97th Congress (Comm. Pub. No. 97-277). Washington, DC: Government Printing Office.

Walker, L. E. (1984). *The battered woman syndrome.* New York: Springer Publishing Co.

Wolf, R. S. (1986). Major findings from three model projects on elderly abuse. In K. A. Pillemer & R. S. Wolf (Eds.), *Elder abuse: Conflict in the family.* Dover, MA: Auburn Publishing Company.

Wolf, R. S., Godkin, M. A., & Pillemer, K. A. (1984). *Elder abuse and neglect: Final report from three model projects.* Worcester, MA: University of Massachusetts Medical Center.

17 Elder Abuse and Neglect: Intervention Strategies

Mary Joy Quinn

In many ways, each case of elder abuse and neglect is uncharted territory and presents almost overwhelming challenges for the practitioner. On the other hand, some cases appear to be simple initially and then become more complex as time progresses and issues unfold. It can be said with certainty that each case is unique. However, there are some general principles that can be applied to each case.

GENERAL PRINCIPLES OF INTERVENTION

In order for elder abuse and neglect cases to be resolved, several disciplines and agencies may be involved.

As can be seen by the case example in Chapter 16, elder abuse and neglect cases can be very complex and involve practitioners of several disciplines and various organizations. In that case, nurses, physicians, social workers, attorneys, police officers, and fire fighters were involved, as were neighbors, relatives, and court personnel. Agencies included community mental health; a home-delivered meals program; two hospitals, including a psychiatric facility and an acute hospital; a nursing home; and eventually a board and care home. Public safety departments (police and fire) were involved, as was, eventually, the probate court.

Practitioners should seek the least restrictive alternative in determining environmental and legal protections for an elder abuse/ neglect victim.

The least restrictive alternative environmentally is living in one's own home with no assistance (Quinn & Tomita, 1986). The more help needed at home, the more intrusions made on the elder and his or her personal freedom. Balancing personal freedom with safety can be a tightrope for the practitioner and those who care about the elder. Many judgment calls may have to be made (and lived with), and there will be ambiguities and gray areas.

In-home help may include informal supports such as friends and neighbors doing shopping or transporting for appointments or may progress to needing paid attendants to come into the home part time or on a full-time, live-in basis. Whenever possible, community services should be brought to the home rather than placing the elder in a facility. The most impaired elder can be maintained at home if he or she is medically stable, if competent, caring attendants can be found, and if there are funds to pay them and someone available to supervise the attendants. However, these conditions cannot always be met, and it may become necessary to impinge further on the elder's personal freedom for safety reasons. It may be necessary to consider placement in group living of some sort if the elder is ambulatory, fairly healthy, and can perform activities of daily living or in a nursing home if the elder has medical needs, is incontinent of bowel and bladder, or is nonambulatory.

The most restrictive alternatives environmentally also include legal action. In those instances, the choices of food, clothing, residence, or medical care are made by someone other than the elder. If the elder has signed a durable power of attorney for health care and subsequently becomes incapacitated, the person designated by the elder as the attorney-in-fact makes decisions about medical care and residence. If the elder is extremely incapacitated and there is no durable power of attorney for health care, it may be necessary to petition the court for the appointment of a guardian or conservator of the person (Quinn & Tomita, 1986).

When looking at legal alternatives, it is important to realize that any legal tool can be abused. Good honest dealings always depend on the person who has the authority. The more restrictive the tool is on the elder's freedom, the more legal protections there are for the elder. The least restrictive tool is, of course, none at all. Some elders need only to have someone help them with bill paying, or they may sign the check after someone has filled it out. Arrangements can be made for the direct deposit of various checks: Social Security, Supplemental Security Income (SSI), civil service annuity, railroad retirement, and checks from the Veterans Administration. In some instances, a representative payee designated by the Social Security Administration may receive federal checks and use them to pay an elder's bills; sometimes agencies perform this service.

Some elders manage their assets through joint tenancy arrangements; they place someone else's name on their bank account(s) or on title to their real property. While this arrangement may work well in some cases and it does avoid probate proceedings following the elder's death, there are dangers, and there are few protections for the elder. Once someone else's name is added to a bank account or real property, the assets legally belong just as much to one person as to another regardless of who the assets belonged to originally.

Still more restrictive is the granting of a power of attorney. There is an element of control on the elder's part because the elder selects the attorney-in-fact and executes the document. There are three types of power of attorney, all of which must be executed when the elder has the legal capacity to do so. The three types are a limited power of attorney, which gives someone else the power to take specific, limited action on behalf of the elder; a general power of attorney, which gives broad powers; and a durable power of attorney, which continues on should the elder lose capacity or competence. Limited and general powers of attorney become invalid once the elder has lost mental capacity. There is no court supervision over power of attorney documents.

Trusts are legal tools that offer another way for elders to designate who will manage their financial affairs by placing the title to their assets into the trust. Elders who have substantial assets may set up a trust and appoint a trustee to administer their financial affairs; this is more restricting than previously mentioned options because only the designated trustee may manage the trust's assets. The trustee may be required to present accountings to the court upon petition of any interested party.

Still more restrictive of personal freedom, but in theory providing more legal protection, are guardianships or conservatorships of estate (Quinn & Tomita, 1986). These legal devices involve probate courts and court supervision, a protection not available with the other legal alternatives. In some states, there is a loss of multiple powers such as the power to vote, to marry, to contract, and to determine residence. Currently, there is a nationwide movement to modify guardianships to make them more flexible and adaptable to individual cases and to make certain that they are not imposed on elders without full due process protections, including bonding.

In the case study cited in Chapter 16, the practitioners made use of the least restrictive alternative both in terms of the elderly woman's place of residence and in terms of how her assets were managed. All efforts were made to maintain her in the home where she had lived for so long; she was returned to the home following the first hospitalization, and several in-home care services were instituted. The woman also attended a community day center specific for older people. Only when those services were refused and a second hospitalization took place was a change in living situation instituted, to a community-based group living setting. Legally, a conservatorship of person and estate was not sought until it became apparent that the elderly woman was incapable of making decisions in her own best interest, that she was not receiving the income to which she was entitled, and that she was being financially abused. Efforts had been made to use the services of a representative payee (a sister) and then to appoint a conservator of person selected by the daughter; that conservator of person proved incapable of preventing further abuse. A trust was drawn up at the request of the daughter with a neutral party acting as trustee, but that too proved unworkable. Thus, a conservatorship with a neutral agency serving as conservator of person and estate was financially necessary.

Principles of Adult Protection

The following principles were arrived at during a 1982 conference entitled "Improving Protective Services for Older Adults." In attendance at the conference were social workers, attorneys, and others who are concerned about services provided to elders who need protection (Collins & La France, 1982).

When interests compete, the practitioner is charged with serving the elder.

In many elder abuse and neglect cases, there are other people, such as landlords, neighbors, and other practitioners, who have concerns and interests in the case. At times, there is concern about morality or eccentricity. However, the focus should always be on the elder and his or her needs and wishes.

When interests compete, the elder is in charge of decision making until he or she delegates that responsibility voluntarily to another or the court grants responsibility to another.

All elders retain full constitutional rights until a court of law declares otherwise. Services cannot be imposed on unwilling elders, and deprivations of personal liberty must be carried out in accordance with due process law.

Freedom is more important than safety.

The elder has a right to be left alone and to live his or her life as desired. The elder also has the right to refuse medical treatment as long as there is mental capacity to do so. It is worth noting that professionals can honestly differ as to whether an elder has the ability to make medical decisions. Only after all other reasonable alternatives have been explored should involuntary intervention and/or court process be employed.

In ideal cases, protection of elders seeks to achieve, simultaneously and in order of importance, freedom, safety, least disruption of life style, and least restrictive care alternative.

It seems clear that services should be provided for the shortest time period possible and only to the extent needed. The chosen intervention should be balanced against the possible impact that it will have on the elder's life style, self-esteem, will to live, and feelings of control and freedom. The elder's self-esteem must be enhanced while safety is provided (Collins & La France, 1982).

SPECIFIC INTERVENTIONS

Detection and Assessment

Over the past decade, several protocols have been developed that help practitioners detect elder abuse and neglect (Anastasio, 1981; Falconi, 1982; Ferguson & Beck, 1983; Fulmer & O'Malley, 1987; Phillips & Rempusheski, 1985; Sengstock & Hwalek, 1983; Tomita, 1982; Wolf, 1986). A well-drawn protocol serves several purposes First, it gives specific structure to medical/social service situations that seem to be mysterious and unmanageable by providing step-by-step guidelines for the detection and assessment of elder abuse and neglect. A protocol also contains information and as such serves as a teaching tool and a reminder of the points to be covered during the process. It also provides an informational baseline about the elder that, if free of jargon, can follow an elder through various medical and/or social service settings and can be understood by practitioners of various disciplines. Finally, a protocol is a legitimate, thoughtful response to the elder abuse reporting laws that have swept the country in the past decade and if used intelligently can curb precipitous diagnosis of elder abuse and neglect and can eliminate inappropriate interventions.

A comprehensive protocol such as the one developed at Harborview Medical Center (Tomita, 1982) contains several sections, including methodology as to preparing to administer the protocol;

specific signs and symptoms of elder abuse and neglect, including high-risk categories; guidelines for administering the protocol to both elder and alleged abuser as well as specific interview questions for both; and specific tools for assessment such as brief mental status questionnaires and checklists to determine the elder's ability to perform activities of daily living. The final part of the protocol offers choices for the diagnosis of elder abuse and neglect: there is no evidence of abuse or neglect, there is a suspicion of abuse or neglect, or there is definitely abuse and neglect (Tomita, 1982).

Interventions

It cannot be emphasized enough that each case of elder abuse and neglect is unique. Therefore, the interventions will need to be tailor made and will depend on such variables as the elder's capabilities, both physical and mental; the urgency of the situation; the amount of cooperation from both elder and alleged abuser; the pathology of the abuser; the intensity and seriousness of the abuse; and the quality of the practitioner-client relationship (Quinn & Tomita, 1986). The choice of intervention also depends on the practitioner's own style and discipline and the policies of his or her agency.

Crisis Intervention

There are emergencies in elder abuse and neglect work. Physically, a client may be found at home in a state of profound neglect, i.e., wasting away, lying in a bed of excrement, or nearly comatose. In these situations, the practitioner must act quickly in securing medical treatment and probably hospitalization. When alleged abusers are present, they must be given the benefit of the doubt, and interventions should consist of gathering information in a nonjudgmental manner and providing information as to what is needed for the elder. The practitioner may have to call for support in the form of medical practitioners, ambulance crews for transport, or, very rarely, law enforcement officers.

There are also financial emergencies where bank accounts are being drained or a joint tenancy account is being dissipated. Practitioners can help the elder interact with bank personnel to halt the abuse and to transfer the assets to a new account that does not provide access to the alleged abuser.

Medical and financial crises can erupt at any time where elder abuse and neglect are concerned. Swift action on the part of practitioners can mean the difference between life and death or between financial comfort and poverty.

Specific Interventions for the Elder

INDIRECT INTERVENTION. In many instances, practitioners will not be able to work directly with elders and/or their caregivers to resolve a case of elder abuse and neglect; the elder or the caregiver may refuse to cooperate, or the practitioner may be only peripherally involved in delivering services. However, indirect intervention in the form of documentation, referral for services, administration of a protocol, and reporting the matter to the official agency mandated by law to receive reports of elder abuse and neglect are also of service to the abused or neglected elder (Quinn & Tomita, 1986). For instance, a documented history of suspicious bruises or falls may be helpful in making a diagnosis of elder abuse and neglect at a later time. If prosecution of the abuser is called for at a later date, the documentation will be in place.

Referral for services also can be helpful. Some community agencies or hospitals have pamphlets that can be given out to elders and caregivers that describe various community services. Or the practitioner may make a direct referral to another agency such as visiting nurses or community mental health so that contact can be made and services offered,

Administering a protocol may be helpful in detecting, assessing, and providing documentation. Here too a service has been performed if the results are kept as part of the elder's file, whether at a day center, a hospital, or an out-patient setting. The protocol would serve as a baseline should the elder become more impaired or there is evidence of repeated abuse.

DIRECT SERVICES. Direct services include counseling the elder, resource linkage and advocacy, and education. The major goal of intervention is to stop the abuse and/or neglect, but other issues are important, such as reducing the elder's isolation and dependency on the caregiver, assisting the elder to accept responsibility for his or her life, and helping the elder learn to set limits on the abuser if the two are to continue to live together, especially if they are living in the elder's house (Quinn & Tomita, 1986).

Counseling the elder will fall to whichever practitioner has contact with the elder. Mental health services are sparse for older people for a variety of reasons. Practitioners may help abused or neglected elders soften self-blame, explore previous episodes of abuse and neglect and devise "escape plans," rehearse new patterns of communicating with the caregiver, or explore how the elder has dealt with past crises. It may be important to counter maladaptive reactions. Some elder abuse and neglect clients generalize their feelings after being victimized and may lose trust in all friends and relatives; practitioners can help to develop trust again by pointing out, for instance, that not all friends are interested in taking money from the elder's bank account. The practitioner may advocate a certain course of action such as a bank account alert or a conversation with the bank manager rather than letting the client maladapt and isolate himself from those friends and relatives who are honest and who care (Quinn & Tomita, 1986).

Over the past several years, there has been a growth in the services that are available to older people. However, most elders do not know what those services are or how to take advantage of them. They may be fearful as well. Practitioners can serve as liaisons in providing information and can help the elder link up with a given service. Some of these services might be chore help, legal services, meals on wheels, help with bill paying, home nursing care, day centers, congregate meal sites, as well as all the community services now offered by many large hospitals. In some instances, the practitioner will need to advocate for the elder with an agency to make certain the elder gets the appropriate service. If there are residual medical problems as the result of physical abuse or neglect, the practitioner can see that the elder gets appropriate care. If financial or legal problems exist, it may be necessary for the elder to retain an attorney or to find an acceptable surrogate money manager.

Teaching an elder about various issues may be indicated, such as social and legal rights, medication management, aspects of certain chronic health conditions, empowerment training such as assertiveness training to strengthen a positive self-image, self-defense classes, and self-care techniques to reduce dependency on the caregiver. It may also be helpful to teach the elder about the nature of abuse and neglect, their recurrent nature, and the increase in severity if there are no interventions (Quinn & Tomita, 1986; Walker, 1984).

SPECIFIC INTERVENTIONS FOR THE ABUSER. Probably the first task the practitioner has in working with abusers is to acknowledge the feelings that are engendered when working with alleged abusers (Quinn, 1985). Those feelings include anger, a need to rescue the elder, a desire to punish the abuser, or contempt that the abuser has "gotten away with it."

Concrete interaction with the abuser may involve resource linkage, education, and actual counseling.

Resource linkage may involve letting the abuser know about caregiver groups that are supportive and informational; these groups also enable caregivers to express feelings of resentment and stress. If the abuser has substance abuse problems, referrals to appropriate agencies may be indicated. Locating a respite center or helping the caregiver arrange for respite will also relieve the caregiver.

Caregivers who are abusive may be able to profit from learning about diseases that are commonly associated with aging and the symptoms that may indicate that the condition is worsening. Other information may be helpful, such as the cycle of violence, informing the caregiver of assistance that he or she may qualify for, realistic expectations of the elder, and utilizing community resources.

A therapeutic plan may involve actual counseling. Some of the themes are confronting dependency issues and the eventual death of the elder, denial and minimization of abuse and neglect, and empowering the alleged abuser by emphasizing self-control and the possibility of changing behavior. Often caregivers complain of not having time for themselves; it is important for practitioners to aid the caregiver in meeting some of his or her own life goals, which may have been interrupted by the caregiving. Anticipatory guidance may be helpful. Caregivers can be asked about difficult situations with the elder that may be coming up in the next month or so, at which time those issues can be discussed and resolutions reached before problems emerge. The caregiver can also be helped to acknowledge the positive benefits of being a caregiver. Throughout the work with the caregiver/abuser, it is important to build in accountability, to combat denial and minimization on the part of the caregiver/abuser, and to avoid letting the caregiver blame others or external events for abusive or neglectful actions. Practitioners also need to be aware that there may come a time when it is necessary to separate the caregiver and the elder for the elder's safety. It may be necessary to find alternative living for one or the other (Quinn & Tomita, 1986).

SUMMARY

Elder abuse and neglect are the latest features of domestic maltreatment to emerge into public awareness. The phenomena share many features with other forms of domestic maltreatment, but taken as a whole, they are unique. Over the past decade, a great deal of work has gone into identifying and assessing the abused elder; now research is refining the earlier work. There is no longer any doubt that elder abuse and neglect exist and are worthy of concern and attention. The solutions will come from many directions: gerontology; other domestic maltreatment literature, research, and clinical intervention strategies; the criminal justice system; the civil courts; medicine; and the social sciences. The need is great, especially given the "graying of America" and the population projections for the near future.

REFERENCES

Anastasio, C. J. (1981, March). Elder abuse: Identification and acute care intervention. Paper presented at the National Conference on Abuse of Older Persons, Boston.

Collins, M., & La France, A. B. (1982). Improving protective services for older Americans: Social worker role. Portland, ME: Human Services Development Institute, Center for Research and Advanced Study, University of Southern Maine.

Falconi, D. (1982). Assessing the abused elderly. Journal of Gerontological Nursing, 8(4), 208–212.

Ferguson, D., & Beck, C. (1983). H.A.L.F. A tool to assess elder abuse within the family. Geriatric Nursing, 4(5), 301–304.

Fulmer, T. T., & O'Malley, T. A. (1987). Inadequate care of the elderly: A health care perspective on abuse and neglect. New York: Springer Publishing Co.

Phillips, L. R., & Rempusheski, V. F. (1985). A decision-making model for diagnosing and intervening in elder abuse and neglect. Nursing Research, 34(3), 134–139.

Quinn, M. J. (1985). Elder abuse and neglect raise new dilemmas. Generations, Quarterly Journal of the American Society on Aging, 10(2), 22–25.

Quinn, M. J., & Tomita, S. K. (1986). Elder abuse and neglect: Causes, diagnosis, and intervention strategies. New York: Springer Publishing Co.

Sengstock, M. C., & Hwalek, M. (1983, November). Sources of information used in measures for the identification of elder abuse. Paper presented at the Annual Meeting of the Gerontological Society of America.

Tomita, S. K. (1982). Detection and treatment of elderly abuse and neglect: A protocol for health care professionals. PT & OT in Geriatrics, 2(2), 37–51.

Walker, L. E. (1984). The battered woman syndrome. New York: Springer Publishing Co.

Wolf, R. S. (1986). Major findings from three model projects on elderly abuse. In K. A. Pillemer & R. S. Wolf (Eds.), Elder abuse: Conflict in the family. Dover, MA: Auburn Publishing Company.

VI Conceptual Models and Conclusion

Constructivist Self-Development Theory as a Framework for Assessing and Treating Victims of Family Violence

18

Lisa McCann
Laurie Anne Pearlman

Over the past ten years, clinicians and researchers have become increasingly aware of the devastating impact of family violence for individuals, families, and communities (e.g., Courtois, 1988; Finkelhor et al., 1983; Gelles & Cornell, 1985). Currently, much attention is focused on understanding why victims of family violence experience the reactions they do, why individuals may experience very different reactions to similar events, and the implications this has for differential treatment strategies. Most theorists in the field of traumatic stress (e.g., Green et al., 1985; Scurfield, 1985; Wilson, 1980) agree that the outcome of trauma is a function of the interaction among the person (pretrauma personality, psychopathology), the situation (characteristics of the stressor), and posttrauma factors (postrecovery environment and social support). However, the precise nature of this interaction has yet to be fully articulated. There is a need for a more comprehensive theoretical model to explain unique response patterns among victims, including a fuller elaboration of the interaction between the person and the situation, and the implications this has for treatment. Our clinical experience with victims of a variety of traumatic life events led us to search for better ways to conceptualize the unique variations in posttrauma reactions across victim groups and to apply the resulting theory systematically to the assessment and treatment of traumatized individuals.

We began our search with a synthesis of the empirical literature on psychological responses to victimization across a variety of victimizing events, including family violence (McCann, Sakheim, & Abrahamson, 1988). This review served as the basis for a new theory that provides a framework for systematic assessment, treatment planning, treatment interventions, and hypothesis-testing research. We

call this theory the Constructivist Self-Development Theory to high-
light its constructivist underpinnings as well as its emphasis on the
development of the self.

In the following sections of this chapter, we briefly explicate the
theory and then discuss its potential applications to the assessment
and treatment of victims of family violence.

CONSTRUCTIVIST SELF-DEVELOPMENT THEORY

In earlier papers (McCann, Pearlman, Sakheim, & Abrahamson, 1988;
McCann, Sakheim, & Abrahamson, 1988), we presented our first
formulations of this theoretical model. In a subsequent elaboration of
the theory (McCann & Pearlman, in press), we broaden the cognitive
portion of our work, which initially focused primarily on cognitive
schemas, to include specific schemas related to one's expectancies
that central psychological needs will be met. In addition, we have
added the concept of the self (resources and capacities), reconcep-
tualized our view of the traumatic memory to focus on the imagery
and verbal systems of memory, and elaborated the importance of the
social and cultural context within which trauma occurs. Finally, we
have used the theory to understand the effects on helpers of working
with traumatized individuals, which we call vicarious traumatization (McCann & Pearlman, 1990).

Constructivist self-development theory is based on the work of
several other theorists, including Murphy (1947; a biosocial theory
of development), Rotter (1954; social learning theory), Kelly (1955;
personal construct theory), Piaget (1971; structural theory), Kohut
(1977; self psychology), and Mahoney (1981; cognitive-constructive
theory). It bears similarities to Epstein's (1985) cognitive experiential
self theory, although it has been developed independently.

Our theory focuses on three psychological dimensions of the
individual who has experienced a trauma. These three dimensions—
the self, the traumatic memories, and the psychological needs and
related cognitive schemas—must be explored and assessed thoroughly as the central part of the therapy process. The person's
unique psychological adaptation to trauma can be understood as a
complex interplay among these factors (see Table 18.1). This view of
trauma is consistent with a constructivist-contextual theoretical
model (Mahoney, 1981). In essence, constructivist theories assume
that individuals create and construct their own personal realities,
which in turn shape their feelings and behavior. A full understanding of an individual's adaptation to trauma must take into account
the unique meanings of the event for the individual.

TABLE 18.1 The Psychological Experience of Trauma

Self
  Resources
    1. Knowing one's needs as distinct from others
    2. Willpower and initiative
    3. Establishing personal boundaries between self/other
    4. Making self-protective judgments
    5. The ability to introspect
    6. Sense of humor
    7. Intelligence
    8. Empathy
  Capacities
    1. Ability to tolerate strong affect
    2. Ability to be alone without being lonely
    3. Ability to calm and soothe oneself
    4. Ability to regulate self-esteem

Psychological needs and schemas about self and others
    1. Safety
    2. Trust/dependency
    3. Independence
    4. Power
    5. Esteem
    6. Intimacy
    7. Frame of reference

Life experience
  Components of whole memories
    Imagery
    Verbal
  Themes of traumatic memories
    Violation
    Betrayal
    Humiliation
    Degradation
    Death and injury
    Helplessness and paralysis
    Loss/confrontation with death
  The meanings of the social and cultural context
    Social class
    Age
    Gender
    Race
    Subculture
    Historical context

Psychological and interpersonal adaptation
  Emotional
    Fear and anxiety   (continued)

TABLE 18.1 (Continued)

  Depression
  Emotional numbing
  Guilt and shame
  Anger
Cognitive
  Perceptual disturbances
  Persistent, distressing thoughts
Biological
  Physiological hyperarousal
  Somatic disturbances
Behavioral
  Sleep disturbance
  Aggression
  Suicidal behavior
  Substance abuse
Interpersonal
  Impaired social functioning
  Sexual problems
  Intimacy problems
  Revictimization
  Victim becomes victimizer

The Self

The self is a hypothetical construct that we use to describe the foundation of the entire psychological experience of the person. Our use of the term is consistent with Kohut's (Baker & Baker, 1987; Kohut, 1977; White & Weiner, 1986). The self comprises various capacities and resources that allow the individual to regulate self-esteem and to maintain an enduring sense of his or her value and worth, as well as to negotiate relationships with others. Severe traumas can disrupt the self capacities and resources, and thus the sense of self-esteem, temporarily or permanently (Brende, 1983; Parson, 1984). The person's ability to integrate and work through traumatic memories is dependent on the stability and cohesiveness of the self.

Psychological Needs and Cognitive Schemas

Psychological needs develop through early experience and serve to motivate human behavior. The cognitive expression of these needs is the schema, which is the basis for an individual's construction of reality (Piaget, 1971). Schemas are the individual's frameworks for understanding himself or herself and the world; they include tacit assumptions, beliefs, and expectations about self and world. They both shape and are shaped by feelings, behaviors, and life experience. Within Rotter's (1954) social learning theory, the individual's behavior is a result of his or her expections for various outcomes and the importance or value he or she places on the expected outcomes. In this regard, the concept of schemas is comparable to Rotter's concept of expectancies. This view is also fundamental to a cognitive-constructive theoretical position (e.g., Mahoney & Lyddon, 1988). The basic schemas for experience reflect one's ideas about causality, the trustworthiness of sense data, identity, and self–world relationships (Mahoney, 1981). We propose that schemas that reflect self–world relationships are impacted by traumatic events and color the unique way the individual interprets and responds to traumatic events. This view is consistent with others in the field of victimization (e.g. Janoff-Bulman, 1985; Roth & Lebowitz, 1988).

Within the area of schemas, we include a brief discussion of the importance of understanding the client's social and cultural context as the client construes it. This context plays an important role in determining how the client will experience a trauma and, particularly in an area such as domestic violence, how the victim's social network responds to the victimization.

The Traumatic Memories

As persons experience life events, they encode these experiences into the verbal and imagery representational systems of memory (Paivio, 1986). The verbal representational system is the system in which all language-related aspects of memory are encoded. Since the visual system is the dominant symbolic system for most sighted individuals (Paivio, 1986, p. 58), most persons will experience imagery as the strongest component of symbolic memory. Thus, the imagery system contains nonverbal representations of experience. Emotion is tied to the imagery system of memory because it is by definition nonverbal. Any of the pieces of a memory may trigger any of the others, consistent with models of state-dependent learning (Eich, 1980; Greenberg & van der Kolk, 1987) and associative memory (Anderson & Bower, 1980; Bower, 1981). The therapy process includes integrating verbal and imagery memory fragments and their associated affects into whole memories that are then in turn integrated into the person's cognitive schemas or meaning systems as well as his or her self-structure.

In essence, we propose that the individual's unique experience of and response to trauma is determined by the self, the psychological needs and cognitive schemas, and the traumatic memory. In the following sections, we describe a hypothesized relation among traumatic experiences, the psychological experience of the person, and psychological adaptation. Finally, we provide a paradigm for systematic assessment and intervention based in constructivist self-development theory.

PSYCHOLOGICAL RESPONSES TO THE EXPERIENCE OF TRAUMA

What are the commonalities in response patterns across victim groups? Our review of the empirical literature on psychological response to victimization (McCann, Sakheim, & Abrahamson, 1988) revealed disruptions in five major realms of psychological and interpersonal functioning. These realms are emotional (fear and anxiety, depression, emotional deadness or numbing, guilt and shame, anger); cognitive (perceptual disturbances, persistent thoughts concerning the event); biological (physiological hyperarousal and somatic disturbances); behavioral (sleep disturbance, aggressive behavior, suicidal behavior, substance abuse, impaired social functioning, severe personality disorders); and interpersonal (sexuality problems, intimacy problems, revictimization, and victim becoming victimizer) (see Table 18.1). Yet despite the converging evidence that victims of family violence may experience many of these reactions, clinicians are well aware of the considerable variations and differences in individuals' responses to similar events. Constructivist self-development theory provides a framework for understanding unique response patterns and for conceptualizing treatment approaches.

We propose that psychological responses to trauma, rather than being viewed as symptoms, should be understood as part of the unique psychological experience of the individual as he or she makes sense of and adapts to traumatic life events. In other words, rather than focusing on the symptoms as the primary problem, clinicians should assume that the symptoms represent disruptions in individuals' psychological experience and self–world relations.

We will now describe guidelines for assessing the three dimensions of the individual—the self, the needs and related schemas, and the traumatic memories—and their relation to the development and understanding of unique responses to trauma.

ASSESSING THE SELF

Although the self might be thought to include all of one's psychological experience, we use it here in a somewhat narrower sense. In our use of the term, the self includes the capacities delineated by self psychology and object relations theorists (Kohut, 1977; Winnicott, 1958) and the resources often referred to as ego resources (Bellak et al., 1973; Murray & Kluckhohn, 1959).

The self capacities all relate to the ability to regulate self-esteem. They include the capacity to tolerate and regulate strong affects without self-fragmentation or acting out; to be alone without being lonely (Winnicott, 1958); to calm oneself through processes of self-soothing; and to moderate self-loathing in the face of criticism or guilt. Self resources determine one's ability to interact successfully in the world. They include the ability to know one's own psychological needs, to demonstrate willpower and initiative, to be aware of and able to establish personal boundaries between self and others, to size up situations or make judgments that are appropriately self-protective, to introspect and reflect on one's experience, to demonstrate a sense of humor and intelligence (Murray & Kluckhohn, 1959), and to empathize with another's experience (Jordan, 1984; Young-Eisendrath & Wiedemann, 1987). Taken together, these capacities and resources suggest the extent to which the self is stable and cohesive and thus the extent to which the client will be able to work through the trauma.

These capacities and resources must be assessed throughout the therapy process. A failure to understand and respect the vulnerabilities within the self can result in a failure in empathy or even re-traumatization. This is most likely to happen when therapists make the mistake of probing for powerful affects prematurely, before the capacities for affect regulation and self-soothing are strong.

The self capacities can be assessed directly over the course of therapy by probing into these areas. For example, the therapist might ask, "When you are very upset, how do you calm yourself? What happens inside you?" Clients who describe being overdependent on outside sources of calm or support or who experience inordinate distress when alone may be evidencing limited or diminished capacities for self-soothing and tolerating solitude. Likewise, certain behaviors may indicate impaired self functions. Destructive acting out, including substance abuse or suicidal behavior, may be clues that the client is unable to modulate strong affects or is experiencing intense periods of self-loathing. Each capacity and resource must be fully understood and explored, having important implications for treatment planning and intervention.

Regardless of whether the capacities of the self were compromised before or after the trauma, the clinician must first determine whether the capacities and resources are strong enough for the client to tolerate the exploration of potentially painful traumatic memories. One may determine that the therapy should initially involve "self-building" without any direct exploration of the trauma-related memories. There is some suggestion in the clinical literature (e.g., Brown & Fromm, 1986) that cases of complicated posttraumatic stress disorder (PTSD) may involve three phases of work: initial stabilization of symptoms, followed by self-building, and then working though the traumatic memories through such techniques as hypnosis or revivification.

SELF-BUILDING

Much has been written about a self-psychology approach to the treatment of self disorders (e.g., Kohut, 1977; White & Weiner, 1986). Only recently has this approach been explicated in the area of victimization (Brown & Fromm, 1986; Parson, 1984; Ulman & Brothers, 1988). It is outside the realm of this paper to describe the complexities of the self-psychology perspective. For the interested reader, Baker and Baker (1987) provide an excellent overview of Kohut's thinking which is succinct and comprehensible.

Our approach to disturbances of the self is twofold. The focus is not on exploring infantile conflicts, as in classical analytic approaches, but rather on understanding the unique ways that individuals regulate self-esteem and maintain self-cohesion in the face of self-shattering experiences such as trauma. This approach, which is fundamentally phenomenological in nature, is critical to conveying the proper respect and understanding of the individual's internal world.

Next, our approach becomes somewhat more eclectic by suggesting that impaired self capacities and resources can be developed or restored through a variety of psychological techniques, in addition to the internalization of empathetic others. For example, a diminished capacity for willpower and initiative might be restored through empowerment techniques such as assertiveness training. An impaired capacity for self-soothing might be restored through imagery work in which the therapist guides the client to soothe, calm, and relate lovingly to the himself or herself. Similarly, it may prove useful to encourage the client to become aware of and value his or her own needs as distinct from others' needs and to become aware of his or her own strengths, processes that have long been a focus of feminist therapy (Young-Eisendrath & Wiedemann, 1987). The process of helping the client to discover his or her strengths is in itself self-building (Young-Eisendrath & Wiedemann, 1987). These are but a few examples of the diversity of techniques that might be employed, depending on the individual and his or her unique strengths and weaknesses. In essence, this approach focuses on strengthening those self capacities and resources that either were undeveloped to begin with or that have been compromised by the trauma so that the traumatic memories can be explored and fully integrated into the individual's meaning system.

ASSESSING PSYCHOLOGICAL NEEDS AND COGNITIVE SCHEMAS

A person's unique experience of trauma will be determined in large part by his or her psychological needs and related schemas about the self and others. The traumatic experience may reinforce or disrupt existing needs and schemas. In our synthesis of the literature on trauma and victimization (McCann, Sakheim, & Abrahamson, 1988), we proposed that persons develop schemas in the five areas of safety, trust, esteem, power, and intimacy. In our later work (McCann & Pearlman, in press), we elaborated on how each of these areas is related to a specific psychological need and expanded the needs of interest to include two more, independence and frame of reference. These need areas are central to many major theories of personality.

Some of these areas may be more emotionally charged than others, depending upon how central each need is for the individual. In addition, the individual's experience of the trauma will depend on which needs are more central. For example, a domestic violence victim with strong trust/dependency needs may experience the abuse as evidence that men can't be trusted, while another survivor with strong needs for security might experience the same event as confirmation that the world is not a safe place.

We refer to a "disturbed" schema as a belief system that results in disturbances within one or more of the five realms of psychological and interpersonal functioning (Table 18.1). We predict that greater psychological disruptions occur when disturbed schemas are overgeneralized and are either inconsistent with or out of proportion to the current situation. For example, a victim of family violence may develop the generalized belief that all men are dangerous, a belief that forecloses the possibility of healthy intimacy with men. Another family violence victim may believe that all people are untrustworthy and unreliable on the basis of her traumatic experience. An extension of such a belief may be a pervasive sense of cynicism and withdrawal from the activities of the world.

Certain feeling states and behavioral patterns may emerge as people make predictions about future life events and behave in ways that confirm these predictions. Below, we describe the hypothesized relation between disturbed schemas and psychological adaptation. These disturbances may occur with respect to the self and with respect to others. We will describe each need area briefly and give examples of disturbed schemas in each area.

Safety

Security, or the need to feel safe and reasonably invulnerable to harm, corresponds to safety schemas. Positive safety schemas include the belief that one can protect oneself from physical and emotional harm, injury, or loss. With respect to others, positive schemas might include the belief that the world and other people are fundamentally safe. Within the area of safety, it is important to listen for themes of unique vulnerability to future harm; chronic, generalized anxiety about potential dangers in the world; and concerns about being unable to find a safe place within oneself or the world.

Examples of disturbed schemas in the area of safety are "I cannot protect myself," "The world is a dangerous place," and "Other people are threatening or dangerous." Sometimes clients will express a belief that there is something about themselves that attracts trouble or brings about harm. The feeling states that often accompany such disturbed schemas are fear, anxiety, and phobias. This may lead to avoidant behavior, resulting in decreased life satisfaction.

Dependency/Trust

Dependency refers to the need to have others prevent frustration and satisfy other needs (Rotter, 1954) and to be treated with understanding and kindness (Gordon, 1976). It is a natural human need that can be expressed in appropriate and mature ways; it should be distinguished from passivity (Young-Eisendrath & Wiedemann,

1987). This need corresponds to trust schemas. Positive schemas in the area of trust may involve the expectancy that one can rely on one's perceptions and judgments and on the word or promise of other persons, consistent with Hochreich and Rotter's (1970) definition of interpersonal trust. Disturbances in the area of trust/dependency can be assessed by listening for themes of betrayal, abandonment, being made a fool of, being disappointed by other people, or being reluctant to ask for help or support from others.

An example of a specific disturbed schema might be the expectancy that one cannot trust one's husband to be faithful. A more generalized disturbed expectancy might be "You can't ever trust men." Other examples of disturbed schemas in the area of trust are "I am a bad judge of character" and "You can't depend on others to be there when you need them." The feeling state most often accompanying disturbed self-trust schemas is self-doubt; when the ability to trust others is impaired, feelings of disappointment, betrayal, or bitterness are common. Behaviorally, the client may be unable to make decisions, may avoid close relationships, and may be suspicious, thus alienating other people.

Independence

Independence refers to the need to control one's own behavior or rewards (Gordon 1976; Rotter, 1954). Positive independence schemas include the belief that one can control one's own thoughts, feelings, and behaviors. The area of independence can be assessed by listening for themes of humiliation, shame, or disappointment in oneself for appearing to be weak, vulnerable, or helpless, as well as an unwillingness to ask others for help. In many individuals, independence and trust/dependency are closely linked. Disturbed schemas may include "I must be in control of my thoughts, feelings, and actions at all times," "I can't tell others when I'm in pain or need help," and "I must be available to others who need me, irrespective of my immediate situation." Clients with unrealistically high expectations for independence tend to overinterpret any signs of emotional vulnerability as a fatal flaw and are resistant to crying or being emotional with anyone because it feels too shameful. Again, it is important to respect these needs and, very gradually, to begin reframing emotional expression as a sign of strength rather than weakness. Behaviorally, such persons may be rigid and overcontrolled, making it difficult to process emotional experiences.

Power

Power refers to the need to direct or exert control over others (Gordon, 1976; Rotter, 1954). Power schemas involve the belief that one can affect or control future outcomes in interpersonal relations. Conflicted needs for power are often revealed through power and control struggles and conflicts concerning assertiveness.

Examples of disturbed power schemas include "I am helpless to control forces outside myself," "I have no influence or control in relationships," and "I must control others or they will control me." The feeling states associated with disturbed power schemas are weakness, helplessness, and depression. A behavioral extension of this may be a learned helplessness pattern, originally conceived by Seligman (1975) and later applied to victims of domestic violence (Walker, 1978).

Esteem

Positive self-esteem is closely tied to the basic human need for recognition or validation. Positive esteem schemas refer to the belief that oneself and others are valuable and worthy of respect (Gordon, 1976; Rotter, 1954). The area of esteem can be assessed by listening for themes concerning self-blame, unworthiness, or badness, and, with regard to others, feelings of contempt for or disillusionment about other people.

Examples of disruptions in these beliefs are "I am bad/flawed/ damaged" and "Everyone I come into contact with is doomed" and "People don't care" or "People are basically out for themselves." Disturbed schemas in the area of self-esteem are likely to be associated with feelings of self-loathing, worthlessness, despair, and futility. The person may engage in self-punishing behaviors, with suicide being the ultimate destruction of the damaged or bad self. Clearly, the strength of the self capacities, particularly the capacity to regulate affect and modulate self-loathing by self-soothing, is central here. A diminished belief in the value of other people is likely to be associated with cynicism, anger, or contempt. Behavioral manifestations may be antisocial life patterns or a general withdrawal from the world.

Intimacy

Human beings have a fundamental need for connection or attachment to other human beings (e.g., Bowlby, 1969). Positive schemas in the area of intimacy may include the belief that one will enjoy being alone, that one can be a friend to oneself, and that one can connect with others in a meaningful, personal way. Panic when alone and an overreliance on drugs, alcohol, sex, food, or spending money as sources of comfort are indications of disturbances in the area of intimacy. The area of intimacy with others can be assessed through exploring the client's internal experience of other people or the world in general. The "reality" of the person's interpersonal world is less important than his or her internalization of this world. Thus, a person who reports having friends may nonetheless exhibit disruptions in this area through statements revealing an inability to understand or feel understood by others.

Disturbed schemas in the area of intimacy may include such beliefs as "I don't feel like I exist unless I'm with other people" and "I'm terrified when I'm alone." With respect to others, examples include "I can't feel close to others" and "I expect to feel disconnected most of the time." The feeling states associated with these disturbed schemas are a pervasive sense of emptiness, loneliness, alienation, or estrangement. These clients may live an isolated existence or find it impossible to tolerate time alone, thus becoming dependent on external sources of soothing, such as sex, drugs, or alcohol (Horner, 1986).

Frame of Reference

The need for a meaningful frame of reference for one's experience is viewed as fundamental within many theories of personality (Epstein, 1985; Fromm, 1955; Jung, 1969; Rogers, 1951). Trauma by definition has the potential to disrupt one's usual ways of making sense of experience, and can challenge one's entire frame of reference. Figley (1983) has noted that trauma survivors often become preoccupied with questions such as "Why did this happen to me?" Examples of disturbed schemas in this area include, "Life just doesn't make sense to me any more," "I've given up trying to understand what happened and why." Feelings of confusion, disorientation, and related generalized distress can be associated with a disturbed frame of reference. Individuals experiencing this disturbance may appear distracted and may behave in ways that appear inconsistent with previous behavior, as the thread that once linked their behaviors has been broken.

Conveying Respect for Central Needs and Disturbed Schemas

The therapist must convey an attitude of respect for the client's central needs and schemas without prematurely challenging those that appear maladaptive. The treatment plan should be sensitive to individual differences in needs and schemas. For example, clients with strong needs for recognition and disturbed schemas in the area of esteem are likely to need empathetic validation and positive mirroring (Kohut, 1977) within the therapy before they can talk about their more shameful, humiliating memories. Likewise, clients with strong needs for independence and high expectancies for personal power may not be ready to delve into painful memories until their fears of vulnerability and loss of control are resolved. Clients with strong security needs and concerns about safety will need to feel that the therapy setting is a safe place and to learn, through imagery or active coping techniques, that they can recreate a sense of safety in their world. Clients with strong dependency needs and trust issues will need to test out their fears that the therapist will disappoint, betray, or abandon them before they can risk becoming too close. Clients with disturbances in the area of intimacy may need to work through their fears around loss and closeness before the next stage of work can begin. Finally, those who have experienced damage to frame of reference will need to regain hope that they can develop a new way of making sense of experience and will need to begin to develop their own answers to questions of causality. A complete understanding of the individual within this context can generate useful hypotheses about the nature of the transference relationship and treatment resistances.

Gently Challenging Disturbed Schemas

In beginning to challenge disturbed schemas, the therapist must always remember that these schemas developed originally as a way of making sense of painful or incomprehensible situations and may have adaptive value for the individual. Furthermore, these schemas may serve as a protection against some emotion or experience that is viewed as dangerous to the self. The clinician thus must first explore how these schemas are adaptive for that individual. This can be accomplished by asking survivors if they could imagine changing their belief systems. The therapist will often learn that these schemas serve as a valued defense.

Within the area of safety, individuals will often express the fear that letting down their guard by viewing the world or other people as not completely dangerous will make them vulnerable to repeated violation. In the words of one client who had seriously disturbed safety schemas, "If I stop believing the world and other people are dangerous, how could I ever live with myself if I allowed myself to get too careless and the same thing happened again?" Likewise, a client with disturbed schemas in the area of trust/dependency may be protecting himself or herself from being betrayed and violated by others. Similarly, disturbed esteem schemas may protect individuals from the awareness that loved ones are to blame for their suffering, as in the case of a victim of domestic violence who cannot fully assimilate the fact that her "loving" husband cruelly betrayed her. Within the area of independence, individuals may be fearful that they will lose their sense of power if they fail to be in control of their emotions and behaviors at all times. Allowing oneself to be emotional, vulnerable, or dependent may be very frightening because it has been associated with being helpless, out of control, and/or victimized. Within the area of power, clients who believe they cannot control others or the environment, as is true of many battered women, may be reluctant to give up this belief and become "empowered" because it may represent a painful loss of a relationship or the possibility that others will punish them. Within the area of intimacy, clients may persist in the belief that they will feel disconnected from others because to change this belief would open them up to the potential for traumatic losses. Connection, which is associated with intense pain and hurt, may thus be far more threatening than enduring a pervasive sense of alienation and estrangement. Finally, the dangers related to giving up a frame of reference such as "I am to blame for everything bad that happens to me" may be in giving up a sense of control over events in one's life.

Thus, one major early goal of therapy is first to understand and acknowledge the adaptive significance of these disturbed schemas. The therapist will continually explore the following questions: "What would it mean if you were to change this belief?" and "What would be frightening about allowing yourself to believe that you could [trust, feel safe, be intimate, etc.]?" The second major goal of therapy is to challenge these disturbed schemas gently by pointing out the painful effects on the client's emotional and interpersonal life of maintaining these schemas. Finally, the therapist should gradually present discrepancies that gently challenge these belief systems. Overall, the goal is to help the individual gradually to develop more positive schemas in the areas that are most important to him or her. This can be accomplished by exploring what it would take to begin to believe that one can feel safe, trust, feel in control, etc., and how the client might test this out in his or her current relationships or life situation.

Restoring Positive Schemas

Specific interventions focused on restoring or building positive schemas will depend on which areas are targeted. For example, positive safety schemas might be enhanced by imagery work focused on finding a safe place in one's mind, by transforming images of danger in fantasy, through systematic desensitization, and with other anxiety-reducing techniques. Within the area of dependency/trust, positive schemas can primarily be encouraged within the context of the therapeutic relationship as well as through testing out how one might begin to trust other people, in small steps. Clients who need to develop more adaptive independence schemas can be encouraged to learn that vulnerability does not always equate with helplessness. Clients who express disturbed schemas around power often respond to traditional methods to enhance a sense of "empowerment," which Walker (1978), for example, has written about with respect to battered women. Disturbances in the area of esteem are at times the most difficult to overcome, largely because these belief systems are often entrenched in early self-conceptions that result from serious injuries to the self. Teaching clients to value themselves, to spend nurturant time alone, to be aware of and acknowledge their positive attributes, and to talk lovingly to themselves can be helpful in gradually building more positive esteem schemas. Within the area of intimacy, clients can be encouraged to experience a sense of connection with the therapist while working through the fears they have about loss and abandonment. Finally, with respect to frame of reference, clients can begin to develop more constructive ways of understanding their experience by gradually testing out alternative attributions of causality and by separating responsibility for what happened from responsibility for the solution (Shaver & Drown, 1986).

Working through disturbed schemas and finding constructive ways to meet important psychological needs is essential work that continues throughout the therapy process. As this work proceeds, and as the therapist and client believe the client is ready to explore the traumatic memories, memory work can be integrated into self work and the need-schema work.

Social and Cultural Context

Individuals' meaning systems are also shaped by their social and cultural context. In agreement with Murphy (1947), we believe that a full understanding of an individual must consider the delicate balance between the inner structure (the psychological experience of the person) and the outer structure (the ecology in which he or she lives). To quote Murphy, "the life process is not simply a series of events within the person but is a field of events in which inner and outer processes constitute a complex totality" (p. 37).

Assessing Social and Cultural Context

The personal meanings of the client's social and cultural background, including social class, age, gender, and race, must be explored as part of the therapy process because this is the context within which the individual experiences his or her phenomenological world. Here, we suggest some of the areas that should be explored and understood as they shape a person's experience of trauma. One's social and cultural background shapes one's needs and schemas about the self, others, and the world. For example, the meanings of dependency/trust may be very different for a black person who has experienced hatred and racism in the world than for a white person who has been insulated from such harmful experiences. Likewise, safety will have very different meanings depending on whether a person is living in a crime-infested city or a middle-class suburb. Furthermore, social class, particularly poverty and deprivation, can have profound negative effects on a person's self-concept and sense of efficacy or power in the world (Albee, 1982). Finally, the person's family and peer relationships, as well as community supports, will have a large impact on whether disturbed schemas are confirmed or gradually disconfirmed through positive experiences. For example, the social support literature would suggest that the victim of domestic violence who develops trustworthy, supportive social networks may be less likely to persist in generalized disturbed schemas than a victim who is socially isolated.

Finally, gender differences in reactions to trauma are an important area for exploration. In this regard, it is important to be sensitive to the meanings of gender to the person, the relationship between sexism and sexual victimization (Russell, 1986), and the different patterns of emotional expressiveness and power relationships in men and women (O'Neil, 1981). Unfortunately, many victims find their disturbed schemas confirmed and their central needs thwarted through the unsupportive or unhelpful reactions of others, even among family or friends who mean well. Symonds (1975) originally spoke of these posttrauma experiences as the "second injury," an area that has received much attention in the victimization literature.

ASSESSING TRAUMATIC MEMORIES

Memories of a traumatic experience are often fragmented. Individuals often experience only pieces of whole memories, such as fragments of images, tactile sensations without images, a flash of feeling without context, phrases that seem out of context, etc. Experiencing recurring, unbidden fragments of memories can be very unsettling, in part because there is often no way of making sense of the experience. For example, a domestic abuse victim may find herself feeling anxious upon smelling a certain odor or seeing a certain television show but be unable to connect her anxiety with anything meaningful. These experiences are often associated with strong, disturbing emotion such as sadness, terror, or rage. Memory fragments may become intrusive or disruptive to the individual's psychological or interpersonal functioning. Those fragments may be stimulated by external stimuli, such as a smell, a sound, or an interaction with someone, or internal stimuli, such as physiological arousal or other emotional states. Below, we describe ways to assess such disturbances.

Assessing the Memory Systems

Disruptions in the Verbal System of Memory

There are many thoughts associated with traumatic events, thoughts that are integral to understanding the whole memory. Statements that the perpetrator made to the victim may become incorporated into the victim's memory of the event as well as his or her schemas. Victims of domestic violence may have internalized denigrating messages given by their abusers. Because of the dynamics of such situations, the abuser is often intimately aware of the victim's vulnerabilities and may play upon them in ways that reinforce low self-esteem.

As clients describe their traumatic memories, in fragments or as whole memories, the therapist must probe into the cognitive process before, during, and after the victimization. Such questions as "What did you think was happening?" "Tell me everything that was going through your mind at that moment," and "What exactly did he say to you?" are examples of probes into the verbal component of memory. The therapeutic challenge is to discover the client's memories of what was said to her and the meanings those statements have for her and then, gradually and gently, to work with the client to explore those meanings in the context of her other life experiences, to develop self capacities, resources, and schemas that will move the client toward greater self-acceptance and stronger self-esteem.

Disruptions in the Imagery System of Memory

Horowitz (1986), drawing on the earlier work of Freud (1926), originally described posttrauma reactions as biphasic. The initial response to trauma is often psychic numbing (Lifton, 1968) or denial. Following this are intrusive symptoms, including unbidden images and emotions. Most recently, it has been suggested that there may be two types of posttrauma reactions, a denial-based disorder and an intrusion-based disorder (Laufer et al., 1985). This view has been incorporated into the revised criteria for PTSD (DSM-III-R; American Psychiatric Association 1987). Individuals experiencing the intrusion-based form of PTSD will be more likely to experience distressing sensory (usually visual imagery) memory fragments.

We believe, as do others (Brett & Ostroff, 1985), that disturbances in imagery are central to the posttraumatic experience, although this is a surprisingly neglected area of research (Singer & Pope, 1978). These disturbances in imagery may take the form of flashbacks, nightmares, or intrusive thoughts (Horowitz, 1986) and are often associated with waves of powerful, upsetting emotions. The images are usually visual, vivid, recurring, and unbidden (Horowitz, 1979). The unbidden images may take a symbolic form, as in the case of a domestic abuse survivor who had haunting dreams and images about being attacked by a man with a hawk's face. Only when she was able to uncover the whole memories, previously repressed, was she able to transform this symbol into the image of her ex-husband's face.

The content of these images appears to be connected to the external characteristics of the traumatic event (see Green et al., 1985). Common themes we observe in traumatic imagery are violation, betrayal, humiliation and degradation, abandonment, death and injury, helplessness and paralysis, loss, and a moment of confrontation with death, a realization that the individual must kill or be killed (literally or figuratively) (see Table 18.1).

The first part of the imagery assessment is to discover whether the client experiences visual images and, if so, when they emerge, how they are handled, and the feelings associated with each component of the image. Early in treatment, clients will often admit to being disturbed by recurrent images but may be reluctant to talk about them. As with the other areas, this resistance should be explored thoroughly and understood, and a therapeutic alliance should be well established before the therapist probes into visual memory fragments.

This is particularly important because the imagery component of memory is a gate to very powerful, sometimes frightening, emotions (Paivio, 1986; Singer & Pope, 1978). Again, the timing of such interventions is largely dependent on the therapist's understanding of the client's self resources and capacities; these must be adequately developed to allow the client to manage the strong feelings that may emerge before the imagery can be explored constructively.

Most often, victims present for treatment with disturbances in emotions, such as depression, sadness, anxiety, guilt, or rage. These feelings may appear to be disconnected to any immediate stimuli, and the connections to traumatic memories may be out of conscious awareness. For example, a survivor who has repressed the traumatic memories of seeing her mother raped by her father in childhood may find herself feeling repulsed while having sex with her partner, an emotion she experiences as inexplicable within that context. On a more conscious level, a battered woman may experience herself feeling a rush of terror or rage with apparently little stimulus. Psychophysiological overreactivity may also be a component of traumatic memories, often provoked by previously neutral stimuli (Kolb, 1984).

Within the ongoing assessment process, the therapist must help the client explore the links among certain feeling states, antecedent cognitions or images, and specific memories. This task is often more difficult than it appears, because some clients will resist making painful connections back to memories. Such indirect methods as asking the client to link these feelings back to other times in his or her life can be productive, as is exploring what is frightening about making these connections. The resistances to exploring feelings may be tied back to self capacities. A client with diminished self capacities may resist this work because it can potentially disrupt an already tenuous sense of self. Such resistances must be respected; if they cannot be understood and worked through, it is very likely that self-building work must be done.

Memory Work

Once the necessary internal strength is built, attention can be turned to the person's internalization of the traumatic memories. In this phase of work, which may be months or even years after therapy begins, the focus is on pulling together the fragmented pieces of memory into whole memories. By this, we mean that the images, thoughts, and feelings can be put together into a meaningful whole, giving new meaning and understanding to what was previously disavowed or unintegrated. The decision to proceed with the memory work can be made by gently testing the client's capacity to approach painful memories and feelings. The client who decompensates, acts out, or experiences disintegrative anxiety upon recollecting memories will need a longer period of self-building or stabilization before memory work can proceed. This process of stabilization has been described in a number of treatment approaches to PTSD (e.g., Brown & Fromm, 1986; Horowitz, 1986).

Individuals' recollections of a traumatic experience range along a continuum from complete recall to complete amnesia. Clinically, one most often sees clients whose memories are fragments. That is, one or more of the pieces is partially or entirely repressed. In our clinical work, we attempt to help victims piece together the distressing images, feelings, and thoughts that, taken together, constitute whole memories. The bothersome fragments must be elaborated out, connected to one another, and then processed as whole memories. This is accomplished by suggesting that clients return to the situation in their imagination, first by asking them about the images they are experiencing, and then—usually through hypnosis or guided imagery—suggesting they return to the experience, with the resources of the therapist and the client's adult self, to reexperience the traumatic memory, but this time feeling what they were not allowed to feel and talking about it as they weren't allowed to do at the time. As part of this process, the client is given the soothing that was missing originally, offered by the therapist and, eventually, by the adult client herself or himself.

Once the fragments are recovered, connected, and worked through, the memories can eventually be laid to rest. The working through is a process of trying to understand what happened and why it happened, reexperiencing the full range of emotions associated with the incident and the accompanying losses, putting the traumatic events and sequelae into the context of the individual's current life, and finally, building a set of positive schemas about the self and others that will enable the person to function better in the future.

SUMMARY AND CONCLUSIONS

The theorized relation among these three dimensions (self resources and capacities, needs and schemas, and traumatic memory) of a person is complex and multifaceted. Their clinical importance is that the therapist must understand the victim of family violence as a whole person in a particular social context in order to help him or her resolve the traumatic memories and maladaptive responses to trauma.

We start with the person's experience of himself or herself within his or her meaningful environment, with particular focus on the self and psychological needs. We presume that a person's self capacities and resources determine, in large part, his or her ability to tolerate painful affects, to soothe and calm himself or herself, and to regulate self-esteem. These capacities may be taxed by the original trauma and yet again when persons reexperience the traumatic memories through fragments of images, thoughts, and feelings. The whole memories cannot be pieced together or integrated into the existing self-structure unless these capacities and resources have been sufficiently strengthened through the internalization of an empathetic, responsive therapist who is respectful of a person's inner resources and vulnerabilities. The traumatic memories must then be understood by fully assessing all components—verbal statements, imagery, and related affect—of these memories. These components of the memories must also be fully linked both to the traumatic experience and to each other. We believe that certain memories of the trauma are linked to characteristic feelings and thoughts. Likewise, self–world relations as reflected by cognitive schemas must be assessed as they are disrupted by trauma and shape the unique way trauma is experienced by the individual. All of this occurs within a broader social and cultural context that has specific meanings for the individual. This complex set of interactions or dynamics within the person, in turn, affects his or her subsequent interactions with others and future life experiences.

REFERENCES

Albee, G. W. (1982). Preventing psychopathology and promoting human potential. *American Psychologist, 37,* 1043–1050.

American Psychiatric Association. (1987). *Diagnostic and statistical manual of mental disorders,* 3rd ed. (revised). Washington, DC: American Psychiatric Association.

Anderson, J. R., & Bower, G. H. (1980). *Human associative memory: A brief edition.* Hillsdale, NJ: Lawrence Erlbaum Associates.

Baker, H. S., & Baker, M. N. (1987). Heinz Kohut's self psychology: An overview. *American Journal of Psychiatry, 144,* 1–9.

Bellak, L., Hurvich, M., & Gediman, H. K. (1973). *Ego functions in schizophrenics, neurotics, and normals.* New York: John Wiley & Sons.

Bower, G. H. (1981). Mood and memory. *American Psychologist, 36,* 129–148.

Bowlby, J. (1969). *Attachment and loss: Vol. 1. Attachment.* London: Hogarth.

Brende, J. O. (1983). A psychodynamic view of character pathology in Vietnam combat veterans. *Bulletin of the Menninger Clinic, 47,* 193–216.

Brett, E. A., & Ostroff, R. (1985). Imagery and posttraumatic stress disorder: An overview. *American Journal of Psychiatry, 142,* 417–424.

Brown, D. P., & Fromm, E. (1986). *Hypnotherapy and hypnoanalysis.* Hillsdale, NJ: Lawrence Erlbaum Associates.

Courtois, C. A. (1988). *Healing the incest wound.* New York: Norton.

Eich, J. E. (1980). The cue dependent nature of state dependent retrieval. *Memory and Cognition, 8,* 157–168.

Epstein, S. (1985). The implications of cognitive-experiential self-theory for research in social psychology and personality. *Journal for the Theory of Social Behavior, 15,* 283–310.

Figley, C. R. (1983). Catastrophes: An overview of family reaction. In C. R. Figley & H. I. McCubbin (Eds.), *Stress and the family: Coping with catastrophe* (Vol. 2, pp. 3–20). New York: Brunner/Mazel.

Finkelhor, D., Gelles, R. J., Hotaling, G. T., & Straus, M. A. (1983). *The dark side of families: Current family violence research.* Beverly Hills, CA: Sage Publications.

Freud, S. (1926). Inhibitions, symptoms, and anxiety. In J. Strachey (Ed.), *The standard edition of the complete psychological works of Freud.* London: Hogarth Press.

Fromm, E. (1955). *The sane society.* New York: Rinehart.

Gelles, R. J., & Cornell, C. P. (1985). *Intimate violence in families.* Beverly Hills, CA: Sage.

Gordon, L. V. (1976). *Survey of interpersonal values examiner's manual,* 2d ed. Chicago: Science Research Associates.

Green, B. L., Wilson, J. P., & Lindy, J. D. (1985). Conceptualizing posttraumatic stress disorder: A psychosocial framework. In C. R. Figley (Ed.), *Trauma and its wake: The study and treatment of post-traumatic stress disorder* (pp. 53–69). New York: Brunner/Mazel.

Greenberg, M. S., & van der Kolk, B. A. (1987). Retrieval and integration of traumatic memories with the "painting cure." In B. A. van der Kolk (Ed.), *Psychological trauma* (pp. 191–215). Washington, DC: American Psychiatric Press.

Hochreich, D. J., & Rotter, J. B. (1970). Have college students become less trusting? *Journal of Personality and Social Psychology, 15,* 211–214.

Horner, A. (1986). *Being and loving.* Northvale, NJ: Jason Aronson.

Horowitz, M. J. (1979). Psychological response to serious life events. In V. Hamilton & D. M. Warburton (Eds.), *Human stress and cognitions.* New York: Wiley.

Horowitz, M. J. (1986). *Stress response syndromes.* New York: Jason Aronson.

Janoff-Bulman, R. (1985). The aftermath of victimization: Rebuilding shattered assumptions. In C. R. Figley (Ed.), *Trauma and its wake: The*

328

study and treatment of post-traumatic stress disorder (pp. 15–35). New York: Brunner/Mazel.

Jordan, J. (1984). *Empathy and self boundaries.* Unpublished manuscript, Stone Center for Developmental Services and Studies, Wellesley, MA.

Jung, C. G. (1969). *The collected works of C. G. Jung: The structure and dynamics of the psyche,* 2d ed., Vol. 8 (R. F. C. Hull, Trans.). Princeton, NJ: Princeton University Press.

Kelly, G. A. (1955). *The psychology of personal constructs* (2 vols.). New York: Norton.

Kohut, H. (1977). *The restoration of the self.* New York: International Universities Press.

Kolb, L. C. (1984). The post-traumatic stress disorders of combat: A subgroup with a conditioned emotional response. *Military Medicine, 149,* 237–243.

Laufer, R. S., Brett, E., & Gallops, M. S. (1985). Symptom patterns associated with posttraumatic stress disorder among Vietnam veterans exposed to war trauma. *American Journal of Psychiatry, 142,* 1304–1311.

Lifton, R. J. (1968). *Death in life: Survivors of Hiroshima.* New York: Random House.

Mahoney, M. J. (1981). Psychotherapy and human change processes. In J. H. Harvey & M. M. Parks (Eds.), *Psychotherapy research and behavior change* (pp. 73–122). Master Lecture Series. Washington, DC: American Psychological Association.

Mahoney, M. J., & Lyddon, W. J. (1988). Recent developments in cognitive approaches to counseling and psychotherapy. *The Counseling Psychologist, 16* (2), 190–234.

McCann, L., & Pearlman, L. A. (1990). Vicarious traumatization: A framework for understanding the psychological effects of working with victims. *Journal of Traumatic Stress, 3*(1), 131–149.

McCann, L., & Pearlman, L. A. (in press). *Through a glass darkly: Transforming the inner experience of trauma.* New York: Brunner/Mazel.

McCann, L., Pearlman, L. A., Sakheim, D. K., & Abrahamson, D. J. (1988). Assessment and treatment of the adult survivor of childhood sexual abuse within a schema framework. In S. M. Sgroi (Ed.), *Vulnerable populations: Evaluation and treatment of sexually abused children and adult survivors* (Vol. 1, pp. 77–101). Lexington, MA: Lexington Books.

McCann, I. L., Sakheim, D. K., & Abrahamson, D. J. (1988). Trauma and victimization: A model of psychological adaptation. *The Counseling Psychologist, 16,* 531–594.

Murphy, G. (1947). *Personality: A biosocial approach to origins and structure.* New York: Harper and Brothers.

Murray, H. A., & Kluckhohn, C. (1959). Outline of a conception of personality. In C. Kluckhohn & H. A. Murray (Eds.), *Personality in nature, society, and culture,* 2d ed. (revised) (pp. 3–49). New York: Alfred A. Knopf.

O'Neil, J. (1981). Male sex-role conflicts, sexism, and masculinity: Implications for men, women, and the counseling psychologists. *The Counseling Psychologist, 9,* 61–80.

Paivio, A. (1986). *Mental representations: A dual coding approach*. New York: Oxford University Press.

Parson, E. R. (1984). The reparation of the self: Clinical and theoretical dimensions in the treatment of Vietnam combat veterans. *Journal of Contemporary Psychotherapy, 14*, 4–56.

Piaget, J. (1971). *Psychology and epistemology: Toward a theory of knowledge*. New York: Viking.

Rogers, C. R. (1951). *Client-centered therapy*. New York: Houghton Mifflin Co.

Roth, S., & Lebowitz, L. (1988). The experience of sexual trauma. *Journal of Traumatic Stress, 1*, 79–107.

Rotter, J. B. (1954). *Social learning and clinical psychology*. Englewood Cliffs, NJ: Prentice-Hall.

Russell, D. E. (1986). *Sexual exploitation: Vol. 155. Sage library of social research*. Beverly Hills, CA: Sage.

Scurfield, R. M. (1985). Post-trauma stress assessment and treatment: Overview and formulations. In C. R. Figley (Ed.), *Trauma and its wake: The study and treatment of post-traumatic stress disorder* (pp. 219–256). New York: Brunner/Mazel.

Seligman, M. E. P. (1975). *Helplessness: On depression, development, and death*. San Francisco: Freeman.

Shaver, K. G., & Drown, D. (1986). On causality, responsibility, and self-blame: A theoretical note. *Journal of Personality and Social Psychology, 50*(4), 697–702.

Singer, J. L., & Pope, K. S. (1978). *The power of human imagination: New methods in psychotherapy*. New York: Plenum Press.

Symonds, M. (1975). The "second injury" to victims. In L. Kivens (Ed.), *Evaluation and change services for survivors* (pp. 36–38). Minneapolis, MN: Minneapolis Medical Research Foundation.

Ulman, R. B., & Brothers, D. (1988). *The shattered self: A psychoanalytic study of trauma*. Hillsdale, NJ: The Analytic Press.

Walker, L. E. V. (1978). Battered women and learned helplessness. *Victimology*, 525–534.

White, M. T., & Weiner, M. B. (1986). *The theory and practice of self-psychology*. New York: Brunner/Mazel.

Wilson, J. P. (1980). Stress and growth: Effects of war on psychosocial development. In C. R. Figley & S. Leventman (Eds.), *Strangers at home: The Vietnam veteran since the war* (pp. 123–165). New York: Praeger.

Winnicott, D. W. (1958). The capacity to be alone. *International Journal of Psychiatry, 39*, 416–440.

Young-Eisendrath, P., & Wiedemann, F. L. (1987). *Female authority: Empowering women through psychotherapy*. New York: The Guilford Press.

The Treatment of the Traumatic Impact of Family Violence: An Integration of Theoretical Perspectives

19

Mary Beth Williams

The authors of this volume have demonstrated, through the utilization of a multiplicity of theoretical orientations, that the treatment of family violence must include trauma-specific techniques. In other words, victims of violence are victims of trauma and therefore need treatment oriented to the specifics of trauma integration. These techniques normalize victim responses to the violence and recognize that responses that were adaptive during the abuse frequently become maladaptive later in life. It is now recognized that the rape trauma syndrome, the battered woman syndrome, the sexual abuse syndrome, among others, are variants of posttraumatic stress syndromes (Caringella-MacDonald, 1988, p. 184). The recognition that family violence is a traumatic stressor that can cause long-term, multifaceted reactions has helped to decrease the use of more stigmatizing, pathological, victim-blaming diagnoses (e.g., borderline personality disorder) and associated inappropriate treatment methods.

Reactions of victims of family violence range from acceptance, to short-term acute disequilibrating reactions, to long-term traumatic stress reactions. The extent of long-term damage is often not immediately recognizable. In many cases, persons who experience an external violent stressor event develop an internal state of psychic traumatization and may attempt to split off, forget, or unconsciously repress their memories of that event or events. Yet later in life, perhaps even after an indefinite period of time, these memories press for expression from their active memory storage center (Lindy, 1986). These memories, according to Figley (1986), are frequently accompanied by questions similar to those that occur at the time(s) of the event(s):

What really happened to me?
Why me? Why was I spared? Why was I included?
How did this happen?
Why in my family?
Why did I stay? Why did I come back, participate, act as I did?
What could I have done to stop the event?
Was I to blame?

Persons also look cognitively at what occurred before, during, and after the event as they attempt to discover the verbal and emotional components of their memories (McCann et al., 1988). Initial research has demonstrated that violence that occurs over a long duration at repeated intervals; involves intrusive acts with force (e.g., more intrusive forms of sexual abuse); is committed by a spouse, parent, or parent figure to whom the victim looks for support and caring; and has elements of sadistic or ritualistic, which abuse increase the likelihood of long-term damage (Briere, 1989).

It is also now recognized that some form of dissociation frequently is a response to the traumatic stressor as a means to forget memories and their associated emotions. This protective, adaptive mechanism ensures that the memories are forgotten, repressed, or disconnected and exist only as pieces, fragments, images, sensations, or flashes. When these pieces start to reappear, perhaps as feeling states (e.g., anxiety) or intrusions (flashbacks, nightmares, behavioral reenactments), the self attempts to defend against them and tries to re-repress the information, feelings, and fragments (Briere, 1989). This process of intrusion and attempts at avoidance/denial is the underlying symptomatic picture of the DSM-III-R diagnosis of posttraumatic stress disorder PTSD (1988, p. 300.89). Symptoms of intrusion and/or avoidance and denial are accompanied by symptoms of hyperarousal, irritability, and hypervigilance. The imagery disturbances that appear are therefore frequently associated with powerful emotions that lead to the physiological hypervigilant reactions.

In Chapter 1, an interactive model of domestic violence was presented. Throughout the book, the authors offer a variety of approaches for intervening in domestic violence to decrease vulnerabilities and stressors or increase resources. The authors of the chapters in this text do not represent a unified perspective. However, they do advocate the use of certain treatment techniques that extend across victim and perpetrator populations and that are also part of posttrauma treatment. Fourteen principles that apply to working with clients who have experienced traumatic family violence will be described and illustrated in this chapter. They include elimination of event evasion (elimination of denial and minimization), emergency responses, extrication from the cycle of violence, empowerment, establishment of trust and rapport, experiential integration, emotional release and experience objectification, enhancement of self and self-esteem, and creative experimentation with a variety of treatment options. Additionally, therapists must be willing to explore their own beliefs and countertransferences and have at least a beginning level of expertise in trauma-oriented techniques before they begin to work with victims and perpetrators of family violence. If this knowledge is lacking, or if they recognize the existence of personal knowledge gaps, they must be willing to educate themselves, on a regular basis, through participation in inservice training programs and appropriate conferences and seminars. This training will help them learn how to establish limits for themselves and their clients while demonstrating empathy so that they can educate those clients about the trauma process and its phenomenology. Each of these fourteen principles will be discussed from the perspective of the various authors in this text. The chapter will conclude with a summary of the most pressing future needs in the family violence treatment and research field.

TREATMENT PRINCIPLES

Elimination of Event Evasion (Elimination of Denial and Minimization)

The core defense utilized by clients who have experienced or perpetrated family violence is denial, which involves repression or dissociation of the memories of their experiences, the experiences themselves, or the associated affects. Acceptance of the reality of the victimization and/or perpetration includes recovering split-off memories and associated affects. This recovery must occur if the traumas can be put in the past. Eleven of the authors in this text discuss, in some manner, the need to eliminate the denial and thereby encourage clients to externalize and recount their experiences.

Little writes that the goal of Gestalt therapy is the acceptance of the reality of the situation without denying the seriousness of the abuse. Acceptance involves becoming aware of and then letting go of rationalized and previously denied parts of life. Gestalt theory terms this process dealing with unfinished business. Hutchins recognizes that abusers must also accept the realities of their actions, deal with their beliefs toward women, and recognize their denial of the abuse as seriously violent.

Stith and Rosen report that families who come to treatment are often unwilling to reveal the existence of family violence, minimizing its contribution to family difficulties. They describe the male belief that wife beating is an acceptable, justified act to maintain a position of power in the family. Jurich similarly describes the typical response to an abusive incident as avoidance, concealment, and minimization. Families of abused adolescents tend to isolate themselves, as do the teens themselves, to avoid detection. Adolescents turn to alcohol or drugs to numb their pain or may be truant or runaway. Most adolescent physical abuse cases, therefore, come to treatment labeled as delinquent or CHINS (child in need of services). Staton discusses the use of multiple media techniques to help clients/patients objectify the events and externalize their abusive encounters.

The focus of Jones's chapter is the involuntary client who does not want help and is not willing to ask for help. Perpetrators of child abuse frequently deny the existence of problems and may resist mandated treatment. The basic social work principle of "starting where the client is" does not work with clients who see help as being forced on them by an external society that has removed their locus of control. These clients are frequently skilled at game playing and try to hook therapists through their use of discounting of the problem, discounting of the significance of the problem, and refusal to consider options or solutions. Getting these clients to accept the reality of the negative impact of their actions and to own their own problems therefore is a major treatment goal.

McCarthy, Fulmer, Lawrence, and Gil, discussing therapeutic interventions with adults who were sexually molested as children, discuss the role of minimization, denial, and dissociation of the traumatic sexual abuse. McCarthy notes that adult survivors generally seek help for other mental health problems and reveal their abuse during the course of therapy, if at all, as a "shameful secret." Confronting the minimization and rationalization of the abuse with the perpetrator is a necessary part of therapy. Lawrence, as she describes her own sexual and physical victimization between the ages of 3 and 16, notes how she buried the pain under her defenses, defenses developed to survive the associated emotional effects of that abuse. Yet she "cried out" through her behaviors of self-destruction, self-mutilation, anorexia, and bodily dysfunction.

The major message of Fulmer's chapter is that spontaneous disclosure of sexual abuse is rare, even after a long course of treatment.

Therefore, a professional must be willing to ask clients/patients about abuse and recognize that denial is more often the norm than the exception. Survivors, she notes, frequently present themselves in a disguised fashion. If this disguise remains the focus of treatment, the therapy will go nowhere. Survivors hide because they have been mandated by perpetrators not to tell, they feel shame, or they may have full or partial amnesia. Fulmer elaborates upon the symptoms, backgrounds, and possible behavioral patterns that may indicate sexual abuse. She describes possible pathological presentations, including borderline personality and anxiety disorders; eating disorders; major depressive episodes; depressive, schizoid, and paranoid life positions; and life-sabotaging cognitions and behaviors.

Gil similarly discusses the role of dissociation in trauma as a disturbance of the normally integrative self functions of identity, memory, and consciousness. Dissociation therefore is a defense mechanism used by victims to survive their abuse and can become a maladaptive habit utilized in a potentially threatening situation later in life.

McCann notes that victims frequently present for treatment with disturbances in emotion (depression, anxiety) that are disconnected from both traumatic memories and the immediate situational stimuli. Exploration of links between feeling states, cognitions, images, and memory fragments are often necessary to link those feelings with past events. The process of internalizing memory fragments into whole memories may take months or years. This process occurs only after the client has a more stabilized sense of self to combat decompensation, acting out, and disintegrative anxiety. Reexperiencing in a safe setting with the resources of a therapist and the client's adult self helps combat the denial and event evasion.

Emergency Responses

When clients/patients begin to experience memory recall or when abuse becomes so traumatic that it can no longer be denied and must be escaped, therapists must frequently utilize emergency-based crisis intervention techniques. A knowledge of these principles and techniques is essential for therapists who work with victims of family violence. Roberts describes crisis intervention principles and notes that all intervenors in the family violence field (law enforcement officers, medical personnel, hot line volunteers, shelter staff, on-line workers) must have a knowledge of these techniques and the accompanying theory base. As Hendricks (1985) notes, crisis counseling must ensure client safety and provide support while examining alternatives and making plans for action.

Extrication from the Cycle of Violence

A third treatment principle/technique is extrication from the cycle of violence. Family violence appears to be intergenerational. Hutchins and Vogler and Stith and Rosen discuss the relationship between growing up in abusive homes or witnessing marital violence and being a member of an abusive family as an adult. Some individuals may learn from their childhood experience that violence is an acceptable way to deal with anger and frustration and cope with stress. Other individuals may repeat the cycle of violence by marrying someone who abuses their children. Lawrence describes her own fears of the intergenerational transmission of violence and her inability, at present, to trust her capacity to be a good parent. It seems clear that the first task in extricating the next generation from repeating the violence is to end the violence in the current generation. Jones notes that gaining commitment to end violence is easier with a voluntary client, a client who is aware that he or she has a problem but is unable to ask for help or is not knowledgeable about available services. Thus, a major task for therapists is to help clients get to a place where they recognize that violence is occurring in their lives and that they are ready to end the violence.

Empowerment of Clients

Client empowerment is the most important end-goal of trauma-oriented treatment. The trauma-aware therapist realizes that clients must be empowered to share responsibility for decision-making in the process of therapy. These clients frequently attempt to maintain rigid control of situations to compensate for their extreme feelings of helplessness. Empowering them to be more in charge of their recoveries through realistic goal-setting helps combat this rigidity (Chu, 1988).

Little, quoting Walker, focuses on reempowerment as a major focus of feminist therapy, therapy that conceptualizes violence against women as a problem of male misuse of power. Clinicians must therefore refuse to accept control of their clients' lives, encouraging them to give up the victim role while accepting responsibility for themselves. Therapists' choice of language in therapy must emphasize client power and help increase self-awareness, self-empowerment, and self-protection.

Hutchins notes that male batterers also characteristically feel powerless and need empowerment if they are to change their abusive behaviors. Stith and Rosen write that the structure of treatment is, in part, determined by the clients' wishes; for example, if a couple chooses to remain together, eventual work with that couple is necessary. Jurich involves parents and adolescents as almost equal partners in planning interventions and designing the family plan of action in therapy. Adolescent input into rules, punishments, and possible exceptions is a necessary aspect of this process.

Jones begins work with involuntary clients by honest contracting, noting the need to avoid games (including the client game of passivity) while stating the limits and extent of the therapist's professional authority. Kramer-Dover empowers child clients for court appearances by rehearsing and familiarizing them with settings and processes. Gil discusses blocking learned helplessness through developing options, exploring choices, mobilizing resources, breaking isolations, and fighting feelings of shame through mutual goal setting. Staton uses nonverbal communication techniques with both children and adults to remove power from the abusive experience itself. Symbolic creating through visual or physical representation of the events helps the person to transform the experience and takes away power from the event. Quinn similarly notes that elders with sound minds have the right to freedom and refusal of treatment. Service providers do not have the right to impose treatment on unwilling persons because freedom is more important than safety.

Establishment of Trust and Rapport

The establishment of trust and rapport in the therapeutic relationship may take years to build to a reasonable level. Traumatized clients frequently expect betrayal and repeatedly test therapists to reinforce their expectations (Chu, 1988). Hutchins and Vogler note that victims of family violence, usually female, are made helpless by their battering partners. The constant betrayal leads to feelings of worthlessness, which inhibit intimacy. Batterers as a population also seem to distrust others and seek closeness only from their victimized partners, closeness that becomes expressed as possessiveness. Stith and Rosen acknowledge that family violence often is not revealed in therapy until one or both of the couple develops trust in the therapeutic relationship.

Establishing rapport is difficult when working with possible abuse, according to Jurich, particularly when reporting of abuse is the legal obligation of the practitioner if abuse is revealed. Jones recognizes that unmotivated clients have generally had damaging prior experiences in relationships and must have empathy, caring, and concern demonstrated over and over before they accept and trust the practitioner.

Staton establishes rapport in the therapeutic setting by using a child's preferred modes of communication to create a common symbolic language—a language in which victims are proficient and comfortable. Kramer-Dover similarly consults with the child victim, keeping the child informed about what is happening without abusing adult power. These children are frequently wary of adults, and initial encounters, which Kramer-Dover describes in detail, affect therapeutic success. The therapist must convey belief and understanding to encourage trust while refraining from touching. Part of this process is to explain methods and procedures, including note taking, to the client.

Gil writes that most adult child sexual abuse survivors have a struggle with trust issues. Lawrence illustrates this struggle by describing her use of self-protective behaviors to prevent others from entering and violating her world and from further exploiting her. She rarely allows touch and finds physical affection to be frightening. A major focus of her therapy has been to teach the small child within (Punky) to trust. In Froning's discussion of Lawrence's recovery, as her present therapist, she describes her own need to make sure that Lawrence's trust is not lost, violated, or disrupted. If a therapist does violate trust, then future therapists (should there even be future therapists) will have even harder struggles to establish rapport. A constant adjustment of therapeutic pace is therefore necessary. If the abuse occurred early in life, the adult has never learned to trust his or her own instincts and/or perceptions and is likely to expect rejection and/or abandonment from the therapist. Froning writes, therefore, that the establishment of trust is central in the search for intimacy. Fulmer similarly notes that trust is the main and constant issue of therapy with adult survivors. Additionally, the hardest part of treatment is to convey to survivors that there is safety both during sessions with the therapist and in life itself.

Experiential Integration

Experiential integration is necessary if the client is to avoid revictimization. Reenactment of the abuse can occur only after safety and trust are established, according to Staton. Reenactment of the event helps to build a new reality and allows the client, as Gil notes, to "go back" and explore the trauma so that he or she can understand it, feel it, and say good-bye to it through abreaction, implosion, and integration of memories, bodily sensations, and affect.

Emotional Release and Experience Objectification

Emotional release and experience objectification are necessary components of the therapeutic process. Victims of family violence, as Roberts writes, have repeatedly been subjected to situations that have emotional components of fear and anguish. Hutchins also describes the emotional scars carried by batterers, scars that are ventilated through anger. Thus, after a nonviolence contract has been established, it is necessary to teach abusers and victims appropriate anger expression and anger management skills, including structured time out. Stith and Rosen describe the use of these techniques to reconnect clients with their own anger-controlling resources.

Staton uses nonverbal communication channels to reintegrate the abuse (i.e., hidden and subjective memories that have been objectified and/or dissociated) and the accompanying feelings. She writes that experiencing and talking about an event is not enough. Events must be replayed with transitional objects until associated meanings and feelings are mastered and denial, self blame, and forgetting are eliminated. Lawrence, in her first-person account, describes her 10-year posttrial odyssey of emotional denial and numbness, guilt, and shame. She has learned to give expression to her little girl within, to grieve and to cry as a healthy expression of her internal pain. Thus, she has "peeled back her layers of defenses" to expose the pain and let go of the anger. Froning also notes that therapy can eventually become a safe place to express anger, and Gil writes that, in therapy, clients must be enabled to express their entire range of emotions, which they have previously avoided out of fear of the associated reexperiencing of the original pain. However, she continues, clients need to be taught pain tolerance during this necessary segment of the therapeutic healing process.

Enhancement of Self and Self-Esteem

Enhancement of self-esteem and development of more self-enhancing beliefs and expectations (schemata) is another goal of therapy with victims and perpetrators of family violence. Stith notes that perpe-

trators often have limited/constrained belief systems that foster violence, and Hutchins and Vogler similarly describe the perpetrators'
chauvinistic thoughts and attitudes. During therapy, victims of family violence learn new beliefs and ways to view themselves that
enhance personal self-esteem. Staton describes the "damaged goods
syndrome" that child sexual abuse victims maintain, seeing themselves as defective with missing parts. She utilizes drawing or clay
to help them represent their alleged "defects" in relation to others.

Froning notes that many sexual abuse survivors view their
bodies as their only contributions to the world. In a search for self-
worth, they offer those bodies again and again in attempts to be
appreciated while, in reality, they are being used and revictimized.
Gil similarly notes that most adult survivors struggle with a negative
or undefined self-image. The broadening of that image and enhancement of self-esteem are major treatment goals, she notes, for the
adult survivor. McCann and Pearlman describe a variety of psychological techniques to help clients develop or restore impaired self-
esteem and self capacities. She notes that this self-building of
previously disturbed schemas is difficult because the schemas are
entrenched in early damaged self-conceptualizations resulting from
serious injuries to the self. These techniques challenge the disturbed
schemas that have evolved to make sense of the traumatic situation
and that may have originally been adaptive in areas of safety, trust/
dependency, independence, power, and esteem. As Stith writes, violence modifies belief systems of victims about themselves, their
relationships with others, and their locus of control over themselves,
events, and others. The modification of stereotypical gender-role beliefs of batterers is part of that process, often through the use of a
cognitive behavioral treatment model and approach, as McCarthy
suggests.

Experimentation with Techniques

Flexible and creative experimentation with varying techniques and
methods of treatment is necessary in work with family violence
victims and perpetrators (Turkus, 1989). The premise of the Hutchins and Vogler chapter is that treatment of the batterer must be
tailored to the man in his individual situation, taking into account
his thoughts, feelings, and actions as well as environment. This
treatment cannot be abstract and general. It must place responsibility
both on the abuser and society as a contributant to the abuse allowing for multiple entry points into the abusive situation. Nevin and

Roberts similarly state that a range of treatment options is essential for effective case management, services that, according to Rogan, can be effectively coordinated through the use of multidisciplinary child abuse teams. These teams make recommendations for evaluations, set conditions for family reunification, and create time lines for supervisory reviews.

As the chapters have indicated, treatment options include individual, family/couple, and group techniques that can be utilized at various stages of the treatment process. The use of groups, especially self-help peer groups such as Incest Survivors Anonymous, Sex Addicts Anonymous, and others, provides an alternative support system to traditional therapy, writes Froning. Battered women's shelters have traditionally used crisis intervention group models for both women victims and their children as forums for expression of feelings and beliefs about family violence, according to Roberts.

Treatment cannot be limited to individual, family, and group treatment alone. Services must also be resource mobilizing and include appropriate court, social service, housing, medical, substance abuse, and vocational referrals. Knowledge of community resources is imperative if a therapist is to work effectively with violence victims and perpetrators. As Kramer-Dover notes, the therapist does not just do therapy with child victims. He or she also consults with child protective service workers, police, school officials, parents, attorneys, and other therapists. Quinn similarly notes the need for involvement of a multitude of disciplines and agencies in the resolution of elder abuse and neglect cases. Each case is unique and needs tailor-made interventions including crisis intervention, indirect intervention and referral, direct counseling, resource linkage, advocacy, and education.

An awareness of and, when appropriate, utilization of adjunct therapies is also important. Staton's chapter in particular discusses the use of visual and kinesthetic modality-oriented therapies that use a variety of materials. The drawing of feelings, problems, and resources; play therapy; puppets; and clay are creative art techniques that can be utilized. Kramer-Dover also describes the use of play and art therapies with child victims of sexual abuse, and Roberts discusses the use of coloring books with children in shelters. Additional adjunct therapies that can be utilized include self-defense training, wilderness/outward bound experiences, and other body-oriented therapies such as massage, exercise, and swimming. These adjuncts help the survivor reclaim his or her body and break isolation. Parenting classes for both partners (abusing and nonabusing) are also excellent.

Exploration of Countertransference and Attitudes

Therapists must be willing to explore their own transference and countertransferences and attitudes toward family violence victims and perpetrators, including children, minorities, gays, and the elderly. It is essential that professionals are aware of their own limits, biases, and needs. Chu (1988) writes that therapist balance is essential: balance between flexibility and limits, acceptance and confrontation, and client and therapist needs.

Fulmer notes that professionals must deal with countertransference issues to prevent overidentification with or distancing from adults who were molested as children. They must overcome their own intense reactions based on the taboo of abuse and taboos against talking about abuse, guarding against voyeurism or inappropriate curiosity, avoiding displays of horror, disbelief, judgment, and denial. Gil similarly stresses the need for therapists who consistently work with violence and trauma to seek consultation and support from others, keeping one's own limits and countertransferences in awareness. Membership in an appropriate support network can be helpful to these practitioners. Additionally, Quinn recognizes that persons who work with the elderly abused client may experience feelings of anger and contempt toward perpetrators, while wanting to rescue the victims.

Expertise and Education

A beginning level of expertise in trauma theory and treatment is essential prior to beginning work in the family violence field. Therapists must have a working knowledge of crisis intervention principles because, as Little writes, typical intervention strategies in family violence focus on the crisis aspects of abuse. A knowledge of the complex cultural factors that maintain violence and minimize batterer responsibility is also important. A knowledge of posttraumatic stress disorder, its phenomenology and differential diagnosis, and a knowledge of reporting policies and state laws are also essential, as is a knowledge of the disguised presentation of abuse. If therapists are to educate clients about trauma, normalizing responses and symptoms in areas of cognition, emotion, interpersonal relationships, body representation, and behavior, they themselves must have training and education.

Staton notes that adult survivors need to be educated as to how they stored the memories of early abuse in their visual and kinesthetic systems. McCarthy teaches all family members in a sexually abusive family system to see themselves as survivors, with responsibility lying with the perpetrators. He stresses that incest therefore cannot become the primary means of self-definition for survivors. Quinn also educates elders about their social and legal rights, the appropriate use of medication, life-management and self-care skills, and the nature of elderly abuse and neglect and its possibility for recurrence. Additionally, Jurich teaches parents of adolescents basic information about adolescent development and family development, including the role of transitional behaviors and normal developmental tasks.

Establishment of Limits and Boundaries

The establishment of limits and boundaries within therapy is essential when dealing with victims as well as perpetrators of family violence. The therapeutic setting must be a stable place that encourages disclosure and contains dysfunctional behavior. Little writes that, through these limits, clients have a safe environment in which they can take risks and increase self-regulation. Establishment of limits is of particular importance with male batterers, who historically are isolated, impulsive, possessive, and dependent. Those limits must ensure the safety of the battered mate and have as their single goal the cessation of abuse. Stith and Rosen help clients to set a similar "bottom line" with spouse abuse that does not permit violence. This "bottom line" is based on an assessment of the lethality of the situation and includes a safety plan and contract that may involve a temporary (if not permanent) separation. Jones notes that the honest use of authority with unmotivated clients must be explicit and includes an awareness of game theories. This process also redirects ownership of problems to the clients themselves.

McCarthy similarly helps the incestuous family to restructure to prevent inappropriate sexual behavior. Each person must assume responsibility for his or her behavior. This abstinence approach, similar to the AA model, keeps communication lines open and acknowledges responsibility for past wrongdoings. Additionally, in this model only the married couple is entitled to make a decision to maintain or terminate a marriage.

Gil sets rules in the therapeutic session that minimize risks for the sexual abuse survivor. In this setting, survivors can say as much or as little as they want. Gil notes, as therapist, that she does not view clients as "crazy," must (at some point) discuss childhood experiences while respecting the pace of the client, will not avoid the subject of abuse altogether (even if the client so desires), and will never hit, hurt, or be sexual with the client. Froning similarly notes that a therapist must be a trustworthy model of stability with appropriate personal boundaries and limits toward the family violence survivor. The therapist's behavior must never include sexual overtures or behaviors, and the therapist and client together must set clear, rules for physical contact, including hugging. Thus, rules must be reiterated on a repeated, regular basis to ensure continuity and safety.

Empathy

Belief in the reality of the client's experiences and resulting empathy from the believing therapist are essential if healing from trauma is to occur. Jones notes that respect for the client is crucial if the relationship between client and therapist is to develop, even when the client is unmotivated. The therapist also functions as empathic teacher, role model, and advocate. McCarthy discusses the importance of genuine clinician empathy toward and respect for all family members in the incestuous situation, including the perpetrator and mother. Belief, no matter how sadistic, bizarre, or abhorrent the abuse, is imperative.

Summary

It is evident that the various authors in this text approach family violence from perspectives that share common treatment goals. Belief in the reality of the violence, empowerment of clients, cognitive and emotional integration, and development of cognitive awareness of the trauma and its short- and long-term consequences are common goals described in many of the chapters. These goals are also paramount to the treatment of those suffering from posttraumatic stress disorder. The editors of this book hope that others, by reading this book, will become aware of the traumatic stress reaction process as it relates to domestic violence, be better able to recognize traumatic reactions, and to integrate the treatment principles and techniques outlined in this book into their work with victims and perpetrators of domestic violence.

NEEDS FOR THE FUTURE

It is imperative to think toward the future, with a goal of eliminating domestic violence and its destructive consequences. The ecological model presented in Chapter 1 demonstrates that domestic violence intervention can be approached from a variety of disciplines and fields and from a variety of perspectives within those fields. The discussion of future needs for eliminating violence and its destruction can also be approached from a variety of different perspectives. The future needs discussed here include sociocultural issues, primary prevention programs, legal system reforms, training, treatment and service coordination, and research. The concluding sections of this chapter deal with some of the changes that are essential for a future without family violence.

Sociocultural Issues

If family violence is to decrease significantly in the coming decades, the American public must come to recognize, en masse, that violence toward all persons is inappropriate, punishable, and worthy of deterrence. Unless social sanctions toward these crimes and toward perpetrators increase, those offenders will continue to believe that they can "get away" with their crimes and will continue to assault their partners, abuse their children and the children of others, and abuse their aging parents (Carmody & Williams, 1987, pp. 35, 36).

Practitioners, through publicizing the long-term, deleterious effects of family violence as well as the staggering incidence of family violence, can help bring public attention and can help to foster public condemnation of all forms of family violence. If violence is to decrease, as Straus et al. (1970) have noted, domestic disarmament must occur. Recognition of and organized condemnation of the amounts of violence in readily available magazines such as *Playboy*, *Penthouse*, and *Hustler*; in children's cartoons; and in heavy metal music (Pulling, 1989) also may be essential if social change is to occur. Federal funding of a national antiabuse, antiviolence campaign could help to combat these cultural attitudes and beliefs and thereby reduce incidence of violence while increasing the reporting of both present and past abuse.

Primary Prevention Programs

One major hope for decreasing the extent of family violence is the development of age-appropriate and content-appropriate primary prevention programs. These programs vary in their audience. They may be designed to build skills in children and teens that would lessen their vulnerability to or build their abilities to avoid the occurrence of child sexual abuse and/or date rape. Other skill-building programs, such as those now being utilized by the U.S. Air Force through its *Family Violence Prevention Resource Guide* (1986) developed by Kathyrn F. Cray, MSW, focus on prevention of spouse and child abuse by teaching adults parenting skills, communication skills, anger-management skills, and stress-management skills.

These primary prevention programs aim to build competence and, especially in child sexual abuse prevention, provide anticipatory guidance should abuse occur (Okin & Borus, 1989). The philosophy of these prevention programs is that the possession of knowledge is empowering. For children, and frequently for parents as well, the most predominant setting for prevention programs is the public school. For example, according to Miller-Perrin & Wurtele (1988), quoting Plummer, over one million children have been trained in the past decade concerning the prevention of child sexual abuse, using a variety of programs.

A major difficulty, particularly with child sexual abuse prevention programs for children, is that there is almost no research support for the conceptual assumptions on which they are based. Tharinger et al. (1988), reviewing 46 programs, have observed that skills and concepts included in those programs are based on what adults believe prevents victimization rather than on the actual processes used to engage and maintain child sexual abuse. Additionally, no clear operational or consensual definitions of major program concepts exists. Also, no publicized research has been undertaken to determine how effective knowledge of these skills can be in warding off abuse (p. 623). Furthermore, there is no evidence that these programs are having an effect on decreasing the incidence of sexual abuse. Thus, the question must be answered as to the fairness and reasonableness of expecting children to prevent their own abuse. It is possible that this type of prevention training can give children a false security, particularly very small children, who do not need to be taught empowerment concepts (p. 626).

In spite of these negatives, however, primary prevention appears to be one of the major ways to decrease the incidence of all types of family violence. Practitioners can help in the development of those programs by translating their practical knowledge into theoretical curricular concepts.

Legal System Reforms

While some change has occurred within the legal system in the past decade, many additional changes still need to occur. More communities need to be made aware of the deterrent effects of arrest of violent spousal abusers as a means to discourage further abusive behaviors. Publicity of successful response programs to domestic violence that have reduced the frequency of the occurrence of violence as well as the severity of injuries when it occurs will help build that awareness. PRIDE (Police Response to Incidents of Domestic Emergencies) in Newport News, Virginia, is one such program. This program views domestic violence as both a public health and police issue and utilizes a preferred arrest policy in which officers can effect an arrest on the scene.

Media presentations of the consequences of domestic violence as well as the extent of marital rape (e.g., "The Burning Bed") are also helping to build public awareness of the incidence and long-term effects of the abuse. Public pressure on legislators has led to the adoption of marital rape laws in a number of states and has resulted in the inclusion of a broader range of offenses as sexual assaults, regardless of victims' gender, sexual orientation, or age. Marlene Young, in a *Sexual Assault Training Handout* (1987) by NOVA (National Organization of Victims' Assistance), notes the need for further enactments of "rape shield laws: laws that forbid the introduction of evidence concerning victims' prior sexual activity" in court trials, laws that allow the use of the rape trauma syndrome as corroborating evidence of crime and demonstrate the impact of rape on the victim, and laws that establish the privacy of communications or confidentiality of communications with rape crisis counselors (p. 3).

Nevins and Roberts note the need for changes in the court system's procedural handling of child sexual abuse cases. Repeated investigatory interviews need to be consolidated into joint interviews. Interviewers should be specialists in the field with training. Videotaping of the first statement, as soon after revelation of abuse as is possible, should be admissible in court in all states (not just in the 14 states in which it is now allowed). Coordination of criminal and juvenile court proceedings should be encouraged, whenever possible, to reduce the number of times a child must testify. Additionally, a reduction in testimony appearances could occur by allowing hearsay evidence to be presented by therapists and other credible witnesses. Judges need to become more active with child victims and should allow supportive, trusted adults to be present during court appearances to lessen the secondary victimization that often occurs during court appearances.

As Hechler (1988) has noted, "not much in the world of child abuse is clear cut" (p. 239). He makes recommendations for legal change as well and believes that panels of expert validators should be chosen (and trained) by the courts to interview children who are alleged to have been sexually abused. Similar panels should be trained and designated to conduct medical examinations of the children. Both medical examinations and investigatory interviews should have standardized protocols. Additionally, the court should ensure public-funded therapy for all possible child abuse victims as well as perpetrators, for both the short and longterm.

Training

Although training in the family violence field has increased within the past decade, there are still many practitioners, volunteers, legal system representatives, and others who are not familiar with the specifics of family violence treatment. More professional education needs to be provided to a wider range of persons in their hometown communities. As Shupe et al. (1987, pp. 124–126) note, this education should be multidimensional and include biological components addressing the role of substances in family violence; psychological components; cultural components addressing existing attitudes; cultural beliefs in "macho men" as role models, as well as violence as a male prerogative; and family system components.

Roberts states that police, hospital staffs, and crisis intervention staffs at shelters need regular, specialized training that teaches the use of adult and child abuse protocols for asking the right questions. Nevin and Roberts similarly note that a need for more diversified and specialized training and education in the practice and administration of programs for youth and children exists. Health care professionals in general and nurses in particular, as well as police and classroom educators, need to participate in multidisciplinary training sessions that teach identification of abuse, mandated referral procedures, and intervention skills. Thus, all mandated referral professionals need to be knowledgeable, as Kramer-Dover writes, concerning their own state reporting laws. These practitioners must become comfortable enough with the subject matter of family violence so that they can ask the necessary questions to uncover its existence.

Treatment and Service Coordination

A variety of services, utilizing multiple theoretical models, need to be made available to all victims and perpetrators of family violence at minimal or no cost. New services need to be developed where none or few exist. Comprehensive trauma centers designed to treat all aspects of family violence need to be developed in major population enters throughout the country so that access to them is made easier. Federal and local funding of these centers through groups such as the United Way could help to reduce fees charged to recipients of services. Additionally, larger corporations need to design specific programs within their employee assistance programs to help victims of crime (as was suggested by the 1982 President's Task Force on Victims of Crime, [Herrington, 1982]).

As Gondolf and Fisher (1988), have written, and as Nevin and Roberts have similarly stated, "abuse must be seen as a common problem needing coordinated, integrated system(s) of community services and interventions" (p. 102). Treatment programs need to be based on common definitions of abuse and neglect for children, partners, and elders, across states, communities, and families, as Quinn has recommended. Additionally, parallels and differences between all types of family violence (elder, spouse, partner, child) need to be made (Finkelhor & Pillemer, 1988, p. 252). Only through the development of a coordinated response to family violence, a response that includes treatment programs designed to fit the individual situations of abusers and victims (as Hutchins and Vogler described) and that takes a clear legal stand and provides a range of treatment options will needed changes occur (Hart, 1984).

Research

The final major area of need in the family violence field is research that investigates the impact of legislative, preventive, and treatment efforts on the incidence and/or recurrence and impact of all types of family violence. Finkelhor et al. (1988) have pointed out the need for family violence research. This research will identify causation, risk factors, and most effective treatment methodologies. These authors list various research needs in each of the major abuse-violence arenas.

Child Physical Abuse

Research in this area includes examination of the effectiveness of parent education prevention programs and their ability to resolve anger in the family. Other areas of research needed examine the following:

1. Long-term mental-health, delinquency, and other effects of physical abuse including rate of recovery from trauma and the role of adult support and other factors in recovery.
2. The impact of various child protective service interventions, including removal of children, removal of perpetrators, and mixed interventions.
3. Public attitudes toward and use of corporal punishment and its relationship to abuse.
4. The economic costs of child abuse in medical, investigatory, court, and counseling services.

Child Sexual Abuse

Research in this area could look at the effectiveness of various types of offender treatments, including self-help groups (SAA), the use of penile plethysmographs in diagnosis, the use of medication to reduce sexual desire, jail as deterrent to reoffending, and cognitive behavioral therapies, over a 5- to 10-year period. The effectiveness of various types of treatments of child victims, including talking therapy, play therapy, visual and kinesthetic therapies (such as those described by Staton), could also be investigated. Additional research needs in this area include the following:

1. The process of recovery from the trauma of sexual abuse in terms of what was helpful and/or harmful, what led to or detracted from recovery over a long-term, postabuse period.
2. The credibility of children's accounts of abuse.
3. The effectiveness of primary prevention programs and their likelihood to reduce victimization, increase reporting, and lessen long-term traumatic impact of the abuse.
4. Prevalence trends.
5. The effectiveness of various methods of community manage-

ment of abuse cases; which models of interdisciplinary teams (such as the one described by Rogan) and systems are most effective and efficient.

Spouse/Partner and Parent/Elder Abuse

Similar areas of investigation could help the practitioner who works with spouse/partner or parent/elder abuse. Research could address what stops and/or prevents recurrence of these types of abuse as well as why some victims seek help. Other areas of research include the following:

1. Community response to abuse in terms of police policy, prosecution, offender treatment, availability of shelter services for partners and the elderly, as well as the availability for nonnursing home alternative living arrangements (adult foster homes) for the elderly.
2. The effectiveness of and need for more prevention education to change those norms that accept violence toward more vulnerable populations and put the elderly, in particular, in a position of nonrespect and nonvalue.
3. Risk factors in the perpetration of family violence (e.g., how do abusers learn to legitimatize their behavior).

CONCLUSIONS

As Marlene Young (1988) has noted, the need is for a greater long-term focus on the effects of serious victimization as well as on determining which intervention strategies work to mitigate and ameliorate those effects. All populations who are victimized or who victimize are entitled to services from trained mental health professionals who have developed standards of professional practice and who abide by a victim-oriented, victim-protecting code of ethics (NOVA, 1985, p. 10). This includes the emotional and physically abused, all children, minorities, gays, lesbians, differently abled, elderly, and others.

The recognition and legitimization of the posttraumatic stress disorder diagnosis is one of the coherent underlying principles of treatment of family violence and this text. While the study of trauma and violence is not new, the field of family violence as trauma is emerging as a specific discipline for both lay persons and professionals involved in its treatment.

REFERENCES

American Psychiatric Association. (1987). *Diagnostic and statistical manual of mental disorders*, 3d ed. (revised). Washington, DC: American Psychiatric Association.

Briere, J. (1989). *Therapy for adults molested as children: Beyond survival.* New York: Springer Publishing.

Caringella-MacDonald, S. (1988). Parallels and pitfalls: The aftermath of legal reform for sexual assault, marital rape, and domestic violence victims. *Journal of International Violence*, 175–189.

Carmody, D. C., & Williams, K. R. (1987). Wife assault and perceptions of sanctions. *Violence and Victims*, 2(1), 25–38.

Chu, J. A. (1988, December). 10 traps for therapists in the treatment of trauma survivors. *Dissociation*, pp. 24–26.

Figley, C. R. (1986). Traumatic stress: The role of the family and social support system. In C. R. Figley (Ed.), *Trauma and its wake: Vol. 2. Traumatic stress theory, research and intervention* (pp. 39–54). New York: Brunner/Mazel.

Finkelhor, D., Hotaling, G. T., & Yelo, K. (1988). *Stopping family violence: Research priorities for the coming decade.* Newbury Park, CA: Sage Publications.

Finkelhor, D., & Pillemer, K. (1988). Elder abuse: Its relation to other forms of domestic violence. In G. T. Hotaling, D. Finkelhor, J. T. Kirkpatrick, & M. A. Straus (Eds.), *Family abuse and its consequences: New directions in research* (pp. 244–254). Newbury Park, CA: Sage Publications.

Gondolf, E. W., & Fisher, E. R. (1988). *Battered women as survivors: An alternative to treating learned helplessness.* Lexington, MA: Lexington Books.

Hart, W. T. (1984). *Attorney General's task force on family violence.* Washington, DC: Department of Justice.

Hechler, D. (1988). *The battle and the backlash: The child sexual abuse war.* Lexington, MA: Lexington Books.

Hendricks, J. E. (1985). *Crisis intervention: Contemporary issues for on-site interveners.* Springfield, IL: Charles C Thomas.

Herrington, L. H. (1982). *President's task force on victims of crime.* Washington, DC: U.S. Government Printing Office.

Lindy, J. D. (1986). An outline for the psychoanalytic psychotherapy of post-traumatic stress disorders. In C. R. Figley (Ed.), *Trauma and its wake: Vol. 2, Traumatic stress theory, research, and intervention.* New York: Brunner/Mazel.

McCann, I. L., Sakheim, D. K., & Abrahamson, D. J. (1988). Trauma and victimization: A model of psychological adaptation. *The Counseling Psychologist*, 16, 531–594.

Miller-Perrin, C. L., & Wurtele, S. K. (1988). The child sexual abuse prevention movement: A critical analysis of primary and secondary approaches. *Clinical Psychology Review*, 313–329.

NOVA. (1985). The aftermath of crime: A mental health crisis. *NOVA Newsletter*, 9(3), 1–11.

NOVA. (undated). *Family violence . . . The crime and its victims.* Washington, DC: National Organization of Victims' Assistance.

Okin, R. L., & Borus, M. D. (1989). Primary, secondary, and tertiary prevention of mental disorders. In H. I. Kaplan & B. J. Sadock (Eds.), *Comprehensive textbook of psychiatry, IV* (Vols. 1 & 2). Baltimore, MD: Williams and Wilkins.

Pulling, P. (1989, June). *History and youth subculture of ritualistic crime.* Paper presented at the Eastern Conference on Dissociation and Multiple Personality Disorder, Alexandria, VA.

Shupe, A., Stacey, W. A., & Hazlewood, L. R. (1987). *Violent men, violent couples: The dynamics of domestic violence.* Lexington, MA: Lexington Books.

Straus, M., Gelles, R., & Steinmetz, S. (1970). *Behind closed doors: Violence in the American family.* Garden City, NY: Doubleday.

Tharinger, D. J., Krivacska, J. J., Laye-McDonough, M., Jamison, L., Vincent, G. G., & Hedlund, A. D. (1988). Prevention of child sexual abuse: An analysis of issues, educational programs, and research findings. *School Psychology Review, 17*(4), 614–637.

Turkus, J. A. (1989, June). *Treating MPD: A model for continuum of care.* Paper presented at the Eastern Conference on Dissociation and Multiple Personality Disorders, Alexandria, VA.

Young, M. A. (1987). *Sexual assault training handout.* Washington, DC: National Organization for Victims' Assistance.

Young, M. A. (1988). Support services for victims. In F. M. Ochberg (Ed.), *Post-traumatic therapy and victims of violence* (pp. 83–110). New York: Brunner/Mazel.

Index

Springer Publishing Company

Violence and Victims

Roland Maiuro, Ph.D., Editor-in-Chief
Irene Hanson Frieze, Ph.D., **Mary Koss**, Ph.D., **Ray Paternoster**, Ph.D.,
Joel S. Milner, Ph.D., Associate Editors
Lenore Walker, Ed.D. & **Daniel Sonkin**, Ph.D., Special Consultants
Angela Browne, Ph.D., Founding Editor

Now it its fifth year of publication, **Violence and Victims** provides a quarterly forum for the latest developments in theory, research, policy, clinical practice, and social services in the area of interpersonal violence and victimization. The editors give special emphasis to original research in familial violence, criminology and criminal justice, the etiology of violent behavior, and the implications for legal and social intervention.

ISSN 0886-6708, Quarterly, Volume 5, 1990
Individual: One Year: $34 ($42 foreign) Two Years: $58 ($68 foreign)
Institution: One Year: $68 ($72 foreign) Two Years: $112 ($120 foreign)

Springer Publishing Company

THERAPY FOR ADULTS MOLESTED AS CHILDREN

Beyond Survival

John Briere, PhD, University of Southern California School of Medicine

"Briere does an excellent job addressing the various problems that therapists may encounter while counseling the survivor and in giving practical techniques for handling such problems.... This book was not written to be read and put away. Instead, it should be used to challenge the ideas of the established professional and as a treatment manual for sexual abuse clinicians. Regardless of its use, it should be considered required reading for anyone who deals with sexual abuse and/or its survivors. Highly recommended!"—*Family Violence Bulletin*

Partial Contents: Post-Sexual Abuse Trauma. "Hysteria," "Borderline Personality Disorder," and the Core Effects of Severe Abuse. Specific Therapy Principles and Techniques. The Specific Problem of Client Dissociation During Therapy. The Trauma Symptom Checklist.

1989 218pp 0-8261-5640-1 hard $29.95 ($33.80 foreign)

BORN UNWANTED

Developmental Effects of Denied Abortion

Henry P. David, PhD, **Zdenek Dytrych**, MD, CSc, **Zdenek Matejcek**, PhD, CSc, and **Vratislav Schuller**, PhD, CSc, Editor

This landmark book establishes that there are adverse effects on children born to mothers who have been refused abortion. Presenting findings from a unique longitudinal study of Prague children, together with related Scandinavian studies, the book documents deviant development and social relations that worsen in adolescence and early adulthood. The authors include an historical and cross cultural overview of the abortion issue and consider unwantedness in demographic and psychological perspective as well as in relation to responsible parenthood. This is an essential reference for all those concerned with psychological development, family planning, and the continuing abortion controversy.

Published jointly with Avicenum, Prague, under the auspices of the World Federation for Mental Health.

1988 144 pp. 0-8261-6080-8 hard $26.95 (foreign $30.00)

Springer Publishing Company

HANDBOOK ON SEXUAL ABUSE OF CHILDREN

Assessment and Treatment Issues

Lenore E.A. Walker, Ed.D., Editor

This ground-breaking volume presents advances in identification assessment, legal alternatives, and treatment of sexually abused children, as well as their families and the offenders. It presents a range of new treatment options including family, community-oriented approaches, and individual therapy.

> *"These papers often challenge traditionally held views; all achieve a high level of clarity and encourage self-examination on the part of the therapist with regard to bias and ignorance..."*
>
> *- Readings*

Complete Contents: The Effects of Childhood Sexual Abuse: A Review of the Issues and Evidence • The Incidence and Prevalence of Intrafamilial and Extrafamilial Sexual Abuse of Female Children • The Psychoanalytic Legacy: From Whence We Come • Assessing the Long-Term Impact of Child Sexual Abuse on Children: Empirical Findings • Correlates of Incest Reported by Adolescent Girls in Treatment for Substance Abuse • Children as Witnesses: What Do They Remember? • Legal Issues in Child Sexual Abuse: Criminal Cases of Neglect and Dependency • Incest Investigation and Treatment Planning by Child Protective Services • New Techniques for Assessment and Evaluation of Sexual Abuse Victims: Using "Anatomically Correct" Dolls and Videotape Procedures • Assessment-Intervention Interface Using the Theme Creation Test for Youths • Guidelines for Assessing Sex Offenders • Play Therapy with Children Who Have Experienced Sexual Assault • Retrospective Incest Therapy for Women • Nonoffending Mothers: A New Conceptualization • A Family System Approach to Treatment • A Developing Behavioral Treatment Model: One Therapist's Perspective Within a Community's Evolving Response • Assessment and Treatment of Sex Offenders in a Community Setting • "Taking Care of Me": Preventing Sexual Abuse in the Hispanic Community • Retrospective Incest for Men: A Personal History

1988   480 pp.   0-8261-5300-3   hard $39.95 (foreign $45.80